Sunset

YOU CAN BUILD

Wiring

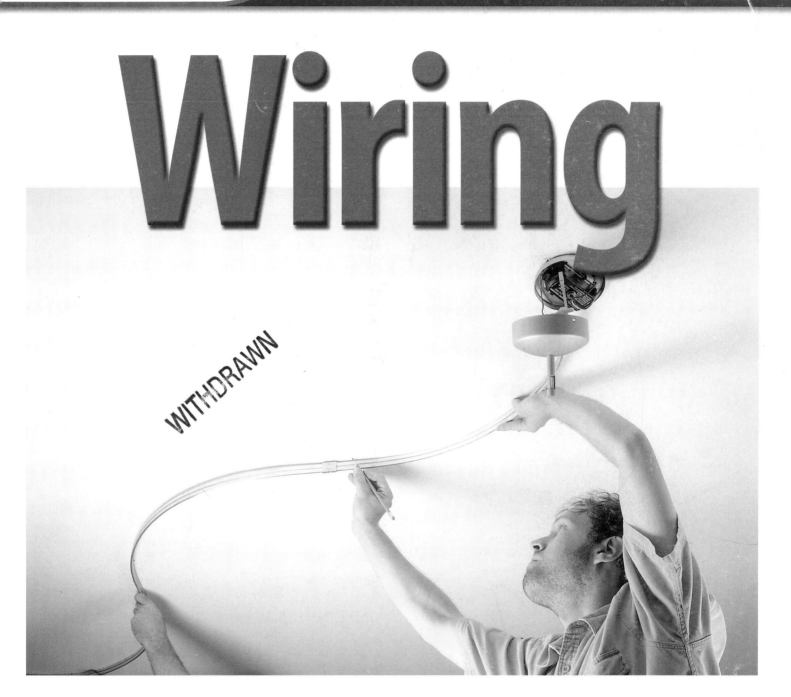

by Esther Ferington,
Brad Kava, and the
Editors of Sunset Books

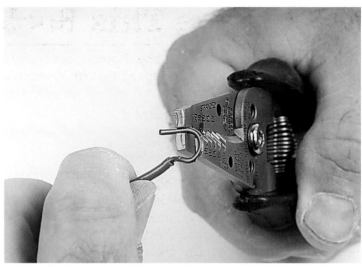

Sunset Books
VP, Editorial Director: Bob Doyle
Art Director: Vasken Guiragossian

Staff for This Book
Managing Editor: Ben Marks
Design & Production: Hespenheide
Design—Laurie Miller, Randy Miyake,
Gabe Manchego
Principal Photographer: Jim Bathie
Illustrator: Anthony Davis
Proofreader: Jennifer Block Martin
Indexer: Marjorie Joy
Prepress Coordinator: Eligio Hernández

Front cover photography by Mark
Rutherford, styling by JoAnn Masaoka
Van Atta

10 9 8 7 6 5 4 3 2 1
First Printing January 2009
Copyright © 2009, Sunset Publishing
Corporation, Menlo Park, CA 94025.
First edition. All rights reserved,
including the right of reproduction
in whole or in part in any form.
ISBN-13: 978-0-376-01596-9
ISBN-10: 0-376-01596-9
Library of Congress Control Number:
2008932360
Printed in the United States of America.

For additional copies of *You Can Build:
Wiring* or any other Sunset book, visit us
at www.sunsetbooks.com.

Note to readers: Almost any do-it-yourself project involves risk of some sort. Your tools, materials, and skills will vary, as will conditions at your project site. Sunset Publishing Corporation and the editors of this book have made every effort to be complete and accurate in the instructions. We will, however, assume no responsibility or liability for injuries, damages, or losses incurred in the course of your home improvement or repair projects. Always follow the manufacturer's operating instructions in the use of tools, check and follow your local building codes, and observe all standard safety precautions.

How to Use This Book

You Can Build: Wiring is organized by chapters, of course, but we have also created a number of repeating features designed to help you successfully and safely complete your home-wiring project.

Safety Notices

On most pages, this is to remind you to turn off the power—and then to test to make sure that you flipped the correct breaker or unplugged the correct fuse—before you do anything. Sometimes, though, the warning is particular to a specific project on a specific page, so please read all boxes carefully and follow their instructions.

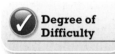

Skill Level Required

Most wiring projects are Easy, but some are Moderate and a few are downright Challenging. The actual Degree of Difficulty will depend on your experience and skills.

Shopping Guides

In some cases, you can use the information in these boxes as the basis for your shopping list before you head off to the home improvement center. In other cases we offer tips and advice to help you shop smart.

What It Will Take

As with the Degree of Difficulty, the time it takes to complete a wiring project will vary with your skill level and experience, but this should help you plan for a quick wiring project that can be completed in under an hour or a weekend-long one.

Preparation Help

Having the tools you need on hand before you begin a project saves time-wasting trips to the home improvement center, so give this box a quick glance before you begin to wire.

For More Info

To save you a trip to the Index, we've placed Related Topics boxes on many pages in *You Can Build: Wiring*. You may want to consult these pages before you begin a project, just in case your wiring job is a bit of a hybrid.

YOU CAN BUILD

Degree of Difficulty
● Moderate

STOP!
Before you replace a switch, turn off power at main service panel and test to verify that power is off.

Stuff to Buy
SWITCH Choose a commercial-rated switch if it will get heavy use
COVER PLATE Pick one that matches your home's décor
ELECTRICAL TAPE

Time Commitment
About 15 minutes

Tools You'll Need
Wire stripper
Screwdriver
Long-nose pliers

Related Topics
Common wiring methods, 28–31
Installing special switches, 110–113
Shutting off & restoring power, 50–51
Special-purpose switches, 108–109
Stripping & joining wire, 54–59

Contents

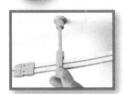

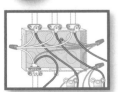

1

Your Wired Home

In this chapter, we help you accomplish home wiring projects safely and with confidence by explaining how electricity works—from the way in which power reaches your home to the importance of grounding. We also show you how to save money on your electric bill and offer tips to help you decide when it's time to call an electrician. The chapter also covers wire and cable types and includes a section on troubleshooting.

Chapter Contents

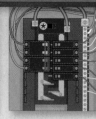

Putting Safety First

If you take the right precautions, household electrical wiring is quite safe to do. Treat your work with caution and respect, and don't rush.

STOP! Cutting the power is a two-step process. First, turn it off; then test to confirm it's off.

Double Protection

Electricians protect themselves in two ways: shutting off power and using safe tools, clothing, and methods. For extra safety, make sure the power is off—but act as though it is still on.

Safety Basics

Never work on or near the thick service wires that bring power into your home's service panel. (Usually there are three wires; older houses may have two.) Do not touch the service wires inside the service panel either.

Work only when you understand the wiring and are sure that the power is off. If you are ever uncertain about this, call an electrician.

The instructions in this book assume that the wiring in your house was done correctly. In real life, this may not always be true. Be on the lookout for substandard wiring and call in a professional if you see anything that looks suspicious.

Shutting Off the Power

If you are working on a lamp or any other portable appliance, unplug it before you start. Don't just turn off the switch, since the wiring will still be live.

For wiring projects, make sure the power is off to the relevant circuit or circuits. (An electrical box may contain wires from more than one circuit, so you may need to shut off more than one circuit to make it safe.)

- With the power still on, turn on a plug-in lamp, a light fixture, or an appliance for each circuit you'll be working on.
- Next, disconnect the circuit or circuits at the service panel. That usually means switching a breaker for each of the circuits involved; for a fuse panel, remove the fuse.
- Test in at least two ways to make sure there is no power in the box, the fixture, or the appliance you'll be working on.

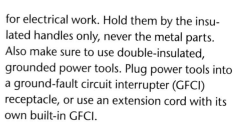

First, check the item you just turned on to make sure that it went off when you cut the power. Then use a voltage tester or voltage detector to verify there is no power present.

- Make sure that nobody accidentally restores the power as you work. Tape a big note on the panel, or, better yet, lock the panel door with a padlock.

The Right Tools & Clothing

Use rubber- or plastic-gripped pliers, strippers, cutters, and screwdrivers that are made for electrical work. Hold them by the insulated handles only, never the metal parts. Also make sure to use double-insulated, grounded power tools. Plug power tools into a ground-fault circuit interrupter (GFCI) receptacle, or use an extension cord with its own built-in GFCI.

Wear rubber-soled shoes, stand on a rubber mat, or do both. Leather gloves will protect your hands from scratches; rubber gloves can provide extra insulation against electrical shock. As with any construction project, protect your eyes with safety glasses if you use a power tool or hammer, or for jobs in tight spaces.

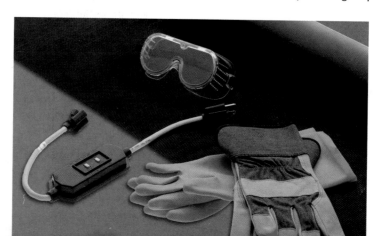

Protective gear you might use includes safety goggles, a GFCI-protected extension cord, rubber gloves, and leather gloves.

The Right Working Conditions

Never work on wiring or electrical projects in damp or wet conditions. Water and electricity are a dangerous mix.

A concrete floor is much more conductive than a wood-framed upstairs floor covered in carpet or vinyl flooring. Stand on dry boards or a rubber mat on top of the concrete, and wear rubber boots.

Codes & Inspections

All new electrical work should be done in accordance with local electrical codes, which are generally tied to the National Electrical Code (or in Canada, the Canadian Electrical Code).

Depending on the type of job you're doing, you may also need to have it inspected by your local building department. Codes and inspections exist to ensure wiring is secure and safe, so always comply with local rules.

Electrical Shock

If you accidentally become part of a live electrical circuit, you'll get a shock—a dangerous and potentially deadly experience. Electrical current flows in a circuit, but it does not need wires to do so. It can return through any conducting object—including a human body— that contacts the earth directly or that touches another conducting object that does so.

There are two basic ways to get an electrical shock. In the first, shown below left, you touch both a live wire and a grounded object—for instance, a metal plumbing fixture, the ground, or a damp basement floor. The shock that you get depends on how conductive the grounded object is. For example, you'll get a really big shock if you are standing in water.

The second way, shown below right, is to touch both a hot wire and a neutral wire, or the ground wire or a metal box connected to the grounding system. In that case, you receive the full force of the circuit's power as it travels through you and back to the service panel.

Grounding may or may not help you in either case. GFCI protection is more likely to shut the power off. But the best way to prevent shock is simple: Make sure there is no power to the circuit or circuits you are working on.

Current travels from hot wire through body to earth

Current travels from hot wire through body to neutral wire

Receptacle Safety

To remove a plug from a receptacle, grasp the plug itself and pull straight out. If you pull by the cord, you may bend the prongs or damage the receptacle.

Very young children may be dangerously interested in open receptacles. If possible, block receptacles with heavy furniture until kids are old enough to learn about household safety.

Protective inserts provide some security, but a determined toddler can remove them. A swivel cover does a better job, because you must twist a plug in order to insert it.

Protective insert

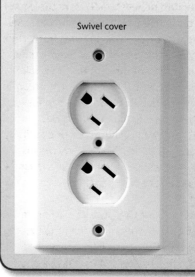

Swivel cover

Conserving Electricity

There are two reasons to conserve electricity: money and the environment. The money part is easy to visualize. Just open your purse or wallet. Use a lot of electricity and you're looking at a lot fewer greenbacks. 'Nuff said.

The Big Picture

The impact of your home-electricity use on the environment is more difficult to get your arms around. In part, that's because the discussion tends to focus on exotic-sounding impacts, such as how global warming is affecting polar bears. So here's a more down-to-earth reason to watch your electricity use: tuna fish sandwiches.

Like all of the fish we eat, tuna contains mercury. In fact, there is so much mercury in fish that the U.S. Food and Drug Administration warns pregnant women, or women considering becoming pregnant, to eat only two servings a week, and to avoid swordfish, mackerel, and other high-mercury species altogether.

Where does all that mercury come from and how does it get into your tuna fish sandwich? Well, it turns out that there's a fair amount of mercury in coal, which is the primary source for most of the world's electricity. When coal is burned to produce electricity, the mercury escapes into the atmosphere, where it remains for years until it finds its way back down to earth and into the food chain. Americans eat a lot of tuna fish sandwiches, which makes this innocuous lunch-time favorite the largest single source of mercury in our diets.

Reducing our energy use and taking advantage of smarter energy technologies can have a tangible impact on the amount of mercury we end up consuming. For example, the editors of *Sunset* magazine recently determined that if every one of their 4.8 million readers did just a few simple things—replacing one incandescent bulb for a compact fluorescent; washing laundry in cold water; unplugging home electronic devices when they are not in use; etc.—the saving would prevent 20 billion pounds of CO_2, and a proportionate amount of mercury, from being sent skyward every year.

In fact, saving energy, whether for the love of money or tuna fish sandwiches, has never been easier. Incandescent light bulbs use about four times as much electricity as CFLs, and almost 10 times as much power as LEDs, so ditching incandescents is an obvious place to start. You can buy an affordable electricity monitor that will tell you how much energy every appliance in your house is using. And you can even link all of your appliances to a device that lets you turn them on or off remotely by phone or computer.

Those are just a few of the new home-wiring improvements described in this book. As you browse through its pages, you may be surprised by how much you can do to lower your home energy expenses and reduce the impact of generating all that energy in the first place. It requires a lot less effort than you might expect. And the pay-off could keep your kids and grandkids in tuna sandwiches for generations to come.

Myths About Lights

Yes, the longest burning light bulb in the world has been shining continuously in Livermore, California for 109 years as of 2009 (www.centennialbulb.org), but that doesn't mean that leaving a light bulb on when leaving a room, rather than turning it off and then turning it back on again, will increase its life span. The television show "Mythbusters" tested a number of incandescent light bulbs and determined that starting up an incandescent does indeed consume 23 seconds worth of power, but that's far less than the myth of a "power surge" using much more.

Turning on fluorescent lights also reduces their life span slightly, but a study by the California Energy Commission reports that fluorescents turned on when needed last longer than those left on constantly.

Here's a simple way to think about it: If you are rinsing dishes at the sink and the doorbell rings, you wouldn't leave the water running to see who it is, right? So why leave the lights on in a room that you are not planning to return to within the next 23 seconds?

Your Energy Savings

Saving the planet and saving money go hand in hand. Here are a number of home-improvement ideas, from light bulbs to insulation, to cut your electricity bill and reduce your carbon footprint.

SMALL STEPS

What to do	What it costs	Why do it
REPLACE incandescent light bulbs with compact fluorescent light bulbs	$1–$20 each	CFLs use 70% less energy and one bulb can save $50–$200 a year
INSTALL an Energy Star–rated programmable thermostat	$29–$100	Save up to 15% on heating and cooling bills
EMPLOY switches and power strips that use motion or power sensors	$20–$50 each	Idle current can account for 1%–2% of energy bills
CLEAN OR REPLACE furnace and air conditioning filters	$2–$20 each	Clean filters can reduce heating/cooling costs by 1%–2%
CAULK AND SEAL walls, ceilings, floors, windows, doors and ductwork	$10–$40 for caulking, weather-stripping, or mastic	Eliminating drafts can save 5%–30% on heating costs
INSULATE older water heaters and pipes	$30–$45 for thermal blanket, pipe insulation and tape	Preventing heat loss can save 4%–9% on water-heating costs
AUDIT your home energy use at www.energystar.gov	$0	The site can suggest ways to cut your energy bill by 20%
BUY a home appliance measuring device	$40	Seeing how much you pay per hour for that old refrigerator makes you realize how much you could save by getting a new one
REPLACE outdoor and even Christmas lights with LEDs	LED Christmas tree lights can cost $30–$40 more than regular ones	LED lights save $1–$11 per 300 hours and last twice as long

GETTING SERIOUS

What to do	What it costs	Why do it
CONTACT a professional to arrange a detailed energy audit	$200–$325 ($0 if your utility company offers one)	Pros can spot waste and suggest cost-effective changes
INSTALL a whole-house fan to lighten load on air-conditioning systems	$180–$230 (not including installation)	Fans can reduce cooling costs by up to 5%
ADD insulation to your attic	50 cents–$1 per sq. ft. (not including installation)	Properly insulated homes use 30%–50% less energy
REPLACE your old refrigerator with an Energy Star–rated refrigerator	$500–$7,300	Today's refrigerators use half the energy of 1992 models
INSTALL Energy Star–rated windows	$150–$600 per standard window (not including installation)	Energy Star windows save up to 15% on heating and cooling costs
PUT IN an Energy Star–rated tankless water heater	$700–$1,200 (not including installation)	Tankless water heaters can be 8%–34% more efficient
PLANT evergreens in the north to block winter winds, and deciduous trees in the south for shade	Trees can cost $25–$150 depending on maturity and size	Landscaping can save 30% in home cooling and heating costs

How Electricity Works

When you turn on a switch, you allow electricity to flow through a household circuit, passing through a light bulb or whatever has been switched on. Home wiring is fundamentally a matter of transporting this current safely and efficiently.

The Circuit Loop

In order to flow, electricity requires a circuit—a continuous, closed path from start to finish, like a circle. The circuit includes the entire route the current travels, from the power source, through a device or appliance, and back to the source. What may look like a maze of wires running through your walls, floors, and ceilings is actually a well organized system composed of these circuits.

Each circuit begins at the service panel, where power enters your home, or a sub-panel. It passes through various receptacles, fixtures, or appliances, then back to the panel where it started.

The current flows to the devices (sometimes called loads) through a hot wire, which is usually covered with black or colored insulation. The current returns from a device through a neutral wire, which usually has white insulation. When a device or an appliance is turned off, the neutral wire has no power flowing through it.

In the simple illustration on the opposite page, turning on the switch connects the two black wires, completing the circuit and allowing electricity to flow through the light. When the switch is turned off, the circuit is broken, electricity stops flowing, and the light goes off.

The power for this pendant light begins at the receptacle near the floor, travels through a switch, and then continues on to the fixture.

Related Topics

Avoiding overloads, 266–267
Calculating usage & capacity, 282–283
The service panel, 16–17

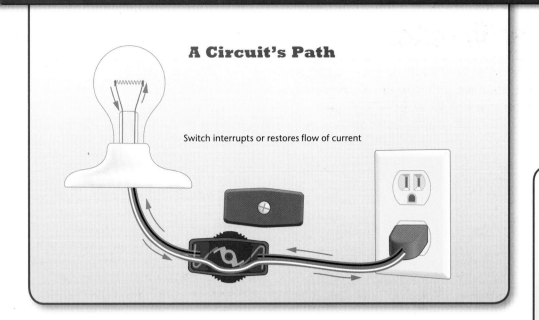

A Circuit's Path

Switch interrupts or restores flow of current

Defining Terms

Like any subject, electrical work uses some specialized terms for the task at hand. Many electrical terms are units of measure.

VOLTS

Water inside a pipe moves because it's under pressure from the water behind it. Electricity is also under pressure, and the force causing the current to flow is measured in volts. Most household electrical circuits carry between 115 and 125 volts (usually 120). Circuits for large appliances, like electric ranges or water heaters, often carry 240 volts.

AMPERES (AMPS)

The current that flows past a given point in one second is measured in amperes, usually called amps. Wires are rated according to the amps they can safely carry without overheating. The larger the wire, the higher its current-carrying capacity.

WATTS

Watts are a measure of energy use (unlike volts and amps, which measure the supply). Watts express the energy per second consumed by an electrical device; a kilowatt is 1000 watts. Household electrical use is usually figured in kilowatt-hours.

CONDUCTORS

A conductor is anything that permits—or conducts—the flow of electricity. Copper, for example, is a very good conductor, so most wires are made of copper. This book uses the terms "conductor" and "wire" interchangeably.

OHMS

Electrical resistance is the property of an electrical circuit that restricts the flow of current. Electrical resistance is measured in ohms. In home electrical systems, the issue of ohms rarely comes up.

RECEPTACLE

Although people often call it an outlet, receptacle is the more precise term for where you plug things in. To an electrician, outlet is a broader term; an outlet could be a receptacle, but it could also be a light or an appliance (see Outlet).

DEVICE

Any electrical receptacle or switch is referred to generally as a device. The term may also apply to something that uses electricity, such as an appliance.

OUTLET

An outlet is any point at which electricity leaves the wiring circuit in order to be used—a wall or ceiling receptacle, a light, or an appliance.

Alternating & Direct Current

In the early days of electricity, some homes used direct current (DC), which flows from a negative pole through an electrical outlet (such as a light bulb) and on to the positive pole. Household batteries, with their negative and positive poles, are the most familiar use of DC these days.

However, direct current can't be transmitted over long distances without a big drop in voltage. Utility companies now provide households with alternating current (AC), which pulses—reverses direction—120 times, or 60 cycles, per second. This is called 60-hertz power. Light bulbs actually flicker as the power cycles, but so fast that the human eye can't detect it.

Volts, Watts, Amps

In terms of household wiring, the relationship between the three basic electrical units is represented in this formula: volts × amps = watts

To put it another way: watts ÷ volts = amps

If you know two of these values, you can figure the third value by multiplying or dividing.

For example:

A 20-amp, 120-volt circuit can deliver 2,400 watts (20 × 120 = 2400).

A microwave oven that uses 1,000 watts of 120-volt power consumes 8.3 amps (1000 ÷ 120 = 8.3).

A 240-volt clothes dryer that pulls 5,600 watts of power requires at least a 23.3-amp circuit (5600 ÷ 240 = 23.3).

How Power Reaches Your Home

Utility companies distribute power to households through overhead wires or underground cables. The voltage is stepped up near the power source, stepped down for power lines, and stepped down again near your house.

STOP!
Note that the service wires coming into the house and into the panel stay hot even when the main shutoff is turned off.

A Long-distance Connection

As shown here, the AC electricity travels first through step-up transformers, which boost the voltage via huge magnetic coils and send it along high-voltage lines into substations. The power then passes through step-down transformers and travels through local power lines to a point near your home. There another step-down transformer converts it to household voltage.

Three-wire & Two-wire Service

Today, most homes have three-wire service. The utility company provides three service lines to your home; two hot wires that each supply electricity at about 120 volts, plus one neutral wire.

With a three-wire service, one hot wire plus the neutral line combine to provide for 120-volt needs, such as light fixtures or wall receptacles. Both hot wires combine with the neutral to provide 240 volts for large appliances like ranges and clothes dryers.

Some older homes still have two-wire service, with one hot wire at 120 volts and a neutral wire. Such a system cannot supply power to 240-volt appliances and is probably ready for an upgrade.

The Service Entrance & Meter

The wires that connect to your home enter through a service head or a buried conduit (pipe). The point of entry is called the service entrance or the service drop.

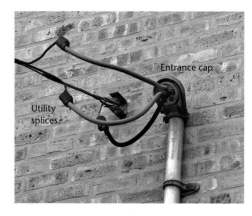

In an overhead entrance, wires typically travel to a service head, which is designed to keep water out. The wires must attach firmly to the house or the pipe before entering the service head; special utility splices join the power company wires to those leading into the house.

Entrance cap

Utility splices

In an underground entrance, wires travel through buried conduit and there may be a transformer in the yard near the house. At the house, the conduit enters via a watertight connection like this L-shaped fitting, known as an LB fitting.

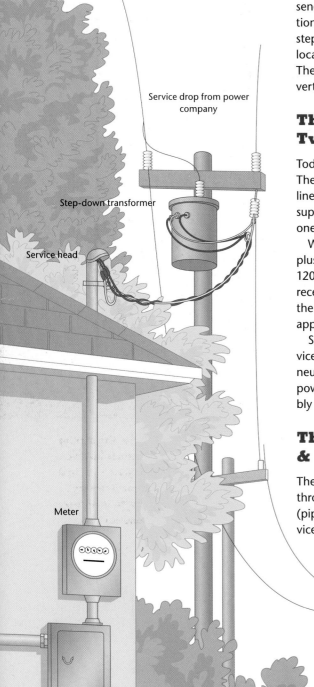

Service drop from power company

Step-down transformer

Service head

Meter

Service entrance panel

Power pole

Substation

Step-down transformer

Related Topic

Meter reading & panel indexing, 34–35

FRONIUS IG

REC

DO NOT OPERATE

Before entering the service panel, the electrical service passes through a meter that is owned, installed, and serviced by the utility company. The meter measures the energy consumed at your house in kilowatt-hours.

The wires then enter the service panel (usually at the top), where they connect to the main shutoff for your house. In some panels, a number of double-pole breakers take the place of a single main shutoff.

Here, the service panel is hidden behind a latched door. The large box to its left is a solar inverter.

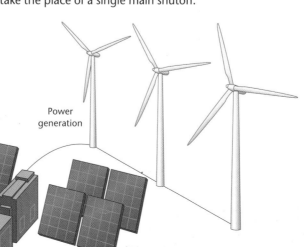

High-voltage power lines

Step-up transformer

Power generation

The Service Panel

The control center for your home electrical system is the service panel, where you go to shut off power to a circuit before working on your home's wiring—or to restore power when a circuit has overloaded.

STOP!
Never replace a fuse or breaker with one of higher amperage.

The service panel is also called the service entrance, fuse box, or breaker box (depending on whether yours has fuses or circuit breakers). It may be on an outside wall below the meter, or on an inside wall, often directly behind the meter.

Panels are commonly mounted in a basement or a garage, and sometimes in a hallway or closet. The type of equipment varies, so don't be concerned if your panel doesn't look like the ones shown here.

The Service Entrance & Main Shutoff

The service panel usually houses the main disconnect or main shutoff, which shuts off power to the entire electrical system. The electrical code allows as many as six circuit breakers to act collectively as the main dis-connect, but your panel may have a single cutoff switch.

Most often, the utility company's two hot wires go to the main disconnect. The neutral wire goes directly to the neutral bus bar, which has terminals for the individual neutral wires of each circuit as well as a terminal for the grounding electrode conductor. This ground wire, which is an important safety feature, runs without interruption to a metal water supply pipe entering your home or to a metal ground rod driven into the earth. Some older homes have ungrounded systems.

The Distribution Center

After passing through the main disconnect, each hot wire connects to one of the two hot bus bars in the distribution center, where energy is divided into branch circuits. Neutrals (with white insulation) and grounds (in bare copper or with green insulation) typically connect to the neutral/ground bus bar. In some panels, there are separate neutral and ground bars.

Some houses also have separate subpanels containing additional circuit breakers or fuses. In most cases, an entire subpanel is controlled by a breaker or fuse in the main service panel.

Fuses & Circuit Breakers

Fuses or circuit breakers both serve the same two functions. When you are working on a wiring project, they act as switches to shut off power to a circuit or circuits so you can work safely. Their other purpose is to

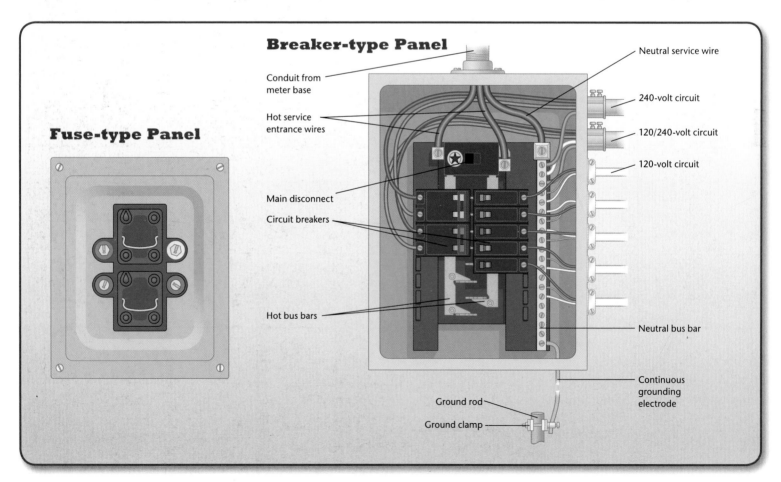

Breaker-type Panel

Conduit from meter base

Hot service entrance wires

Main disconnect

Circuit breakers

Fuse-type Panel

Hot bus bars

Neutral service wire

240-volt circuit

120/240-volt circuit

120-volt circuit

Neutral bus bar

Continuous grounding electrode

Ground rod

Ground clamp

protect circuits from being damaged by an overload. When wiring is forced to carry more current than it can safely handle, fuses blow or circuit breakers trip, disconnecting the electricity. That can happen when you operate too many appliances on one circuit, as a result of a short circuit, or (rarely) due to a sudden surge from the utility company.

The amperage rating of a fuse or breaker must match the circuit it protects. For example, a circuit using 12-gauge (sometimes called #12) wire is rated to carry 20 amps, so it requires a 20-amp breaker or fuse. A circuit with 14-gauge wire, which is rated for 15 amps, requires a 15-amp breaker or fuse. A 240- volt circuit using 10-gauge wire, which is rated for 30 amps, requires a 30-amp breaker or fuse.

When excess current causes a fuse to blow or a breaker to trip, you'll need to remedy whatever caused the problem. After that, you can reset a tripped circuit breaker by flipping or pushing the toggle. Once a fuse blows, however, it is ruined and must be replaced. Discard it and put in a new one.

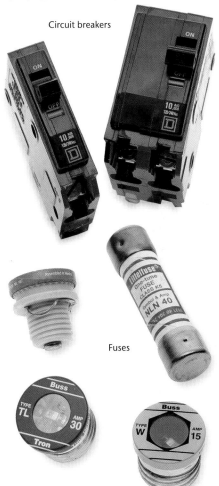

Circuit breakers

Fuses

In kitchens, it's common to have multiple circuits for lights and appliances.

Breaker Panels

The breaker panels shown here are typical 100-amp and 200-amp panels. On most panels, the amperage is written on the main disconnect or on the interior of the panel cover.

Many new or remodeled homes have a 200-amp panel. But if your panel only carries 100 amps, don't worry on that account. Your home probably doesn't need more than 100 amps unless it has several heavy electricity users, like electric heat, central air, an electric range, and an electric water heater.

Circuit Wiring

The 200-amp breaker panel, below middle and right, is shown with and without a cover in place. With the cover removed, you can see the wires that lead to the circuits of your home.

A 120-volt circuit consists of one hot wire (with black, red, or colored insulation) and one neutral wire (white). The hot wire originates at a circuit breaker connected to one of the two hot bus bars, while the neutral wire connects to the neutral bus bar. A 240-volt circuit requires two hot wires, so it attaches to a breaker block that connects to both of the hot bus bars.

Different Panel Layouts

Not all panels are laid out the same way. In this 200-amp breaker panel, the three service wires enter at the top right. The two hot wires go to the center of the panel and attach to the hot bus bars, one on each side. The neutral wire (marked with pieces of white tape) attaches to the neutral bus bar, lower on the right.

Other panels may have neutral/ground bus bars on the sides, and some have separate bus bars for the neutral (white-insulated) wires and the grounds (bare copper or green-insulated).

Fuse Panels

In an older home, you may find a fuse panel. The fuse panel on the opposite page is rated at 100 amps, enough for a medium-size home. As long as the wiring is correct, it is safe.

However, this particular panel can only divide service into eight 120-volt circuits—not enough for a home with a modern kitchen and other electrical outlets—and there is just one 240-volt circuit (on the right, marked "main range"). To add modern kitchen appliances, electrical heat, air conditioning, or other amenities, you might need to upgrade to a breaker panel with slots for more circuits.

This panel has no ground wires. The ground path is provided by the armored sheathing instead. There is also no single

This 100-amp panel provides space for only 12 breakers, making it too small for an average-to-large home with numerous electrical appliances.

This 200-amp panel has space for 17 more 120-volt circuit breakers.

The same 200-amp panel, without its cover.

main disconnect. Pulling out the fuse block labeled "main lights" will shut off the power to all the 120-volt circuits, but not the 240-volt circuit.

With the cover off, this panel is a tangle of wires with no visible bus bars. Hot wires lead to terminals connected to individual fuses, and there is a neutral bus bar in the center of the panel.

This fuse panel is limited to eight 120-volt circuits. Fuses are color-coded, but check for the written amp rating as well. Fuse panel with cover off shown below.

In a laundry area, the dryer is often plugged into a 240-volt circuit, while the washer plugs into a 120-volt circuit.

Branch Circuits

Power connects to the individual branch circuits of your house wiring at the service panel. Branch circuits then feed power to different parts of your home.

Circuit Basics

Most circuits carry 120 volts and provide power to multiple outlets. These circuits are commonly 15-amp circuits, using 14-gauge (#14) wire, or 20-amp circuits with 12-gauge (#12) wire.

To avoid an overload that will trip a circuit breaker or blow a fuse, aim for a load of no more than 80 percent of the amperage on a given circuit. You'll find, for example, that a 15-amp circuit that's powering an air conditioner should not also be used for a microwave oven; if both appliances are used at the same time, they are likely to overload it.

What Do the Circuits Control?

In some homes, circuits are divided by usage rather than rooms. For example, there may be a circuit for lights (usually 15 amps) that supplies two or three rooms and a receptacle circuit (usually 20 amps) that supplies the outlets in more than one room.

In other homes, circuits are divided by living space, with a single 15-amp circuit supplying both the lights and the receptacles for a single room—or for one room and parts of others.

Special Circuit Needs

Certain circuits have special configurations. A 240-volt circuit almost always supplies a single appliance. Some 120-volt circuits may supply only one receptacle—say, for a computer or sensitive electronic equipment.

In some cases, a duplex outlet—the most common type, with room for two plugs—may be split between two circuits. This prevents overloading when two heavy-use appliances are plugged in.

Many local codes incorporate special circuit-loading rules, especially for kitchens. A modern kitchen typically has five or more circuits—one for lights, one for the dishwasher and garbage disposer, one for the refrigerator, and two for the receptacles.

Rooms with just a few lights and receptacles are often connected to a single circuit.

A kitchen is an example of a room where the circuits are divided by usage.

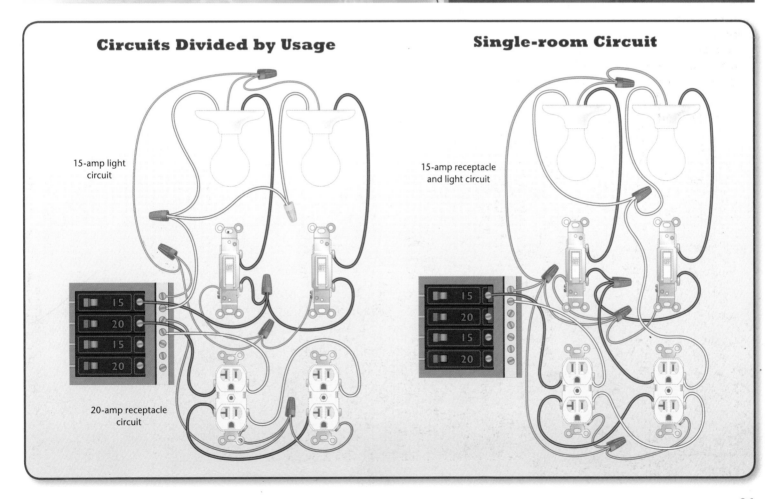

Circuits Divided by Usage

15-amp light circuit

20-amp receptacle circuit

Single-room Circuit

15-amp receptacle and light circuit

Grounding

Grounding protects you and your home from electric shock or fire. Metal parts of a circuit with which you might come into contact are connected to the earth.

There's an easy way to check whether your home wiring is adequately grounded. Plug a receptacle analyzer into six or seven outlets throughout the house. It will tell you, among other things, whether or not each one is grounded.

Understanding Ground Faults

Grounding is a crucial safeguard when an electrical problem called a ground fault occurs. That can happen wherever there is damaged wiring. You can also cause a ground fault if you fail to shut off the power and then work on open wiring—a dangerous mistake.

The illustration below, top, shows how grounding works in a typical three-wire system. When a power cord is frayed or damaged, a hot, energized wire may touch metal (here, the metal housing of an appliance). The metal is then energized, making it hazardous.

When this occurs, the current returns to the service panel through the ground wire, rather than the neutral wire. It then travels harmlessly into the earth through a thick house ground wire attached to a grounding rod or a metal water pipe.

At the same time, because the hot wire is now connected directly to the ground through the metal housing, it creates a "short" circuit. The resulting excess current trips the circuit breaker or blows the fuse.

Grounding Through Metal Conduit or Sheathing

If your home system uses conduit or armored cable, the service panel may not have a ground wire. Instead, the conduit or sheathing acts as the ground path. The result is the same: a blown fuse or tripped breaker, with the excess voltage traveling harmlessly into the earth.

Ungrounded Systems

Some homes built before the 1940s have ungrounded systems. Such a system is usually permitted if the wiring is sound, but any additions to it must typically be grounded.

If your home is ungrounded, be extra careful with your equipment, check and replace any frayed wiring, and call in an electrician for inspections every few years. Also make sure that your outlets have two slots and no grounding hole; the hole will only give a false sense of security. To make an outlet safer, install a GFCI receptacle.

Service Ground Connections

The main ground wire for your house should be connected firmly to a grounding rod or rods, a metal cold-water pipe, or both.

The grounding system will not work if any connections are loose. All connections should be made with clamps designed for grounding. If you suspect a problem with your grounding connections, call an electrician.

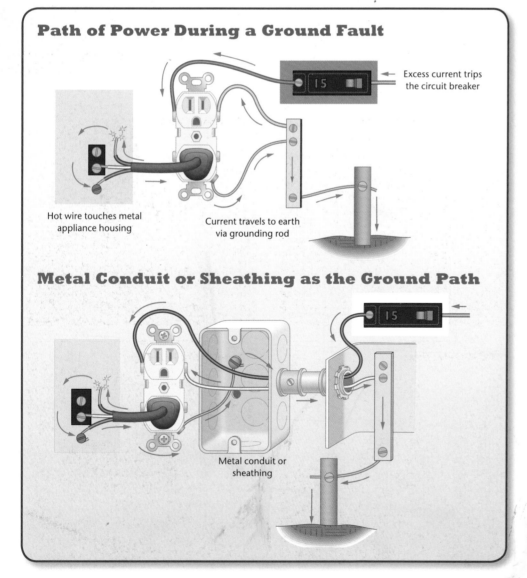

Path of Power During a Ground Fault

Excess current trips the circuit breaker

Hot wire touches metal appliance housing

Current travels to earth via grounding rod

Metal Conduit or Sheathing as the Ground Path

Metal conduit or sheathing

Related Topics

Other safety measures, 24–25
The service panel, 16–17

In electrical terms, being connected to the earth means being properly grounded.

In the service panel, the house ground wire—a thick wire that is either bare or green insulated—connects to a neutral/ground bus bar. The wire leads from the service panel to the grounding rod(s) or cold-water pipe.

GROUNDING RODS

Rods extend 8 feet into the ground; modern codes call for two or more rods. Setups vary by locality. This one has a green-marked ground wire clamped to the rod, and a copper strip connected to the metal conduit and rod.

COLD-WATER CONNECTIONS

Water pipes lead into the earth and connect to the city water system, making for good grounding. If the pipe is attached to a water meter with nonmetal parts, however, the grounding path will be interrupted. In that case, a jumper cable solves the problem.

OTHER METHODS

In some areas, grounding rods may be embedded in the house's concrete foundation. In regions with rocky soil, a large metal plate may be used in place of a rod.

Service-panel Connection

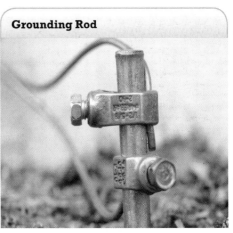

Grounding Rod

Cold-water Pipe

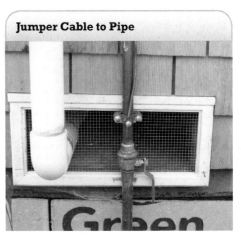

Jumper Cable to Pipe

Other Safety Measures

Over the years, electrical codes have changed, almost always in the direction of greater attention to safety. Here are some key points to bear in mind.

GFCI receptacles in kitchens are required by code in most areas.

Polarized Outlets & Plugs

In a polarized system, each slot of a receptacle or outlet carries only one kind of current. You can spot a polarized receptacle by the difference in the slots—one is longer than the other. The shorter slot connects to the hot wire, which brings power into the receptacle, and the longer slot is for the neutral wire, which carries power back to the service panel.

Polarized systems have been around since the 1920s, so most houses are polarized, even if the system is ungrounded.

Similarly, a modern electrical plug has a shorter prong connected to the appliance's hot wire and a wider one connected to the neutral wire. The plug can be inserted in only one way, so that the switch safely controls the current.

If either the plug or the receptacle is incorrectly wired, the wiring in the appliance will remain energized even when it is switched off—a dangerous situation. When you are rewiring a lamp or appliance, be careful that you attach the hot wire to the short prong.

Related Topics

Rewiring a lamp, 246–249

Lamp Plugged into a Polarized Receptacle

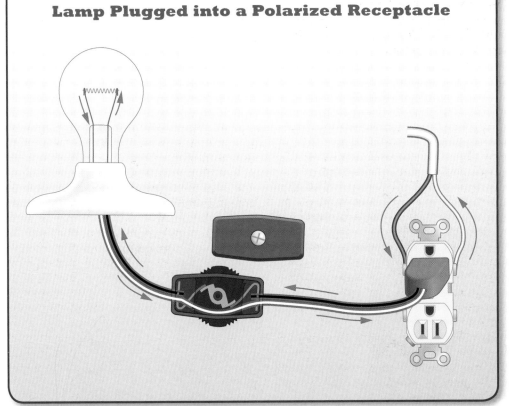

Protection Against Arc Faults

Faulty wiring, such as frayed insulation or a loose connection, can cause electricity to jump—arc—from the hot wire to a metal surface, a neutral wire, or a ground wire.

Common causes of arc faults include a nail pounded through lamp cords and cords of all types with cracked or missing insulation. In either case, the arc fault occurs when wires in the cord to come into contact with each other. An arc fault can also happen if a wire comes loose from a receptacle or a switch, or if wiring inside an electrical box has damaged insulation and contacts the metal box.

An arc fault creates a fire hazard more often than it causes shock; frayed lamp cords are a leading cause of house fires.

A GFCI will usually shut off in the event of an arc fault, but an arc-fault circuit interrupter (AFCI) is more reliable. Hire an electrician if you'd like to add AFCI circuit breakers to your house (there are no AFCI receptacles). Most codes require AFCI breakers for circuits that control bedrooms. You may want to have them installed for living-area circuits as well.

GFCI Protection

A ground-fault circuit interrupter (GFCI) provides excellent protection against electric shock in many circumstances. It senses even a very small imbalance in the amounts of incoming and outgoing current and instantly opens the circuit, cutting off power. GFCIs are built to trip in $\frac{1}{40}$ of a second if there is ground fault of .005 ampere or more.

The most common way to provide GFCI protection is with a GFCI receptacle. Any GFCI receptacle monitors the flow of electricity at that outlet. For example, a hair dryer that gets wet will instantly trip the GFCI it is plugged into. A GFCI receptacle can also be wired to monitor all devices installed in the circuit from that point onward (called downstream).

You can also hire an electrician to install a GFCI circuit breaker, which protects the entire circuit. This is more expensive, but it is also more reliable.

Most electrical codes require GFCI receptacles or breakers for bathrooms, kitchens, garages, basements, and outdoor locations —in other words, any potentially damp spot.

Arc-fault Situations

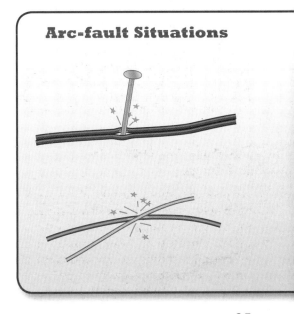

Looking Inside

Opening a switch or receptacle box, or detaching a light fixture may be a little scary at first—which is mostly a good thing. But once you've learned to work safely, you will be able to open boxes with more confidence.

Pulling Out a Receptacle

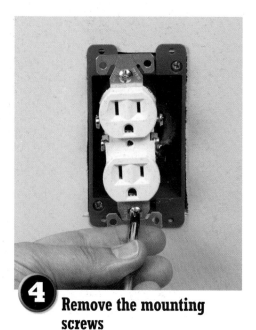

① Test to confirm power is off
- Insert probes into each set of receptacle slots

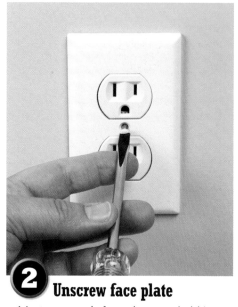

② Unscrew face plate
- Most receptacle face plates are held in place by a single screw
- Most face plates for light switches have two screws

③ Remove the face plate
- Pull it straight away from the wall

④ Remove the mounting screws
- Keep screws attached to the fixture tabs to avoid losing them

⑤ Pull out the receptacle
- Grasp the receptacle by its plastic parts, pull out gently
- If it's wired correctly, you should be able to pull it out several inches

Test & Test Again

When you open a box, test for power both before and after you remove the cover, since more than one circuit may be present. Test a receptacle for power with a voltage tester, receptacle analyzer, or a voltage detector. Test a switch or a fixture for power with a voltage detector. A 240-volt receptacle carries twice the power of a standard 120-volt model, making it very dangerous. It's better to avoid removing the cover of a 240-volt receptacle; if you must do so, use extreme caution.

Related Topics

Shutting off & restoring
power, 50–51
Testing methods, 52–53

Removing a Light Fixture

1 Detach the fixture

- Shut off the power; test it is off with a voltage detector
- Remove the lamp cover or globe, usually by loosening setscrews
- Remove light bulbs
- Release the mounting screws; for a threaded pipe, unscrew the nut

2 Pull out the fixture

- Use a sharp knife to slice any paint or caulk holding it in place
- Pull out the fixture
- Let a very light fixture hang from its wires; support others with a stepladder or on a coat hanger
- Test again for power in the box

Device Puller

A device puller has a strong magnet to grab a device, plus a hefty plastic handle to keep you well protected from shock when you pull it out. This example is a switch puller; you can also buy a receptacle puller.

Removing a Panel Cover

If you suspect a major problem at your service panel, call in an electrician. Otherwise, there is no need to shut off power to a service panel before you remove the cover. In most cases, you simply remove four or six screws and pull the panel off.

Common Wiring Methods

At first glance, the wires in a box may seem tangled, because they are crammed into a small space. The arrangement is clearer once you pull out a device and see how they connect.

Receptacles

Most receptacles are duplex outlets—outlets that have room for two different plugs. Usually, each plug-in space includes a hole to accept a grounding prong. Old homes with an ungrounded system lack the grounding hole.

The silver-colored terminals on a receptacle are for the neutral (white) wires; the brass-colored terminals correspond to the hot (black or colored) wires. Ground wires attach to the grounding screw.

MIDDLE-RUN & END-RUN WIRING

Typically, a single cable supplies power to a series of receptacles chained together on the same circuit.

A receptacle in the middle of the run has wires that carry power both to the receptacle and on to the next box. The wires may attach to wire nuts and only two terminals, as shown here. More commonly, the wires are attached to all four terminals.

An end-run receptacle has wires attached on only two terminals.

PLASTIC OR METAL BOXES

Receptacles can be installed in plastic or metal boxes; metal is more common in older construction.

Metal Box with BX Cable

Plastic Box with NM Cable

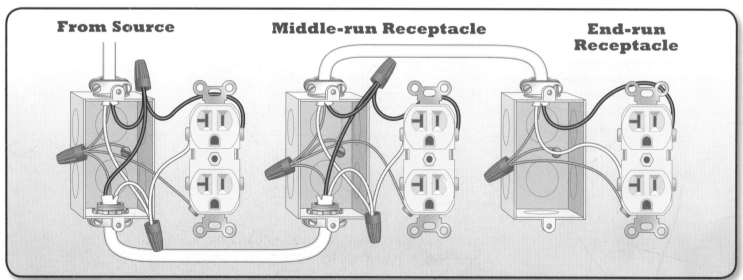

From Source　　　**Middle-run Receptacle**　　　**End-run Receptacle**

Cable is usually attached to a metal box with a cable clamp, which screws onto the box. The clamp squeezes nonmetallic (NM) cable or holds metal armored cable or conduit with a setscrew.

With BX armored cable (opposite, top left), the metal sheathing acts as the ground connector, making it especially important to clamp the cable tightly to the box. Make sure that the nut on the clamp is screwed down tight; if you have access outside the box, check that the clamp is attached tightly to the cable. Many homes wired with metal conduit do not have ground wires.

In the photo on the opposite page, top right, NM cable runs into a plastic box. Since there is no cable clamp on a plastic box, the cable should be stapled in place a foot or so from the box. No metal-clad cables are approved for plastic boxes.

GROUNDING METAL BOXES

Receptacles connect to the house grounding system in different ways. In a metal box, a ground wire should attach to the receptacle and to the box, using either a green grounding screw or a grounding clip. Grounding clips can come loose, so check that they are attached firmly. A grounding screw is more reliable, but you should still make sure it is tight.

If the box is plastic, the ground wire is connected only to the receptacle. The ground wire in the plastic box shown in the NM cable on the opposite page is bare copper; others may be covered in green insulation.

Grounding Boxes

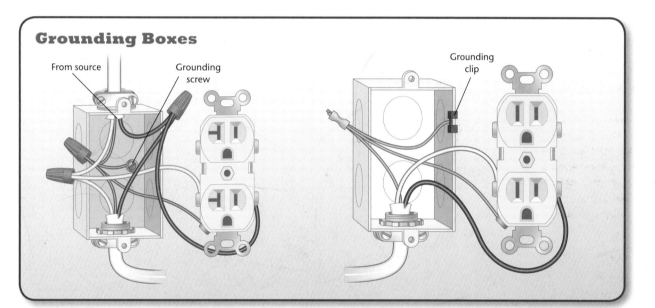

From source | Grounding screw | Grounding clip

Split Receptacles

When you examine the wiring for a receptacle, check between the terminal screws. If the tab between them has been broken and each terminal is connected to a different cable, you have a split receptacle. This may mean that each outlet is on a different circuit, or that one outlet is always hot and the other is controlled by a wall switch.

The tab between the terminals has been broken off.

A 20-amp receptacle's neutral slot is T-shaped.

LEFT: A bank of switches and a thermostat are conveniently located.
RIGHT: A three-way switch at the bottom of a stairway.

Switch Wiring

Switches interrupt the flow of electricity through the hot wire, allowing you to supply or cut off power to a fixture.

THROUGH-SWITCH & SWITCH-LOOP WIRING

A standard single-pole switch, which controls one or more lights from a single location, may be wired in two ways.

The most common way is through-switch wiring. Power runs to the switch box, then to the fixture box. In the switch box, the hot wire passes through the switch but the neutral wire goes directly to the fixture.

Switch-loop wiring is more common in older homes. Both the black and the white wires leading from the fixture box to the switch box attach to the switch, forming a loop. Both wires are hot, so the white wire is marked with black paint or tape in the switch box.

GROUNDING

Modern codes require that switches be grounded just like receptacles. If the switch has a grounding screw, the ground wire is fastened with it.

THREE-WAY SWITCHES

If you can control a fixture from two different switches, then those switches are three-ways. In the example on the opposite page, the circuit is completed by the two black wires on the right. The red wire connects the two switches and the neutral wires connect the source to the fixture.

Related Topics

Common wiring configurations, 272–279
Grounding, 22–23
Smart & wireless switches, 152–153
Special-purpose switches, 108–109
Switches, 104–105
Three- and four-way switches, 268–271

Through-switch Wiring

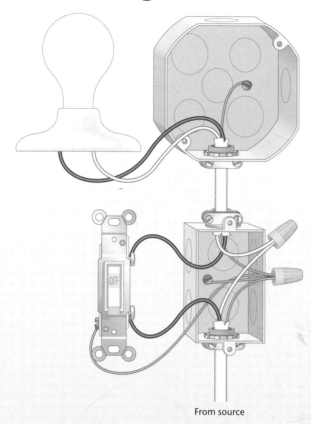

From source

Switch-loop Wiring

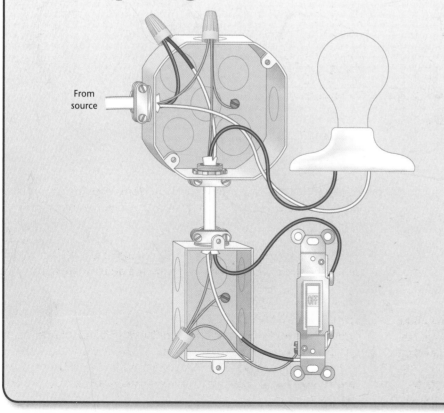

From source

Connecting to a Grounding Screw

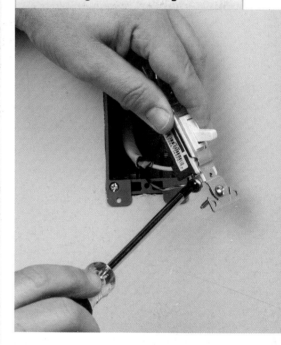

Three-way Switch

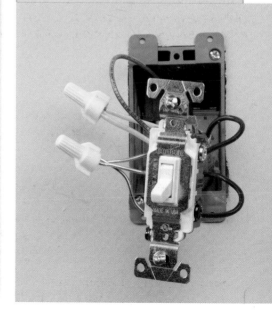

Cable & Wire Types

Most home wiring is hidden in the walls, but you can probably get a good look at your cables and wires at the service panel and in unfinished areas like the attic, garage, basement, or utility room.

Single-conductor Wires

Solid-core wire

Stranded wire

Multiconductor Cables

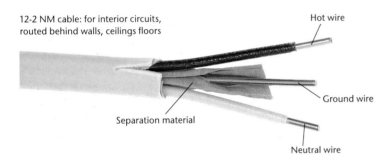

12-2 NM cable: for interior circuits, routed behind walls, ceilings floors

Hot wire

Ground wire

Separation material

Neutral wire

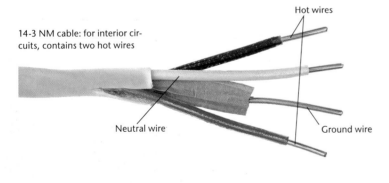

14-3 NM cable: for interior circuits, contains two hot wires

Hot wires

Neutral wire

Ground wire

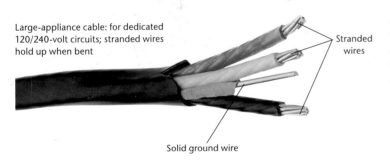

Large-appliance cable: for dedicated 120/240-volt circuits; stranded wires hold up when bent

Stranded wires

Solid ground wire

Cable Basics

Most household wiring uses solid-core wire. However, some thicker wires for 240-volt circuits are stranded.

Electrical cable typically combines a neutral wire, one or two hot wires, and a ground wire inside a plastic or metal covering called sheathing.

The individual hot and neutral wires (also called conductors) within a cable are usually insulated from one another by a color-coded thermoplastic insulation, which doesn't carry current. Neutral wires are white or gray, while hot wires are black, red, or another color. The ground wire may be bare or green-insulated.

NM Cable

Nonmetallic sheathed cable, or NM, is the standard choice for interior projects in many parts of the country. It is also often referred to as Romex, which is the trademarked name of one brand of NM. NM cable should be installed in dry locations only.

Older NM cable is rated at 140 degrees F (60 degrees C). Newer cable, labeled NM-B, can withstand temperatures of 194 degrees F (90 degrees C), making it safe even near heating sources. A beefier, black-sheathed NM cable, sometimes called large-appliance cable, has stranded wires, which can be bent numerous times without breaking.

Newer NM cable may also be color-coded to make it easy to tell whether it contains 14-gauge (#14) or 12-gauge

(#12) wires. Yellow-sheathed cable has #12 wires. Cable with #14 wires is typically white.

Underground feed (UF) cable has a sheathing bonded to the individual wires to make it moisture-resistant. As the name indicates, it is used for underground outdoor wiring.

Armored Cable

Older armored cable, called BX, has no ground wire. Instead, the spiral metal sheathing serves as the ground path. A newer armored cable, Type MC, has a green-insulated ground wire.

Wires

Cable is identified by the number and size of the wires it contains. For example, a cable with two 14-gauge (#14) wires (one neutral and one hot) and a ground wire is called two-wire cable—or, more specifically, 14-2 with ground.

The number "14" refers to the diameter of the metal conductor, not including the insulation. The larger a wire's diameter, the larger its current-carrying capacity, or ampacity, and the lower its gauge number. For instance, #14 has an ampacity of 15, whereas #12 can carry 20 amps. These numbers appear on the cable sheathing, as well as on the individual wires protected within the sheathing.

Individual wires labeled THHN are suitable for dry locations only and rated for 194 degrees F (90 degrees C). Those labeled THWN are rated for 167

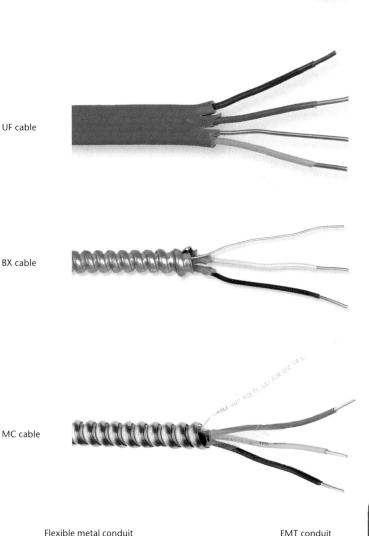

Color-coded
NM cable

UF cable

BX cable

MC cable

Flexible metal conduit
(Greenfield)

EMT conduit
and fittings

Related Topics

Working with NM cable, 62–63
Working with armored cable,
  64–65
Working with conduit, 66–67

degrees F (75 degrees C) and suitable for damp locations.

Copper is the best and most commonly used metal for electrical wires. Some homes from the 1960s and 1970s have aluminum wire, which does not conduct as well and so is thicker.

Conduit

Pipe-like conduit protects individual wires from moisture and physical harm. It is often used where wiring is exposed, such as in a garage, basement, or utility room. In some parts of the country, NM cable is not allowed by code and conduit is required for all wiring.

Conduit has two advantages over NM. It offers more protection from nails or screws driven into walls, and if it's wide enough, you can pull new wires through for changes or upgrades. However, conduit costs more and takes more time to install than NM or armored cable.

Thinwall metal conduit, called Type EMT, has long been the standard preference for interior wiring. Flexible metal conduit, sometimes referred to by the trademark Greenfield, is similar to armored cable, but you supply the wires. It is often used where EMT would be difficult to route and for water heaters and other large appliances.

Rigid nonmetal conduit, made from PVC plastic, is often allowed for interior installations. It is not the same as PVC plumbing pipe.

The larger the conduit, the more wires it can hold. So it makes sense to plan ahead. When you want to add service, you may be able to pull additional wires through a sufficiently wide conduit and thus avoid cutting into walls.

Knob-and-Tube Wiring

Old knob-and-tube wiring consists of separate hot and neutral wires threaded through porcelain knobs and tubes. It has no ground wire, so all the receptacles connected to it are ungrounded.

Although it's no longer legal in new construction, knob-and-tube wiring may be allowed to remain in existing installations. Many electricians consider it safe as long as it is left undisturbed. However, if you have the opportunity, it is a good idea to replace it with NM or other cable, and to provide a ground.

Meter Reading & Panel Indexing

You can tackle the wiring jobs on this page with a pad and pencil. Reading your meter helps track your usage (and check your bill); labeling your house circuits at the panel will make any project easier.

STOP!
A circuit index (map) at your service panel can be a great time-saver—but no index is guaranteed accurate. When you turn off a circuit based on the index, you'll still need to check the box where you're working to be sure power is off.

Reading the Meter

Most electric meters have four or five dials, which alternate between clockwise and counterclockwise. To read a meter, record the numbers indicated for each dial, from left to right. It's almost—but not quite—as easy as it sounds!

When the pointer is between two numbers, write down the smaller number.

When the pointer appears to be directly on a number, check the next dial to the right. If the pointer of that next dial is on zero or has passed zero, go back to the original dial and record the number that pointer is on. But if the pointer on the next dial has not reached zero, go back to the original dial and record the number preceding the one indicated there.

In the example below, the pointer on the first dial is between 0 and 1, so the number to record is 0. The next dial pointer is between 4 and 5, so the number is 4.

The pointer of the third dial is almost on 2, so look at the fourth dial. That pointer has passed 9 but not quite reached 0. For the third dial, then, record the number 1. For the fourth dial, the number is 9.

On the last dial, with the pointer between 7 and 8, the number is 7. The reading is therefore 04197 kilowatt-hours.

To calculate the number of kilowatt-hours consumed during a certain period, subtract the meter reading at the start of the period from the reading at the end. You can use this method to check your utility bills.

Electric companies often have tiered charges. The first 500 or so kilowatts are charged at one rate and additional kilowatts are charged at a higher rate, which may vary depending on the time of year.

Indexing Your Service Panel

A circuit index or map makes it easier to shut off power to a wiring area you want to

0

4

1

9

7

Time Commitment

Meter reading: Less than 5 minutes, with practice
Indexing a panel: 1 to 2 hours, depending on house size

Tools You'll Need

Pencil
Paper
Two cell phones or walkie-talkies
Small lamp, plug-in radio, or outlet tester

Related Topics

Avoiding overloads, 266–267
Calculating usage & capacity, 282–283
Planning a large project, 280–281

work on. You may be lucky enough to inherit an index from a previous owner, although old indexes are not always accurate. The index may be inside the service panel door or written on labels beside the breakers or fuses.

To create your own index, first turn off computers, televisions, and anything else that could be damaged as the power goes on and off. Then turn on every light and ceiling fixture.

If possible, recruit a helper to index the circuits. A pair of cell phones or walkie-talk-ies will simplify the job, though if the home is small, you can call to each other. Also equip your helper with a plug-in radio, lamp, or outlet tester to check the power at each wall and ceiling outlet.

Station yourself at the service panel, with the panel door open. Write down numbers for each breaker (or fuse, for a fuse panel). Leave room to note what's on each circuit.

Turn off the first circuit breaker, or remove the first fuse. Your helper should tell you which lights have turned off and also check the outlets and appliances to find out which ones have no power. Write down this information. Then restore power to that circuit, and check the next one.

It may seem tiresome to check all the receptacles in the house, but circuits sometimes go in unexpected directions. Don't forget to check outdoor receptacles, as well as those in the garage or attic. Major appliances commonly have their own 240-volt circuits.

Once you're done, transfer your findings to a circuit index and firmly attach it to the panel.

Circuit Index

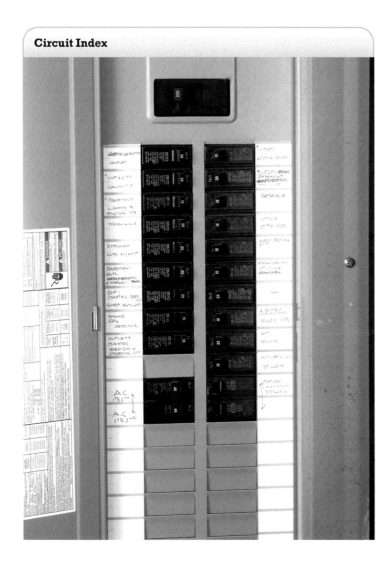

Indexing Your Circuits

Inspecting Your Wiring

If you're about to buy (or sell) your house, it's a good idea to have a pro inspect it. At other times, taking a look yourself can help you spot potential hazards and plan upgrades or repairs. If you discover troublesome situations, call an electrician.

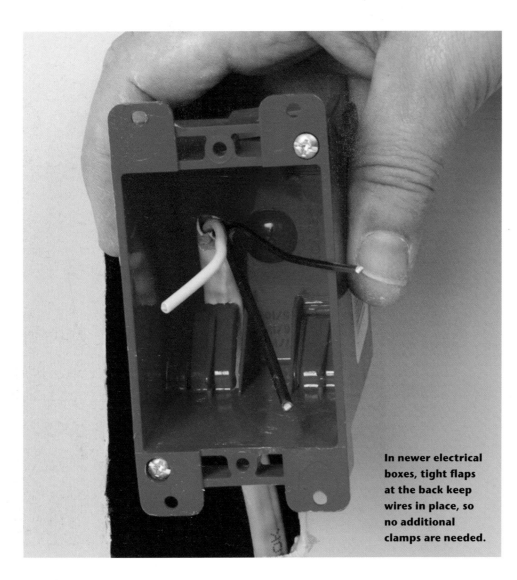

In newer electrical boxes, tight flaps at the back keep wires in place, so no additional clamps are needed.

Frayed Cord

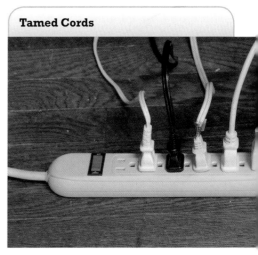

Tamed Cords

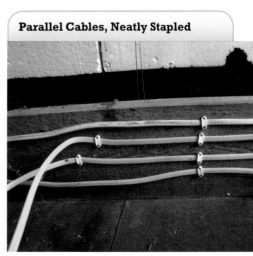

Parallel Cables, Neatly Stapled

Surface Inspection

Look first at exposed materials: boxes and cables in utility areas, lamps and appliance cords, receptacles and fixtures.

LAMP & APPLIANCE CORDS

If a cord is frayed, or the insulation is brittle and cracked, it should be replaced rather than patched with tape. Also replace cracked or otherwise damaged plugs. To prevent future damage, avoid running cords under a rug.

TANGLED CORDS

Especially under a computer desk, cords can become a confusing mess. Use power strips to keep them organized. Some strips have surge protection. Many have mini-circuit breakers, which shut off power during an overload so the rest of the circuit is not affected.

ACCESS TO SERVICE PANEL

A service panel or subpanel should be out of children's reach, but it also should be easy for adults to get to. Keep the path to any panel clear.

CABLE RUNS

Exposed electrical cables (in basements and garages, for example) should be firmly attached to the framing of the house, running in parallel rather than crossing. The cable staples should be insulated or rounded so they don't dig into the sheathing. When cables run across joists, some inspectors require that they go through holes rather than being stapled to the undersides. Never hang clothes or anything else from electrical cables.

BOX WITH NO COVER PLATE

It's not uncommon for a plate to be left off a switch or receptacle after a repair, but it's really not a good idea. Dust and lint can collect in the box, creating a fire hazard. And there is a real risk of electrical shock, especially for curious children. Take a minute to install that cover plate.

UNBOXED WIRING

Codes require that electrical connections be made inside an electrical box or inside a fixture with a built-in box. Unboxed connections are exposed to damage and present a fire hazard.

UNCLAMPED CABLE

Because most plastic boxes do not have cable clamps to hold the cable firmly, NM cable should be stapled to the framing within a foot of a plastic box.

Where cable enters a metal box, it must be attached to the box via a cable clamp. Otherwise, it could be nicked by the box hole's edges. Unclamped armored cable or conduit may render a part of the system ungrounded.

APPLIANCE CONNECTIONS

Major appliances have built-in electrical boxes where cables can be clamped and splices are protected. These water heater connections should have been made inside the heater's box, and the cable should be clamped.

OPEN KNOCKOUT PLUG

Although it's less dangerous than a missing cover plate, a partly open or missing knockout plug on the side of a box provides an opening for little fingers and allows dust inside. Cover such a hole by tapping in a goof plug.

Unsecured Cable

Partly Open Plug

Missing Cover Plate

Connection Outside a Box

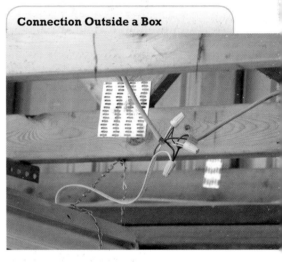

Out-of-place Appliance Connections

PHONE CONNECTIONS

Telephone wiring carries very little power, so it's generally considered OK for splices like those shown at right to occur outside boxes. (Observe routine cautions if you're working on it, though.) Splices in a box are preferable because they are better protected.

USING A RECEPTACLE ANALYZER

A receptacle analyzer, sometimes called a circuit analyzer or outlet tester, tells you whether a receptacle's plug is grounded and correctly wired for polarization. If an analyzer indicates that a single receptacle (or one side of a duplex outlet) is wrongly wired, shut off power and either correct the wiring or replace the receptacle. You may need to tighten grounding connections, or perhaps the neutral and hot wires are not on the correct terminals. If several receptacles test ungrounded, call in a professional electrician, as there may be a problem with the system ground.

NICKED WIRE END

If a wire was nicked during stripping, or if it was bent several times, the metal loses strength and can break. Cut the wire, restrip it, and reattach it.

TOO MUCH STRIPPED WIRE

Only the part of the wire that touches the terminal screw should be stripped (and maybe ⅛ inch more). Exposed wire may touch the metal box and cause a short. Cut the wire, restrip it, and reattach it.

CABLE CLAMPS

Make sure that NM cable inside a metal box has some sheathing visible just inside the box. This ensures that the cable clamp is grasping the sheathing so that it cannot damage the individual wires.

ARMORED CABLE BUSHINGS

The cut ends of sheathing on BX or MC armored cable have sharp edges that can easily nick wire insulation—creating the danger of short circuits or fire. Check inside the box for a little red bushing that protects the wires. If it is missing, slip one on and push it down. If it is there but raised, push it down so it encases the wires. The bushing shown on the opposite page is pushed correctly onto the sheathing, even though it is at an angle.

If you see a number of armored-cable connections without protective bushings, call in a professional.

COBWEBS & COCOONS

Spiders, moths, and other creatures can create a mess, and sometimes a short circuit, if they get into a box. Brush out debris and make sure the box is well sealed.

Older Wiring

In older homes, be on the lookout for these unpleasant surprises.

BLACKENED INSULATION

Old cloth insulation can darken over time. In the switch box on the opposite page, it is impossible to tell which wire is black and which is white. Since those colors indicate which wire is hot and which is neutral, the dark insulation could cause dangerous miswiring. Identify the wires and protect them with insulation sleeves.

CEILING BOX USED AS A JUNCTION BOX

In some old homes, power travels through the ceiling boxes first, so a small pancake box like the one on the opposite page may contain wires from two or more circuits. As long as the wiring is well spliced and firmly attached, this is considered safe. Test carefully before working on this type of wiring.

PUSH-BUTTON SWITCH

A push-button switch is charming, but it won't last forever. Replace it if you see sparks or hear a pop when you operate it.

MIXED CABLES

A mix of different cable types isn't uncommon in an older house. Here, metal conduit, cloth NM cable, and armored cable enter the same fuse box. As long as the connections are secure and the wires are well insulated, such a mixture is not unsafe.

SHORT WIRES

In some older boxes, the wires are just too short to connect easily. Use pigtails to lengthen the wires. Or install a dimmer switch or other specialty switch that has wire leads rather than screw terminals.

TANGLED JUNCTION BOX

Don't be alarmed if you find a nest of wires in a large box. It's safe as long as the connections are firm and no bare wire is exposed.

Splices in Phone Wiring

Testing a Receptacle

A Well-clamped Cable

Visible sheathing

Push-button Switch

Lots of Tangled Wires

Nicked Wire End

Armored Cable Bushing

Blackened Insulation

Pancake Box

Too Much Stripped Wire

Dirty Panel

A Remedy for Short Wires

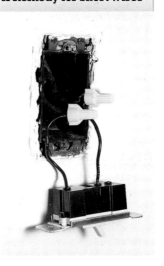

A Mixture of Cables

When & How to Hire a Pro

This book will enable you to replace existing service, add new service, and solve most electrical problems. However, there are times when it's best to turn to a pro.

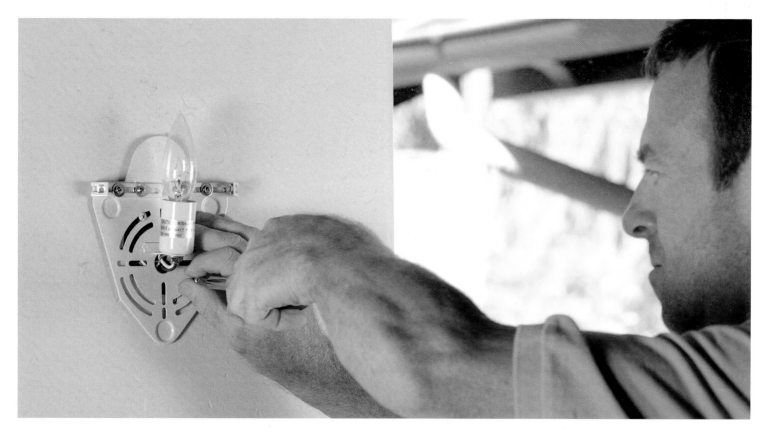

Installing light fixtures requires a knowledge of wiring techniques, as well as basic carpentry skills.

ARE YOU ALLOWED TO DO THE WORK?

In some municipalities, it is illegal for a homeowner to undertake certain kinds of electrical installations—for example, to add new service that involves running new cable. If this is the situation in your area, you will need to hire a pro.

DOING PART OF THE WORK YOURSELF

Your local building department may have some specific rules about what you can and cannot do. For instance, you may be able to do all wiring up to the point at which the circuits are connected to the service panel, but the final hookup may have to be done by a licensed electrician.

ALWAYS HIRE A PRO WHEN...

Be sure to hire a pro—or the power company—when the work involves live wires. Have a professional perform any installations in which you cannot shut off power before doing the work. This includes working on the service entrance or the electrical meter. Installing a new service panel falls under the same category.

Also hire a pro to advise you, at least, on a major project that calls for more than two new circuits. An experienced electrician can evaluate your needs and plan for circuits that will be correctly loaded.

You should also hire a pro whenever you don't feel confident about doing a job or decide that it is too ambitious for the spare time you have available.

CONTRACTING WITH A PRO

Any electrician you hire should be licensed in your area and insured. To obtain a fair price, get quotes from two or three electricians. Make sure the quotes include the materials to be used; the type and number of devices, appliances, and fixtures; and the locations of the installations.

The contract should spell out when the work will be finished, with incentives or penalties to ensure timely completion. Be sure to hold back a significant final payment until the job is done to your satisfaction.

WORKING WITH AN INSPECTOR

When you need an inspection, be sure to have everything ready and open for viewing. If, for instance, you cover cable with drywall before you are supposed to, the inspector may require you to tear it out.

When you talk to the inspector, take notes, then follow the instructions to the letter. Never argue with an inspector; you have very little chance of victory.

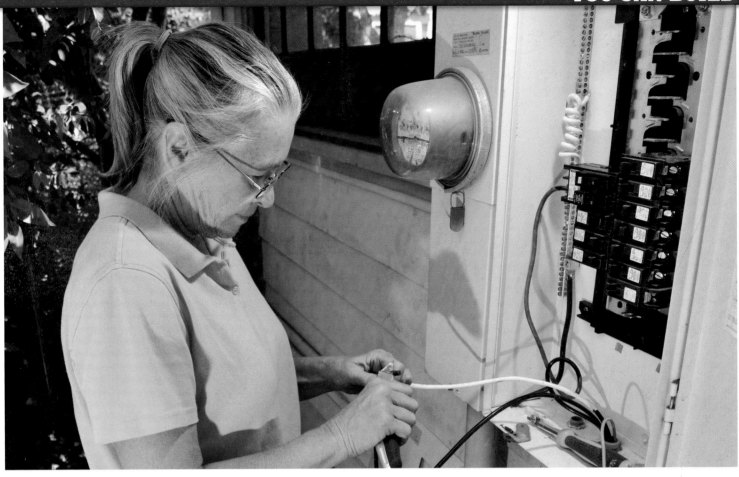

In most cases, working on the service panel is best left to a pro.

CODE & PERMITS

The National Electrical Code (usually called the NEC or simply "The Code") spells out the wiring methods and materials for all electrical work. This code forms the basis for all regulations applied to electrical installations.

The information in this book complies with guidelines set out by the NEC. Some cities, counties, and states amend the code to suit their particular purposes. As a result, specific regulations can vary by location—even from town to town.

In Canada, wiring requirements may differ from those listed in this book. Before beginning any work, check the Canadian Electrical Code.

In most areas, you must get an electrical permit before installing new service that calls for a new circuit. You may also need to get a permit to run new cable even when there is no new circuit. And some building departments require that you obtain a permit just to replace a light fixture or a receptacle. Check with your local building department.

It's not "cheating" to make notes when wiring home electronics; experts do it all the time.

Tools & Skills

I n this chapter, we show you all the tools you'll need to per-

form everything from simple wiring tasks like changing a

receptacle to more complicated projects requiring new cable and

conduit. We also explain the steps to take to shut off power, as

well as the testing methods to make sure you are wiring safely;

the techniques for stripping and joining wire; and the best ways

to work with armored cable.

Chapter Contents

Working with NM Cable
page 62

Working with Armored Cable
page 64

Wiring with Conduit
page 66

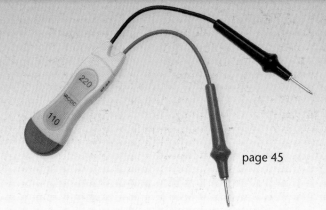

page 45

Basic Wiring Tools

Most wiring projects don't require lots of tools, so you can spend a bit more for high-quality equipment that feels solid and safe. Use tools made for electrical work, with rubber-insulated grips.

STOP!

Always use electrician's tools, which have rubber grips to protect you from shock in case the power has been accidentally left on. For additional safety, consider tools with extra insulation that's molded to keep your hand away from the metal part of the tool. Bright-colored tools labeled "1000" offer the greatest safety. They can absorb a shock of as much as 1,000 volts, and the shafts and handles are insulated. No matter which tool you use, shut off the power before getting to work.

Basic Hand Tools

Lineman's pliers cut wires easily, and the jaws hold stripped wires securely. Use them to neatly twist wires together before you add a wire nut.

Long-nose pliers can be used to bend wire ends to hook around screw terminals, and they also cut wire. Buy a pair that's big enough to fit comfortably in your hand.

Diagonal cutters, or dikes, make closer, cleaner cuts, although you can probably make do without them.

Wire strippers are essential. They remove thermoplastic insulation from wire ends without damaging the wire, and you can also use them to bend wire ends into hook shapes. Although professionals sometimes strip wires with other tools, that requires experience; always use wire strippers for your projects.

A multipurpose tool can be used to cut wire, strip insulation, and attach crimp connectors, but doesn't do so as well as tools designed for each task.

A basic screwdriver collection should include Phillips heads in #1 and #2 sizes, plus small and large slot heads. A spinning, or rotary, screwdriver makes quick work of removing and reinstalling small screws. A power screwdriver—or, better, a cordless drill—with interchangeable tips is even easier to use.

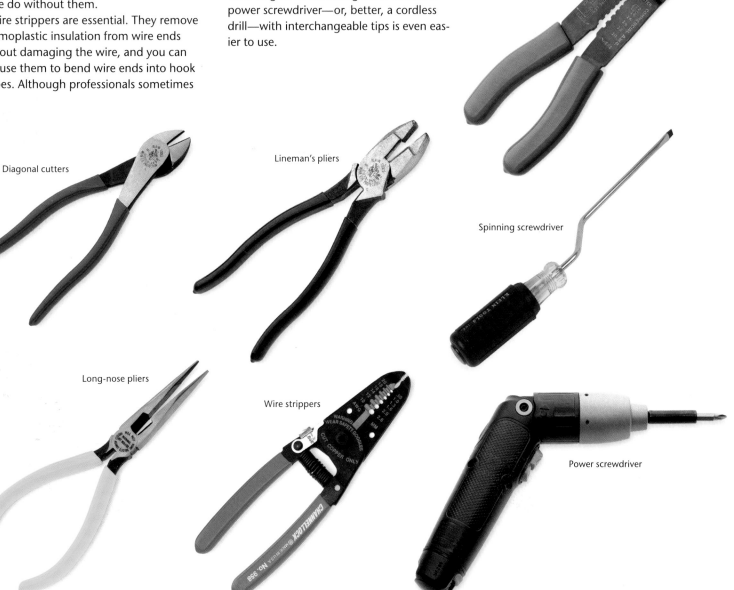

Multipurpose tool

Diagonal cutters

Lineman's pliers

Spinning screwdriver

Long-nose pliers

Wire strippers

Power screwdriver

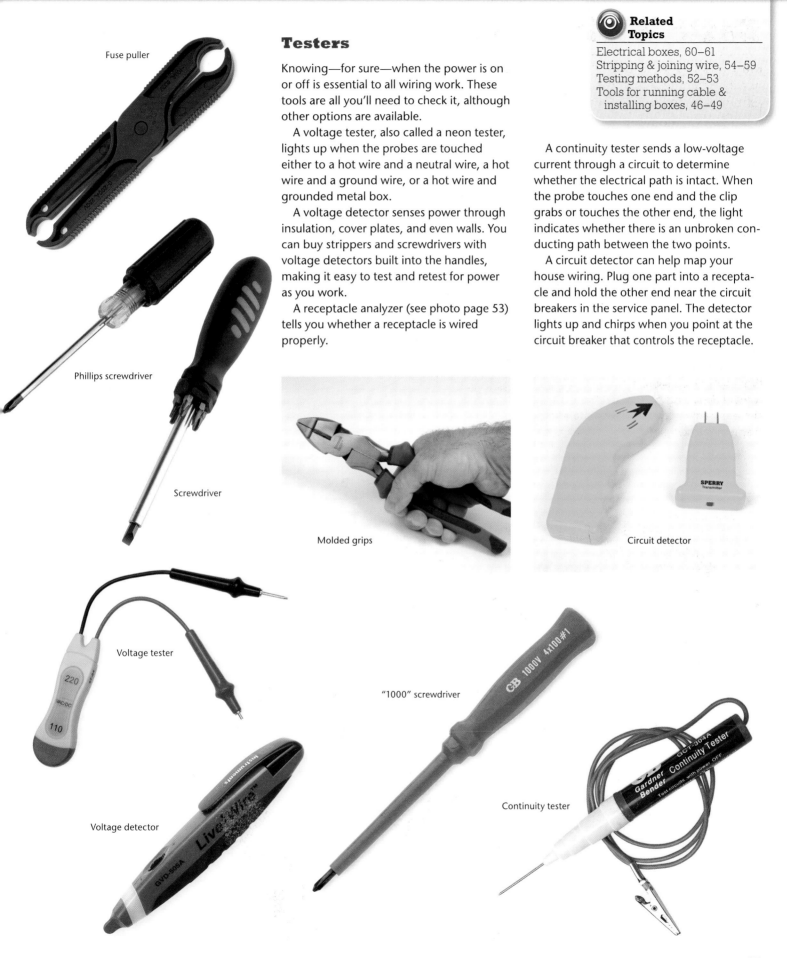

Fuse puller

Phillips screwdriver

Screwdriver

Related Topics

Electrical boxes, 60–61
Stripping & joining wire, 54–59
Testing methods, 52–53
Tools for running cable &
   installing boxes, 46–49

Testers

Knowing—for sure—when the power is on or off is essential to all wiring work. These tools are all you'll need to check it, although other options are available.

A voltage tester, also called a neon tester, lights up when the probes are touched either to a hot wire and a neutral wire, a hot wire and a ground wire, or a hot wire and grounded metal box.

A voltage detector senses power through insulation, cover plates, and even walls. You can buy strippers and screwdrivers with voltage detectors built into the handles, making it easy to test and retest for power as you work.

A receptacle analyzer (see photo page 53) tells you whether a receptacle is wired properly.

A continuity tester sends a low-voltage current through a circuit to determine whether the electrical path is intact. When the probe touches one end and the clip grabs or touches the other end, the light indicates whether there is an unbroken conducting path between the two points.

A circuit detector can help map your house wiring. Plug one part into a receptacle and hold the other end near the circuit breakers in the service panel. The detector lights up and chirps when you point at the circuit breaker that controls the receptacle.

Molded grips

Circuit detector

Voltage tester

"1000" screwdriver

Voltage detector

Continuity tester

Basic Wiring Tools **45**

Tools for Running Cable & Installing Boxes

You'll need many of these tools to install new service. You may also require excavating tools to run outdoor cable, or special tools for low-voltage phone and networking lines.

Tools for Stripping & Cutting

Strip sheathing from NM cable with cable strippers or cable rippers; both tools do the job faster and run less risk of causing damage than improvised attempts with a knife and diagonal cutters. Cable strippers look like wire strippers, but they have 14-2 and 12-2 cable slots. Cable rippers come in light- and heavy-duty versions.

Cut through the sheathing of armored cable with an armored-cable cutter—never a hacksaw, which could damage the wires inside.

Cut metal conduit with a hacksaw, then remove the burrs inside the conduit with a reaming tool. Alternatively, use an electrician's tubing cutter. Never use a standard plumbing tubing cutter on conduit; it will leave sharp ridges inside the pipe that could damage wire insulation.

Cut plastic (PVC) conduit with a PVC cutter. Or use a hacksaw or any carpentry saw, followed by a knife to remove burrs from inside the pipe.

Cable rippers

Reaming tool

Armored-cable cutter

PVC cutter

Cable strippers

Electrician's tubing cutter

Hacksaw

Testing Tools

A standard voltage tester and voltage detector are all you need for most installations, but you may choose to buy some professional testing tools, too. A snap-around tester allows you to determine the voltage in a line without touching bare wires. A pro-quality plug-in tester tells you everything that a receptacle analyzer tells you, plus more information about the circuit, such as whether there is a slow leak called a high-resistance short.

FISH TAPE & FISHING TOOL

Use fish tape to pull wires through conduit or to tug NM or armored cable through finished walls. For a cable job, you may need a fishing drill bit, made of a long bit, a bender to direct the bit, and a pulling attachment that grabs onto the cable. Instead of using fish tape, you can also try a length of NM cable or ½-inch PEX plumbing pipe.

Fish tape

Snap-around tester

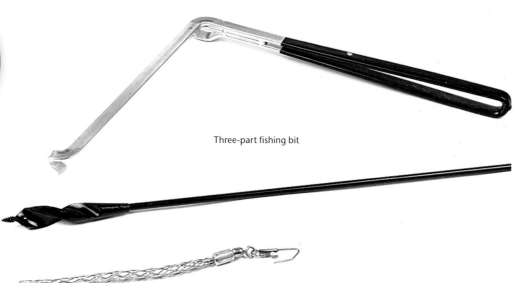
Three-part fishing bit

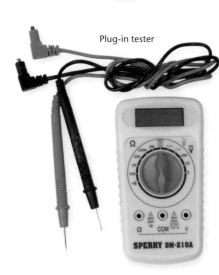
Plug-in tester

Bending Conduit

To shape metal conduit with a conduit bender, first measure the distance to the bend and add a few inches to be safe. Follow the directions that come with your bender to determine where to place that point on the conduit against the markings on the tool. Slip the conduit into the bender and hold the conduit on the floor as you bend it to the desired angle. This bender has marks that help you make bends at the correct angles.

Carpentry Tools

The carpentry tools you'll need depend on whether you are running cable through finished walls or unfinished framing.

Handsaws are safer when you must cut blindly into a finished wall. (With a power saw, you're more likely to cut into a hidden cable, duct, or pipe.) Use a hand drywall saw, also called a jab saw, to cut through drywall. Once you know where it's safe to cut, a saber saw, also called a jigsaw, works better and cuts faster on plaster. A reciprocating saw comes in handy for demolition and cutting notches in corners.

For demolition and general carpentry, use a claw hammer and a flat pry bar. A flexible flashlight helps you look inside walls and ceilings, and a stud finder can locate wood framing inside a wall, as well as hidden electrical and plumbing lines.

Cordless drills are convenient to use, but corded drills often have more power.

Drills with a 3/8-inch chuck generally have less power than 1/2-inch drills. If you need to drill through many joists or studs, consider renting or buying a 1/2-inch drill with a cord. A right-angle model makes it easier to work in tight spots and to drill straight holes. A handle on the side helps you steady the drill as you work with large bits.

Spade bits are fine for drilling a handful of holes through joists and studs, but if you have lots of drilling to do, use an auger bit. Both bits are large enough that it's a good idea to use a variable-speed drill for better control.

Claw hammer

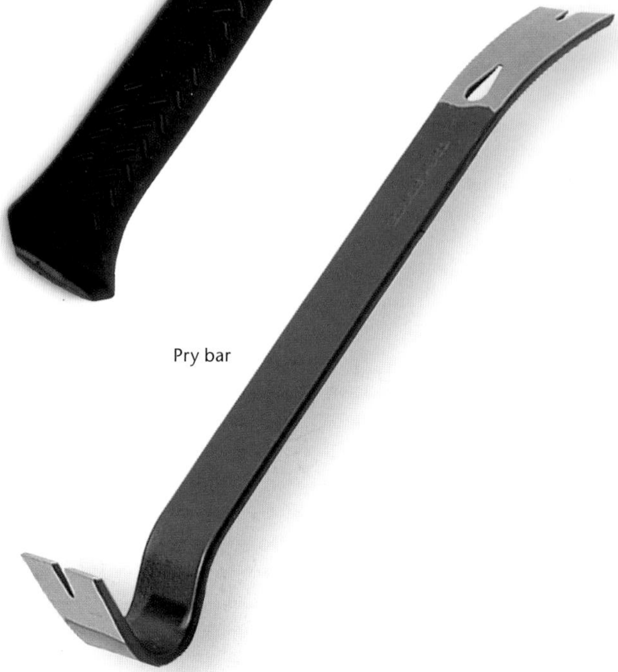

Pry bar

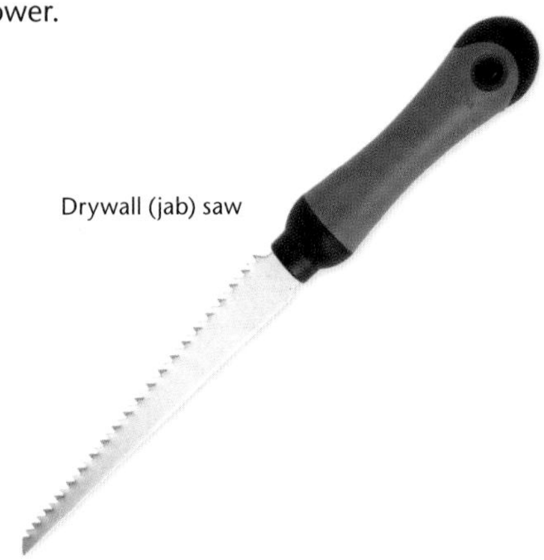

Drywall (jab) saw

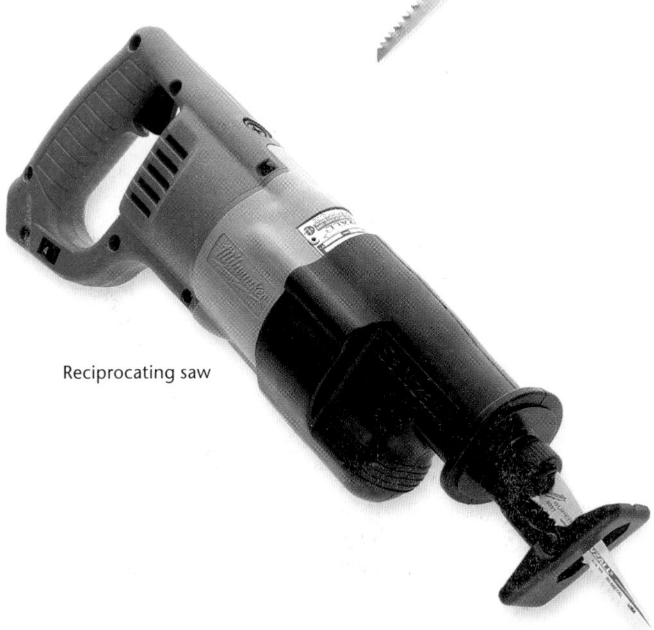

Reciprocating saw

Saber saw (jigsaw)

Related Topics

Wiring in finished rooms, 130–135

Wiring in unfinished framing, 140–141

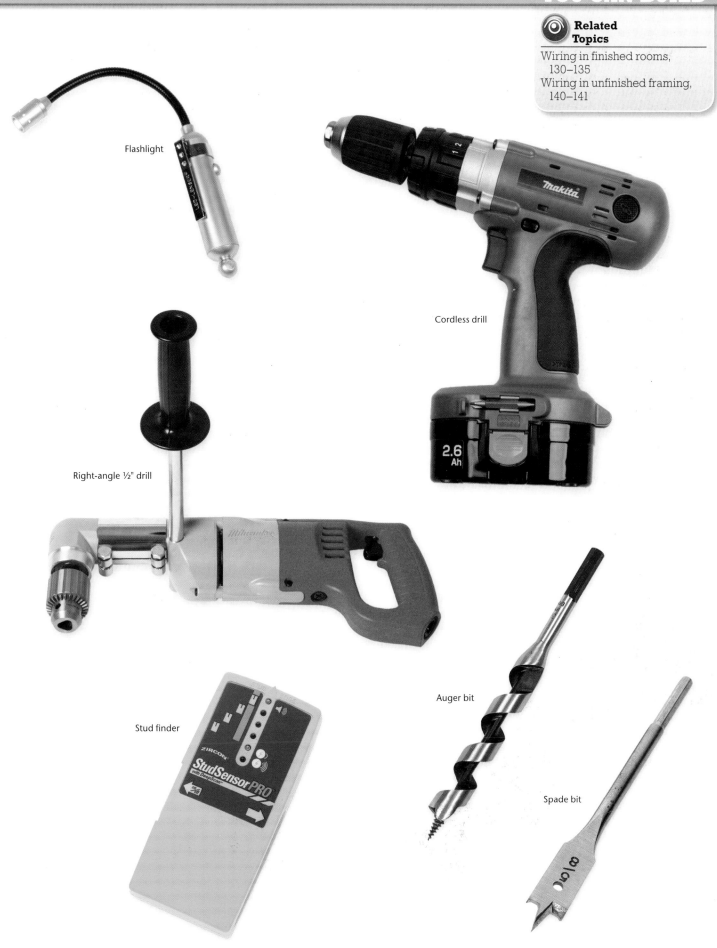

Flashlight

Cordless drill

2.6 Ah

Right-angle ½" drill

Stud finder

Auger bit

Spade bit

Shutting Off & Restoring Power

Before you start work on a wiring project, go to the service panel or subpanel to shut off power to the circuit (or circuits) that are involved. If you cannot easily find the correct fuse or breaker, use a process of elimination; when shutting off a circuit does not turn off the outlet, restore power to the circuit and try another.

STOP!
When you're turning off power to a circuit to start a wiring project, always confirm at the project site that the power is really off.

You may also need to deal with a fuse or breaker if you suddenly find yourself in partial darkness due to an overloaded circuit. To restore power, you'll need to reduce the load on the circuit and then replace the fuse or reset the breaker.

Fuses

There are two basic types of fuses: plug and cartridge. To turn off power to a circuit protected by a plug (screw-in) fuse, turn the fuse counterclockwise several times. Turn it with your fingers; no tool is needed. To restore power, rotate the fuse clockwise by hand. Seat it securely, but don't overtighten it.

To turn off a circuit protected by a cartridge fuse, pull out the fuse block by its wire handle.

Fuse block

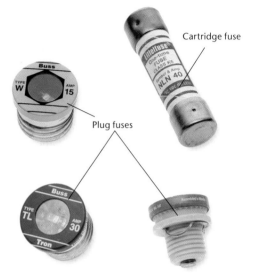

Cartridge fuse

Plug fuses

BLOWN FUSES

A fuse has a thin metal strip through which current passes into a circuit. If too much current starts to flow, the metal melts, cutting off the current—and destroying the fuse in the process.

A blown fuse must always be replaced. Never replace a fuse with a higher-rated fuse. For example, if the circuit is rated for 15 amps, use a 15-amp fuse.

Keep a supply of replacement fuses. If you are suspicious of a fuse, throw it out. Replace it with a fuse you know is good—not an old blown fuse that's lying around the panel.

Older plug fuses have metal screw-in bases; most have been replaced by S-type fuses, which have ceramic bases. Before using an S-type fuse in a socket for the first time, you must screw in a correctly rated S-type ring. The ring is a safety feature that makes it impossible to install a fuse with a higher rating. Once the ring is installed, it can't be removed.

To replace a cartridge fuse, pull out the fuse block, then remove one fuse at a time with a plastic fuse puller or your fingers. Test the fuse with a continuity tester; if the tester doesn't light, the fuse needs to be replaced.

> ### Breaker-type Plug Fuse
>
> This fuse acts like a circuit breaker. When the circuit overloads, the little button pops out. To restore power, push the button back in. Check to see whether this device is approved for use in your area, as some electricians consider them unreliable.

S-type fuse

> ### Testing a Cartridge Fuse

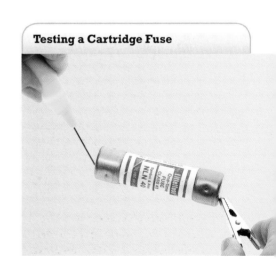

Circuit Breakers

To turn off a circuit using a circuit breaker, locate the breaker protecting the circuit and flip the toggle to the "off" position. (With some breakers, you push in, rather than to the side.) Flipping a breaker may take more force than flipping a light switch.

If a breaker has tripped, its toggle may be in the "off" position, or the situation may be less obvious. There may be a tab next to the toggle that pops out or turns red to indicate when the breaker is off. To restore power, flip the breaker on. You may need to flip it fully off (push hard), then on.

Most breakers protect 120-volt circuits for lights and receptacles. For a high-voltage appliance, you may see a double-pole 240-volt breaker or a pair of 120-volt breakers tied together with metal clips.

An S-type fuse ring in the socket ensures that this 20-amp fuse will not fit into a 15-amp circuit, thus preventing an unsafe situation.

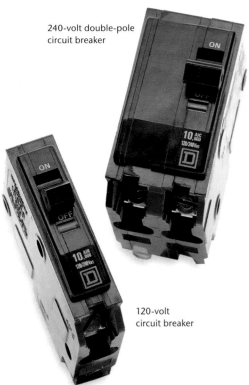

240-volt double-pole circuit breaker

120-volt circuit breaker

If you're not sure whether a plug fuse has blown, use this small tester to check for continuity inside the fuse. If the light doesn't come on, the fuse should be replaced.

Plug fuses often provide a clue to what made them blow. An overload melts the bridge; a short circuit blackens the glass.

In case of an electric fire or other emergency, shut off the main breaker. It's usually at the top of the service panel.

Testing Methods

Some testers help you determine quickly whether the power is on. Others spot any gaps in a fixture's or device's wiring or circuitry.

STOP!
Whenever you're working with wiring, make it an ironclad rule to check first that power to the area you're working on is turned off at the service panel.

VOLTAGE TESTER

Before you touch anything in a box, use a voltage tester (also called a neon tester) to make sure power is off. With the cover plate still in place, check a receptacle by poking the tester probes into the slots.

After opening the box, if the box is metal, move the device well away and test again before touching any bare wires. Touch the probes to the hot and neutral wires, as well as to the hot and ground wires. If the box is metal, also touch the probes to the hot wire and the box. Take care not to bridge between the device and a metal box.

When using a voltage tester, be sure to press firmly to avoid a false negative. Poke deep into receptacle holes and twist the probes to either side to ensure you are touching the metal parts inside.

TESTING A HIGH-VOLTAGE RECEPTACLE

For a high-voltage receptacle, use a tester that can handle 240 volts. That much power would blow out a simple one-level neon tester. When you poke the probes into the two hot (vertical) slots, the tester should read 240 volts. With the probes inserted into one hot slot and either the grounding or neutral slot, the reading should be 120 volts.

VOLTAGE DETECTOR

A voltage detector allows you to test for power without having to touch any bare metal—or even remove cover plates. Be aware, however, that it is not as reliable as a voltage tester. Purchase a high-quality detector with a sensitivity adjustment. Hold the detector against a cable or device you know is hot, then turn the adjustment knob until the tool lights up. If the tool lights up against nonelectrified metal, turn down the adjustment.

STUD FINDER

Many stud finders, also called wall sensors, can detect the presence of power in addition to studs within a wall. Although the readings are not absolutely guaranteed reli-

Testing Before Removing Cover Plate

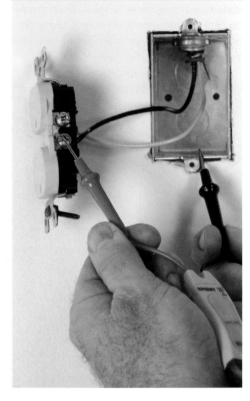

Testing After Removing Cover Plate

able, this tool can help you avoid cutting into a hidden live wire.

RECEPTACLE ANALYZER

If you were to buy just one electrical tool, it should be a receptacle analyzer. Plug in an analyzer to verify that a receptacle is correctly wired. It will tell you whether the receptacle is on and also whether it is grounded and polarized. You can also buy an analyzer for GFCI receptacles.

CONTINUITY TESTER

A battery-powered continuity tester sends a low-voltage current through a circuit to determine whether the electrical path is intact. Use one to test switches, lamps, appliances, cartridge fuses, and any other electrical device. Before you use a continuity tester, shut off power to the circuit (or

unplug the lamp or appliance you are testing) and test to make very sure the power is off. Attach the tester's alligator clip to one end of the wiring, then touch the probe to the other end. The tool's light will glow if there is an unbroken path between the two.

SCREWDRIVER-TYPE TESTER

A voltage-and-continuity tester is used different ways for different jobs. To test for power, insert the probe into the hot slot of a receptacle or touch the hot wire in a box—of course, without touching the wiring yourself. Press the clip, and the light glows if there is power.

To test for continuity, the device actually uses your body as part of the circuit (which is perfectly safe; it's a very small amount of current). Touch the screwdriver-like probe

Related Topics

Grounding, 22–23
High-voltage receptacles, 122–123
Other safety measures, 24–25
Shutting off & restoring power, 50–51

to one end of a circuit, touch the other end with your finger, and lightly press down on the tester's clip. If the circuit is unbroken, the light will glow.

As a bonus, you can use the screwdriver to remove or install cover-plate screws.

Multitester

Electricians often use a multitester, also called a voltage meter or VOM. In addition to determining continuity, it measures voltage, including low-voltage current and resistance in ohms. Some models have a clamp-on ammeter that detects current passing through a closed cable or an appliance cord. A digital multitester is easier to use and more accurate. Some meters require you to set the voltage range before testing, while others switch (or "range") automatically.

Be cautious when you use the multitester. If you didn't turn off the right circuit, or if two circuits travel through a box, or if there's a short in the system, the wires may still be hot. Hold tester probes by their insulation, and do not touch the metal parts. Otherwise you may get a shock or cause a short circuit.

Sperry Multitester

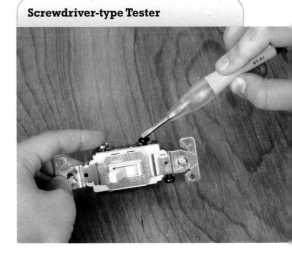

Testing 240-volt Receptacle

Stud Finder

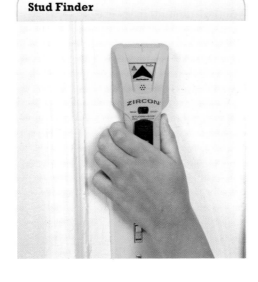

Receptacle Analyzer

Continuity Tester

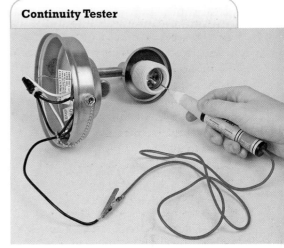

Voltage Detector

Screwdriver-type Tester

Stripping & Joining Wires

For basic wiring projects, you may need to strip wire ends, bend the ends into loops, connect them to terminals, and splice wires together. The next six pages show you how to do those tasks.

Stripping Wire Ends

Don't try to strip a wire end with a knife; it won't go well, and you may nick the wire—or a finger. Many electricians strip wires with diagonal cutters, but if you're a beginner, you risk nicking the wire that way, too. The tools shown on these pages enable you to strip wire cleanly, safely, and quickly.

If you do create a fairly deep nick in a wire, you need to start over. The nick will weaken the wire and may cause it to break later. Just cut the wire behind the nick and strip it again. Surface nicks, like the ones visible in the four steps on the opposite page, are not a concern.

HOW MUCH TO STRIP

To form a question-mark loop, strip 1 inch of insulation from the wire's end. If you will be poking the wire into the back of a receptacle, use the gauge on the back of the receptacle to determine how much insulation to strip. To join two wires in a splice, strip ¾ inch from each. To splice three or more wires, strip 1 inch.

USING STRIPPERS

Insert the wire into the hole in the strippers that corresponds to the wire's diameter. (You may have to look closely; there are often numbers at each side of the hole, one for solid-core wire and one for stranded wire.) Squeeze the strippers, rock them back and forth to make sure they cut all around the wire's insulation, and pull the insulation off. It should come off fairly easily.

If you must loosen your grip before you can slide off the insulation, the tool is digging in too deeply and may be nicking the wire. If so, you probably need to use a larger hole on the stripper.

USING A MULTITOOL

With this tool, it's easier to spot the right hole for the wire. But it may be awkward to work in tight situations, which are common when working in boxes.

USING ONE-HOLE STRIPPERS

You may find one-hole strippers the simplest to use. Adjust the size of the hole to

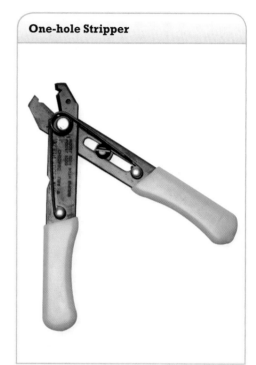

One-hole Stripper

Measuring Wire

Stripping Wire

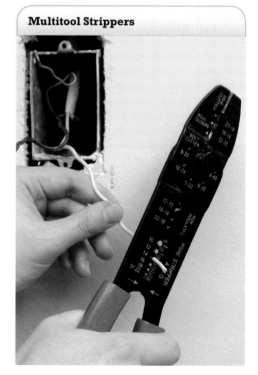

Multitool Strippers

Related Topics

Inspecting your wiring, 36–39
Common wiring methods, 28–31

match the wire you are working with, and readjust it when you change wire sizes. Or buy two or three tools, one for each size of wire you expect to use.

Looping the Ends

To attach a stripped wire end to a screw-down terminal, you must first form it into a loop. With a bit of practice, you can perform these four steps in just a few seconds—or use a looping screwdriver instead.

MAKING A QUESTION-MARK LOOP
To make a question-mark shape loop, first strip a full inch of insulation from the wire end. When working with #12 or thicker wire, you may find it better to strip 1⅛ inches.

LOOPING SCREWDRIVER
This specialized screwdriver has a small metal pin jutting from its handle. Place the tip of the stripped wire between the screwdriver shaft and the pin. Then twist the screwdriver until you have a loop the right size for fitting over a terminal.

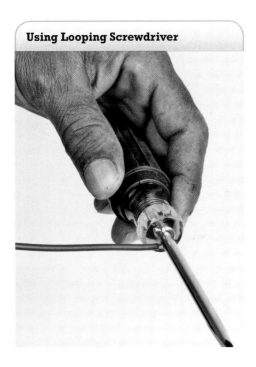

Using Looping Screwdriver

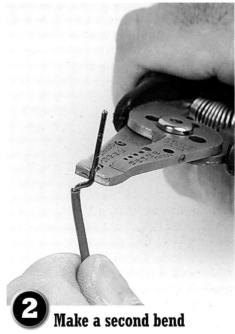

1 **Bend the wire nearly 90 degrees**
- Use the tip of a pair of strippers or long-nose pliers

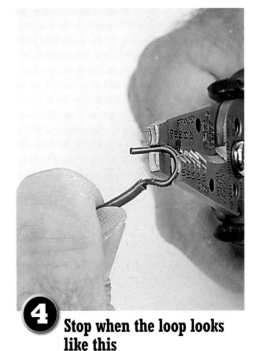

2 **Make a second bend**
- Slide the tool over about ⅛ inch
- Bend the wire at about 45 degrees

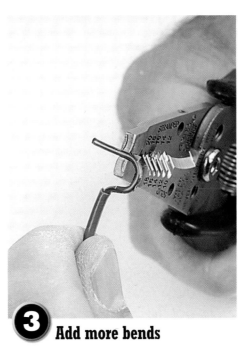

3 **Add more bends**
- Slide the tool over ⅛ inch and bend again
- Repeat several times

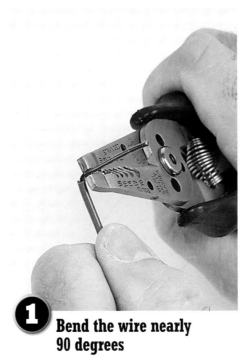

4 **Stop when the loop looks like this**
- Make the opening just wide enough to slip over a terminal screw

Electrical Tape

Technically known as electrician's tape, electrical tape comes in several colors, but there's rarely a reason to use anything but the standard black. Spend a little more for commercial-grade tape, which is thicker and stickier than standard-grade tape. The cheaper tape is much more likely to come loose.

You can buy electrical tape in a dispenser that makes it easier to cut it off, cut the tape with a knife (though that sometimes is awkward), or simply tear the tape. Tearing creates a wrinkled end that can be smoothed when the tape is applied, but that may require more effort than simply cutting the tape neatly to begin with.

Squeezing Wire Around Terminal

Squeezing Wire Around Terminal

Attaching Wire to a Screw-down Terminal

Standard receptacles have terminals with screws; you tighten the screws to hold down looped wire ends. Be sure to attach hot wires to the brass terminals and neutral wires to the silver-colored terminals on a receptacle.

To attach a looped wire end, slip it under the appropriate screw head on the receptacle; the screw should already be unscrewed all the way, but if not, loosen it yourself. Holding the wire in place, use strippers or long-nose pliers to squeeze it fairly tightly against the screw threads.

Ideally, the stripped wire should wrap fully around the screw threads, with no bare wire protruding past the screw head. You don't need to achieve perfection, but try to come close enough so that the terminal grabs plenty of stripped wire and there is no more than ⅛ inch of exposed wire. If you are having trouble achieving this, you may need to strip more insulation or start over and strip a little less.

Tighten the screw firmly. Also tighten down any terminal screws that you will not use.

Wrapping with Tape

Some building departments require that screw-down terminals be wrapped with electrician's tape as an extra measure of safety inside the box. Once the connections are made, slip the end of the tape under a mounting screw and pull it fairly taut as you wrap it around the device body. Wrap two layers of tape, then cut or tear the tape and press it down firmly to make sure it will not come loose.

Push-in Terminals: Good & Bad

Some receptacles and switches have holes into which wires can be inserted, instead of terminals around which wire must be looped. A 15-amp receptacle has holes sized for #14 wire, and a 20-amp receptacle has wider holes to accommodate #12 wire.

Tightening Screw

Wrapping with Tape

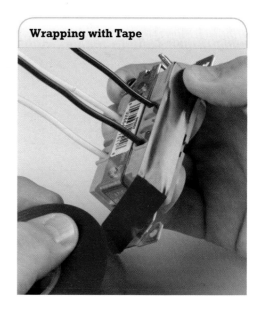

A device like this saves you the trouble of looping the wire end and wrapping with tape, but be careful when you select it. High-end versions have setscrews to tighten on the wire after it's inserted, making a connection you can really believe in. Standard versions lack the setscrews, so wires poked into them occasionally come loose, sometimes with disastrous results. It's worth paying more for the high-end type with the setscrews, which typically costs four times as much as a standard one.

Reliable Push-in

Cheap Push-in

Receptacles and switches should be easy to find and convenient to users.

Wrapping the Connection

After adding a wire nut to a splice, many electricians wrap the bottom with two layers of electrical tape, both to add protection and to ensure that the nut will not unscrew.

Splicing Wires

Spliced wire ends should be wrapped together tightly. The usual way is to twist them first, then add a wire nut as shown here. Alternatively, you can join the wires simply by tightly twisting on a wire nut. Once the wires have been spliced, protect the splice with a wrapping of electrical tape.

STOP!

Any wire nut should have metal threads inside to grab tightly and conduct power. Some light fixtures, for example, come with plastic-only wire nuts. Throw them out and use metal-threaded nuts instead.

TWISTING THREE OR FOUR WIRES

When twisting more than two wires together, strip off an inch (rather than ¾ inch) of insulation from each wire. Hold the wires next to each other, grab all the tips with lineman's pliers, and twist. Forming a firm splice is tricky, but you'll get the hang of it after a few tries.

NUT-ONLY METHOD

Some pros believe that twisting overstresses the wires, weakening the splice. To join untwisted wires with a wire nut, hold the wires firmly together with the ends aligned. Poke them firmly into the nut until you can feel that the wires are in all the way. Twist the nut clockwise until you twist the wires with the nut itself. Hold the nut and pull on each wire to make sure both are well attached.

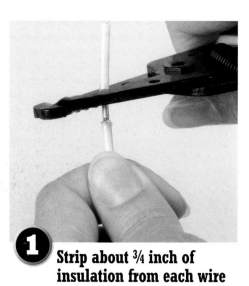

1 Strip about ¾ inch of insulation from each wire

- Check for nicks that may weaken it
- Cut and restrip a wire with nicks like those shown

2 Grip both wires

- Align the stripped ends and align the insulation edges
- Hold the ends with lineman's pliers and twist clockwise
- Hold the wires tightly in one hand as you continue twisting with the pliers
- Avoid overtwisting, which may weaken it

Twisting Three Wires

3 Cut the ends

- Tug the wires to make sure the connection is firm
- Cut the ends at an angle with lineman's pliers or diagonal cutters

4 Attach a wire nut

- Insert the cut ends deep into the wire nut
- Twist the nut clockwise until it stops
- Tug again to check the connection
- If bare wire is exposed below the wire nut, either try again or wrap with electrical tape

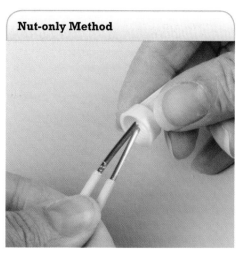

Nut-only Method

STRANDED TO SOLID

When installing a light fixture, you often need to splice the fixture's stranded wire to the house's solid-core wire. There are two techniques. For the first method, as shown below, the tip of the stranded wire should extend slightly past the tip of the solid wire. Twist the stranded wire around the solid wire, then insert the wires all the way into the wire nut and twist clockwise. Test by pulling on each wire.

For the second method, first insert the stranded wire into the nut. Then insert the solid wire and twist. Again, test the connection by pulling on both wires.

PIGTAIL SPLICE

A pigtail splice connects two or three wires together, with one—the pigtail, or jumper wire—connecting to a terminal on a device or box. A wire nut secures the splice. You may use the splice to reduce the number of wires from three to two, as only one wire should be connected to a terminal. A pigtail

can also extend a wire or attach bare ground wires to a grounding terminal on a box. Usually 6 to 8 inches long, a pigtail must be at least as thick as the other wires in the splice.

You can make your own pigtails out of short lengths of wire, or buy a ready-made pigtail with a wire nut attached.

GROUNDING

A grounding wire nut is green and has a hole in the top. Cut one bare grounding wire about 4 inches shorter than the other, screw on the wire nut so the long wire protrudes, then attach the long wire to the grounding terminal. For a metal box with no ground wire attached to it, use a grounding pigtail. Screw the pigtail's wire nut onto the grounding wires, and attach the other end to the box with a grounding screw.

COMPRESSION SLEEVE

A compression sleeve is used only for grounding splices, since the metal is exposed. Check with your local building department to see if compression sleeves are required for wire splices. If they are not, don't use them. A wire nut is just as good, and can be removed.

To install one, twist the wire ends clockwise at least one and a half turns. Snip the ends so they are even. Slip a compression sleeve onto the ends and crimp it with a multipurpose tool or a crimping tool. If code requires it, add a wire nut.

Grounding Wire Nut

Twisting Wires

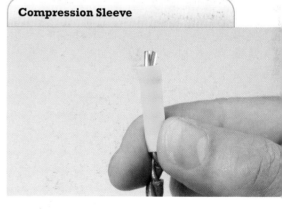

Compression Sleeve

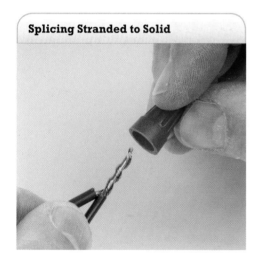

Splicing Stranded to Solid

Plug with Pigtail Attached

Grounding Pigtail

Choosing Wire Nuts

All wire splices should be secured and protected with a wire nut. Simply applying electrical tape without a wire nut is forbidden by code because it does not produce a secure splice. Use wire nuts of the correct size for the number and gauge of the wires you are splicing, as indicated on the wire nut packaging. Keep a selection of nuts on hand.

Electrical Boxes

Wherever you splice wires or connect to a terminal, the connection must be made in an approved electrical box. Many boxes are interchangeable. For example, the same box could be used as a receptacle box, a junction box, or a switch box.

The assortment of boxes on the opposite page is just a sampling of the variety that is available. Rectangular boxes that hold switches or receptacles are sometimes called switch boxes. Square outlet boxes or junction boxes may hold devices or just wiring splices. Octagonal or round boxes are used most often for ceiling fixtures.

Outdoor wiring requires weather-tight boxes.

The volume of each box determines how many wires of a particular size may be brought into it. Consult the table at right to make sure the box you choose is large enough for your purposes. When in doubt, buy a larger box.

METAL OR PLASTIC

Metal boxes are sturdier, and you should attach a ground wire to them. Plastic boxes cost less and don't require grounding. They are made of tough nylon and are fairly strong. Use plastic boxes with NM cable only; armored cable (AC or MC) and metal conduit require metal boxes. Some electrical codes allow special PVC plastic boxes for exposed indoor and outdoor wiring with PVC conduit.

NEW OR OLD WORK

For mounting purposes, boxes fall into two main categories. New-work boxes are used where there's no wall or ceiling covering to contend with and the framing is more accessible. They are attached directly to exposed studs or joists. Cut-in (or old-work) boxes are used when wall or ceiling materials are in place. They come with brackets or spring-mounted ears designed expressly for remodeling work.

BOX SIZES

A one-gang box is wide enough for one receptacle or switch. Two-, three-, and even four-gang boxes accommodate those numbers of devices. Metal gangable boxes can be disassembled and reassembled to produce boxes of multiple gangs.

ATTACHING CABLE TO BOXES

Cables attach to boxes in three basic ways.
- Most plastic boxes have tabs that loosely hold the cable, which must be stapled outside the box to nearby wood framing.
- Many metal boxes and some plastic ones have knockout holes, usually ½ inch in diameter, to accommodate cable clamps. The clamps secure cable or conduit via straps or setscrews and attach to the box with a nut
- Some boxes have built-in clamps that secure the cable when you tighten a screw.

Number of Conductors* Per Box

Size	Number of conductors			
	#14	#12	#10	#8
Round or octagonal boxes				
4" × 1¼"	6	5	5	4
4" × 1½"	7	6	6	5
4" × 2⅛"	10	9	8	7
Square boxes				
4" × 1¼"	9	8	7	6
4" × 1½"	10	9	8	7
4" × 2⅛"	15	13	12	10
4¹¹/₁₆" × 1¼"	12	11	10	8
4¹¹/₁₆" × 1½"	14	13	11	9
Rectangular boxes				
3" × 2" × 2¼"	5	4	4	3
3" × 2" × 2½"	6	5	5	4
3" × 2" × 2¾"	7	6	5	4
3" × 2" × 3½"	9	8	7	6
4" × 2⅛" × 1½"	5	4	4	3
4" × 2⅛" × 1⅛"	6	5	5	4
4" × 2⅛" × 2⅛"	7	6	5	4

*Count all grounding wires as one conductor. Count each receptacle, switch, fixture stud, cable clamp, and hickey (a threaded electrical fitting) as one conductor. Count each wire entering and leaving the box without a splice as one conductor. Don't count pigtails (jumper wires).

Related Topics
Cable connections, 144–145
New electrical boxes, 138–139
Outdoor wiring, 170–171

Ceiling Boxes

This type of ceiling cut-in box has metal spring flanges that hold tight to the back surface of drywall or plaster when you tighten the mounting screws.

This new-work ceiling box has a hanger bar that attaches to a joist on either side. You can slide the box along the bar to place it where you wish.

Known as a pancake box, this type of electrical box can attach to a hanger bar, a joist, or even a wooden ceiling. It accommodates only one two-wire cable.

The heavy-duty bar for this cut-in box can be inserted through a hole in drywall or plaster. You turn the rod to clamp it firmly to the joists on either side, then attach a ceiling box to the bar.

Wall Boxes

Nail-on boxes are convenient for new construction. Some come with nails already attached; others have mounting plates with holes to drive nails or screws through.

This nail-on box's mounting plate can be adjusted to the thickness of different wall finishes.

You can remove the plate on one side of this gangable box and attach it to another to produce a two-gang box. Adjustable ears (which are removable) allow it to be mounted on either wooden or plaster-and-lath walls. This example has integral cable clamps; others have knockouts to accommodate clamps.

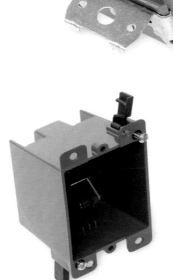

This common type of cut-in (old-work) box mounts with clamps that move forward and grab the back of the drywall when you tighten screws.

When a square box like this is used as a junction box, housing only wire splices, it is covered with a blank cover. Use an adapter plate (this one is a single-gang plate) to turn it into a switch or receptacle box. An extender ring adds depth.

Working with NM Cable

Nonmetallic (NM) cable is inexpensive and quick to install, and it's the most commonly used cable throughout much of the country. However, in some areas, conduit or armored cable is required and NM cable is not allowed, so check with local codes.

STOP!
Test any cable ripper on a scrap piece to make sure it cuts through the sheathing, but does not nick or score the wire insulation. Adjust the ripper as needed before working on the real thing.

Modern NM cable is color-coded so that an inspector can quickly tell that you've installed cable with the correct wire gauge. Typically, #12 wire has yellow sheathing and #14 cable has white or gray sheathing.

On these pages we show how to strip the cable's sheathing—a very different task from stripping the insulation on individual wires. Two-wire cable is fairly flat, with a channel down its center through which you can run a knife or cable ripper. Three-wire cable is round, and its sheathing is a bit trickier to strip. Underground feed cable, used for outdoor installations, is also non-metallic, but stripping it is difficult.

Four Ways to Strip Two-wire Sheathing

Use diagonal cutters or lineman's pliers to cut NM cable to length. Then strip it using one of the four methods shown here, each using a different stripping tool.

Whichever tool you use, don't rest the cable on your knee or thigh when you work. Cut away from your body, not toward it. In most cases, plan to strip 8 to 10 inches of sheathing to provide ample wire length inside the box.

CABLE STRIPPERS

Using strippers made for NM cable, insert the cable into the correct slot—either 12-2 or 14-2. (A multipurpose tool may have the same type of slot.) Squeeze the stripper handle, give it a quick twist, and pull the cable sheathing off while continuing to squeeze the stripper handle. If you accidentally put 12-2 cable into the 14-2 slot, you will nick the wire insulation; cut the cable and start again.

SQUEEZE-TYPE CABLE RIPPER

Follow these three steps to strip cable sheathing with a squeeze-type cable ripper.

Cable Strippers

1 Score the cable
- Slide a cable ripper up the cable
- Press the handles of the ripper together and pull it toward the cable end

2 Peel the sheathing
- Bend the cable back to crack sheathing
- Peel back sheathing and paper strip
- Confirm the wire insulation is undamaged

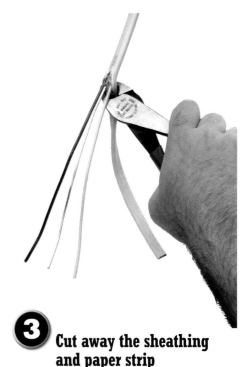

3 Cut away the sheathing and paper strip
- Use diagonal cutters or strippers

Related Topics
Cable connections, 144–145
Stripping & joining wire, 54–59

Utility Knife

You can also use a utility knife to strip a cable.

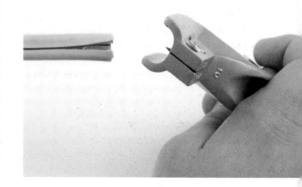
Using a Cable Ripper

1 Slice the sheathing

- Lay the cable flat on a board
- Poke a utility-knife blade into the center channel, just deep enough to cut through the sheathing
- Slice along the cable

2 Remove the sheathing and paper strip

- Peel back the sheathing and the paper strip
- Cut them away with diagonal cutters or strippers
- If you use the knife to cut them off, slice away from the wires

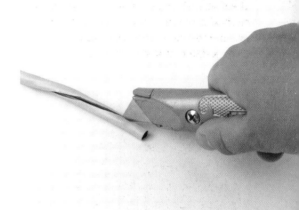
Stripping Three-wire Sheathing

HEAVY-DUTY CABLE RIPPER

This type of cable ripper has a blade with an adjustable depth. Place the cable on a flat surface, fit the tool over the cable, and press down to insert the blade into the center of the cable. Keep pressing as you slice along the cable. Separate and cut the sheathing and the paper strip.

Stripping Three-wire Sheathing

Three-wire cable is round rather than flat, making it more difficult to strip its sheathing without damaging wire insulation. Using one of the following techniques, practice on scrap pieces until you are confident you will not damage wire insulation.

- Pros often use cable strippers. Squeeze gently (it takes practice to get the depth

right) and twist about halfway around the cable. Then strip the sheathing off.
- Adjust heavy-duty cable rippers carefully, so that they just barely slice through the sheathing, and strip as you would for two-wire cable. (Squeeze-type rippers are not recommended for three-wire cable.)
- Slice with a utility knife. Since there is no central channel with three-wire cable, follow the curve of the twisted wires.

Clamping NM Cable

Use a clamp made for NM cable. It may be a separate clamp like this one, a clamp built into a box, or a plastic clamp. Whichever clamp you use, be sure it does not touch any individual wires. A short length of sheathing should be visible inside the box.

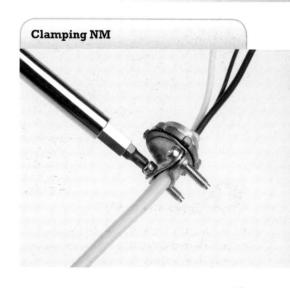
Clamping NM

Working with Armored Cable

Cable with a flexible metal sheathing is variously called armored cable, AC cable, or MC cable. It offers wiring some protection against nails that may poke through walls and other possible sources of damage.

While installing wiring in an older home, you may run into BX type armored cable, which has no ground wire, only a thin bonding strip. Though BX cable sheathing is commonly used for the ground path, the bonding strip was actually meant to act as the ground. Modern armored cable has a green-insulated ground wire.

Stripping & Connecting Armored Cable

1 Cut sheathing with an armored-cable cutter

- Slip the cable into the cutter
- Turn the adjusting knob until it holds the cable firmly
- Squeeze the tool and turn the crank to cut sheathing

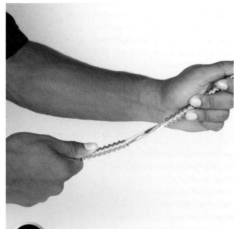

2 Remove the sheathing

- Twist and pull off the waste end of the sheathing
- Make sure the wire insulation is undamaged. If not, cut the cable and try again, turning the knob counterclockwise for a shallower cut

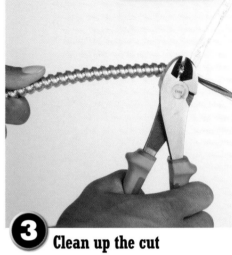

3 Clean up the cut

- Undo and remove the plastic wrapping
- Use diagonal cutters to trim sharp sheathing edges

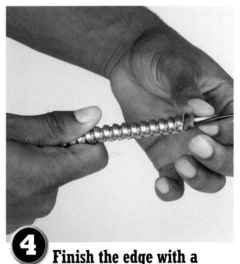

4 Finish the edge with a bushing

- Slip a plastic bushing over the wires
- Press it down tightly inside the sheathing to protect wires from the sheathing's cut end

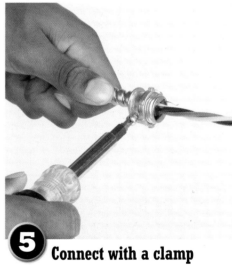

5 Connect with a clamp

- To connect to a box, use a cable clamp made for armored cable
- Slide it far enough that the bushing is visible; if necessary, trim the sheathing further
- Tighten the setscrew and tug to check the connection

Other Methods

An armored-cable cutter is definitely the best way to strip armored cable sheathing because it won't damage wire insulation. But if you don't have one, and you need to strip only one or two cables, you can use a hack saw or the "bend and twist" method below.

HACK SAW

Holding the blade at an angle to the cable, cut just barely through one of the coils. Rotate the cable so you can continue cutting without damaging wire insulation. You don't need to cut all around the cable, just completely through a ridge, which represents a coil. Once you have cut enough, you can easily pull off the sheathing. Finish the job by trimming and adding a bushing, as in Steps 3 through 5 on the opposite page.

Cutting Cable with Hack Saw

Bend & Twist

1 Bend the cable

- Bend the cable with your hand (if you're strong) or slip-joint pliers
- Stop when the cable breaks slightly, with the metal separating so you can glimpse wires inside

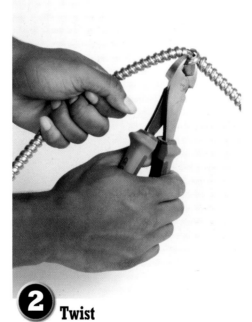

2 Twist

- Grasp the cable firmly on both sides, with your hands or with two pliers
- Twist until part of the coil pops out far enough so you can insert cutters

3 Cut

- Cut the sheathing with diagonal cutters
- Inspect the wires closely to make sure you have not nicked any insulation
- Trim the cut and add a bushing, as in Steps 3 through 5

Wiring with Conduit

Codes sometimes require that wiring in exposed locations be enclosed in conduit; in some areas, in fact, all wiring must be done with conduit. For interior wiring, thinwall metal conduit (EMT) is still the most common type.

In some older installations, metal conduit was used as a ground path. Today it is common to run a green-insulated grounding wire.

Make sure the conduit you choose is wide enough to accommodate the wires you will pull through it. As a general rule, ½-inch conduit is large enough for up to six #12 or #14 wires, four #10 wires, or two #8 wires. If you need to run more wires, use ¾-inch conduit instead.

These pages show how to run conduit on a wall surface. To run conduit through framing, cut holes as you would for cable.

Routing Logistics

Before you install conduit, first install the switches, receptacles, and junction and fixture boxes. Then run the conduit between the boxes. If a run of conduit will include a total of more than 360 degrees of bends, install a pulling elbow—a fitting that with an opening through which you can access the wiring partway along the run—along the line. Consider adding some pulling elbows even for a run with 360 degrees or less.

At a T intersection, where a conduit run splits in two and there is no device or fixture, install a junction box and cover it with a blank plate.

If you have a lot of conduit to run, buy a conduit bender and learn how to use it. It takes practice to get the bends just right and to learn how to measure the lengths. For a small project, make your turns using fittings instead. Make sure the boxes have knockouts that accept the fittings.

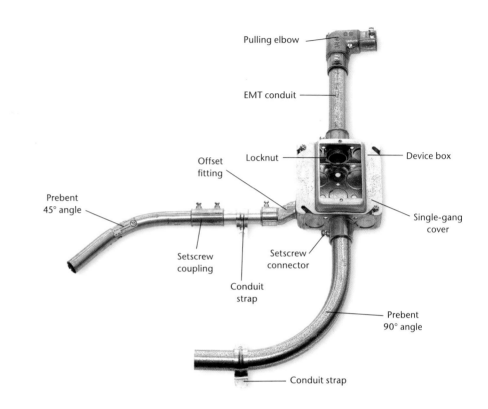

Pulling elbow · EMT conduit · Offset fitting · Locknut · Device box · Prebent 45° angle · Setscrew coupling · Setscrew connector · Conduit strap · Single-gang cover · Prebent 90° angle · Conduit strap

Installing Metal Boxes & EMT Conduit

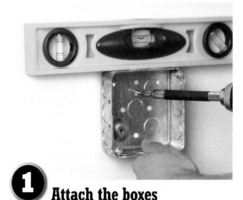

❶ Attach the boxes

- Make sure the conduit will follow straight lines from box to box, measuring from the floor or using a level
- Drive screws through the backs of boxes and into framing members where possible; otherwise, plan to use a conduit strap on a nearby stud to anchor the installation
- On a masonry wall, drill holes with a masonry bit and drive masonry screws

❷ Add offset fittings

- Attach offset fittings where the conduit will attach, so it will be snug to the wall
- Use setscrew fittings for most interior applications; you may need compression fittings in damp conditions

3 Mark for the cut

- If possible, hold the conduit in position and mark it for cutting, rather than using a tape measure
- If a conduit needs a bend, add the fitting or make the bend first, then mark for the cut afterwards
- Mark so the conduit will slip the correct distance into the fitting, usually 1 inch

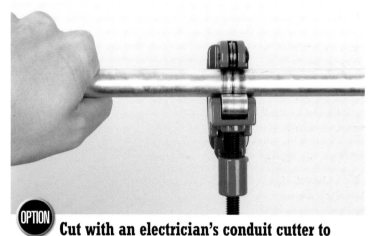

OPTION Cut with an electrician's conduit cutter to avoid sharp burrs

- Slip the pipe into the cutter
- Tighten the knob until the pipe seats firmly against the two guide wheels and the cutting wheel, but avoid overtightening
- Rotate the tool around the pipe a full turn
- Tighten the knob, rotate again; repeat several times
- Step down on one side of the pipe and pull up the other side to snap it

4 Cut, then ream

- Cut at the mark with a hacksaw
- Use a conduit reaming tool to remove all the burrs inside the pipe; be thorough, since sharp edges would slice through insulation when the wires are pulled through

5 Put the conduit in place

- Slide the conduit pipe into the fitting
- Tighten the setscrew
- Tug the pipe to make sure it is seated and the screw is tight

6 Attach the conduit

- Anchor the conduit to the wall using one- or two-hole straps with screws driven into studs
- On a masonry wall, use masonry screws or lag shields

Wiring with Conduit **67**

Using Greenfield

Greenfield is the common term for flexible metal conduit. It is required in many places for short runs wherever cable is exposed, such as for the whips (lengths of flexible cable) that lead to water heaters, dishwashers, garbage disposers, and other appliances. Even if Greenfield is not required, you may choose to install it in a garage or basement where cable is not covered by drywall. If your locality requires metal conduit, Greenfield is typically allowed only for short runs.

Cut Greenfield with a hacksaw and ream the inside smooth, just as you would for EMT. Support it with a conduit strap within 8 inches of a box or fitting and at intervals no greater than 4 feet.

In installations where NM cable emerges from the wall to travel to an appliance, the exposed cable may be protected by Greenfield. Strip the sheathing, then slide Greenfield over the exposed wires.

Installing PVC Conduit

Several types of nonmetallic conduit are available, but Schedule 40 PVC is the one most homeowners use. It's rigid and flame retardant, and it resists heat and sunlight. In some areas it is more common than EMT. Be sure to use PVC conduit made for electrical work—not PVC irrigation or water-supply pipe.

Install boxes first, then cut conduit lengths and assemble fittings to run between the boxes (you cannot bend PVC pipe, except with a specialized heater). Measure for cutting the conduit the same way you would for EMT conduit.

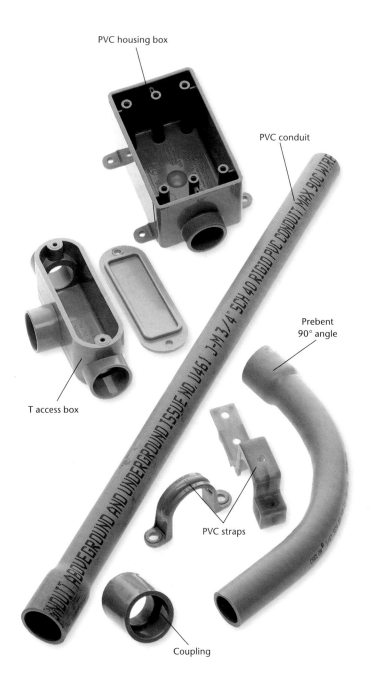

PVC housing box

PVC conduit

Prebent 90° angle

T access box

PVC straps

Coupling

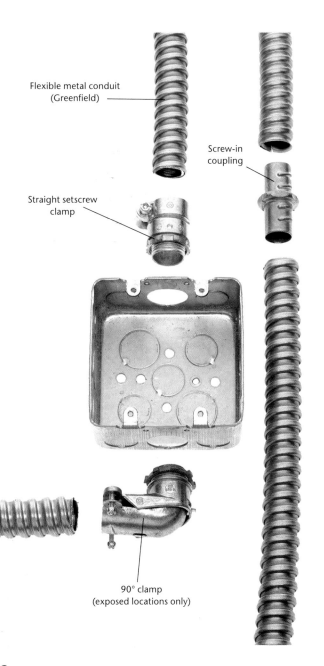

Flexible metal conduit (Greenfield)

Screw-in coupling

Straight setscrew clamp

90° clamp (exposed locations only)

CUTTING & DEBURRING

You can cut PVC conduit with a hacksaw, hand saw, or power saw, but a PVC cutter works quickly and makes less of a mess. After cutting, use a knife or reaming tool to remove any burrs inside the pipe.

JOINING

PVC cement works extremely fast, so prepare carefully before you apply it. (Once cemented, the joints cannot be disassembled.)

Dry-fit five or six lengths of conduit and fittings without the cement to make sure they fit correctly. Disassemble the pieces, placing them in the correct order so you don't get confused as you join them.

To make each connection, apply electrician's (medium body) PVC cement, not plumbing cement or primer, to the inside of the fitting and the outside of the pipe. Immediately press the pipe into the fitting, then hold it still for a count of 10. Wipe away any excess cement.

SUPPORTING

Attach PVC straps to the conduit every 4 feet or so. Drive the strap nails into studs, or drill holes and tap in special masonry straps, as shown.

Pulling Wires

Unreel and push a fish tape through the conduit until it pokes through at a box or a pulling elbow. Strip differing amounts of insulation from the wires. For example, strip 6 inches from one, 8 inches from the second, and 10 inches from the third. This staggering arrangement makes for less of a bulge at the point of attachment, which makes the cable easier to pull through the conduit. Fold the wires over the fish tape and wrap them tightly with electrician's tape. Reel in the fish tape to pull the wires through the conduit.

If you have a long, complex route to follow, fish the wires in several stages, working toward a pulling elbow or a box, then moving on.

To avoid kinking or scraping insulation, have someone feed in the wires as you pull. You can also buy special pulling lubricant to make the job go better.

Cutting PVC Conduit

Supporting PVC Conduit

Joining PVC Conduit #1

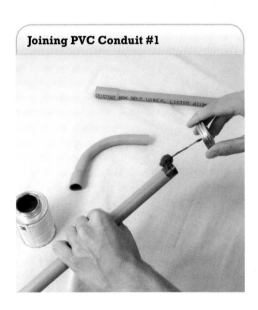

Taping Wire & Fish Tape

Joining PVC Conduit #2

Using Fish Tape

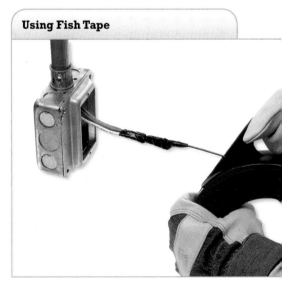

3 Replacing Light Fixtures & Ceiling Fans

In this chapter, we show you how to light up your home, inside and out. We begin by helping you choose the latest light bulbs, followed by step-by-step installation instructions for light fixtures and track lighting on your ceiling, as well as vanity and sconce fixtures on your wall. In addition, you'll learn how to wire low-voltage rail and cable lights, exterior motion-sensor lights, and a switched ceiling fan.

Chapter Contents

**Sconce &
Vanity Lights**
page 86

Ceiling Fans
page 88

**Installing a
Ceiling Fan**
page 90

**Halogen
Under-cabinet
Lights**
page 92

**Motion-
sensor
Exterior
Light**
page 94

**Low-voltage
Outdoor
Lighting**
page 96

**Installing
Low-voltage
Lights**
page 98

Light Bulbs

At a home improvement store, the light bulb display may take up 30 or more feet of aisle space. If your bulbs are casting too much or too little light, or producing a light that makes your walls appear the wrong color, try a different type of light bulb.

Incandescent bulbs

Choosing Bulbs

Be sure to get a bulb with the right base. Most fixtures use bulbs with medium bases, but some have smaller sockets made for candelabra or other base sizes. Some halogen bulbs have bases with pins.

INCANDESCENTS

Incandescents, the old standard light bulbs, are now available in many varieties. A typical incandescent bulb produces a warm, yellowish glow. A frosted bulb creates less glare than a clear bulb. A soft pink bulb does not cast a pink light, but it does provide a slightly warmer tone. A blue-tinted bulb produces cooler light that's closer to daylight. Incandescents also come in flood or spot bulbs for recessed fixtures.

HALOGENS

Low-voltage halogen bulbs are typically very small and have pins that poke into a fixture's socket, rather than screwing in. They tend to get quite hot. Standard-voltage halogens have a distinctive shape and screw into a standard medium-base socket. Halogens save money by using less energy and lasting longer, but they cost more to buy.

FLUORESCENTS

Fluorescents use much less energy and last longer than incandescents, and they may save more money than halogens. Many produce a cool light, but you can also buy bulbs that cast a light almost as warm as that of an incandescent.

Fluorescent bulbs come in various shapes that screw into standard sockets. Test to be sure a bulb fits your fixture or lamp. Bulbs with twisted shapes are typically bulky, while compact (CFL) or mini bulbs are about the same size as incandescents.

LEDS

Because the typical LED bulbs (left) costs more than $75, and many utilities are offering customers attractive incentives to switch from incandescents to CFLs, it's not likely that LEDs will become the preferred bulb in most homes any time soon. But LEDs last about 10 times as long as an incandescent, which makes them excellent choices for lights in difficult-to-reach places. They are also suitable for exterior use since LEDs don't mind the cold. And they use very little energy, making them good companions for solar or battery-powered fixtures.

Kelvin, CRI, & Full-spectrum Ratings

Sometimes, though not always, ratings are printed on a bulb or its packaging.

A bulb's Kelvin (K) rating indicates the color of its light. The lower the rating, the warmer (more yellow) it will be. Full daylight is about 5,000K; light on a cloudy day is about 8,000K. A standard incandescent bulb is typically about 2,700K, while blue-tinted incandescents may be about 3,500K. Fluorescent bulbs and tubes range from 4,000K to 8,000K.

The Color Rendering Index (CRI) measures how closely a light renders the true colors of objects. A rating of 100 is perfect, and 85 or higher is considered very accurate.

Terms such as "full-spectrum," "daylight," and "plant bulb" generally refer to lighting that resembles light from the sun, with about 5,000K and a CRI of 85 or more. Choose lighting that feels good to you. In some rooms, you may prefer to have light that is colder—that is, more like sunlight. In other areas you may appreciate light with a warmer, cozier feel.

Fluorescent bulbs

Halogen bulbs

Handling Bulbs

Most of the time, when a bulb burns out, you turn off the light, unscrew the old bulb, and screw in a new one.

The rules are a little different for halogens. When changing a small halogen bulb, remove the old bulb (after it cools) with a rag or wearing a glove. Avoid touching the glass in the new bulb with your fingers; finger oils will shorten its life.

If any type of light bulb is cracked, watch out for tiny shards, which can make for painful splinters. Wipe the area around a broken bulb with a damp paper towel. Gently wrap newspaper around the broken bulb and press on the newspaper as you unscrew it. Use the paper to wrap and discard the bulb.

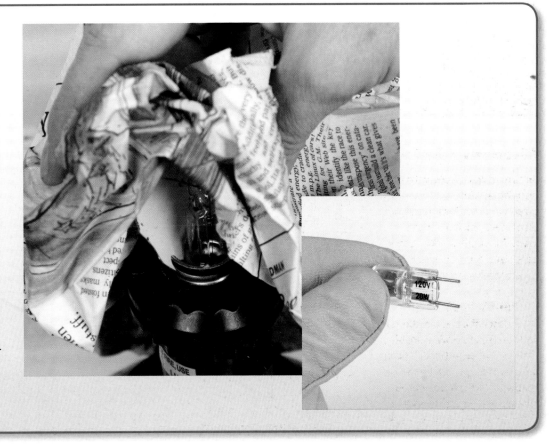

Installing a Flush Light Fixture

Replacing an old light fixture with a new one is usually a straightforward task. The canopy of the fixture attaches to a flat metal strap in the ceiling box. Most new fixtures come with a strap, but you may be able to attach to the old one.

Before You Begin

Shut off power to the existing fixture at the service panel. Flip the switch to verify that the light does not come on, then test for power before you remove the fixture. Take out the old fixture and verify again that power is off.

If the house wires are long enough, cut them just behind where they join to the old fixture's leads and strip the new ends. Otherwise, remove the wire nut and any electrical tape, inspect the wiring for damaged insulation, and make repairs as needed.

1 Screw on the new strap

2 Ground the fixture

- Wrap the house's grounding wire tightly around the threads of the grounding screw
- If the fixture has a grounding lead, wrap it, too
- Tighten the grounding screw

3 Connect black to hot

- Bring together the fixture's black lead and the house's hot (black or colored) wire
- Twist the lead around the wire with the lead about $1/8$ inch longer than the wire
- Twist on a wire nut; you may choose to wrap tape around the open end of the nut

4 Connect white to white

- Splice the white lead to the white house wire

5 Secure the canopy

- Carefully fold the connected wires into the box
- Attach the canopy to the strap
- Tighten the screws

6 Add light bulbs

- Use light bulbs with no greater wattage than that indicated on the fixture
- Restore power and test that the light works
- To attach a bowl-type globe, slip it into place and secure it with the decorative fastener or fasteners

Stuff to Buy

FIXTURE Choose a fixture with a canopy at least as wide as the old one, to avoid repainting; make sure the wattage is high enough to illuminate the room to your liking

LIGHT BULBS Be sure to get the correct wattage for the fixture

BASIC SUPPLIES Electrical tape and appropriately sized wire nuts

Time Commitment

One to two hours

Tools You'll Need

Screwdriver
Wire stripper
Lineman's pliers

Related Topics

Chandeliers & pendant lights, 80–81
Repairing wiring in boxes, 260–261
Shutting off & restoring power, 50–51
Stripping & joining wire, 54–59
Testing methods, 52–53

Alternative Arrangement

Some fixtures have a canopy that covers the mounting screws.

Flush light fixtures are popular in closets because they take up so little space.

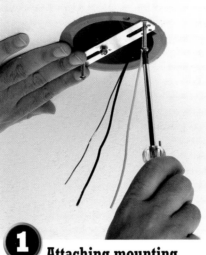

1 Attaching mounting hardware

- Screw on the strap
- Just start the mounting screws in their holes

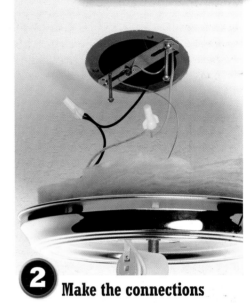

2 Make the connections

- Attach the ground wire and ground lead to the grounding screw
- Splice the hot wires and splice the neutral wires

3 Position the canopy

- Push up the canopy so the screw heads come through the wide part of the keyhole-shaped holes
- Rotate it to put the screw heads over the narrow part
- Tighten the screws

4 Add the bulb or bulbs and the globe

Track Lighting

Track lighting lets you decide where to run the tracks, where to put the lights on the tracks, and how to point them. When you install the lights in a kitchen or other work area, make sure they don't shine on the head of the person who works there.

Sample Track Layouts

Using standard L connectors with tracks, you can create an L or box shape. Other shapes call for a T connector or a cross connector, which may need to be special-ordered.

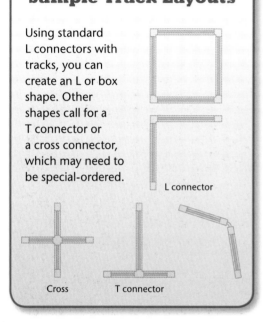

L connector

Cross   T connector

Before You Begin

Starting at a standard ceiling box that is controlled by a wall switch, you can run tracks in any arrangement you choose. Plan your layout, then determine the tracks and connectors you need.

Shut off power to the existing fixture at the service panel. Flip the switch to verify that the light does not come on, then test for power before and after you remove the fixture.

These track lights illuminate the countertop as well as the inside of the cabinets when the doors are open.

1 Wire the track connector

- Remove the old fixture
- Splice the track connector's ground lead to the house's ground wire with a wire nut (with some models, attach grounds to a grounding screw)
- With wire nuts, splice the black lead to the hot (black or colored) wire, and the white to the white

3 Measure and locate

- For a track parallel to a wall, measure and make layout marks using the distance you measured in Step 2
- Position the marks so the track will just cover them
- Use a stud finder to locate the joists
- If the track runs across the joists, mark their locations
- If it runs parallel to a joist, you will probably need toggle bolts (Step 6)
- For a plaster ceiling, consult with your local hardware store

2 Attach the mounting plate

- Tighten screws to attach the plate to the ceiling box
- To run a track parallel to a wall, measure from the wall to a screw that will be used to attach it (Step 5)

4 Add fittings

- Remove the end cap of each track wherever you will install a fitting
- Either slide fittings onto the tracks before you install them, or add fittings later (Step 7)
- Slip the first track into the connector and tighten the setscrews
- For an 8-foot track, have a helper support the other end

Stuff to Buy

TRACKS, CONNECTORS, LIGHTS Plan your layout, then make your list—typically, 4- or 8-foot track sections, 90-degree elbows, floating connectors (which go anywhere along a track), and live-end connectors (at the track end). You can also special-order T, 45-degree, flexible, and cross connectors. Buy white if you plan to paint.

TOGGLE BOLTS Use these if you are running parallel to a joist instead of across joists

LIGHT BULBS Use track-lighting bulbs and buy the specified wattage

BASIC SUPPLIES Electrical tape and appropriately sized wire nuts

 Time Commitment

Half a day to plan the layout, half a day to install

 Tools You'll Need

Cordless screwdriver or drill with screwdriver bit
Wire stripper
Lineman's pliers
Pencil
Tape measure
Stud finder

 Related Topics

Grounding, 22–23
Recessed canister lights, 160–163
Shutting off & restoring power, 50–51
Stripping & joining wire, 54–59

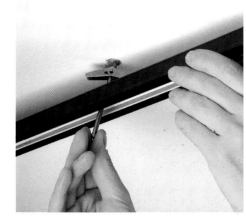

5 **Attach the track**

• Align the track with the layout marks
• If the track runs across joists, drive screws into every possible joist, penetrating at least 1½ inches
• If it parallels a joist, use toggle bolts every 16 inches or so; follow the directions that come with the toggle bolts to drill holes, insert bolts, add the nuts, and tighten the bolts

6 **Add the other tracks**

• Slide a connector on the end of the installed track
• Remove the end cap from the next track; slide it onto the other end of the connector
• Screw all the tracks to the ceiling, adding connectors as needed
• Make sure all ends are connected to a fitting or an end cap

7 **Secure the electrical connector**

• At the box, slip the mounting plate's electrical connector into the track
• Twist until it snaps to make a secure electrical connection
• Snap the canopy over the mounting plate

8 **Add lights**

• Attach lights in the same way as the electrical connector, by slipping in and twisting
• If you want to change a light's position, remove it first; don't slide it

Fluorescent Fixtures

Fluorescent fixtures are a dependable, inexpensive choice favored in basements, utility rooms, work areas, and occasionally kitchens.

Degree of Difficulty

● Easy

STOP!

Always turn off power to the circuit you are working on, then double-check at the project site before and after removing the fixture to make sure the power is off.

How to Do It

After making sure the power is off, remove the old fixture. If you find that you have a ceiling box, feed the cable through the large knockout in the fixture's top or side. Firmly secure the fixture to the ceiling or wall and then make the connections.

You can also install a fluorescent where there is no box, as long as there is a cable coming through the ceiling or wall. The fixture itself acts as the electrical box.

Safety Tip

Fluorescent tubes are coated inside with a tiny amount of mercury, so handle them carefully to avoid breaking them. If a tube does break, wear protective clothing, open a window to vent the room, and wrap the shards in a double plastic bag. Local regulations may require you to dispose of old fluorescents at a special recycling site.

The fluorescents in this garage and workshop provide lots of light economically and efficiently.

Stuff to Buy

FLUORESCENT FIXTURE
FLUORESCENT TUBES Make sure to buy the type and wattage specified on the fixture packaging
TOGGLE BOLTS Use these if you are running parallel to a joist instead of across joists
BASIC SUPPLIES Electrical tape and appropriately sized wire nuts

 Time Commitment

One to two hours

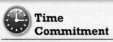 **Tools You'll Need**

Screwdriver (or cordless drill with screwdriver bit)
Wire stripper
Lineman's pliers
Stud finder

 Related Topics

Cable connections, 144–145
Shutting off & restoring power, 50–51
Stripping & joining wire, 54–59
Working with armored cable, 64–65

1 Place the fixture

- Use a stud finder to locate ceiling joists
- Knock out the large hole in the fixture's body and feed the wires through it

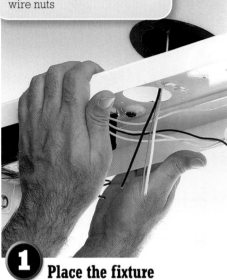

2 Fasten the fixture

- Drive screws to attach the fixture to ceiling joists
- If joists are not conveniently placed, use toggle bolts

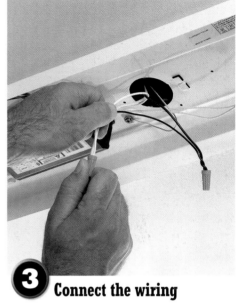

3 Connect the wiring

- Connect the house's ground wire to the grounding terminal on the fixture
- Splice the fixture's black wire to the house's hot (black or colored) wire
- Splice the neutral wires
- Fold up the wires carefully and snap on the electrical cover

4 Add tubes and test the fixture

- Slip the ends of the fluorescent tubes into the tube holders
- Restore power, and test (you may need to twist the tubes again)
- Snap the diffusing panel into place

Cable Connection

If you find a cable, but no electrical box, when you remove an old fixture, proceed as follows:
- Match the cable's clamp to the correct size of knockout plug in the new fixture, and remove the plug
- Slip the clamp through the hole, thread the nut over the wires, and tighten the nut
- Attach the fixture body to the ceiling or wall, slipping the cable clamp through the opening
- Splice the wires
- Attach the cover as shown at left

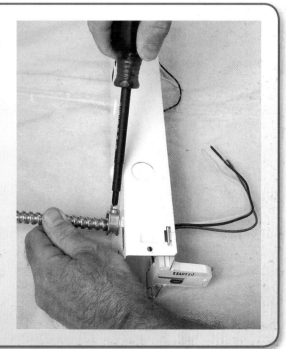

Chandeliers & Pendant Lights

Modest-sized chandeliers and pendant lights can be hung safely from a securely fastened standard ceiling box. Once the power is off and the old fixture is removed, tug on the box with pliers; it should feel as though it can handle more than the fixture's weight.

STOP!
Always turn off power to the circuit you are working on, then double-check at the project site before and after removing the fixture to make sure the power is off.

Installation Tip

With the power off to the circuit, place the fixture on a ladder, or on a board anchored to a ladder, to support it while you work. If possible, support the fixture near to the desired finish height.

This modern, flying-saucer-like fixture proves that chandeliers don't have to be dripping with cut crystals and gilt.

Securing Ceiling Fixtures

If the box is not firmly attached, you may be able to drive a screw through the box at an angle into a joist, or there may be a framing member directly above it into which you can drive a screw.

For a heavy chandelier (or if the existing box is insecure), install a fan-rated box instead.

Chandeliers and pendants mount in several ways; follow the instructions that come with the one you purchase for details. In each case, you need to cut the chain or cord to length, prepare some hardware, then run the wiring and make the attachments. Small pendants with a thick cord rather than a chain simply attach directly to a standard strap, with no stud. You can also attach pendants to rail or track systems.

Position pendants 1 or 2 feet above eye level when you install them above dining tables or countertops.

1 **Connect mounting plate**

- Read the installation instructions to understand wire paths, hardware, and order of assembly
- Adjust cable length as necessary
- Connect wires on mounting plate to wires in ceiling box

Stuff to Buy

CHANDELIER OR PENDANT LIGHT For fixtures hanging over a dining table or counter, choose heavily frosted or solid-color globes so they don't shine into people's eyes

LIGHT BULBS Check the fixture packaging for the correct wattage; also make sure to get the correct base type

BASIC SUPPLIES Electrical tape and appropriately sized wire nuts

 Time Commitment

One to two hours

 **Tools You'll Need**

Screwdriver (or cordless drill with screwdriver bit)
Tape measure
Wire stripper
Lineman's pliers

 Related Topics

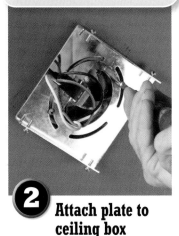

2 ### Attach plate to ceiling box

- Tighten setscrews part way into the sides of mounting plate
- Secure mounting plate to ceiling box; position so fixture will be parallel to walls
- Open a link to shorten the chain or slip it over a mounting ring to protect the finish

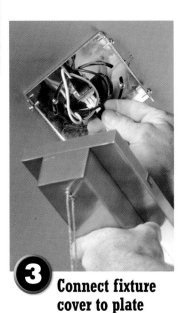

3 ### Connect fixture cover to plate

- The wires for this fixture plug directly into the mounting plate

A pair of simple pendant lights turns this kitchen table into a friendly place for after-school projects and homework.

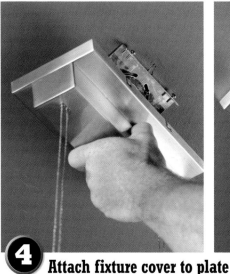

4 ### Attach fixture cover to plate

- Place the fixture over the setscrews one side at a time
- Partially tighten one side, tighten the other side, then finish tightening the first

5 ### Enjoy your fixture

- This chandelier is like four pendants, directing light straight down on a dining room table

Low-voltage Interior Lights

Low-voltage light systems have a sleek, modern look. They begin with a transformer, which attaches to a standard ceiling box and steps down the power to 12 volts or so.

Your LV Choices

The rail light shown below and on the opposite page has a bendable track and lights that slide along it to suit your lighting needs. Cable lights, also called trapeze lights (see page 84) must be installed in straight lines, but they are easy to adjust.

Both styles come in kits that include the transformer, the rail or cables, and several lights. A variety of other lights can be special-ordered. You can also buy low-voltage systems that plug into a standard receptacle and are controlled by a cord switch. Keep in mind that low-voltage halogen lights get hot, so install them well away from flammables and out of the reach of curious children.

In a kitchen, rail lights can provide general illumination or shine directly onto a counter or table. Rail lights can also be installed on a wall, where they may provide stylish task lighting for a work surface, or accent lighting to highlight artwork. You will need a wall-mounted electrical box for rail lights on a wall.

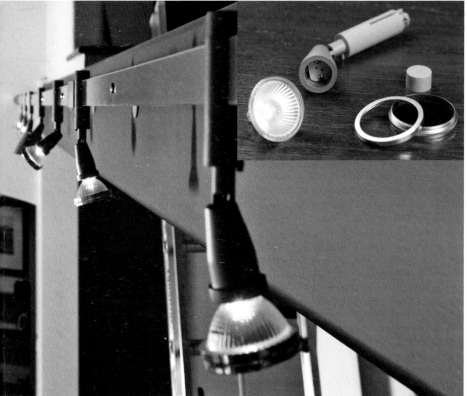

1 Install the transformer

- Remove the old fixture from the box
- Splice the transformer and the house's ground wires, or attach the wires to a grounding screw if there is one
- Splice the transformer's black lead to the house's hot wire and the white to the white (neutral)
- Fold the wires into the box
- Mount the transformer's plate to the box with mounting screws
- Push the canopy over the plate and attach it with screws

Rail or ribbon lights have a high-tech look that complements home-entertainment systems and contemporary interior design.

Stuff to Buy

LOW-VOLTAGE LIGHTING KIT
Choose either rail lights or cable lights

BASIC SUPPLIES Electrical tape and appropriately sized wire nuts

Time Commitment

Most of a day

Tools You'll Need

Screwdriver
Wire stripper
Lineman's pliers
Allen wrench

Related Topics

Grounding, 22–23
Shutting off & restoring power, 50–51
Stripping & joining wire, 54–59

② Bend the rail

- To plan the route for your rail, assemble it directly below where it will go
- Use a large bowl or bucket to help you make even bends; bending by hand may produce unattractive shapes
- Try bending two end pieces to about the same arc, then bend the middle piece to a tighter or more open arc

③ Cut or join rails

- To cut a rail, use a hacksaw
- To join rail lengths, snap them together by pushing their ends into a rail joiner, then use an Allen wrench to tighten the setscrews

④ Mark for posts

- Use a pencil to mark the rail for mounting posts no more than 32 inches apart
- Working with a helper, lift the shaped rail into position near the ceiling (it will rest against the center of the transformer at one point)
- Mark the ceiling for the post locations

⑤ Install posts

- At each mark, drive a drywall anchor into the ceiling; tap with a hammer, then finish with a screwdriver
- Drive a screw to anchor a threaded washer
- Remove the post's cap, then screw the post into the threaded washer
- Turn the post so the rail can slide through it

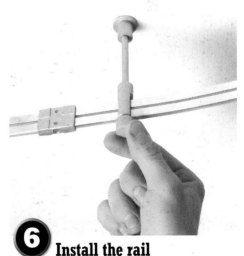

⑥ Install the rail

- Slide the rail through the posts, then screw the caps on
- To install each light, remove the fixture cap, slide the light onto the rail, and screw the cap back on
- To reposition a light, unscrew the cap first
- Restore power and test the lighting

Cable Lights

Also called trapeze lights, cable systems feature small halogen fixtures perched atop and/or hanging from two low-voltage cables. These lights work well in places like kitchens, where ambient light needs to be augmented by targeted lighting over task areas.

This crisscrossing pair of cable lights illuminates a high-ceilinged entry hallway.

The Typical Cable-light Kit

Like rail lights, cable lights are usually sold in kits, although you can build your own by purchasing individual parts. They include:

TRANSFORMERS

Transformers convert 110/120-volt household current to 12 volts, which is the current that runs through the cables. Some transformers are wired to their 110/120-volt source (the input) and the cable lights (the output). Others plug into wall receptacles and are only wired to the cable lights. Be sure to purchase a transformer that is noise-free (some people end up replacing transformers because of annoying, background hums). Output wires from the transformer are usually attached to the cables (to make them hot) with special connectors called power feeds.

CABLE

Some cable is sold with insulation on it, and that's important if your cables are running close to metal that could cause them to short. But in most cases, uninsulated wire is better. It makes the relocation of the lights on the cables simpler because you don't have to pierce the insulation in each new location to make a connection. There's generally little or no price difference between the two cable types.

MOUNTING HARDWARE

Different types of hardware are sold depending on whether you plan to attach your cables to a ceiling or a wall. Buy tensioners, which are basically turnbuckles, to tighten your cable after it has been installed. Some so-called "dead-end" pieces, which are typically designed for walls, also include built-in turnbuckles.

POSTS

If mounting hardware is attached to the ceiling, you will need a post at each end of the cable's run. Posts are sold in pairs since you have two cables. Some wall-mounted systems such as the one on the opposite page don't require posts, but you can add posts to engineer a turn in the middle of a cable's run.

HEADS

Have some fun with the fixtures that attach to the cables. Head styles range from simple pin spots to space-age designs to bugs. Colored glass shades can be selected to enhance a room's existing color scheme.

Stuff to Buy

CABLE LIGHT KIT
LIGHT BULBS Be sure to match the wattage and type of bulb on the fixture package
BASIC SUPPLIES Electrical tape and appropriately sized wire nuts

 **Time Commitment**

Two to four hours

 Tools You'll Need

Screwdriver
Wire stripper
Lineman's pliers
Stud finder

 Related Topics

Shutting off & restoring power, 50–51
Stripping & joining wire, 54–59
Testing methods, 52–53

1 Wire the transformer

- With the power off, wire the transformer
- Follow all instructions supplied by lighting manufacturer

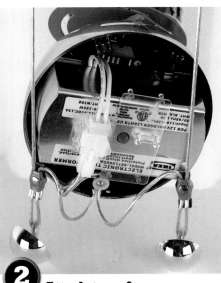

2 Attach transformer to cables

- In this kit, the power feeds also act as cable tensioners
- Here a plug connects the transformer's output wires with the actual cable

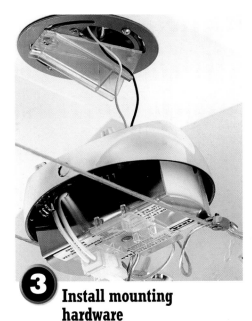

3 Install mounting hardware

- The housing for this transformer slides onto a plastic wedge, which is attached to a plate that's screwed to the electrical box

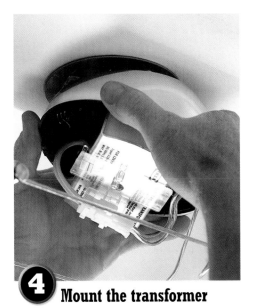

4 Mount the transformer

- The round housing for this transformer comes in two parts
- The first part mounts to the electrical box

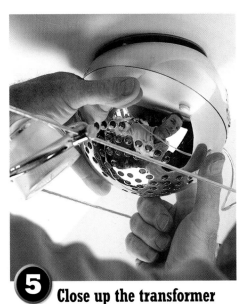

5 Close up the transformer

- The second part adds a decorative, globe cover
- Follow all instructions supplied by manufacturer to secure the transformer in its housing

6 Add lights

- Place halogen fixtures along the cables
- Reposition them as needed to illuminate task areas or artwork

Sconce & Vanity Lights

Sconces are wall lights, often pointing upward or downward to produce ambient light. In a bathroom, some people prefer vanity lighting over a bathroom cabinet or mirror while others find that a sconce on either side of a mirror creates fewer shadows.

Before You Begin

Replacing old vanity or sconce lights is a simple way to update a room or area that you use every day. Wall lights are wired in the same way as ceiling lights. The box behind a wall light may be a round or octagonal ceiling box or a rectangular switch or receptacle box. As long as the fixture covers the box, either a ceiling or receptacle box works fine.

Many vanity lights, including the one shown on the opposite page, are wired like the fluorescent fixture on pages 78–79 and the under-cabinet fixture on pages 166–169. In these cases, the fixture itself acts as an electrical box. Check codes in your area before assuming you can do this.

In general, the placement of a vanity light is a simpler decision than the placement of a sconce. After all, there is really only one place to put a vanity light (above a mirror), whereas a sconce can go just about anywhere. To test the quality of the light from a sconce in a bathroom, find a table lamp whose shade and wattage are similar to the sconce you are considering. Place it on a table or shelf and then stand in front of your bathroom to gauge its effectiveness (if you have a pair of table lamps for this purpose, all the better).

Outside of the bathroom, sconce placement is trickier. That's because many of the most interesting sconce designs are decidedly three-dimensional, which means they may project themselves farther into a room or hallway than you might imagine. Before purchasing a sconce, measure your space carefully, especially in hallways where clearances are tight. Before you install your purchase, hold it in place as family members walk past it to make sure that you are not about to position a sconce at head or eye level where it could do some serious, if unintended, damage.

Installing a Sconce

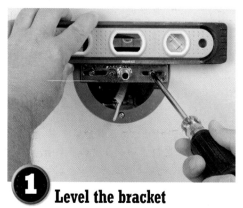

❶ Level the bracket

- With the power off, remove the old fixture
- Attach sconce bracket to electrical box
- Check the level of the bracket and adjust as necessary

❷ Attach the grounds

- In this case, the ground in the cable and the fixture can both be connected to the bracket, or use a wire nut if required by code
- If the box is metal, pigtail the ground to the grounding screw

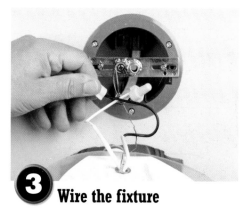

❸ Wire the fixture

- Splice the fixture's hot lead to the house's hot wire, then splice the neutrals
- Fold the wires into the box behind the bracket
- This sconce has a center stud; tighten the mounting nut partway before leveling the fixture

❹ Level the sconce

- After leveling the sconce, finish tightening the mounting nut
- Add a light bulb, restore power, and test the light

Sconces decorate a wall while they illuminate a room with indirect light.

Stuff to Buy

VANITY OR SCONCE LIGHTING FIXTURES

LIGHT BULBS Be sure to match the wattage and type of bulb on the fixture package

TOGGLE BOLTS Use these if you won't be attaching to framing inside the wall

BASIC SUPPLIES Electrical tape and appropriately sized wire nuts

 Time Commitment

One to two hours

 **Tools You'll Need**

Screwdriver
Wire stripper
Lineman's pliers
Stud finder

 Related Topics

Cable connections, 144–145
Fluorescent fixtures, 78–79
Shutting off & restoring power, 50–51
Stripping & joining wire, 54–59
Testing methods, 52–53

Installing a Vanity Light

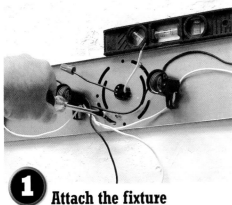

1 Attach the fixture

- For a wall-mounted box, remove a large knockout in the fixture and thread the wires through the hole; if there is only a cable, clamp it to a small knockout
- If there is a box, drive mounting screws through the fixture and into the box's threaded holes, checking for level as you work

2 Connect the wires

- Splice the ground wires, or connect the house ground wire to the grounding screw on the fixture
- Splice the hot wires, then splice the neutral wires

3 Secure the fixture

- Check again for level, then drive screws into framing to attach the fixture to the wall
- Alternatively, use toggle bolts

4 Add cover and bulbs

- Install the decorative cover
- Add light bulbs of the wattage specified by the manufacturer

Vanity lights are typically placed above bathroom mirrors to double their effect.

Ceiling Fans

Installing a ceiling fan is one of the most popular do-it-yourself wiring projects. Many people choose a fan that includes a light unit—either a single light or several individual ones—but you can also install a fan that has no lights.

Box Mounted to Brace

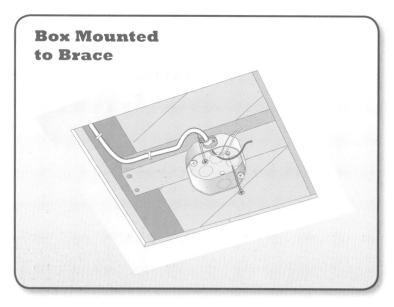

Securing It Safely

A ceiling fan is heavy—some types are very heavy—and it vibrates, which puts stress on hardware. An improperly installed fan can come loose and fall. There are two possible ways to ensure that a fan is attached securely. The most common method is to mount it to a heavy-duty fan-rated box, which has deep threads that will hold the fan tight and not come loose. The box itself must be securely attached to a framing member or two in the ceiling. Or, install a bracket between two joists and attach the box to that, as we have done here.

The second approach is to attach the fan directly to framing in the ceiling. One method is shown in the illustration above. Here, a 2-by-4 brace is attached to the ceiling joists on each side. The fan's bracket will be attached both to the electrical box and to the brace with long screws.

Fan Switches

If you want to control a fan and light separately, there are several options.

WIRELESS REMOTES

This is an increasingly popular choice. Many fans are sold with a sending unit that can be installed inside the fan's canopy so you can control the fan and the light using a battery-powered remote-control unit.

To save money on heating in the winter, set your fan to the up position to force warm air, which rises, back down into a room.

Switch-loop Wiring for Light & Fan

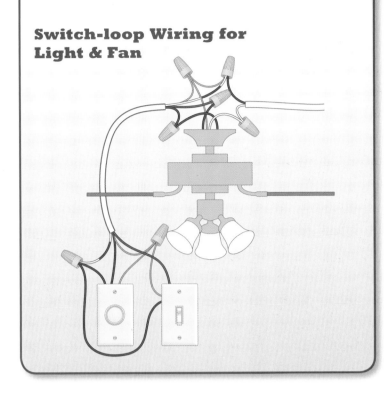

WALL SWITCHES

If you have three-wire cable (one black, one red, and one white wire, plus the ground) running from the switch to the ceiling box, you can install two switches, as shown on the following pages, or install a special wall switch that controls the fan and the light separately.

FAN WITH CUSTOM SWITCH

Some ceiling fans have their own wall switches that control the light and fan separately even though there is only two-wire cable running from the ceiling box to the switch box. You will pay extra for this feature.

PULL CHAINS

Most fans have separate pull chains for the fan and the light, and the fan typically has three speeds. If you simply wire the fan as you would a light fixture, you can use the pull chains to set the fan to the desired speed and to turn the light on or off, then use the wall switch to turn both elements on and off.

Choosing the Right Size

Ceiling fans come in different sizes for use in different areas. They're most efficient in rooms with 8-foot ceilings. See the table below for general guidelines. For example, in a 10-by-12-foot room (120 square feet), a 42-inch fan would be appropriate.

For adequate air movement, the blades should be at least 12 inches from the ceiling and 24 inches from any wall. For safety, they should be at least 7 feet above the floor or they may hit a person's raised arm. You can buy "wall hugger" fans that mount closer to the ceiling for rooms with low overhead, but they will be less efficient in moving air. For high or sloped ceilings, downrod extensions are available in lengths of up to 6 feet.

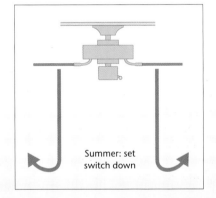

Summer: set switch down

Winter: set switch up

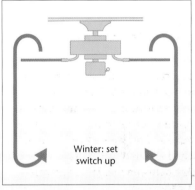

Fan clearances

SEASONAL TUNING

In warm weather, set the reversing switch (on the side of the fan) to the down position, which causes the blades to turn counterclockwise and push air down, cooling you with a direct breeze. In winter, push the switch up to turn the blades clockwise. This will pull the lower, cooler air upward, distributing the warmer air near the ceiling throughout the room without causing a draft. Always wait for the fan blades to come to a complete stop before flipping the reversing switch.

Room Size	Fan Diameter
Up to 64 sq. ft.	36 inches
Up to 144 sq. ft.	42 inches
Up to 225 sq. ft.	44 inches
Up to 400 sq. ft.	52 inches

Installing a Ceiling Fan

Here are steps for installing a common ceiling fan using through-switch wiring (the power source is a receptacle below the wall switches) and a metal brace. Other fans have different hardware, but the procedures are essentially the same.

1 Assemble the fan

- Attach the blades to the irons, then mount the irons to the motor
- Double check with a screwdriver to make sure everything is tight
- Every ceiling fan is different; follow assembly instructions carefully

2 Check the ceiling brace

- Most braces adjust to 24 inches
- Prongs on the ends sink into ceiling joists
- Kits include hardware to attach brace to box

3 Cut the ceiling

- Use a hole saw to cut an opening for the ceiling-fan box

4 Install the brace

- Insert brace into ceiling
- Position it between joists
- Hand tighten until pins begin to dig into joists

5 Connect the cable

- Thread cable from power source through box
- Slip collar around cable to protect it from box edges
- Finish tightening brace with adjustable pliers, as needed

6 Attach the box

- Slip box-mounting hardware over the brace
- Screw box to hardware; make sure it's tight

7 Preparing the wires

- Separate wires in cable
- Attach ground to box
- Leave enough slack to attach to fixture

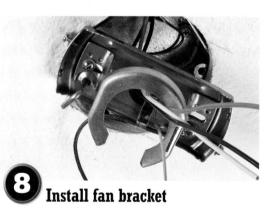

8 Install fan bracket

- This fan has a bracket that attaches to the box
- Thread wires through hole in bracket

9 Wire the fan

- Connect ground wire to bracket and fixture
- Connect neutrals and each set of hot wires; one is for the fan, the other is for the light

Stuff to Buy

CEILING FAN
FAN-RATED BOX
METAL BRACE If you cannot attach the box to a ceiling joist or a wooden brace between two joists
WIRE NUTS

 **Time Commitment**

A weekend, including drywall repairs and paint

 Tools You'll Need

Screwdriver
Wire stripper
Hole saw and drill
Jigsaw or drywall saw

 Related Topics

Cable connections, 144–145
New electrical boxes, 138–139
Shutting off & restoring power, 50–51
Stripping & joining wire, 54–59
Tapping into power, 136–137
Wiring in finished rooms, 130–135

10 Secure fan to bracket

- Attach cover to hide wires and bracket
- If the fan is heavy, ask a helper to support its weight

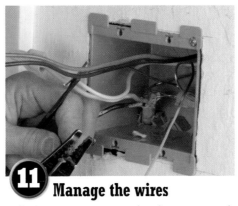

11 Manage the wires

- Connect source ground to fixture ground
- Make two pigtails for grounds to switches
- Connect source neutral to fixture neutral
- Connect source hot to two pigtails, each of which will connect to a switch (one for the fan, one for the fan light)

12 Wire the first switch

- Connect the first hot fixture wire and one of the hot source pigtails to one of the switches
- Connect one of the ground pigtails to the first switch

13 Wire the second switch

- Connect the second hot source pigtail to the second switch
- Connect the second hot fixture wire to the second switch
- Connect remaining ground pigtail to second switch

14 Attach switches to box

- Push wires into box gently but firmly to make room for the switch

15 Install face plate

Like many fan-light combos, this one comes with a pair of pull chains, in case you don't want to install wall switches.

Halogen Under-cabinet Lights

There are many ways to add light to a counter made dark by overhanging cabinets. Halogen lights are a popular solution. The unit shown here uses standard voltage. You can also buy units with transformers so you can install low-voltage lamps.

Cords vs. Cordless

The under-cabinet lights shown below and on the opposite page do leave you with visible wiring—stapled cords, which are safe because they carry low voltage, and some balled-up thin cord from the switch. Most people don't mind the visible wiring if it is tucked under the cabinet. For a cord-free installation, consider under-cabinet fluorescents or tracks, both of which usually require you to run cables through the walls.

Safety Tip

Halogens get hot, so install the lights where children cannot reach them.

❶ Insert the bulbs

- Disassemble the lamps by unscrewing the covers, taking care not to touch the bulbs with your fingers
- Set the lights on the counter under where you want to install them

Under-cabinet halogens are barely visible, but they throw a lot of light where it's needed.

Stuff to Buy

HALOGEN UNDER-CABINET LIGHTS Either buy them as a kit that includes lamps, extension cord, plugs, insulated staples, and a switch, or buy the lamps and switch separately
BASIC SUPPLIES Electrical tape and appropriately sized wire nuts

 Time Commitment

About two hours

 Tools You'll Need

Screwdriver
Diagonal cutters
Tack hammer

 **Related Topics**

Hardwired under-cabinet lights, 166–169
Shutting off & restoring power, 50–51
Stripping & joining wire, 54–59
Testing methods, 52–53

❷ Attach the lights

- Positioning the lights under the cabinets about 8 inches from the wall, attach them with short screws
- Take care the screws don't poke into the cabinet

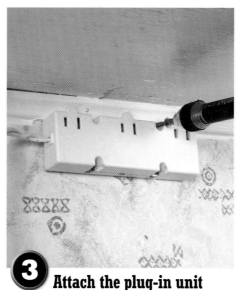

❸ Attach the plug-in unit

- Drive screws to attach the plug-in unit in a central location
- If you install it inside a cabinet, drill holes to run cords to the lamps

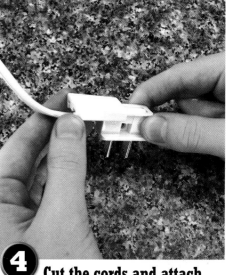

❹ Cut the cords and attach to plugs

- For each lamp, run the cord straight back to the wall and then along the cabinet to the plug-in unit
- Cut the cord long enough to follow that path, with about 2 inches of slack
- Slide the cover off a plug and insert the cut end of the cord; follow the instructions so that the ribbed (neutral) wire attaches to the wide plug blade
- Snap the cover into place to make the electrical connection

❺ Anchor the cords

- Using the insulated staples provided, attach the cords to the cabinet; you can use one staple to attach two cords
- Keep the cords straight and fairly taut and avoid twisting them
- Plug the cords into the plug-in unit, then plug in the unit

❻ Connect the switch

- Connect the thin cord from the switch to the plug-in unit, then attach it to the wall using its self-stick tape
- Ball up the cord as neatly as possible, tuck it away, and secure it with insulated staples

Mini Halogens on Tracks

For a different look, consider mini halogen lights. Designed for narrow tracks, these small bulbs can be hidden under a counter to provide ambient light for a room, while also illuminating the counter below.

Motion-sensor Exterior Light

Degree of Difficulty

● Easy

For a small investment of time and money, you can replace an old exterior light with one that turns on at night when it senses motion. Many motion-sensor lights allow you to adjust the sensor's sensitivity as well as how long the light stays on.

STOP!
Always turn off power to the circuit you are working on, then double-check at the project site before and after removing the fixture to make sure the power is off.

A Simple Installation

For the replacement project described here, you will need an electrical box for an existing light that is controlled by a wall switch.

1 Attach the mounting strap

- With the power off, remove the existing fixture
- Check that the box is well sealed against water and won't admit cold air into the house; apply caulk or mortar as needed
- If there is no ground wire for a metal box, attach a grounding pigtail
- Screw the fixture's mounting strap to the box

2 Wire the fixture

- Thread the house wires through the fixture's rubber gasket
- Splice the fixture's black lead to the house's hot (black or colored) wire
- Splice the white lead to the house's white wire
- As always, make sure the wire nuts cover all bare wire; you may choose to wrap tape around the open end of the nuts

3 Attach the fixture

- Carefully push the wiring into the box
- Align the gasket so it seals the light against the wall
- Drive one or two screws to anchor the light
- It may take several tries to get the wires inside and the gasket positioned just right

4 Caulk the joint

- Apply a bead of exterior caulk all around the light's body
- With a finger, gently smooth the caulk so it seals completely

Stuff to Buy

MOTION-SENSOR LIGHT
LIGHT BULB Be sure to get the appropriate type and wattage for outdoor use
BASIC SUPPLIES Electrical tape and appropriately sized wire nuts; local codes may require weather-tight wire nuts for outdoor installations
EXTERIOR CAULK

Time Commitment

Two hours to install and adjust

Tools You'll Need

Screwdriver
Wire stripper
Lineman's pliers

Related Topics

A new light & switch, 164–165
Outdoor wiring, 170–171
Shutting off & restoring power, 50–51
Stripping & joining wire, 54–59

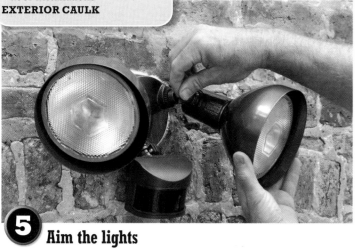

5 Aim the lights

- Loosen the ring nut that allows you to swivel each socket
- Position the base and tighten the nut
- Loosen the wing nut that controls the light's position, adjust the light, and re-tighten the nut
- Test at night to make sure the light illuminates the desired area, such as a path, but won't shine in your eyes, passing drivers' eyes, or your neighbors' windows

6 Adjust the sensor

- Experiment to adjust the sensor so it turns on when someone approaches (including you with a bag of groceries), but does not bother neighbors
- Aim the sensor in the desired direction—upward for broad coverage, downward to cover a smaller area
- Using the controls at the bottom, adjust the range to determine how wide an area will be sensed
- Set the amount of time you want the lights to stay on after motion is detected
- On some units, choose whether to add detection areas under the light or outside the space where it shines

The table below this exterior motion-sensor fixture is just inside the light's main coverage area, which means it's illuminated but not flooded with light.

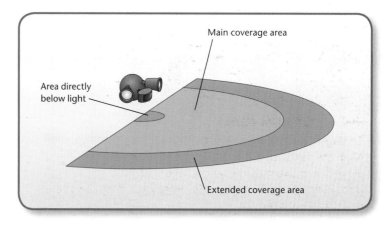

Main coverage area

Area directly below light

Extended coverage area

Low-voltage Outdoor Lighting

Attractive, well-placed lighting will make your yard, deck, or patio an inviting place at night. Low-voltage lights are not as bright as the standard variety, but they are usually strong enough to provide path illumination and ambience.

A Typical Low-voltage System

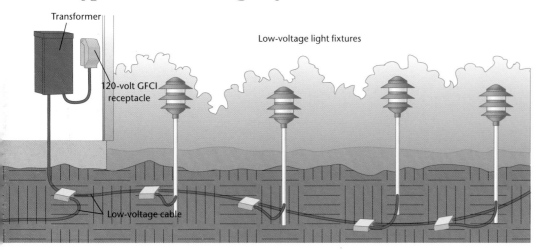

Transformer

120-volt GFCI receptacle

Low-voltage light fixtures

Low-voltage cable

Lighting the Path

Outdoor Lighting Techniques

Most yards benefit from a combination of three or more of the following lighting techniques. In general, you can use low-voltage lighting to achieve them, but you may need standard-voltage lights for large areas or more dramatic effects.

The Solar Option

Solar lights collect power from sunlight, store it in a rechargeable battery, and shine at night. The brightness and duration of the light depend on how much sunlight has been collected. It may take several days for the battery to build up full power. Older solar lights were feeble, but the latest models shine brighter and last longer.

Standalone solar lights can be placed wherever there is sunlight, even on a table; you can also buy kits with several lights powered by a single collector. A kit lets you place the solar collector in a sunny place while putting the lights in shadier spots.

Related Topics
Avoiding overloads, 266–267
Outdoor wiring, 170–171

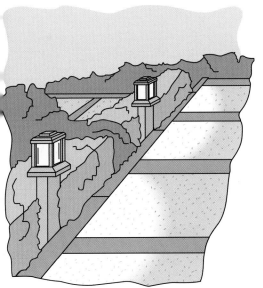

SILHOUETTING

To silhouette a tree, shrub, or bed of flowers, aim a spotlight or wall washer at a fence or wall from close behind the plant.

PATH LIGHTING

Low fixtures provide soft pools of light directly below them. They may be placed in a garden but are most often used to light a walkway. If you don't like the runway effect, illuminate part of the path with downlighting or spread lighting.

SPREAD LIGHTING

Spread fixtures are short, but cover a fairly large area. Place these in planting beds to light up surrounding shrubbery.

DIFFUSED LIGHTING

Low lighting is often enough for low-traffic areas. You can light railings and fences indirectly, either from underneath or from behind, to outline the edges of the structures.

DOWNLIGHTING

Downlighting is a good way to accentuate trees, flowers, and shrubs. Position lights above the plants and shine them down for gentle illumination. You can also use this method to light pathways, porches, and patios.

Installing Low-voltage Lights

Degree of Difficulty

● Easy

Most low-voltage lighting kits contain everything you need. The cord carries only 12 volts, so you do not need an electrical permit. But you do need to plug into an outdoor electrical receptacle, which should be GFCI protected.

STOP!
Always turn off power to the circuit you are working on, then double-check at the project site before and after removing the fixture to make sure the power is off.

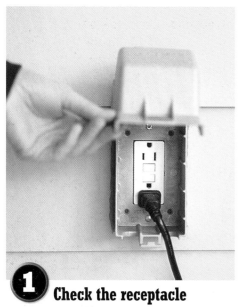

① Check the receptacle

- Make sure your receptacle is GFCI protected
- If necessary, install an in-use cover to keep out rain

② Install the transformer

- Place the transformer near the receptacle, and where it won't get bumped
- Mount it with screws driven into siding or another stable surface

③ Place the fixtures

- Experiment with the light fixtures to choose a final placement
- Lay out the cord, running it past the lights

④ Attach the cords

- Join each light's cord to the main cord with the connectors provided

⑤ Install the lights

- Poke each light into the ground
- Cover the wires with mulch or soil

⑥ Program the system

- Connect the wires
- Program the lights to come on when it gets dark or to follow a schedule

Stuff to Buy

LOW-VOLTAGE LIGHTING KIT
Purchase a kit with as many lights as you want, up to a dozen; for more than that, buy another kit, as one transformer may not suffice. Check whether the transformer has the ability to set the lights on a timer or on a photocell that senses when it gets dark.
WIRE STAPLES Use outdoor-rated wire staples for deck-mounted installations; they tap in with a hammer

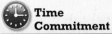

Time Commitment

Two to four hours, depending on project

Tools You'll Need

Drill
Small hammer
Jigsaw

Related Topics

Installing a GFCI receptacle, 120–121
Outdoor wiring, 170–171

Low-voltage Deck Lighting

Installing deck-mounted lights is only a little more complicated than poking landscaping lights in the ground. Install the transformer near a receptacle, ideally underneath the deck.

Where possible, hide the cable by running it under the decking, through holes drilled in framing, or through channels routed in posts or rails. You can cover a channel with trim. Fasten wires with wire staples that are made for exterior use. Pull the wires fairly taut and position them neatly before you fasten them.

Installing a Riser Light

- Remove a stair tread
- Outline the hole for the light on the riser
- Drill a hole near one corner, then cut the shape with a jigsaw
- Insert the light's box, make the connections, and screw on the cover
- Test light before you reinstall the tread

Installing a Post Cap Light

- Bore a hole through the post with a long drill bit, or cut a channel in the side and cover with trim
- Thread the wire through
- Make the connections
- Slip the light over the post
- Hold it in place with small nails or screws

Fastening Wires

- Hide cable by running it under decking or deck-skirt framing
- Fasten wires with staples made for exterior use
- Pull the wires fairly taut and before you fasten them

Transformer Under Deck

- A deck gives you plenty of places to hide a transformer
- Mount the transformer as close as you can to an exterior receptacle

4 Replacing Switches & Receptacles

In this chapter, we show you how to wire a variety of switches—from standard, 120-volt switches to dimmer switches wired with leads. You'll also learn how to choose the right receptacle based on power needs and location. GFCI receptacles are covered, as are split-circuit receptacles. Finally, we explain how to add switches and receptacles without tearing up your walls.

Chapter Contents

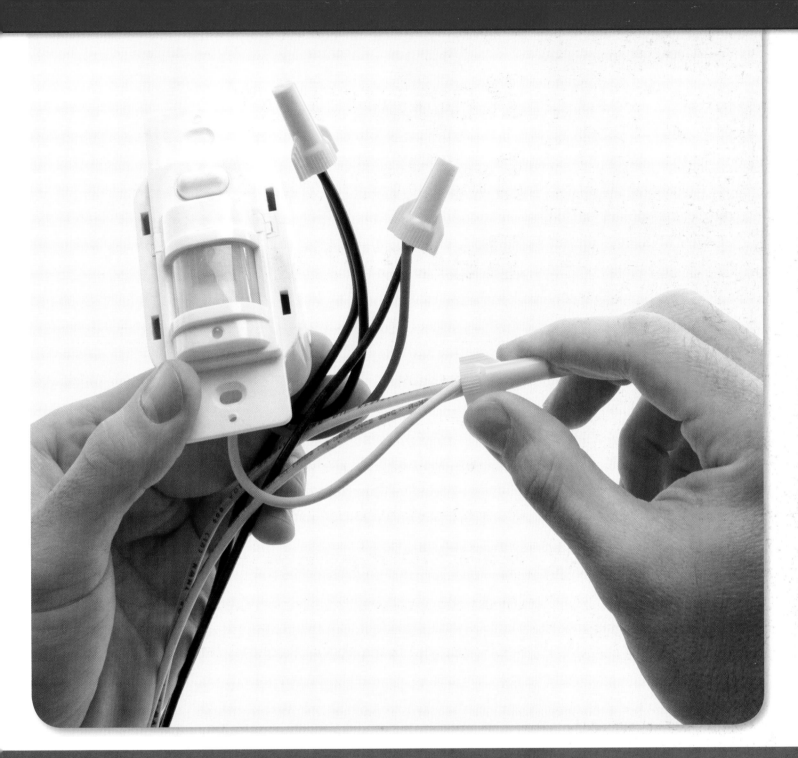

Split-circuit Receptacles
page 118

Installing a GFCI Receptacle
page 120

High-voltage Receptacles
page 122

Surface-mounted Wiring
page 124

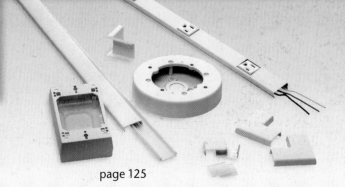

page 125

Cover Plates

A cover plate protects you from live wiring and puts a finished surface on the wall. Install the plate flush against the wall, firmly attached and straight.

Choosing Cover Plates

The most common choice for cover plates is ivory-colored or white plastic. You can buy plates for one, two, or three switches or receptacles, or a combination of them.

STYLES

Most cover plates are chosen to blend with the wall, but you can also use plates to add a style or color accent. Options include ceramic, stone, plastic, wood, and coated metal.

PLATES FOR PROBLEM AREAS

For an uneven wall, which causes the plate to flex, or a location that may get bumped, use an unbreakable flexible nylon plate. If a standard plate fails to cover a blemish in the wall, try an oversized one (top right).

Unbreakable Cover Plate

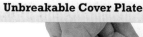

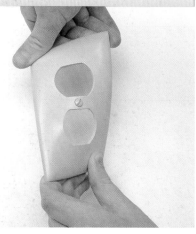

Painting or Papering a Plate

You can paint a cover plate or cover it with wallpaper. It's best to paint the plate off the wall; if you paint it on the wall, protect the receptacle or switch with masking tape first. For wallpaper, cut the wallpaper to size with a slight excess in each direction, then tuck the excess behind the plate.

Straightening a Skewed Cover Plate

If a cover plate does not look straight, remove it. Slightly loosen one or two mounting screws and make adjustments, checking with a level as you work. Replace the plate and tighten the screws.

It can be tricky to align both devices for a double or two-gang cover plate. The tool shown at right does the aligning for you.

Sealing Against the Wall

If the cover plate won't sit flat on one or two sides, try tightening the screws. (If the plate cracks, try an unbreakable one.) If that doesn't work, remove the plate, apply joint compound to the area, sand it smooth, and prime and paint. Alternatively, caulk around the plate. The result is less attractive, but much less time-consuming.

If there is a gap behind the entire cover plate and the wall, try removing the plate and tightening the device's mounting screws. It may help to break off the little tabs on either side of each screw. If that doesn't work, the electrical box is protruding from the wall. Use joint compound to build up the wall around the box.

Fixing an Uneven Wall

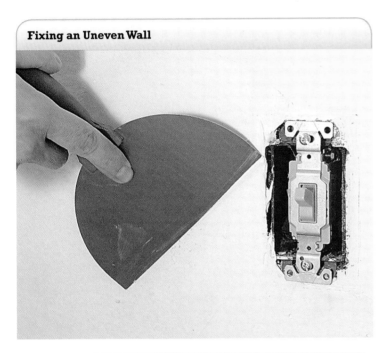

Two-gang Aligning Tool

Caulking a Plate

Breaking Off Tabs

Switches

Most switches will last for decades without needing replacement. However, if a switch fails to operate a light reliably, you can investigate to find the source of the problem. New switches, for replacement or in new construction, come in several varieties.

STOP!
Always turn off power to the circuit you are working on. Double-check at the project site before and after removing the cover plate to make sure the power is off.

Testing Switches

To test a switch, first shut off power to the circuit and test that power is off. Pull out the switch and tighten any loose connections. If you see any breaks or deep nicks in the wires, cut the wires behind the damage, then restrip and reattach them. If the connections are secure, the switch may be faulty. Disconnect the switch from all wiring and check it with a continuity tester as follows.

SINGLE-POLE SWITCH

Flip the switch on. Attach the continuity tester's clip to one terminal and touch the probe to the other one. The light should glow. Flip the switch off, and the light should not glow. If either test fails, replace the switch.

THREE-WAY SWITCH

Attach the continuity tester's clip to the common terminal (usually darker colored or marked with a C). With the probe touching another terminal, the tester's light should glow when the switch is in one position but not the other. Test the other noncommon terminal the same way. If any of the tests fail, replace the switch.

MECHANICAL TIMER SWITCH

For a mechanical timer switch, attach the tester's clip to a lead or terminal, touch the probe to the other one, and turn the dial to the "on" position.

Most special switches—including dimmers, motion-sensor switches, and electronically programmable switches—have tiny circuit boards that require electricity in order to work. That means you can't test most special switches using a continuity tester.

Testing a Single-pole Switch

Testing a Three-way Switch

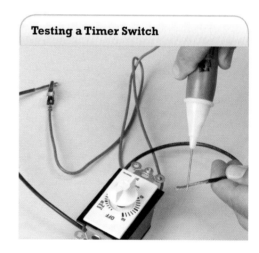

Testing a Timer Switch

Choosing Standard Switches

Switches are rated by amperage and voltage. Almost all residential lights use 15-amp, 120-volt switches. If the fixture you are switching uses 20 amps (with 12-gauge wire), use a 20-amp switch. A 240-volt switch is rare, but might be used, for example, to control an air conditioner.

Older switches (right) did not have grounding terminals, because the plastic toggles were considered shockproof. Nowadays, grounded switches are required for all new installations. If you are replacing an ungrounded switch, hook up the ground wires if possible.

Ungrounded Single-pole Switch

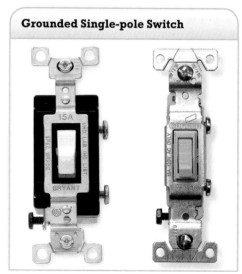

Grounded Single-pole Switch

Related Topics

Common wiring methods, 28–31
Installing special switches, 110–113
Looking inside, 26–27
Special-purpose switches, 108–109
Stripping & joining wire, 54–59

SINGLE-POLE & THREE-WAYS

Most residential switches are single-pole types, with toggle that has "on" and "off" labels and controls a light or lights from a single location. A single-pole switch has two terminals, not counting the ground. The hot wire is connected to both terminals; when you flip the switch, you open or close the connection between the wires, thereby shutting power off or turning it on.

A number of special-purpose switches—dimmers, pilot switches, timers, motion sensors, and so on—can expand the basic on-off function. Most standard switches are wired with screw-down terminals.

To control a light, several lights, or a receptacle from two locations, you'll need two three-way switches, which do not have "on" and "off" written on their toggles. A three-way can turn the light on or off when it is in either the up or down position. It has three terminals, not including the ground.

In the unusual case where a light is controlled from three locations, two three-way switches and one four-way are used.

SWITCH GRADES

You may need only inexpensive "residential" or "contractor" switches, which work fine and last a very long time in most situations. For heavier-duty service, look for somewhat pricier switches labeled "heavy-duty," "commercial," or "spec."

Instead of terminals, special-purpose switches often have stranded leads, which are spliced to the house wires with wire nuts.

VARIATIONS

A switch-receptacle has both a switch and a receptacle that fit into the space of a single device. This combination device can be wired so that the receptacle is always hot, or the receptacle can be controlled by the switch.

Dimmer switches, once called rheostats, allow you to turn the brightness all the way up or off, or to any gradation in between. Dimmers can both set mood and save energy, but they don't controls the levels of most new compact fluorescents, so check the specs of your CFLs before installing a dimmer.

Decora-style Switch

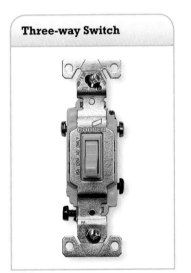
Three-way Switch

Four-way Switch

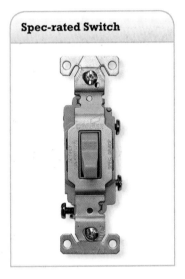
Spec-rated Switch

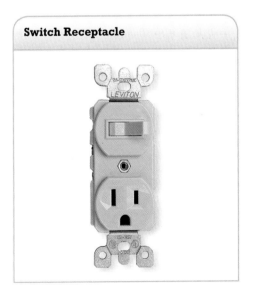
Switch Receptacle

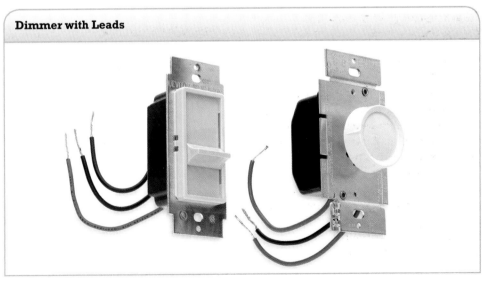
Dimmer with Leads

Replacing a Single-pole Switch

Degree of Difficulty

✓

● Easy

Replacing a light switch is so easy and inexpensive that you may choose to do it just to change its color or style. Switches usually last a lifetime, but if yours is loose, cracked, or just plain ugly, replace it. The project shown here is an example of switch-loop wiring.

STOP!
Before you replace a switch, turn off power at main service panel and test to verify that power is off.

Two Types of Wiring You May Find

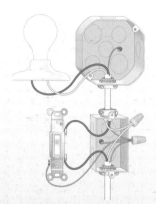

THROUGH-SWITCH WIRING
- Attach black wires to terminals
- Leave white wires alone

SWITCH-LOOP WIRING
- White wire is also hot
- Mark with black paint or tape for safety

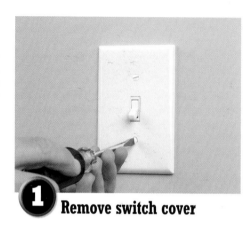

1 **Remove switch cover**

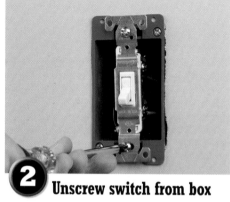

2 **Unscrew switch from box**
- Remove mounting screws from box
- Slowly pull switch at mounting straps

3 **Test for power**
- Touch probes to terminal screws to confirm that power is off
- For more on testing, see pages 52–53

4 **Snip the wires**
- Rebending wire ends can cause them to crack
- If wires are long enough, cut ends close to switch

Short wires?

If the wires are so short that snipping their ends will make it difficult to wire the new switch, loosen the terminal screws and back the wires out, taking care to bend the wires as little as possible.

NOTE

Quick Inspection

If you notice lots of cracked or missing insulation on wires, or signs of heat caused by wire coming in contact with the electrical box, see pages 260–261 for additional repair instructions.

Stuff to Buy

SWITCH Choose a commercial-rated switch if it will get heavy use
COVER PLATE Pick one that matches your home's décor
ELECTRICAL TAPE

Time Commitment

About 15 minutes

Tools You'll Need

Wire stripper
Screwdriver
Long-nose pliers

Related Topics

Common wiring methods, 28–31
Installing special switches, 110–113
Shutting off & restoring power, 50–51
Special-purpose switches, 108–109
Stripping & joining wire, 54–59

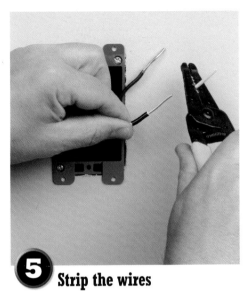

5 Strip the wires

- Strip about 1 inch of insulation from wires
- Form clockwise loops so they will wrap easily around screws
- For detailed instructions on stripping and looping, see pages 111–112

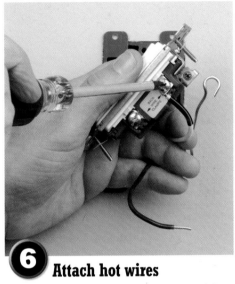

6 Attach hot wires

- Use long-nose pliers to wrap wires around terminal screws
- Tighten with screwdriver until secure

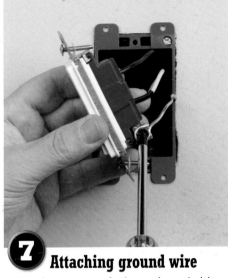

7 Attaching ground wire

- Attach one ground wire to the switch's grounding terminal
- If the switch is in a metal box, also ground to the box
- For more on grounding, see pages 22–23

8 Mount the switch

- Carefully fold the wires back into the box
- Gently push the new switch into place
- Tighten mounting screws most of the way
- Use a level to make sure the switch is plumb
- Finish tightening the screws

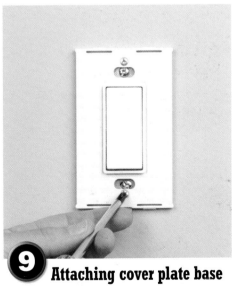

9 Attaching cover plate base

- This cover plate has two pieces to hide the screws

10 Press on cover plate

Special-purpose Switches

You can enhance your control over light fixtures and fans with specialty switches. Dimmers let you vary lighting levels, while timers and sensors do some or all of the switching automatically.

Dimmer Options

In addition to basic rotary or sliding dimmer switches, you can buy more sophisticated dimmers with a variety of options. Most are rated for 600 watts. For a large chandelier whose bulbs total more than that, install a heavy-duty dimmer that can handle the wattage.

If you have a light controlled by two three-way switches and you want to use one or two dimmers, read the three-way dimmer's instructions carefully. Some three-way dimmers can be installed on only one of the switches; the other switch must be a standard toggle. Others can be installed at both locations.

Toggle Switch with Sliding Dimmer	Digital Fade Dimmer	Smart Dimmer

These switches allow you to set a desired brightness level with the dimmer, so the switch retains that setting while you turn the toggle off and on.	This switch remembers the last brightness setting you chose, but also allows you to tap twice for brightness or press and hold for gradual fading. A "delayed off" feature keeps the light on for a few seconds while you leave the room.	This dimmer has many of the same features as the digital fade, but it turns the fixture on when you press the top, and off when you press the bottom. It allows you to set the brightness even when the light is off.

Related Topics

Common wiring methods, 28–31

Installing special switches, 110–113

Replacing a single-pole switch, 106–107

Stripping & joining wire, 54–59

Timer Switches

Timer switches may turn a light on and off at predetermined times (including dusk or dawn for some units) or simply shut it off after a certain interval.

Shutoff Timer

Use a shutoff timer for an item that you do not want left on indefinitely. The amount of time it can be set to stay on depends on the model. The most common use is for a bathroom heating unit or vent fan, but you may also want to use it for a bright porch light.

Countdown Timers

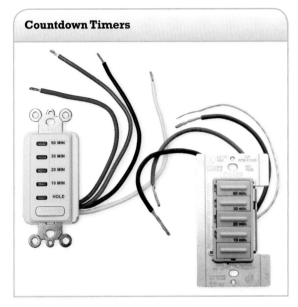

A countdown timer is like a shutoff timer, but with more features. Choose among 10-, 20-, 30-, or 60-minute intervals, or choose to leave the light on until you turn it off. Mechanical models have a separate push switch for each interval (above, right), while electronic models use a single switch (above, left).

Programmable Timer

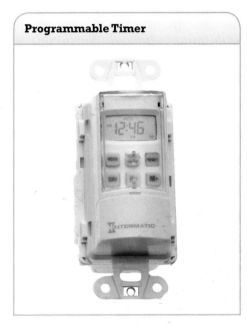

Programmable timers add a level of sophistication, providing multiple daily settings for security lights, a fan, radio, or TV.

Helpful Switches

Some switches seem to do more than what you ask of them, as these two examples demonstrate.

Pilot Switch

A pilot switch has a small red light that glows when the fixture or appliance is on. Use it for fixtures or appliances that you won't see or hear directly, like an attic light or fan, a garage or basement light, or outdoor lighting.

Motion-sensor Switch

Used for security, convenience, or energy savings, a motion-sensor switch turns on a light or lights when it detects movement in a room or a part of the yard, then shuts power off after an interval during which no motion is detected. The better models allow you to adjust the sensitivity and the interval and include a manual on-off switch.

Installing Special Switches

You can wire most dimmers and many special-purpose switches by simply connecting the hot wires to the switch, which come with their own leads (short stranded wires attached to the device). Just splice hot wires to switch leads and tighten with wire nuts.

STOP!
Always turn off power to the circuit you are working on. Flip the switch to verify the light does not come on, then test for power before and after removing it.

Switch-loop Wiring

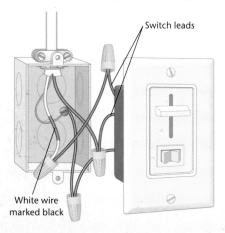

Switch leads

White wire marked black

Through-switch Wiring

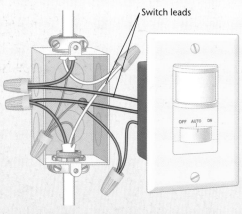

Switch leads

Through-switch Wiring

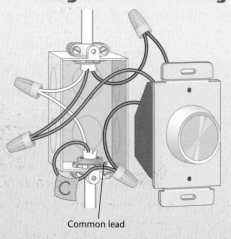

Common lead

Switch-loop & Through-switch Wiring

If you have only one white and one black or colored wire (plus the grounds) entering the box, you have switch-loop (or end-line) wiring and the white wire should be marked black. If you have two black or colored wires connected to the switch and two or more white wires that are spliced together, you have through-switch wiring. In either case, splice the dimmer's leads to the two switched wires (or to one black wire and one white wire marked black), as shown at top left.

Wiring a Three-way Dimmer

If the fixture is controlled by a pair of three-way switches, either replace only one of them with a standard three-way dimmer and leave the other switch as a toggle, or invest in a pair of three-way dimmers made be used in both locations (they are more expensive). No other special-purpose switches can be installed onto a three-way setup.

Before snipping or removing the wires from the existing three-way switch, tag the wire that leads to the common terminal. Follow the switch manufacturer's instructions to splice the wires to the leads or attach wires to terminals. Be sure to attach the common wire to the common lead or terminal. (Note: For simplicity, the ground wires are not shown in this illustration.)

Pro Tips

- Special-purpose switches are usually larger than the single-pole switches they replace, so they may not fit in the existing box.
- Some of these switches require a neutral, which means they cannot be installed if you have switch-loop wiring. For them, there must be two cables in the box, indicating through-switch wiring.
- Many special switches come only in single-pole versions, while others can be installed as one or both of a pair of three-way switches.
- Don't rush headlong into changing a switch. Before you snip or remove any wires, examine the wiring arrangement and make sure you understand it. Compare the new switch with the old to understand which wire will go where. It often helps to tag at least some of the wires with symbols indicating the terminals where they belong.

Tools You'll Need

Screwdriver
Wire stripper
Lineman's pliers

Related Topics

Common wiring methods, 28–31
Looking inside, 26–27
Repairing wiring in boxes, 260–261
Replacing a single-pole switch, 106–107
Shutting off & restoring power, 50–51
Stripping & joining wire, 54–59
Testing methods, 52–53

Wiring a Through-switch Dimmer

❶ Remove cover
- Make sure the power to the circuit is off

❷ Assess the wiring
- This is an example of through-switch wiring

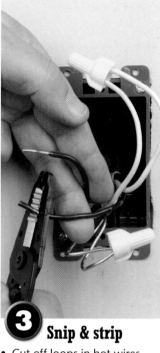

❸ Snip & strip
- Cut off loops in hot wires
- Strip about ¾" of insulation
- Strip insulation from the switch leads as needed

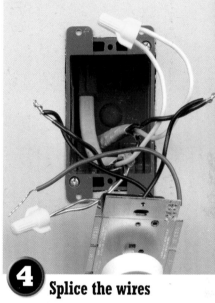

❹ Splice the wires
- Wrap the stranded leads around the solid-core house wires

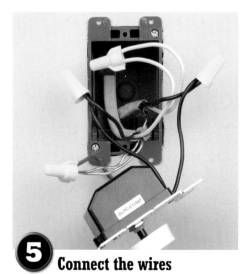

❺ Connect the wires
- Secure all wires with nuts
- If the old switch was ungrounded, add a grounding pigtail if necessary

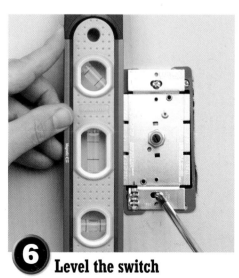

❻ Level the switch
- Tuck the wires into the box, taking care not to loosen the wire nuts
- Place the switch and drive the mounting screws, adjusting it to plumb as you work

❼ Attach new cover plate
- Pull the knob straight off to attach the cover plate
- Push the knob back on, then restore power and test

Wiring Other Specialty Switches

Some specialty switches are wired just like a simple dimmer. Other switches such as electronic-timer and pilot-light switches are examples of switches that can be installed only if there are two cables—and therefore a pair of neutral wires—in the box.

Finding the Feed Wire

Before you can make the connections to a switch that uses neutral wires, you need to find which wire is the feed wire—the hot wire bringing power into the box. The feed wire usually enters at the bottom. Turn off the power and remove the old switch. To test, separate the wires so there is no danger that they will touch each other or anything metal. Keeping other people out of the room, restore power and carefully touch one probe of a voltage tester to a black wire and one to the white wire from the same cable. If the tester glows, that's the feed wire. You might cap it with a wire nut. Shut off power before continuing.

Timer Switch

Some models have poke-in terminals, others have stranded leads. Motion-sensor switches and programmable switches are also wired this way.

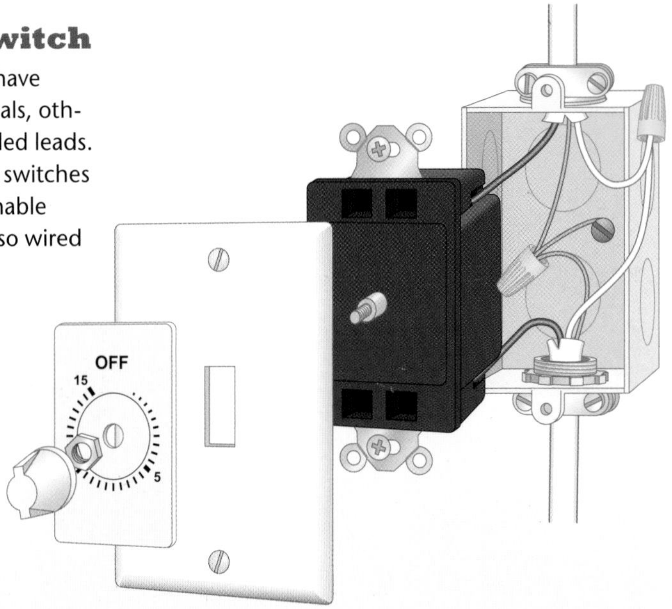

Pilot-light Switch

A pilot-light switch has a connecting tab on one side. Connect the grounds. Use a pigtail to connect the white wire to the silver terminal. Connect the feed wire to the dark brass terminal labeled "common," then connect the other black wire to the lighter-colored brass terminal.

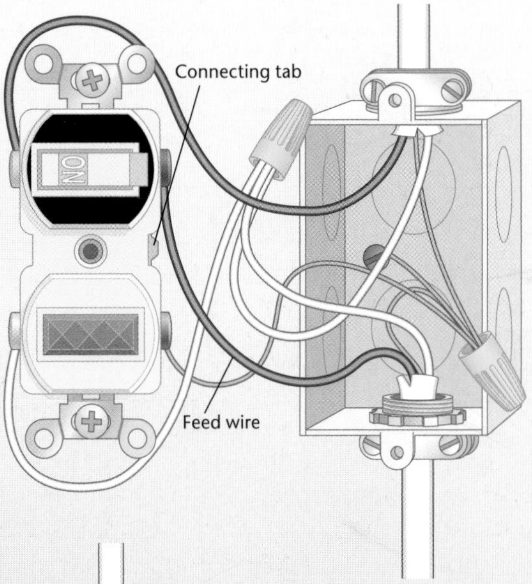

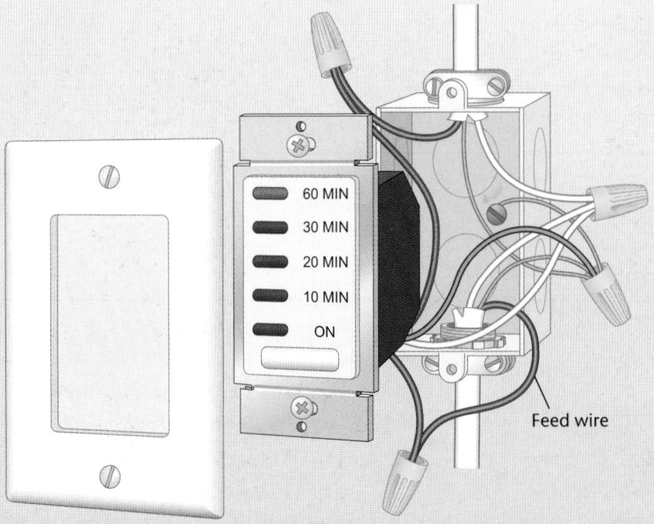

Connecting tab

Feed wire

Electronic Timer

For an electronic timer, splice the wires to the leads as shown. There are separate leads for the feed wire and the hot wire leading to the fixture.

Feed wire

Outlet Controlled by Switch

Feed wire

Connecting tab

Outlet Always Hot

Connecting tab

Feed wire

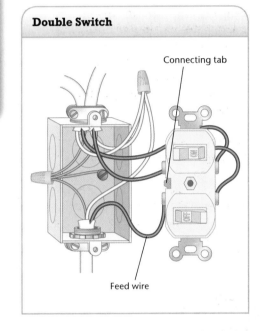

Double Switch

Connecting tab

Feed wire

Wiring a Switch-outlet

You can replace a receptacle, most likely one near a countertop, with a switch-outlet. You may want the outlet to be controlled by the switch. Or, if a switch has through-switch wiring, you can put in a switch-outlet that has an always-hot outlet.

To make the switch control the outlet, connect the grounds. Use a pigtail to attach the neutral wire to the silver terminal. Connect the feed wire to the brass screw on the side with no connecting tab, then hook the other hot wire (leading to other receptacles) to a brass terminal on the side with the connecting tab.

For an always-hot outlet, also connect the grounds and use a pigtail to connect the neutral wire to the silver terminal. Then, connect the feed wire to a terminal on the side with the connecting tab, and connect the other hot wire to a terminal on the side with no connecting tab.

Double Switch

If you want to replace a double switch, tag the wires to indicate which terminal each goes to. Three cables may enter the box—one bringing power and the other two leading to two different fixtures. Or there may be a single three-wire cable (with a white, black, and red wire) that carries power to two fixtures.

Connect the grounds. Connect the neutral wires together; they do not attach to

the switch. Attach the feed wire to a terminal on the side with the connecting tab. Attach the other two hot wires to each of the terminals on the side with no connecting tab.

Two cables, or a three-wire cable, may bring power from two different circuits. In that case, the switch's connecting tab is broken off and a separate feed wire connects to each of the terminals on the side with the broken tab. To replace the switch, you will need to break off the connecting tab and wire the new switch just like the old one.

Two Switches in a Box

If two switches share a two-gang box, there are a number of possible wiring configurations. The one shown here is the most common, with a single power source supplying both switches. If your arrangement is different, tag the wires and connect them to the new switches the same way they were connected to the old switches.

Connect the grounds and leave the white wires spliced together. Use pigtails to connect the feed line to each of the switches. Connect the other hot wires to the other terminals.

Two Switches in a Box

Cables lead to separate fixtures

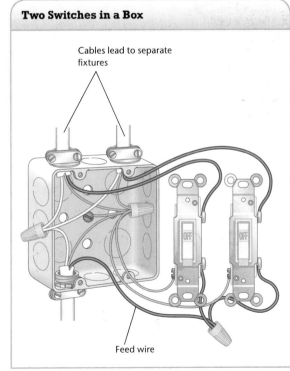

Feed wire

Receptacles

Like switches, most receptacles last a long time without giving any trouble. However, if a receptacle does not consistently provide power, you can check for the source of the problem. New receptacles come in the varieties shown here.

STOP!
Always turn off power to the circuit you are working on. Double-check at the project site before and after removing the cover plate to make sure the power is off.

Troubleshooting Receptacles

If a receptacle is unreliable, shut off power to the circuit and test that power is off. Pull out the receptacle. Check that the wires are fastened securely and not deeply nicked or broken.

Test the receptacle while it is still wired and attached to the box. Note that the wiring, rather than the receptacle, may be faulty. If the tester tells you the receptacle is not polarized, check that the wires are on the correct terminals. Neutrals must be connected to silver terminals, hot wires to brass terminals.

If the receptacle still sometimes fails to deliver power, or if you see sparks or hear a popping sound when plugging something in, replace it.

Code Requirements

Code requires that all new receptacles for 15- or 20-amp, 120-volt branch circuits (most of the circuits in your home) be of the three-hole, grounding type shown on these pages. The specific amperage and voltage a receptacle is suited for are stamped on its front. Most receptacles are for use with copper wire only. Receptacles marked AL-CU may be used with either copper or aluminum wire.

Receptacle Grades

Home improvement centers often sell inexpensive "residential" or "contractor" receptacles, which work fine and last a very long time in most situations. For heavier-duty service—for example, if the receptacle will get bumped or if people tend to yank plugs out by the cord—buy "heavy-duty," "commercial," or "spec" receptacles. These receptacles typically have poke-in terminals that include setscrews, which clamp the wire ends securely. (Less expensive, lighter-duty receptacles should be wired with screw-down terminals even if they also have poke-in holes.)

15-amp Duplex Receptacle

20-amp Duplex Receptacle

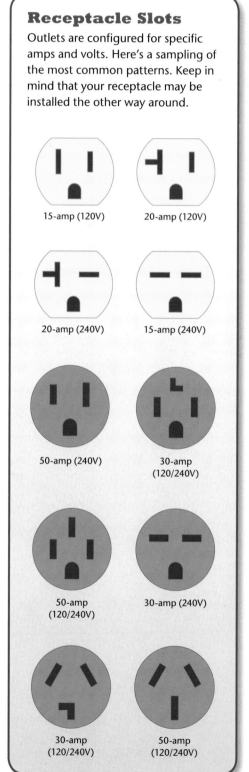

Receptacle Slots

Outlets are configured for specific amps and volts. Here's a sampling of the most common patterns. Keep in mind that your receptacle may be installed the other way around.

15-amp (120V)

20-amp (120V)

20-amp (240V)

15-amp (240V)

50-amp (240V)

30-amp (120/240V)

50-amp (120/240V)

30-amp (240V)

30-amp (120/240V)

50-amp (120/240V)

120-volt Duplex Receptacles

Grounded duplex receptacles consist of an upper and lower outlet, each with three slots. The longer (neutral) slot accepts the wide prong of a three-prong plug, the smaller (hot) slot is for the narrow prong, and the U-shaped grounding slot is for the grounding prong. The silver terminals are for the neutral wires, and the brass terminals are for hot wires. A green grounding screw is for the grounding wire.

GFCI Receptacle

A ground-fault circuit interrupter (GFCI or sometimes GFI) receptacle can be installed in place of a standard 120-volt receptacle. GFCIs are required in kitchens, bathrooms, garages, and any other exposed, damp areas where ground faults are most likely. Whenever the amounts of incoming and outgoing current are not equal, such as during a ground fault or current leakage, the GFCI opens the circuit instantly, cutting off power.

A GFCI receptacle protects you against shock, but only if it is fully functional. Every month or so, press the test button. If the power does not shut off, replace the GFCI.

High-voltage Receptacles

To ensure that no one will plug a 120-volt appliance into a 240-volt receptacle, higher-voltage circuits use special receptacles into which only matching plugs fit. These are available in both 240-volt and 120/240-volt models (often labeled "125/250"). The latter, often servicing a kitchen range or clothes dryer, combine 240-volt power for the appliance's motor or heating units and 120-volt power for timers and controls.

Some 240-volt receptacles can be installed in a standard electrical box; others are floor-mounted. Industrial-grade versions have a locking device that holds the plug in the slots—a safety measure for stationary power tools and other heavy equipment. Three-hole high-voltage receptacles have two slots for hot prongs and one for the grounding prong. There is no neutral. Four-hole high-voltage receptacles have two slots for hots, one for the ground, and another for a neutral.

Because recent codes often call for a neutral wire in addition to two hots and a ground, newer clothes dryers and other high-voltage equipment typically have four-prong plugs, which will not fit into older three-hole receptacles. If you have such an appliance, you may need to install a new high-voltage receptacle.

Related Topics

50-amp (120/240 volt) Box-mounted Receptacle

GFCI Receptacle

30-amp (120/240 volt) Floor-mounted Receptacle

20-amp (240 volt) Receptacle

Twist-lock High-voltage Receptacle

Replacing a 120-volt Receptacle

Replacing a receptacle is only a little more difficult than replacing a switch, so it is not uncommon to do it simply to update a room's color or style. In addition to the traditional devices with the rounded outlets, styles include rectangular "decora" models.

Receptacles On a Circuit

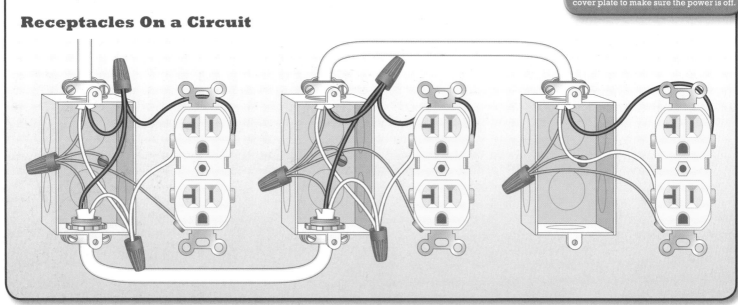

Choosing the Right Receptacle

Check the circuit breaker or fuse and the wire thickness to determine the correct amperage for the receptacle. On a 20-amp circuit with #12 wire, install a 20-amp receptacle. On a 15-amp circuit with #14 wire, install a 15-amp receptacle.

After shutting off power and pulling the receptacle out (see pages 26–27, Step 1), make sure you understand the wiring configuration before snipping or removing the wires. A receptacle at the end of a run will connect to only two wires (plus the ground). A middle-run receptacle connects to four wires (plus the ground). You may need to upgrade the grounding connections (see pages 22–23 and 25). If the receptacle is on two circuits, or if one of its outlets is controlled by a switch, the connecting tab on the hot side will be removed. See pages 118–119 for replacing a split-circuit receptacle.

Replacing a Standard Receptacle

① Shut off power and test
• Push the probes all of the way into the outlets

② Unfasten receptacle from box
• Unscrew the face plate
• Unscrew the receptacle from the box
• Test again at terminals for power

③ Remove receptacle from box
• Pull gently but firmly on the receptacle
• Carefully note the connections of all the wires in the box before disconnecting

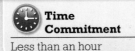 **Time Commitment**
Less than an hour

 **Tools You'll Need**
Level
Screwdriver
Wire stripper
Voltage tester

 Related Topics
Common wiring methods, 28–31
Installing a GFCI receptacle, 120–121
Receptacles, 114–115
Split-circuit receptacles, 118–119
Stripping & joining wire, 54–59

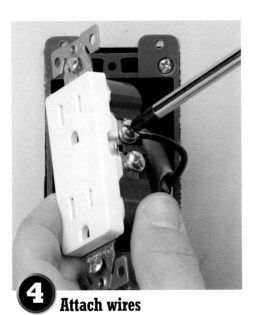

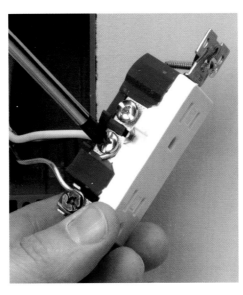

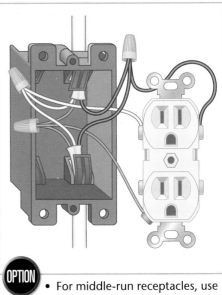

4 Attach wires

- Rebending weakens wire, so use existing loops if possible
- If the box is metal, be sure to attach the ground wire to it
- Hot wires always attach to one side of a receptacle, neutral wires to the other

OPTION
- For middle-run receptacles, use pigtails and wire nuts

5 Level the receptacle

- Use a level before tightening screws to box
- Carefully fold the wires back into the box and press the receptacle into place

6 Attach new face plate

Pro Tip

If the box's threads are stripped so a device's mounting screw spins around without grabbing tightly, replace the screw with a #6 or #8 flathead (not a pan-head) machine screw. A short drywall screw will also work.

Split-circuit Receptacles

A split-circuit receptacle, as the name suggests, has a different power source for each plug-in outlet. You can identify a split-circuit receptacle because the connecting tab will be broken on the hot side and different hot wires connect to each hot terminal.

Split-circuit Receptacles on a Circuit

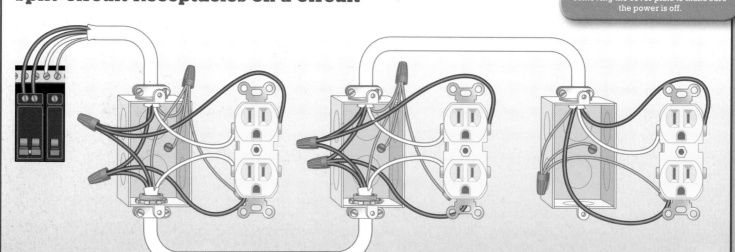

Where & When to Use Them

This is a good arrangement for a series of receptacles above a workbench, where you may plug two heavy-use tools or appliances into the same receptacle. Because the two plugs are on different circuits, they will not cause a circuit overload. Some local codes require this arrangement (rather than GFCI receptacles) for the receptacles above a kitchen counter.

Another reason for wiring the receptacle this way is so that one outlet is always on and the other is controlled by a switch. For example, in a bedroom with no overhead light, this allows you to turn a lamp on and off with a wall switch, while using the other outlet as a more typical always-on house outlet.

In some localities, a split-circuit receptacle in a kitchen is required by code.

Time Commitment
About an hour

Tools You'll Need
Screwdriver
Wire stripper
Lineman's pliers

Related Topics
Common wiring methods, 28–31
Installing a GFCI receptacle, 120–121
Receptacles, 114–115
Replacing a 120-volt receptacle, 116–117
Shutting off & restoring power, 50–51
Stripping & joining wire, 54–59

Replacing a Split-circuit Receptacle

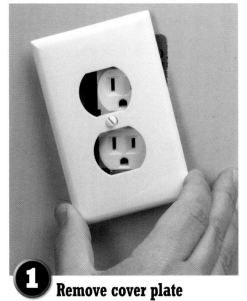

1 Remove cover plate
- Shut off the power and test the receptacle
- Unscrew cover plate and set it aside

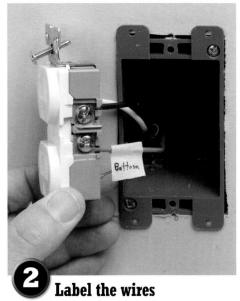

2 Label the wires
- Pull out the receptacle without removing the wires
- Label each wire to show how it should be connected to the new one
- Undo wires and remove the receptacle

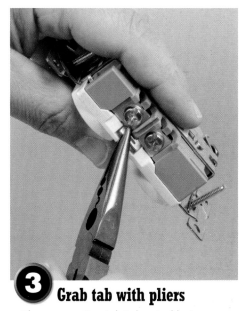

3 Grab tab with pliers
- The connecting tab is located between the two hot terminals of the new receptacle
- Use needle-nose pliers to get a good grip

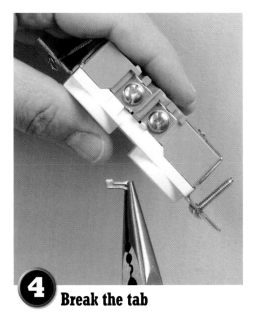

4 Break the tab
- Bend tab back and forth to weaken it
- When it bends easily, give it a twist to break it

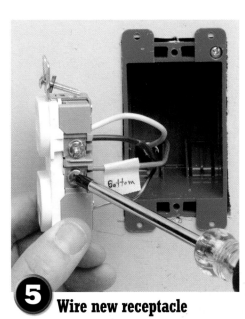

5 Wire new receptacle
- Attach the ground wire
- Follow labels to attach the neutral and hot wires

6 Attach new cover plate
- Restore power and test the outlets

Installing a GFCI Receptacle

A ground-fault circuit interrupter receptacle, or GFCI, offers excellent protection against shock and is required by many codes for areas that could become damp, such as bathrooms, kitchen counters, garages, and outdoor locations.

GFCI receptacles are common in kitchens, especially near sinks.

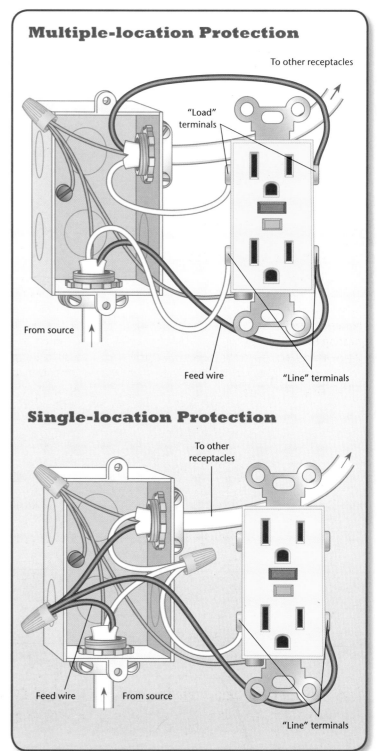

Multiple-location Protection

To other receptacles

"Load" terminals

From source

Feed wire

"Line" terminals

Single-location Protection

To other receptacles

Feed wire   From source

"Line" terminals

The Benefits of GFCIs

A GFCI receptacle can be wired to protect a single location—only those items plugged into the receptacle itself. Or it can be wired to protect multiple locations, shutting down devices downstream on the same circuit. See the illustrations at right for the two types of wiring.

Wiring a GFCI is similar to wiring a standard receptacle, except the terminals are labeled "line" (the incoming power) and "load" (power going out to other devices). To protect a single location, attach the incoming pair of black and white wires to the hot and white (or neutral) terminals on the line end.

For multiple-location protection, the incoming wires are connected in the same way, but the outgoing pair of hot and neutral wires attach to the "load" end. If a downstream receptacle experiences a current irregularity, the upstream GFCI will shut down, thereby shutting off the downstream receptacles as well.

When replacing an existing receptacle with a GFCI receptacle, you generally follow the procedures for a standard receptacle replacement. The steps shown here emphasize the procedures that are particular to a GFCI installation.

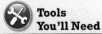 Time Commitment	Tools You'll Need	Related Topics
About an hour	Screwdriver Wire stripper Voltage tester Lineman's pliers	Common wiring methods, 28–31 Receptacles, 114–115 Replacing a 120-volt receptacle, 116–117 Split-circuit receptacles, 118–119 Stripping & joining wire, 54–59

Wiring a GFCI Receptacle for Multiple-location Protection

1 Remove the old receptacle

- Shut off power to the circuit
- Test the receptacle to make sure you have flipped the correct breaker
- Note where wires are attached before disconnecting them
- If you are replacing a screw-down receptacle with a poke-in type, snip off loops
- Strip ¾ inch of insulation

2 Attach "line" side first

- Connect the feed wire to the brass terminal (it may be labeled hot) on the "line" end of receptacle
- Connect the neutral wire from the feed wire's cable to the silver terminals (it may be labeled white) on the "line" end
- Attach the other hot wire (it feeds receptacles downstream) to the brass (hot) terminal on the "load" end of receptacle

- Attach the other neutral wire to the silver (white) terminal on the "load" end
- Restore power, push the reset button, and test for power in the GFCI receptacle and downstream receptacles
- Press the test button and confirm it cuts off power at the GFCI receptacle and downstream receptacles
- Shut off power

3 Install GFCI receptacle in box

- Press the GFCI into position
- Check for plumb or level as you drive the mounting screws
- Add a box extender if it will not fit

4 Attach plate cover

- Restore power and test again

High-voltage Receptacles

Moveable high-voltage appliances—window air conditioners, electric ranges, and electric dryers, for instance—have cords that plug into 240-volt receptacles. The slot configurations of these receptacles are designed to ensure you can't plug in a wrong appliance.

STOP! Always turn off power to the circuit you are working on. Double-check at the project site before and after removing the cover plate to make sure the power is off.

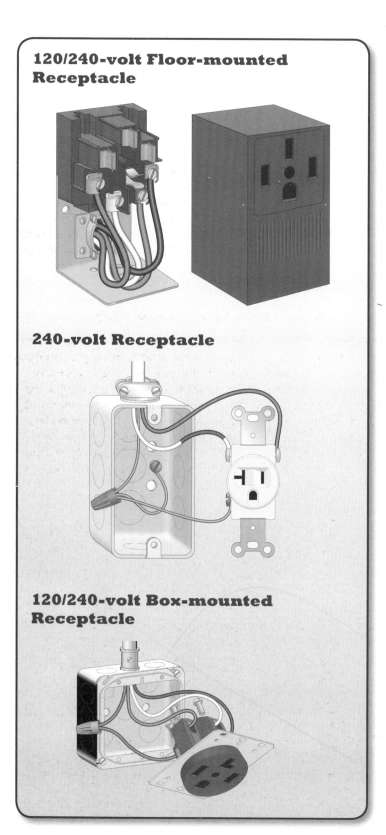

120/240-volt Floor-mounted Receptacle

240-volt Receptacle

120/240-volt Box-mounted Receptacle

How Power Is Delivered

At the service panel, a high-voltage receptacle connects to a double-pole circuit breaker or a fuse block, which connects to both hot bus bars in order to supply twice the power of a 120-volt receptacle.

If one of your 240-volt appliances fails or becomes unreliable, the fault is most often in the appliance or its cord. Sometimes, however, a receptacle fails and needs to be replaced. You should also replace any damaged high-voltage receptacle.

High-voltage receptacles may connect to two or three wires, in addition to the ground wire. The wires should be thick enough to handle the current without overheating: 12-gauge wire for 20 amps, 10-gauge wire for 30 amps, and 8-gauge wire for 40 amps.

The three illustrations at left show the most common types of 240-volt receptacles. Because household current can vary slightly, receptacles are typically rated for 250 and 125 volts, though they usually supply 240 and 120 volts. If your house wires are aluminum, they require special connections.

Note: 240-volt wiring is no more difficult to install than 120-volt wiring, but the danger of shock or fire is far greater. If you are at all uncertain about your understanding or abilities, call an electrician.

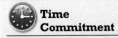 Time Commitment	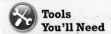 Tools You'll Need	Related Topics
About two hours	Voltage tester that can handle 240 volts Screwdriver Wire stripper Lineman's pliers	Common wiring methods, 28–31 Installing a GFCI receptacle, 120–121 Receptacles, 114–115 Replacing a 120-volt receptacle, 116–117 Shutting off & restoring power, 50–51 Split-circuit receptacles, 118–119 Stripping & joining wire, 54–59

Testing a High-voltage Receptacle

When you test a live high-voltage receptacle, take precautions. Use a voltage tester that can handle 240 as well as 120 volts. With the circuit on, poking the probes into two hot slots should yield a reading of 240 volts. Poking into a hot slot and a neutral or ground slot should yield 120 volts. If you have a fuse service panel and one of the two cartridge fuses in a fuse block is blown, half the power will be gone; in that case, poking into two hots will yield a reading of only 120 volts.

Stripping & Attaching Thick Wires

Before you remove wires from the old receptacle, check the new one to make sure you will know where to put each wire. Most receptacles indicate which color wire goes into each terminal, but you may need to tag

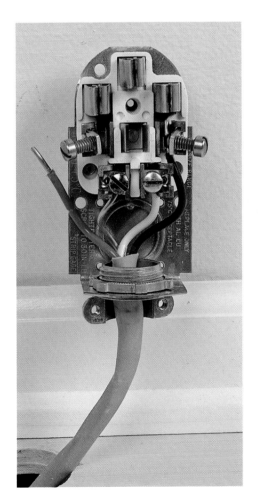

two or more wires so you don't forget their locations.

A 20-amp air-conditioning receptacle connects to 12-gauge wire, which can be stripped with standard strippers. However, 30- and 40-amp receptacles use thicker wire that is likely stranded rather than solid. If the stripped wire is in good condition—in most cases it has not been bent—there is no need to clip the wire ends and restrip. If the bare wire is nicked or has been bent several times, use lineman's pliers or diagonal cut-

ters to snip off just the bare wire end (the wires are often short). Carefully pare away the insulation using a knife. Work slowly to avoid cutting into the bare wire.

Many high-voltage receptacles attach with poke-in terminals. Arrange the wires so they are tangled as little as possible. Insert each wire end fully into its terminal so little or no bare wire is exposed, then tighten the hold-down screw.

Floor Mounting

Position a floor-mounted receptacle so there will be plenty of room for the plug once you slide the range, dryer, or other appliance into position. If the old receptacle is in the way of your new appliance, you may need to cut a channel in the floor to reposition the receptacle. In that case, you may need to disconnect conduit, sheathing, or a box in order to move the receptacle, or hire an electrician.

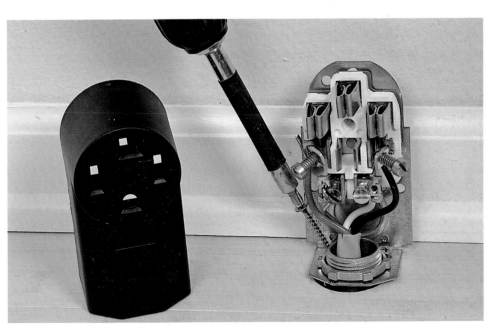

Surface-mounted Wiring

Surface-mounting wiring (often called raceway) allows you to add new receptacles, switches, and lights without running electrical cable through the walls. Instead, wires run through protective metal or plastic channels and boxes mounted on walls and ceilings.

Degree of Difficulty
● Easy

STOP!
Always turn off power to the circuit you are working on. Double-check at the project site before and after removing the cover plate to make sure the power is off.

A pocket office under a flight of stairs is a perfect place for surface-mounted wiring.

When & Where to Use It

Correctly installed, surface-mounted wiring is safe and approved by most local codes, but check with your building department to be sure it is up to code in your locale. Although surface-mounted wiring saves you the mess and labor of digging into finished surfaces, some people consider it too industrial-looking for a living area. It is more often used in utility areas such as basements, laundry rooms, and workshops.

Avoid Overloading

As with any new wiring, make sure the new service you install will not overload the circuit and trip a breaker (or blow a fuse). The steps that start on page 126, for example, show how to tap into an existing receptacle and install a new ceiling light with a switch. If the light is rated for 100 watts, this adds less than one amp to the circuit's load (100 amps divided by 120 volts equals 0.83 amps). However, if you add receptacles or a high-wattage chandelier or ceiling fan, the additional load is more of a factor.

The Components

Make a rough drawing showing the receptacle you plan to tap into, the devices and fixtures you want to install, the distances between all the parts, and any turns you need to make. Then assemble the parts you need, using the drawing for reference.

The metal raceway shown in these steps must be installed in sequence. Cut one channel, install it onto a box's base plate, then proceed to the next channel and the fitting or base plate that attaches to its other end. If you have a very long run, use straight connectors to join two tracks.

With other systems, you can attach the base plates first, then cut the channels to fit between them.

Stuff to Buy

CHANNELS May be one piece, or may have a wall-mounted part and a cover

MOUNTING CLIPS OR SCREWS Depends on the channel type

STARTER BOXES These have a base plate with an access hole in the back; for tapping into an existing wall receptacle

RECEPTACLE & SWITCH BOXES These have solid base plates and may be deeper than starter boxes

FITTINGS You can buy them for inside, outside, and surface corners

FIXTURE BOXES Make sure your light or fan has a canopy that will mount attractively to the fixture box

THHN-RATED WIRE Buy 14-gauge for a 15-amp circuit or 12-gauge for a 20-amp circuit

Time Commitment

The better part of a day

Tools You'll Need

Cordless screwdriver
Level
Hacksaw
File
Light hammer
Wire stripper
Lineman's pliers

Related Topics

Calculating usage & capacity, 282–283
Common wiring methods, 28–31
Receptacles, 114–115
Replacing a 120-volt receptacle, 116–117
Replacing a single-pole switch, 106–107
Shutting off & restoring power, 50–51
Stripping & joining wire, 54–59
Testing methods, 52–53

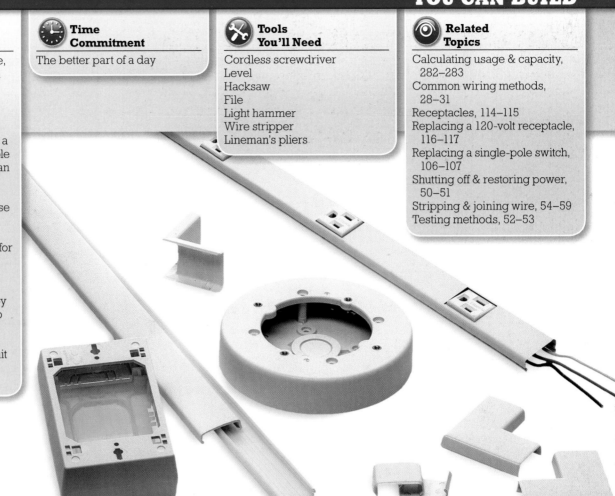

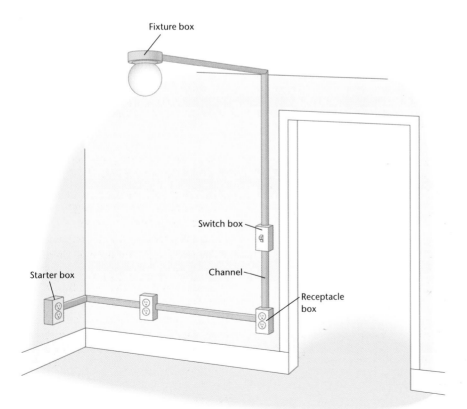

Fixture box

Switch box

Channel

Starter box

Receptacle box

Raceways come in both plastic and metal. You can also special-order components with wide channels or built-in receptacles.

Painting Raceway

Metal channels can be painted easily with latex or alkyd paint. Plastic channels can be painted if you first lightly sand them (ideally, before you attach them to the wall) and then apply an alcohol- or alkyd-based primer.

Installing Surface-mounted Wiring

STOP!
Always turn off power to the circuit you are working on. Double-check at the project site before and after removing the cover plate to make sure the power is off.

1 **Pull out the receptacle**

- Shut off power to the circuit
- Determine how you will tap into the receptacle (Step 12); you may want to prepare pigtails at this point
- Unscrew the mounting screws, pull the receptacle out, and test again
- Attach the base plate.

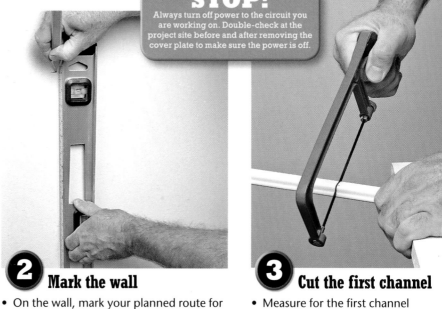

2 **Mark the wall**

- On the wall, mark your planned route for the channels
- Also mark for the receptacle, switch, and fixture boxes
- You may want to use a level and mark the wall with faint pencil lines

3 **Cut the first channel**

- Measure for the first channel
- Cut the first channel with a hacksaw and file any burrs; for two-part channels, cut the cover and wall-mounted part separately if necessary

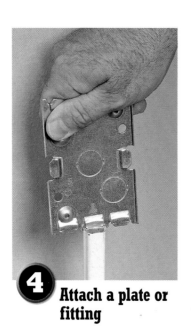

4 **Attach a plate or fitting**

- Attach a base plate (as shown) or fitting at the end of the channel
- Slip the tab into the rear of the channel and press down
- You may need to tap with a hammer

5 **Place fasteners**

- Hold the channel in position and mark for clips and box-mounting screws
- Clips should be no more than 30 inches apart on a wall and 16 inches apart on a ceiling
- Install the clips or screws
- Where you cannot drive a screw into a stud or joist, use a plastic anchor

OPTION

- You can use straps instead of clips
- Hold the channel and drive screws into both of a strap's holes

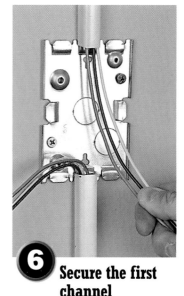

6 **Secure the first channel**

- Position the track over the clip or clips
- Make sure it is correctly aligned with the boxes
- Press or tap the track until it snaps onto the clips
- Drive screws to attach the base plate to the wall

7 Add remaining wall channels

- Continue attaching track
- At an inside corner, slide the base plate of a corner piece onto the end of the track; holding the track, mark the noncorner end, then cut it
- Attach clips; snap the channel onto the clips
- Do not add covers for boxes or corners yet

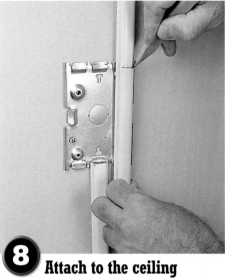

8 Attach to the ceiling

- Slip a ceiling box onto a channel as you would a wall box
- To hang a heavy light fixture, use a stud finder and position the box so you can attach it with screws driven into a joist
- For a lightweight fixture, use toggle bolts
- If the channel runs across joists, attach clips with screws driven into the joists; otherwise, use toggle bolts or plastic drywall anchors

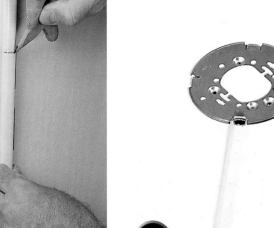

9 Fish the wires

- Fish black, white, and green wires through each track by simply pushing the wires
- Leave 12 inches of wire protruding at each box so you'll have plenty to work with
- Don't scrape off insulation when you pull wires through boxes

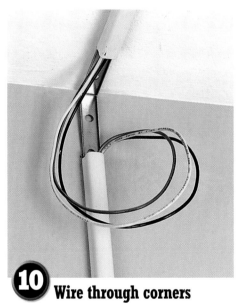

10 Wire through corners

- Run the wires continuously through a corner
- Don't make splices anywhere but in a box

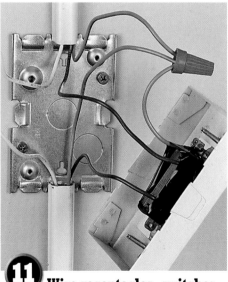

11 Wire receptacles, switches, and fixtures

- Make the usual wiring connections for receptacles, switches, and fixtures
- Attach the track covers at any corners

12 Connect to the receptacle

- Tap into the old receptacle
- If receptacle has open terminals (shown), attach new wires
- If all the receptacle terminals are used, attach with pigtails
- Mount the receptacle, restore power, and test before attaching cover plate

5

New Electrical Lines

In this chapter, we help you tackle the tricky challenge of wiring in finished rooms—from cutting access holes in your walls and ceiling to fishing wire to patching those holes so that you can enjoy your new fixtures. We also show you the steps required to use one receptacle as a power source for a second, and we make sure you know how to attach cable safely and securely to any electrical box.

Chapter Contents

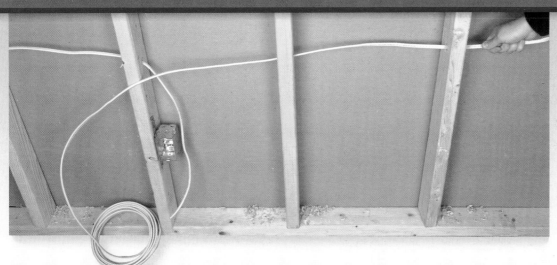

page 143

Wiring in Finished Rooms

Projects like adding a light or a receptacle are typically done in a room with walls and ceilings that are finished with drywall or plaster. The techniques on the following pages are aimed at minimizing damage to wall surfaces.

✓ **Degree of Difficulty**

● Moderate

STOP!
Always turn off power to the circuit you will be tapping into. Before you begin any connection, double-check to make sure the power is off.

What to Do First

When working in a finished room, the usual order of work is:

- Plan how you will tap into power
- Cut holes for the new fixture, switch, and receptacle boxes
- Cut channels in the walls and drill holes as needed, then run cable from box hole to box hole
- Run cable into the boxes and mount the boxes
- Connect the new switches, receptacles, and fixtures
- Connect the power

Consult with your local inspector to make sure the method you choose conforms to codes. For a project using a plastic box and NM cable, for example, you may be required to staple the cable to the stud

about 8 inches from the box—something that requires opening the wall.

Planning Wiring Paths

Having settled on where you will tap into power and how you'll open the finished wall or ceiling, you can plan wiring paths. Sketch out the full installation. Even if your project is simple, the inspector will probably want a drawing that shows the location of each proposed switch, receptacle, light fixture, and appliance.

The cable may need to travel through studs, joists, and other framing members, all of which are hidden inside the wall. Spend some time with a stud finder to locate the framing—and for heating and air-conditioning ducts, plumbing pipes, and electrical cables or conduit.

Switches or receptacles, which are usually attached to studs, can be good starting points for finding the framing. Studs and joists are usually spaced 16 inches apart, but in older homes, the spacing may be fairly random, and in some newer homes it may be 24 rather than 16 inches. Some homes have horizontal fire blocks spanning from stud to stud about halfway up the wall. The exterior wall of a newer masonry home is usually framed with 2 by 4s between the brick veneer and the interior wall finish. On an older masonry home, however, there may be only furring strips (typically about 1 inch thick) nailed

If the box you tap into for power is in a location with finished walls, you might have to cut several small access holes along the new line's route. Before you cut, plan how you will repair the wall.

directly to the brick. This does not allow much space for running cable, much less installing boxes.

Choose Simplest Solutions

Where possible, run cable and install boxes in places like an attic floor and the ceiling of an unfinished basement, where wall, ceiling, or floor coverings are attached to only one side of the framing. Then you can work from the uncovered side, running cable along joists or beams

If you are building a built-in in a bathroom, use it as a opportunity to hide a plug so that hair dryers and other appliances can be stowed when not in use.

Stuff to Buy

BOXES Electrical boxes for fixtures and devices
CABLE Measure for your cable needs, then add 20 percent; for cable placed under molding (not inside of framing), consider armored cable for protection from nails
FIXTURES, DEVICES, COVER PLATES
FASTENERS Don't forget cable clamps and staples

Tools You'll Need

Stud finder
Drywall saw
Jigsaw (for plaster)
Putty knife and small pry bar (for molding)
Fish tape
Cordless drill and bits
Screwdriver
Wire stripper
Lineman's pliers

Related Topics

Calculating usage & capacity, 282–283
New electrical boxes, 138–139
Common wiring configurations, 272–279
Common wiring methods, 28–31
Wiring in unfinished framing, 140–141
Stripping & joining wire, 54–59
Tapping into power, 136–137
Testing methods, 52–53

or drilling holes and threading cable through them. You can also fish cable through finished walls from these locations.

If you will be cutting through wall or ceiling coverings, look through the following pages to estimate how many holes you need to cut. Remember to consider running wires behind moldings.

Once you've planned your installation, take your drawing to the building inspector, who can tell you what materials are required by code.

Start by either pulling out the device box you want to tap into or removing a knockout so you can access the box while it is still in place. Cut holes for the new boxes. Remove moldings or cut access holes, then run the cable and install the boxes.

Some cut-in boxes, also called remodel or old-work boxes (see pages 60–61), come with hole-cutting templates. If yours doesn't, trace the box's outline on the wall or ceiling, omitting any brackets or ears meant to grab the face of the drywall or plaster. Be precise, as an oversized hole will require patching and may not leave enough wall or ceiling surface for anchoring the box.

To make a tidy cut in drywall, use a drywall saw (also called a jab saw). Drill starter holes as shown, or hit the saw handle with the palm of your hand to poke the blade in. You may need to use a utility knife to clean away burrs or to slightly enlarge the hole.

Pro Tip

Before you cut, drill a small test hole where you want the new box. Bend a 9-inch length of stiff wire into a 90-degree angle at its midpoint, push one end of the wire through the hole, and rotate it. If the wire bumps into something, move over a few inches; try again until you find an unobstructed location.

Perils of Plaster

Removing plaster can create an amazing amount of garbage, not to mention clouds of dust. Close doors to other rooms, cover nearby rugs and furniture, and wear a dust mask.

Most plaster is anchored to wood lath, 3/8-inch-thick slats that run across the studs or joists with 3/8-inch gaps between them. Making a clean cut in plaster can be difficult because the lath vibrates as you saw and may crack the plaster. Drill access holes at the corners of the box outline, then use a knife to score the surface. Change knife blades often. Cut with a jigsaw, pressing firmly against the plaster as you cut.

Cutting Through Plaster

Mark the Wall

Cutting Through Drywall

Hooking wire to fish tape

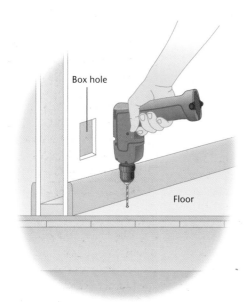

Making a smooth, tight splice

Routing Cable with Access

After cutting the hole for the new box, but before mounting the box, run cable from the area of the power source to the new box location—don't connect it to power yet, of course. When possible, pull the cable from its packaging, run it, and cut it to length at the new location. If you must cut the cable ahead of time, cut it several feet longer than needed.

With luck, you'll be able to fish cable from above your location (in an attic) or below it (in a basement). But when you work in an attic, don't put your weight on the fragile surface between the joists. You can easily put your foot through the ceiling.

FISHING TECHNIQUES

To route cable through covered walls and ceilings, you're going to need some "fishing gear." For short distances, you can use a straightened coat hanger or a piece of 12-gauge wire with one end bent into a hook. Or you may have good luck with NM cable (12-3 works well because it keeps its shape). But the best tool, especially for longer runs, is usually a fish tape, which comes on a 25- or 50-foot reel. For long cable runs, you may need a pair of fish tapes.

To attach cable to a fish tape, first strip off several inches of sheathing. Then bend the wire ends around the hook on the fish tape and wrap the connection with electrician's tape, making the splice as smooth and thin as you can.

In most cases, you'll find it easier to pull wires from a smaller to a larger hole.

SHORT RUNS

Drill a small guide hole, in line with the hole you cut for the box, up through the ceiling or down through the floor to mark the location. Then, from the basement or attic, measure the distance from the guide hole to the center of the wall and drill a ¾-inch hole through the floor plate or ceiling plate into the access area behind the box. (A ceiling plate is usually double the thickness of a floor plate.)

Run fish tape through the drilled hole and up (or down) until you can see it, and pull it through the box hole. Use electrical tape to attach the cable to the fishing line as smoothly and seamlessly as possible. Draw it through the drilled hole and out through the box hole.

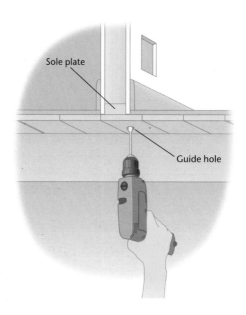

Box hole

Floor

Sole plate

Guide hole

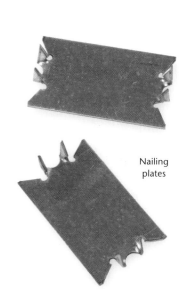

Nailing plates

Pulling Fish Tape

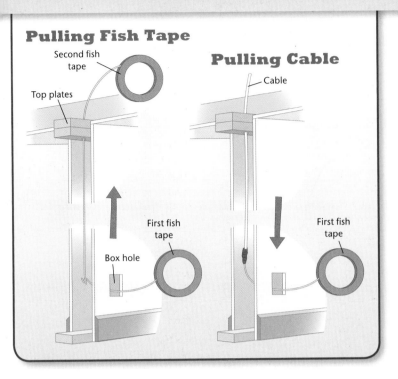

Second fish tape

Top plates

Pulling Cable

Cable

First fish tape

Box hole

First fish tape

LONG RUNS

For distances of more than 2 feet, you'll need a helper and two fish tapes. Have your helper hold a flashlight in the box while you peer through the drilled hole. If you can't see the light beam, a fire block or some other obstruction is in the way. Either drill through the block (you may need to cut through the wall near the block to gain access) or cut through the wall and notch the block.

Slip the cable through the block. Install a protective metal nailing plate on the block before you refinish the wall; this protects the cable from nails as the finished surface is reattached. Also install protective nailing plates in any situation where cable passes through wood less than 1½ inches from the surface.

FISHING FROM ABOVE AND BELOW

Fish tapes have hooked ends that are fairly easy to join. Run the first tape in through the box hole and a second fish tape down through a hole in the top plates. Have a helper wiggle and move the box-hole tape while you do the same from above, until the two tapes are hooked together in the wall. Gently tug on the second tape to bring the hooked first tape up through the wall. Detach the second tape and replace it with the cable. Then, pulling slowly from the box hole, work it down through the wall.

Routing Cable Without Access

If you cannot get behind a finished surface via a basement or attic, use one of these techniques.

INSIDE A WALL

Neatly cut a straight, narrow strip of wall covering to expose studs. Save the cut-away piece of drywall. Drill through the center of each stud (a long fishing drill bit may enable you to drill through a hidden stud, thereby eliminating an additional hole in the wall). Run the cable through the wall and through the box holes.

BEHIND A BASEBOARD

First, remove the baseboard as needed. Then cut away the drywall behind it, taking care not to cut above the height of the molding. Either cut a channel, or cut the drywall all the way to the floor. Keep the cut-away piece. If possible, drill holes through the centers of the studs to run the cable through. Otherwise, cut notches about

Working with Molding

When routing cable behind window, door, or baseboard molding, keep these points in mind:

- Armored cable provides better protection against nails than NM cable. It's also tougher to bend and work with.
- Molding may split as you remove or reinstall it, so before you begin, make sure you can buy replacement pieces.
- Before removing molding, use a utility knife or a putty knife to break the paint bond between the molding and the wall or ceiling.
- To remove a baseboard, slip a putty knife blade behind the molding and push a wood shim behind the blade to protect the wall. Then use a small pry bar to pry the baseboard away from the wall. Continue along the wall with the pry bar and shim until you can pull off the entire length.
- When you nail the molding back on, position nails above and below the cable and any nailing plates you may have installed.

1 inch deep instead. Run the cable and cover the studs with protective plates if they are within 1½ inches of the finished wall surface. Replace the drywall piece and reinstall the baseboard.

Inside a Wall

Box hole

Box hole

Wall studs

Cable

Behind a Baseboard

Box hole

Existing box

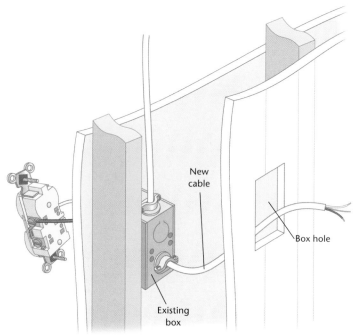

Installing Back-to-back Devices

When cutting a new box hole on a wall behind an existing device, offset the new hole a few inches from the first. Remove the existing device and route the new cable through a knockout hole in that box directly to the new hole.

New cable

Box hole

Existing box

As a part of this remodel, an extra switch was added next to a bench (foreground) by tapping into power at an existing switch by the door.

Running Cable Around a Doorway

Routing around a door calls for a fair amount of carpentry. First, remove the door casing (the molding that runs around the doorway and rests against the jamb and the wall); also remove nearby baseboard as needed. Run cable between jamb and rough framing, notching spacer blocks or shims wherever necessary. If possible, push the cable into the cavity so it is at least 1½ inches from the finished side of the casing.

Test the wiring before you replace the door casing and baseboard. If you're adding or replacing a door, install the jamb and door, then the wiring.

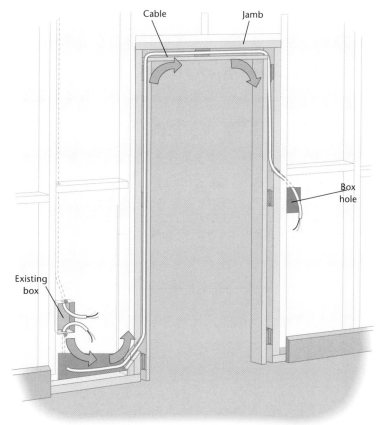

Cable

Jamb

Box hole

Existing box

Routing Cable for a Switched Ceiling Light

Here's an example of a project that uses several cable-running techniques from the preceding pages. In this case, cable runs parallel to ceiling joists. To run it across joists, cut access holes.

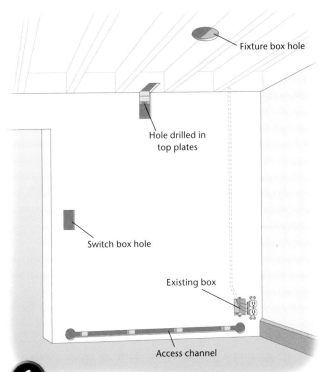

Fixture box hole

Hole drilled in top plates

Switch box hole

Existing box

Access channel

1 Cut the holes and channel

- Make sure the new light will not overload the circuit and plan how to tap into power
- Mark the fixture box's location between two ceiling joists and cut that hole
- Cut a hole for the switch box (for all cuts, save the cut-out pieces for reuse)
- Cut into the corner of the wall and ceiling for an access hole, and cut a notch or drill a hole through the wall's top plates
- Carefully remove the baseboard; cut an access channel behind it between the switch box location and the existing power source

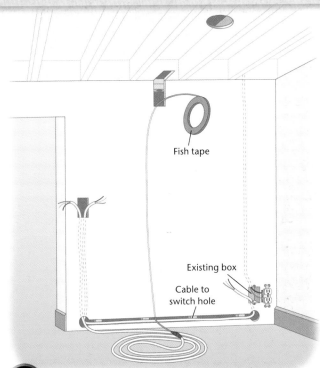

Fish tape

Existing box

Cable to switch hole

2 Run cable to the switch hole

- Run a cable between the power source and the switch box's hole
- Fish a second cable from the switch hole to the access hole, via the baseboard area

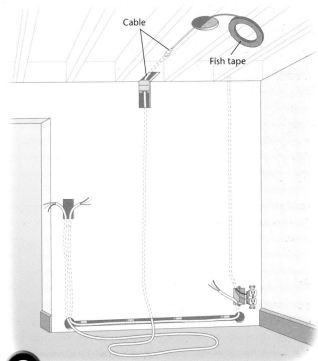

Cable

Fish tape

3 Run cable to the fixture hole

- Fish from the fixture box hole to the access hole via the hole in the top plates
- Attach the second cable to the fish tape
- Pull it through the access hole, top plates, and fixture box hole

Tapping into Power

One of the most common eyesores in a home is a tangle of extension cords and power strips plugged into a room's lone receptacle. Adding a second receptacle by tapping into the first is not a beginner project, but it's not especially difficult either.

STOP!
Always turn off power to the circuits you are working on. Double-check at the project site to make sure the power is off.

1 Getting started

- Turn power off at breaker and test to confirm
- Remove baseboard with flat pry bar
- Identify stud locations based on nail holes under baseboard, or drive small nails where they won't show to locate studs

2 Score drywall

- Drill pilot holes at either end of the channel you will cut for the cable
- Do not drill above the height of the baseboard where it will show
- Score parallel lines between the pilot holes to make cutting easier

3 Cut drywall

- Follow scoring lines with a drywall saw
- Either cut a channel, as shown, or remove the drywall all the way to the floor

4 Remove drywall

- Save the cut-away piece
- If possible, drill holes through the centers of the studs to run the cable
- If drilling is not feasible, cut notches about 1 inch deep instead

5 Cut new hole

- Measure height of first box to find location for the new one
- Draw outline of the back of the box on the drywall and cut it out

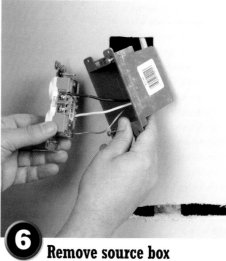

6 Remove source box

- If screw or nail heads are accessible inside the box, try removing them from framing
- If screw or nail heads are not accessible, cut them with a reciprocating saw
- Replace the box with one designed for cut-in work

 **Stuff to Buy**

RECEPTACLE
CUT-IN BOX
BASIC SUPPLIES Wire nuts, electrical tape, cable

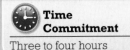 **Time Commitment**

Three to four hours

 Tools You'll Need

Drywall saw
Lineman's pliers
Pry bar
Reciprocating saw
Screwdriver
Utility knife
Wire stripper

 Related Topics

Cable connections, 144–145
Calculating usage & capacity, 282–283
Replacing a 120-volt receptacle, 116–117
Tools for running cable & installing boxes, 46–49

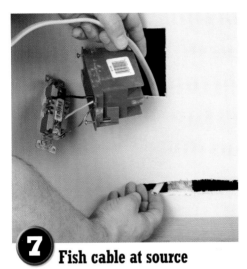

7 Fish cable at source

- Run source cable into the new cut-in box and connect to receptacle terminals
- Cut a length of NM cable a few feet longer than the distance between the two holes
- Bend cable slightly so it pushes easily from the receptacle hole to the channel

8 Fish cable at load

- Run cable along the floor, then bend it slightly to make it easy to push from the channel up to and through the new hole
- Push the cable into notches cut in the studs
- Make sure you have enough extra cable at either end to complete your wiring

9 Wire source receptacle

- Secure the new cut-in box to the wall
- Attach the load hot and neutral wires to the receptacle's open brass and silver terminals
- Connect the load ground with a pigtail and wire nut

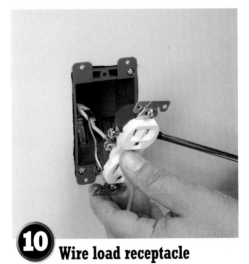

10 Wire load receptacle

- Push the cable into the box and strip the wires
- Attach the new ground wire to the receptacle's ground screw, and to the box if it is metal
- Wire the new hot and the neutral wires to their respective brass and silver terminals

11 Replace drywall

- Cover the cable running through the notches in the studs with protective plates since they are within 1½ inches of a finished wall surface
- Carefully replace the piece of drywall to fill in the channel

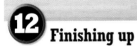

12 Finishing up

- Secure receptacles to their boxes if you have not already done so
- Cover receptacles with face plates
- Replace baseboard

New Electrical Boxes

Once you've cut a hole and routed the cable, the remaining jobs are: running cable into the box, mounting the box, making the wiring connections, and doing any patch work. The first steps can be done pretty quickly, but patching holes in a wall takes time.

STOP! Always turn off power to the circuit you will be tapping into. Before you begin any connection, double-check to make sure the power is off.

How to Install Them

Ideally, cable run into a plastic box with no clamps should be stapled to a stud or joist. If both sides of the wall or ceiling are covered, this won't be possible without cutting through the surface. The inspector may allow you to run the cable anyway, or you may be required to install a box that has clamps.

Always leave at least 8 inches of cable extending into the box for connections. You can always cut it shorter later.

Before mounting the box, insert the cable or cables through a knockout hole. To remove a knockout plug, tap with a hammer, pliers, or a screwdriver. Then twist it off with the pliers. Attach a cable clamp made for your type of cable. (Either attach the cable to the clamp first, then slip the cable through the knockout hole and tighten the clamp's nut, or attach the clamp to the box first, slide the cable through the clamp, and tighten the screws.) For a plastic box, you may need to loosen the grabbing tab by poking it with a screwdriver, then push the cable through.

How you mount the new box will depend on its type. Several cut-in boxes used for remodeling are shown here.

CEILING BOX WITH METAL SPRING EARS

Once this box is mounted, it can't be removed, so make sure the hole is the right size, and run the cable into the box before you install it. To lock the box into place, tighten the screws at the back. This pushes the spring's teeth into the back side of the ceiling.

SADDLE BOX

The easiest type to install if you are cutting a hole for a new box, a saddle box works when the ceiling hole is centered under a joist. Attach the cable to the box, slip the box up onto the joist, and drive a screw to anchor it. When you install the fan's bracket, you will drive long screws that also grab the joist.

PLASTER CUT-IN BOX

To attach to a plaster wall, consider a box with ears. Cut away just enough of the plaster (but not the lath) to accommodate the ears, then screw the ears to the lath.

Other plaster cut-in boxes have side clamps that tighten against the back of the plaster.

Fan-rated Boxes

A ceiling fan is heavy and it vibrates, so it needs to be attached firmly. Page 90 shows how to achieve a strong connection by attaching the fan's bracket directly to a framing member in the ceiling. The more common method, and perhaps the only method approved by your local building department, is to attach a fan-rated ceiling box to one or two framing members.

Fan-rated boxes have either extra-strong threads or bolts, or holes positioned so you can screw the fan's mounting bracket directly to a ceiling joist. Choose a fan box to suit your situation and to match your fan's mounting hardware.

Cut-in Wall Box with Wing Clamps

1 **Install the box**
- Fold the box's wings flat
- Slip the box into the hole

2 **Secure it to wall**
- Press box firmly against wall as you drive in screws
- As you tighten, wings pivot against back of wall

Tools You'll Need

Screwdriver
Lineman's pliers
Cordless screwdriver
Putty knife
Taping knife

Related Topics

Electrical boxes, 60–61
Installing a ceiling fan, 90–93
Shutting off & restoring power, 50–51
Stripping & joining wire, 54–59
Wiring in unfinished framing, 140–141

Installing a Fan-rated Box

1 Inspect the box

- Cut a small hole alongside the box
- Take care not to cut wires
- Use a flashlight to locate the cable

2 Remove box

- If the box is mounted with nails, insert a short board or dowel into the box, pound up until box is loose, then remove with a flat pry bar
- Or, cut through the nails or screws using a reciprocating saw with a short blade

3 Install brace

- Turn screw on end of brace to adjust it to ¼ inch less than distance between joists
- Position it at a 90-degree angle to the joists
- Its feet should rest on top of drywall or plaster
- Turn the brace's tube until end spikes are fully embedded in joists

4 Secure box to brace

- Attach the cable to the box
- Secure box to brace, using hardware provided
- Tighten nuts and screws firmly
- Connect wires and mount fan to box

Patching Walls & Ceilings

Be sure not to patch the walls until electrical inspections are complete and your work is approved. If you cover up anything that the inspector wants to see, you may be required to cut holes in the wall all over again. For small repairs to walls or ceilings, use a taping knife and spackling compound. For a larger section, use a piece of drywall to fill the hole. If there is no framing to nail to, attach wood cleats to the sides of existing framing members. In either case, allow compound to dry, then sand and apply another layer until wall looks and feels smooth. Then prime and paint.

1 Cut drywall

- Attach it with drywall screws
- Seat the heads so they do not protrude

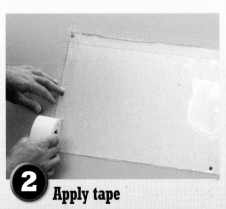

2 Apply tape

- Wipe the surface so it's free of dust
- Use fiberglass tape on all joints

3 Seal it

- Apply joint compound with a taping knife
- Smooth and feather the edges

Wiring in Unfinished Framing

If you are working in new framing, or if you have chosen to expose old framing by removing a part of the wall or ceiling, installing boxes and running cable is much easier than with finished surfaces in place.

STOP!
Always turn off power to the circuit you will be tapping into. Before you begin any connection, double-check to make sure the power is off.

It's relatively simple to convert a garage into a well-wired sewing room if the framing is unfinished when you begin.

Box Locations & Wiring Paths

Local codes may specify exact heights for switches and receptacles. As a general rule, receptacles should be 12 to 18 inches above the floor and switches 46 to 50 inches above the floor. (Measurements are to the centers of the boxes.) For universal (or wheelchair) access, receptacles are often placed at mid-height, however.

In most cases, ¾-inch-diameter holes for the cable should be drilled in the centers of 2-by-4 studs (which are 3½ inches wide). The hole should be at least 1¼ inches from the edge of the stud, so that after ½-inch drywall is installed, the hole will be at least 1¾ inches from the wall surface.

When you run cable horizontally through studs, use a spacer, such as a scrap piece of wood, to maintain holes that are the same height. Avoid bending the cable sharply.

On a ceiling joist, drill holes at least 2 inches from the edge. If you drill closer to the edge, or if you cut a notch instead of drilling a hole, install a protective nailing plate.

Cable must be stapled or supported with straps every 4½ feet, and within 12 inches of each metal box and 8 inches of each plastic box. Use insulated cable staples of the correct size for the type of cable, and take care not to smash the cable as you work.

Nailing Plates

Stapled Cable

Materials

Nonmetallic (NM) sheathed cable is used for new work in most locales. However, in some areas, conduit or armored cable may be required. Plastic boxes are often allowed, but increasingly, metal boxes are required or at least recommended.

Order of Work

- Complete the framing
- Install the rough plumbing pipes and heating ducts
- Run the rough wiring (boxes and cable)
- Add any wall insulation
- Cover the framing with drywall or plaster
- Add the plumbing fixtures and the finish wiring (switches, receptacles, fixtures)

Door & Window Routing

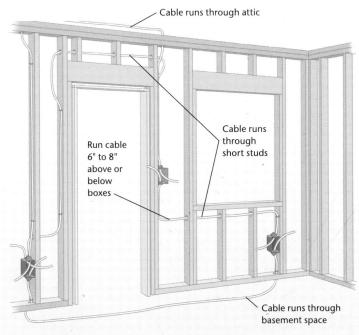

Cable runs through attic

Run cable 6" to 8" above or below boxes

Cable runs through short studs

Cable runs through basement space

Wall & Ceiling Routing

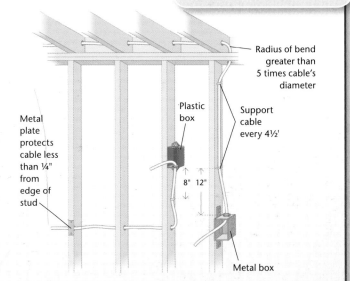

Radius of bend greater than 5 times cable's diameter

Plastic box

Support cable every 4½'

Metal plate protects cable less than ¼" from edge of stud

8" 12"

Metal box

Corners

At an intersection where wall studs meet, if the corner is hollow, drill holes from both sides, then feed or fish the cable through. If the corner is solid, you might need to drill larger holes, or cut notches and cover them with protective nailing plates. Often the best solution is to route cable above or below the area.

Corners

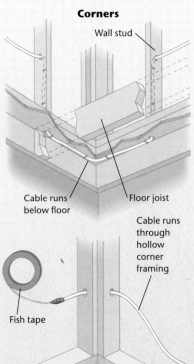

Wall stud

Cable runs below floor

Floor joist

Cable runs through hollow corner framing

Fish tape

Up in the Attic

In the attic, NM cable running across the joists at an angle should be protected by guard strips. It can also pass through holes in the joists, though this may make it more difficult to install attic insulation. Where cable runs parallel to joists, you can staple it to the side of a joist.

An Attic Overview

Cable runs through holes in joist

Cable stapled to sides of joists

Cable runs across joists (protect with guard strips if near opening)

Down in the Basement

Cable is often routed along a basement ceiling, which is the floor of the room above. If it's going across the joists, you can run it through holes drilled in the joists, staple it to running boards nailed in place across joists, or staple it to a beam or other structural member.

Basement Basics

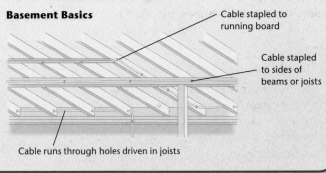

Cable stapled to running board

Cable stapled to sides of beams or joists

Cable runs through holes driven in joists

Boxes & Cable

Having made a detailed wiring plan, you are ready to install the boxes and run the cable. It's easy to make a location mistake or forget a box, so electricians generally write the type and size of the boxes on studs or joists, install the boxes, and then double-check everything before the drywallers show up.

STOP!
Always turn off power to the circuit you will be tapping into. Before you begin any connection, double-check to make sure the power is off.

Attaching Boxes

Besides choosing the right boxes, take note of how fixtures or devices attach to the boxes. Some boxes have holes for mounting screws, while others require that you add an adapter plate, also called a mud plate. For a single switch or receptacle, pros often install large two-gang boxes and then attach a single-gang mud ring. That leaves more room inside the box, which makes wiring easier. Also plan how you will clamp the cable to the box. If you are installing a ceiling fan or a heavy chandelier—or to allow for that possibility in the future—use a fan-rated

ceiling box and attach it firmly to the framing.

Some fixtures, such as recessed canister lights and some bathroom fans, do not require an electrical box. Install such a fixture so its edge will be flush with the ceiling's finished surface.

Running Cable

Following your plan drawing, mark the positions of holes on studs and joists. Where a series of holes will be at the same height, use a guide made of a scrap board or two with a notch cut on top. Most people can

center the drilled hole within the width of the framing member without a guide. As long as you're within half an inch, it's close enough.

You could drill the holes with a spade bit on a 3/8-inch drill, but the going will be slow and it may be difficult to drill straight holes. A 1/2-inch right-angle drill with an auger bit works better.

Where possible, pull the cable from a coil or from the box, and cut it to length when you have finished pulling. If you must cut it ahead of time, add at least 4 feet, or 2 feet

Measuring Height

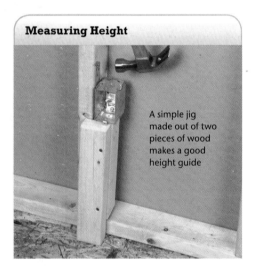

A simple jig made out of two pieces of wood makes a good height guide

Measuring Depth

Hold a scrap piece of the finish material in place as you attach the box

Adjustable Flange

Secure the flange to the stud, then use a screwdriver to adjust the box in or out

Ceiling Box with Spiked Flange

Anchor the box with the tap of a hammer, then drive nails or screws

Adjustable Hanger Bar

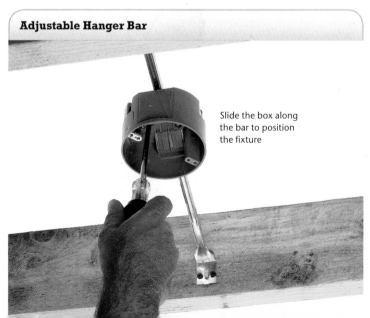

Slide the box along the bar to position the fixture

Related Topics

Cable & wire types, 32–33
Wiring in finished rooms, 130–135
Wiring in unfinished framing, 140–141
Wiring with conduit, 66–69

for each box. When a cable goes to a service panel or a subpanel, add at least 6 feet (4 for the panel and 2 for the box), so you can route the wires around the panel's perimeter.

Work carefully so you do not kink or twist the cable during installation. If you're having trouble, try pulling cable from the box and straightening it before you run it.

When you're finished pulling, the cable should not droop between studs or joists, but it should not be banjo-string taut either. Drive a staple within 8 inches of a plastic box or 12 inches of a metal box and allow some slack.

Pulling Cable

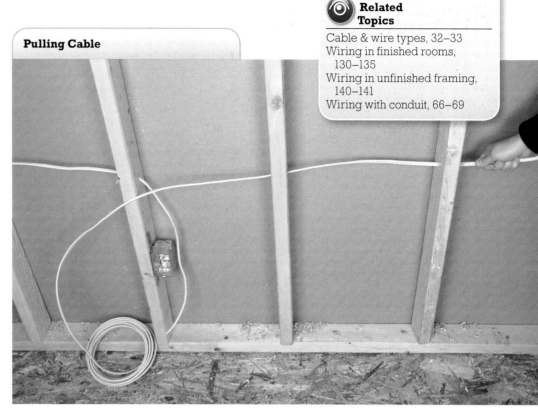

Drilling with a Height Guide

Cable Stapled Near a Box

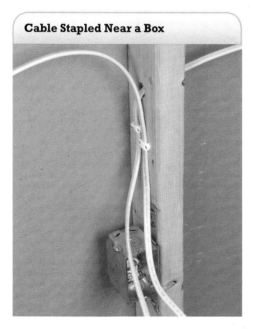

Filling the Holes

Cable holes that run between rooms—usually at bottom or top plates—should be filled with a special fire-stop sealant, available in caulk tubes. This inhibits fire from spreading from room to room. When a hole goes outside, or into an attic, fill the hole with foam insulation.

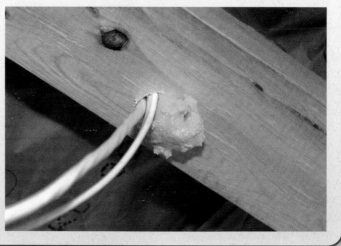

Cable Connections

How you secure a length of cable to an electrical box will depend entirely on the box. Some plastic boxes have hinged slots that hold cable in place by compression. Other boxes, whether made of metal or plastic, are designed for metal or plastic clamps.

STOP!
Always turn off power to the circuit you will be tapping into. Before you begin any connection, double-check to make sure the power is off.

Metal Boxes

If your box is metal, you must clamp the cable to it. Some metal boxes have built-in clamps, while others have knockouts that you remove to attach separate clamps.

Strip the sheathing before you poke the cable into the box. Before you insert the wires, check to make sure no insulation was nicked. Insert the wires far enough so you see ½ inch or so of sheathing inside the box. The clamp should grasp the sheathing, not individual wires.

Be sure to allow yourself plenty of wiring length inside the box—6 inches at least, but you may want to allow 8 or more in case you make mistakes and have to cut and restrip the wires.

Plastic Box with Metal Clamp

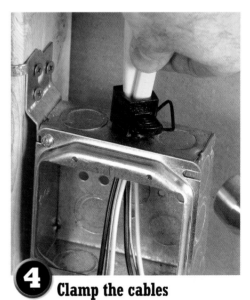

Thread and secure cable to a plastic box using a metal clamp in the same way as you would to a metal box using a metal clamp (see opposite page).

Attaching Plastic Cable Clamps

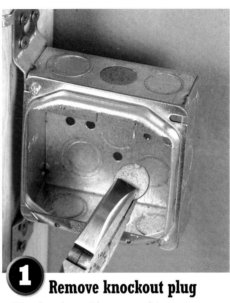

1 Remove knockout plug
- Tap the plug with a screwdriver
- Twist off the slug with lineman's pliers

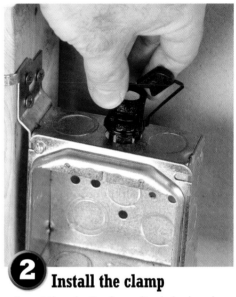

2 Install the clamp
- Insert the plastic clamp firmly by hand
- If necessary, tap with a hammer

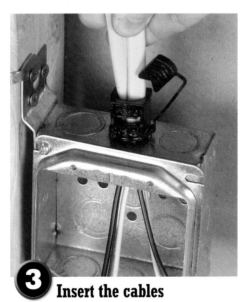

3 Insert the cables
- Thread the cables through the clamp (plastic clamps have room for two)
- Make sure you can see a little sheathing inside the box, at the bottom of the clamp

4 Clamp the cables
- Insert the clamp's tab into the slot; don't worry if it breaks off from the thin strip holding it to the clamp
- Hold the cables in place and tap the tab with a hammer until it firmly grabs the cables

ATTACHING METAL CABLE CLAMPS

Start by stripping cable and removing a knockout plug. You can install metal clamps in either of the two ways shown here.

Option A Attach the clamp to the cable sheathing, ½ inch or so above the edge of the sheathing, by tightening the two screws. Thread the wires through the knockout hole and slip the clamp's threads through the hole. Then slide the locknut up around the wires and tighten the nut.

Option B First attach the cable clamp to the box, then slide the stripped cable through the clamp until ½ inch of sheathing is visible inside the box. Tighten the screws that hold the cable.

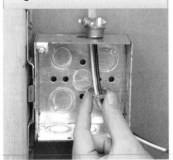

Option A

Option B

Plastic Boxes

Most plastic boxes have hinged knockouts instead of clamps, so you staple the cable near the box rather than clamp it directly to the box. Some plastic boxes have built-in clamps or knockout holes like those in metal boxes.

Hinged knockouts are like trap doors, with tabs that grab a cable and make it difficult (though not impossible) for it to slide back out. You may need to use a screwdriver tip to open the trap door. Open it gently so you don't overbend the tab. Hold the wires tightly together to poke them through the knockout. It helps to give the wires a slight bend so they curve away from the bottom of the box and out the front as you push. Staple the cable within 8 inches of the box. Some inspectors may want you to leave several inches of slack in the cable between the staple and the box.

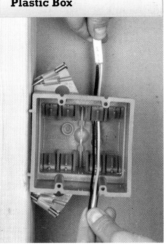

Plastic Box

Making a Greenfield Whip

For running power to an appliance that is occasionally moved, such as a water heater or dishwasher, exposed NM cable may not be allowed. Instead, you may be required to install a Greenfield whip—a length of flexible metal conduit, also called Greenfield, that protects the cable running to the appliance.

1 Strip the sheathing

• Strip a long section of cable sheathing—enough to reach the appliance, plus 2 or 3 feet to allow it to move
• If you find it difficult to strip so much sheathing at once, strip it in sections

2 Cover with Greenfield

• Cut a piece of Greenfield to length and slide it over the wires
• Keep sliding for several more inches over the sheathed part of the cable

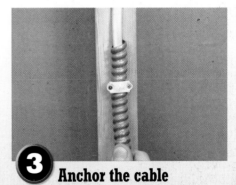

3 Anchor the cable

• Staple over the Greenfield and over the cable
• Tug to make sure both staples are firmly attached

6

Lights, Indoors & Out

In this chapter, we help you choose the right light fixtures for your home, whether you are lighting a bedroom, a living room, a kitchen, or a bathroom. We also show you how to install canister lights in a ceiling, how to add a new light and switch to a finished room, and we explain your options for under-cabinet lighting. Finally, we go outside to help you safely wire exterior fixtures.

Chapter Contents

Choosing Light Fixtures

Home improvement and lighting stores offer a wide variety of lighting types for different functions. Most of those lighting options also come in a range of design styles. Here's a rough guide to some of the many choices available.

Choosing Lights to Suit Your Needs

Using similar fixtures throughout a home can unify the decor. If you're installing more than one fixture, consider using lighting "families" that include ceiling fixtures, sconces, pendants, track lights, and even lamps.

Tastes and habits change over the years, so it's smart to make your lighting system adaptable. Movable or adjustable lamps are one option, but systems and even recessed downlights can be altered as well. With a change of trim, a regular built-in downlight can be transformed into an accent light or a wall-washing light.

When you select a particular fixture, consider how it directs light, and whether that suits your needs for that location. Does it create a narrow, focused beam, a broad, diffuse spread, or something in between?

Take measurements of your top choices, then hold bowls or boxes of the same sizes in place at home to evaluate the scale. Globes may seem smaller in the store than in your home.

When calculating cost, consider more than just the price of the fixture. The electricity the bulbs or tubes use is an ongoing expense to evaluate as well. Also, some fixtures are more efficient than others, providing more light for the amount of electricity consumed.

All light fixtures need to be cleaned regularly and the bulbs changed. Kitchens, work areas, and bathrooms demand fixtures that are easy to reach and clean. For hard-to-reach areas, such as above stairs, a fixture with a long-lived fluorescent or halogen bulb is a good choice.

CHANDELIERS & PENDANTS

Stylish chandeliers and pendants add sparkle in high-ceilinged entry areas, above dining tables, and in breakfast nooks. Such decorative fixtures can provide direct or diffused light or a combination of the two. It's always a good idea to wire these fixtures to

This coordinated suite—pendant light over the stairs, chandelier over the table, sconce on the wall—provides ambient light.

a dimmer so you can fine-tune the light to suit your mood. Swags—chain-suspended pendants with cords and plugs—are a movable alternative.

For any fixture that hangs down, clearance is a consideration. A pendant used over a table should be at least 12 inches narrower than the table to prevent bumped heads. Chandeliers should hang about 30 inches above a table. In an entry space, be sure a chandelier will allow safe passage for tall people.

FLUSH-MOUNTED FIXTURES

Flush-mounted fixtures are especially good at providing diffuse ambient light. Most come with their own mounting hardware, adaptable to any standard fixture box. Consider how a fixture bounces light off a

wall or ceiling to make sure the light will be directed where you want it. Most flush-mounted fixtures still use incandescent bulbs, but fluorescent options are more common as the quality of fluorescent products improves. Some screw-in fluorescent bulbs are the same size as incandescents, so they fit into any fixture.

WALL SCONCES

Available in a huge array of styles, sconces are great for halls (provided they don't impede traffic) and for indirect lighting in living spaces. They often come in pairs that can flank a fireplace, door, or bed. Place sconces about 5½ feet above the floor and keep them away from corners, where they can create hot spots.

Related Topics

Light bulbs, 72–73

Chandeliers

Flush-mounted Fixtures

Wall Sconces

Low-voltage rail lights are often used to supplement rows of recessed canister lights.

Many ceiling fans also include a light, which means you can install two switches for each of these types of fixtures.

LOW-VOLTAGE RAIL & CABLE LIGHTS

After illuminating shops and showrooms for years, low-voltage lights are increasingly popular with homeowners. The diminutive fixtures are designed to be at once striking and discreet.

A cable light system has four basic components: transformer, cables, lights, and mounting hardware. Many manufacturers offer kits that can be installed by homeowners, while more elaborate systems may require professional installation. Rail systems, such as the one above, are also sold in kits. Rails are packaged straight so they can be bent to fit your particular lighting needs.

CEILING FANS

To reduce your dependence on air conditioning, consider overhead fans. Fans can also be handy in cooler months to mix warm and cool air, adding comfort to your home.

Chose a blade width based on the size of the room and how much of a breeze you want to create. The fan may come with its own light, or you may choose a separate light kit. Either way, be sure it is rated for the bulb wattage you need. The fan and light may be controlled separately with a special wall switch, pull-chain switches, or remote controls. Fans come in a variety of styles, including sleek, simple designs, more ornamental looks, or bright or pastel colors for a child's room.

BATHROOM MIRROR LIGHTS

Bath fixtures should provide shadow-free task lighting and warm, smooth-toned color temperature. The classic choice is theater lighting: strings of incandescent globes on a strip base. Other options include vertical fluorescent tubes, incandescent tubes, and sconces.

UNDER-CABINET TASK LIGHTS

In a kitchen, flat, narrow lights can fit under wall cabinets and shine on the counter below. Fluorescents are popular in both plug-in and hardwired versions and can be as shallow as $1^3/_{16}$ inches. Lengths from 12 inches on up are available, and some can be ganged together to make longer runs.

Ceiling Fans

Bathroom Mirror Lights

Under-cabinet Task Lights

Track Lights

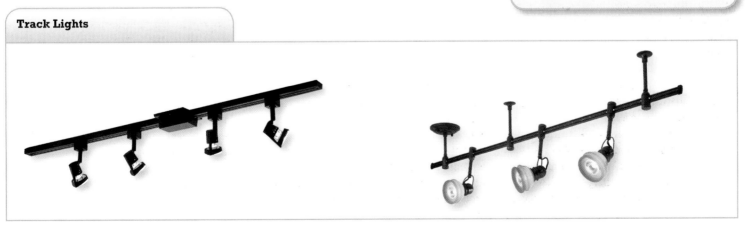

Halogen strips and round lights also work for under-cabinet use, particularly if you want to dim them.

TRACK LIGHTS

Available in varying lengths, tracks are, essentially, electrical lines that extend from an electrical box or plug into a wall outlet. Matching fixtures can be mounted anywhere along each line, offering versatility and ease of installation. Newer models are smaller and more stylish, especially those designed for low-voltage halogen bulbs.

Tracks can accommodate clip-on lamps, low-voltage spotlights, and pendant fixtures, as well as a large selection of standard spots. Low-voltage tracks require a transformer to dial down the electrical output of standard wiring from 120 volts to the lower voltage some halogen bulbs require.

You can modify light output or keep it out of people's eyes with track fixture accessories. Lenses focus or diffuse light, louvers cut glare, and baffles and barn doors cut or shape light output. Filters add subtle or not-so-subtle color accents.

For safety, avoid track lighting in damp areas such as bathrooms or laundry rooms.

Controls

Dimmers and control panels can help you adjust light for different uses and decorative effects. Dimmers, sometimes called rheostats, are also energy savers. Be aware, though, that some light sources, notably fluorescents, can be difficult or very expensive to dim, so check the options as you shop.

Smart & Wireless Switches

Thanks to the growing selection of switches that require no new wiring, you can manage your home lighting from across the room, across the street, or across the continent. Some of these switches let you control your heating and cooling, too.

The Lagotek Home Intelligence Platform lets you control lights, home audio, air conditioning, and heat.

Your Options

Smart switches range from the "clap on clap off" number you can buy at your corner drugstore to sophisticated systems that let you light up your porch and five rooms when you pull into your driveway. There are surprisingly affordable systems that plug into your PC and allow you to control home appliances, heating, and lighting from anywhere in the world. They will also automate your home's power consumption, letting you select the most effective energy-saving schedule.

LIGHTS ONLY

The most common type of smart or wireless switch is one that's designed to turn a plug-in lamp on or off. Typically the wireless kit consists of a module that plugs into a standard receptacle—the lamp plugs into the module. The module contains a receiver that can be switched on or off by a transmitter, usually inside a key fob or an unwired switch that can be surface-mounted wherever it's most convenient. For this reason, wireless switches are great for situations that require universal design. Most wireless remotes are powered by a battery; more expensive models are equipped with a micro-generator that makes enough electricity from the act of pressing the switch to power its transmitter.

When installing any plug-in switch, be sure that the receptacle you plug it into is always hot. Don't plug it into a receptacle that is controlled by a wall switch.

HOME SYSTEMS

If money is no object, the Lagotek Home Intelligence Platform is for you. This state-of-the-art home-automation system can be run by voice commands to change heating and cooling settings—day or night—for maximum energy efficiency. You can also use it to control lights, home audio, and video-surveillance cameras. There's even a vacation-mode setting, in which the system remembers how your lights were operated during the two previous weeks and imitates it, as if you were still there.

On the low end, X10.com makes inexpensive systems that control your lights, heating, and cooling via the electrical wires they are plugged into. Use your home PC to run the system, or access it over the Internet from anywhere. For example, if you are at work and the weather shifts unexpectedly, you can change your home's climate remotely so that your house will be cool, or warm, when you get home.

Lutron, the company that made the first light dimmer in 1961 with mood in mind, now picks up the green theme, noting that making a light 25 percent dimmer saves 20 percent in energy and adds to the lifespan of your bulb. Lutron also has complete house packages that install into existing wires and allow you to control the lights from panels in the house, or from your car's visor.

Wireless Remote

This type of switch allows you to control a lamp, television, radio, or appliance from as far as 100 feet away, since its radio signal passes through walls and ceilings. Often called a keychain remote, the sending unit easily fastens to a keychain, so it provides a convenient way to turn on a light when you approach your home.

Touch-pad Dimmer

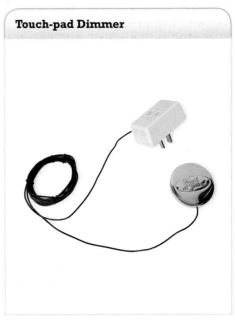

This device allows you to control a lamp by touching a pad located wherever you choose on a wall. It has a "soft-start" feature that causes the bulb to brighten gradually, which helps bulbs last longer.

Touch Dimmer

This one seems to work like magic. Unplug a lamp, unscrew the bulb, screw in the unit, then screw the bulb into the unit. Plug the lamp back in, and you can now turn the light on or off or adjust the brightness level simply by touching the lamp's base.

Tabletop Timer

Plug in the timer, then plug a lamp into the timer's plug. Some units simply turn on and off once or twice a day. Others can be programmed to turn a lamp on and off at various times to fool would-be intruders while you are away.

Wall-mounted Switches

Some wireless switches look very much like standard wall switches but require no wiring. The type shown above has a module that plugs into a receptacle. Plug a lamp into the module, and you now have a lamp that can be controlled by a transmitter in a wireless wall switch.

Lighting, Room by Room

Home lighting is the art of painting light and shadow onto a dark canvas. The challenge is to determine where light is needed and to direct it there in a way that avoids glare while offering good illumination.

In this corner, a pendant illuminates a table, recessed spots light up a wall, and even a collection jelly beans and gumballs are lit.

A floor reading light and a table lamp put light where the owners of this home need it. Ceiling spots are used for fill, while a mirror over the fireplace is a passive light source.

Layers of Light

Professionals divide lighting into four categories or layers. Working with these layers builds flexibility into your lighting scheme, letting you dial the light in a room up or down to suit your mood.

TASK LIGHTING

Task lighting is bright light that illuminates a particular space where an activity takes place, such as reading, sewing, or preparing food. It's often achieved with individual fixtures directed onto the work surface in a tight pattern.

Adjustability is important for task lighting. So is shielding (hiding the bulb from direct sight). It's best to aim the light at an angle so it won't cause hot spots or throw shadows onto the work area. Where possible, it's better to have two or more light sources rather than one.

ACCENT LIGHTING

Like task lighting, accent lighting focuses on a specific space, but it's used to set a mood or to spotlight architectural features or artwork. Beam spread, intensity, and color are considerations for accent light. Low-voltage halogen bulbs, available in a wide variety of intensities and beam patterns, produce especially clean, white accent light.

AMBIENT LIGHTING

With ambient or fill lighting, the undefined areas of a room are filled with a soft level of light—enough for someone to watch television or navigate safely through the room. An ambient glow not only makes a room more inviting, but it helps people look their best, filling in harsh shadows created by stronger point sources.

Ambient lighting usually comes from a fixture that provides diffuse illumination—typically, a central overhead fixture. Directional fixtures aimed at a wall can also produce a wash of soft light.

Architectural features containing built-in lights, such as coves, cornices, valances, and soffits, are increasingly common. These work well as shields, blocking the lights from view while allowing illumination to fill a room with a pleasant ambient glow.

DECORATIVE LIGHTING

Decorative lighting is the only type that draws attention to itself. The classic chandelier is a good example. More recent

Avoiding Glare

When choosing where to place your light fixtures, consider the glare factor. Direct glare, such as the light from a bare light bulb, is the worst kind. Shades and covers diffuse the light and cut the glare. Recessing a fixture can also remedy the problem. Watch out for reflected glare as well. A fixture directly opposite a flat, shiny surface like a dining room table or a computer monitor can create "veiling" glare. Try adjusting the light's position, if possible; improving its shielding capacity, perhaps with a new globe or shade; or using different bulbs. A dimmer can also reduce reflected light to a comfortable level. A chandelier creates a special challenge. Hang it about 30 inches above the table surface to minimize the effects of reflected glare from the tabletop surface.

As you make other choices for your home, keep in mind that shiny surfaces like ceramic tiles or semigloss paint reflect light and can create uncomfortable glare.

options include low-voltage pendant fixtures, neon lights, and fiber optics. Decorative strip lights can add sparkle and warmth to a room while highlighting architectural lines.

Lighting Up a Living Room

To make your living room comfortable, use well shielded task lighting for reading or handwork; accent lighting for artwork, collections, or architectural features; and soft, adjustable ambient light throughout.

Recessed canister downlights can complement both contemporary and traditional decor and are most often used for accenting or for lighting casual tasks. Choose adjustable downlights that can be adapted as your furnishings and art change. If you're retrofitting, cable lights or other low-voltage tracks are good alternatives. Pharmacy lamps with adjustable necks and built-in dimmers are also favorites for efficient task lighting.

Options for ambient light include wall sconces, movable torchère-style floor lamps, wall washers, and traditional floor and table lamps. Built-in architectural fixtures like valances, soffits, and coves can be effective ambient sources, too.

Use dimmer switches to suit different living room uses. Three- and four-way switches add functionality as you enter one way and exit another. You may want floor receptacles in a living room so lamps can be near furnishings in the center of the room.

Illuminating Entries

Entries make first impressions. Light them warmly to make them inviting, but don't overlight them. And minimize glare by shielding porch and entry fixtures.

The main rule is to keep it simple. To draw attention to attractive features in a room beyond the entry, let the entry lights serve as a quiet complement rather than a separate focus of interest. To make an entry look bigger, use uplighting aimed at the ceiling, or add mirrors.

Hidden downlights brighten a collection of black-and-white photographs. A strip light tucked beneath the floating shelf's lip adds a soft glow.

Recessed ceiling lights are not enough in a kitchen, which is where the powerful pendant lights over the kitchen island come in.

Another use for pendants is to create a casual dining area, like the one at the end of this kitchen counter.

A row of visually unobtrusive pendants lights up a slender island counter.

Lighting Up a Kitchen

Kitchens need flexible lighting that's suitable both for a late-night snack and for full-scale entertaining. Multiple sources and dimmer controls let you use the light you need, from full work lighting to a warm glow after hours.

Task lighting for the sink, countertops, and cooktop is essential. Plan for strong, shadowless light over each work area. In most cases, shielded strip lights under the cabinets—hidden behind a trim strip or a valence—are the best way to light counter areas. Track lighting, recessed canisters, or pendants can illuminate the sink and work islands.

It was once common to install a simple flush light or two in a kitchen ceiling. Nowadays, ceiling lights are often splashier and even a bit decorative. Pendants are especially popular; place them over a breakfast nook, an island, or anywhere they won't present a traffic hazard.

Fluorescent tubes are unrivaled for energy efficiency and are long lasting as well. Some jurisdictions require fluorescent lighting for general kitchen illumination. Fluorescent fixtures with long tubes can be placed in soffits atop cabinets or in overhead coves. Fixtures that use fluorescent bulbs, on the other hand, come in most any style.

Illuminating the Dining Room

The table is the focus of the dining room. You can illuminate it with a traditional chandelier, modern pendants, recessed canister lights,

This pendant is prominent enough to be considered a chandelier, which is controlled by a dimmer switch to vary the mood. Recessed ceiling and display spots contribute ambient light.

Rope lights brighten the niche in the foreground, while a spot lights up an object in an alcove.

or a combination. To prevent unpleasant glare and shadows, avoid using a decorative fixture like a chandelier as the room's only light source. Instead, add softer fill lights on the walls or ceiling. Wall sconces, built-in cove lights, or torchère-style floor lamps work well. Accent light on paintings or display niches can also double as ambient fill.

Hallways & Stairs

Keep it simple in lighting hallways and stairs. Recessed canister lights are popular, as are tracks and opaque pendants. If the hall is wide enough, consider sconces. A hallway can make an exciting gallery for art, but be sure the light is dimmable—or consider a second set of fixtures for soft illumination. Where a fixture is difficult to reach, install extended-life bulbs.

With any stairs, even just two steps to another level, it's important to provide adequate light for safety. The edge of each tread and the depth of each step should be clearly defined. One way to achieve this is to combine a recessed canister or flush light over the stairs (to light the edges) with a softer light projected from the landing below (to define the depth). Another option is to build low-voltage fixtures into the wall just above every third or fourth step. Lights hidden in a handrail can also illuminate treads. For a main landing or entry stairs, consider decorative and accent lighting as well.

For either halls or stairs, plan to install three- or four-way switches at each end or hallway opening. A dimmer can replace one switch for decorative lighting control.

When there's no ceiling, such as in this hallway between a wall and a stairway, sconces light the way.

Lighting Bedrooms

The traditional approach to bedroom lighting was a central overhead globe and a plug-in table lamp or two. Today's large, open master suites, however, are more like living rooms and benefit in the same way from multiple layers of light. Even a basic bedroom is more comfortable with a little flexibility in the lighting design. Add soft, fill light with decorative sconces, torchères, or built-in cove lighting. If you're replacing an existing ceiling globe, consider an opaque pendant that directs light up and off the ceiling.

Check to ensure that glare won't be a problem for someone reclining in bed. Overhead fixtures should be carefully aimed and fitted, as needed, with tight trim covers and baffles or louvers. Bright, directional reading lights beside the bed should be adjustable and well shielded. Alternatively, use a pair of dimmable low-voltage downlights, cross-aimed like overhead airline lights, to prevent shadows.

Translucent shoji closet panels are a glowing wall of light. Subtly lit from behind, they are also washed from above in the front.

Lighting Up a Bathroom

The trick to lighting bathrooms is to supply task lighting that's gently flattering yet bright enough for personal grooming. Lights around a mirror should spread light over a person's face rather than the mirror surface. To avoid heavy shadows, place lights at the sides of the mirror, not just the top. Options include theater makeup bars,

Bedroom Light Switches

A bedside switch to turn off main room lights is handy. A second switch can control night-lights. A recent innovation is a bedside master switch that can control computerized security lights both indoors and out.

A skylight gives this bathroom a cheery feel. Sconces and ceiling fixtures provide focused light.

Lights on either side of a mirror help eliminate shadows. These sconces also feature shades to reduce glare.

wall sconces, or tubes mounted vertically. Choose warm-toned tubes or bulbs for accurate makeup light and good skin tones. Some mirror units have their own integral tubes, light diffusers, or swing-out makeup mirrors with separate light sources.

Energy-efficient fluorescent lights are required for general bathroom lighting in some locales. For a large bathroom, consider adding indirect sources for fill lights, perhaps built into architectural features, or try translucent diffusers and other bounce lighting to spread soft, even illumination.

Multiple light sources and controls allow you to alternate between morning efficiency and nighttime serenity. Consider dimmers here. Also provide low-energy nighttime lighting for safety and convenience.

Tub, shower, and toilet compartments may need their own light fixtures. Bath and shower lights must be sealed and approved for wet locations. Any light fixture within reach of water should be protected by a GFCI (ground-fault circuit interrupter) to prevent electrical shock.

Work Space or Home Office

Make sure your work surface is free of heavy shadows, which can cause eyestrain. Combine diffuse ambient lighting and adjustable task lighting to avoid excessive contrasts between a work area and the rest of a room.

If your space includes a computer, it's best if the lighting, including natural light, comes from the side. Light behind the monitor can cause eyestrain, while light in front can bounce glare off the screen. If ambient light is too bright, it may reflect off the wall or ceiling to throw glare onto the computer screen. One solution is to put ambient lights on dimmers so they can be dialed down as needed.

Canister lights are complemented by high-mounted sconces that serve as uplights.

This rustic home office sports task lights as well as recessed downlights and uplights hidden in bookcase soffits.

Recessed Lighting in Large Rooms

Recessed lights have an understated appeal and work especially well in large rooms with high ceilings. Like stars in the ceiling sky, they provide subtle dots of ambient light. As a general rule, recessed can lights should be spaced 6 feet apart in a grid pattern, but spacing will vary with the size of the room, the intensity of the lights, and the height of the ceiling (the higher the lights, the wider the circle of illumination they cast below).

Using graph paper, draft rough plans for light placement. Make a scale drawing of the room, then add dots spaced 5 or 6 feet apart. Using a compass, draw circles around the dots to represent a lighting radius of 4 feet for an 8-foot-high ceiling or 5 feet for a 10-foot ceiling (for a total diameter of 8 or 10 feet, respectively). This exercise gives you a general idea of how the light in the room will be distributed. Many people prefer to concentrate more light in the center of the room than along the perimeter, for example.

Keep your plans flexible, because you'll probably find that ceiling joists require you to move lights a few inches one way or the other as you install them.

Recessed Canister Lights

Recessed canister lights—also called can lights, downlights, or pot lights—provide ample illumination without calling attention to themselves. Unobtrusive and versatile, they're a good choice for both modern and traditional decors.

Planning the Wiring

If you already have a ceiling fixture with a wall switch, you can probably use the existing switch. Remove the fixture and run the cable from the fixture box into a canister light, then run cable from that light to the others. If there is no existing fixture with a switch, you will need to run cable from a power source to a switch box, then run cable from the switch box up into the ceiling and on to each of the can lights. In some cases, adding an extra canister light or two can make it easier to run cable.

If you want to control the lights with a pair of three-way switches, make sure the first light's junction box is large enough to handle the extra wires. Run three-wire cable from the switches to one fixture only, and run two-wire cable from that fixture to all the others.

Trims & Accessories

Some lights come with their own trims, but most do not. Purchase trims that are sized to match the fixtures (it's fine to mix them within a room). In addition to an open trim, which exposes the bulb to view, you can choose trims with white or black baffles and special reflective finishes, which accentuate or downplay the bulb's brightness. A watertight lens is a good choice for a damp area like a bathroom or above a sink. An eyeball trim swivels so you can point it at a painting or at an area of the wall you want to accentuate.

The only part of a canister light that you will actually is the trim.

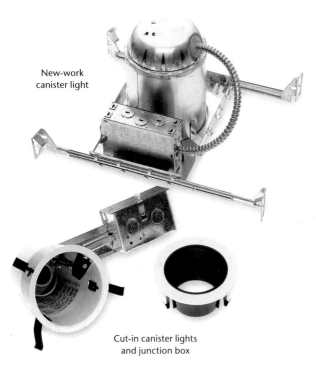

New-work canister light

Cut-in canister lights and junction box

Stuff to Buy

RECESSED CAN LIGHTS
Lights come in 4-, 5-, and 6-inch diameters and may use incandescent flood bulbs or fluorescent or halogen bulbs. Most are 7 inches tall and fit a ceiling with 2-by-8 joists; for 2-by-6 joists, buy low-clearance fixtures.

Time Commitment

Varies depending on the number of lights; about half a day

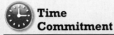

Tools You'll Need

Screwdriver
Wire stripper
Lineman's pliers
Drywall knife
Jigsaw (for plaster ceiling)

Related Topics

Choosing light fixtures, 148–151
Calculating usage & capacity, 282–283
Shutting off & restoring power, 50–51
Stripping & joining wire, 54–59
Tapping into power, 136–137
Wiring in finished rooms, 130–135

Installing Cut-in Canister Lights

1 Mark locations

- Measuring from nearby walls, lightly mark the preferred light locations
- Drill a small hole in each mark, insert a bent wire a little longer than the radius (half-diameter) of the fixture
- Rotate the wire to check for obstructions; relocate the mark as needed
- For an insulated ceiling, use a stud finder or cut a hole you can reach through

2 Trace the shapes

- Carefully trace the hole from the fixture's template
- If there is no template, either use a compass or trace the canister and then make the hole a little smaller

3 Cut the holes

- Cut the hole with a drywall saw, taking care not to make it bigger
- For a plaster ceiling, use a jigsaw

OPTION Using a hole saw

- If you have to cut a lot of holes, use a hole saw made for canister installations
- Adjust the saw to the correct diameter and practice several times in scrap drywall
- Testing the results with a canister before making cuts in your ceiling

④ Run the cable

- Run cable from the switch box to the first hole, then on to the next holes
- Where possible, run cable parallel to the joists
- Using a fishing bit may cut down on the notches or holes you need to cut

⑤ Leave extra cable

- Allow yourself 16 inches of cable, or more, at each opening

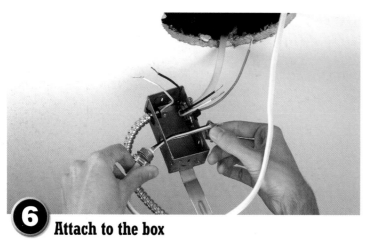

⑥ Attach to the box

- Remove the cover from the junction box
- Remove knockouts as needed; except for the last light in a series, there will be two cables entering the box
- Strip 6 inches of sheathing from the cable
- Connect the cable to the box with a cable clamp

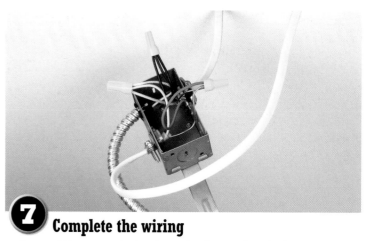

⑦ Complete the wiring

- Connect the ground wires to each other and to the box
- Strip and splice the neutral wires and the hot wires
- Fold the wires back into the box and replace the box cover.

⑧ Insert the box and fixture

- If necessary for fit, pull the mounting clips into the box
- Thread the cables, the box, and then the fixture up through the hole
- Rotate the fixture as needed to keep the box from hitting a joist

⑨ Clamp the light in place

- Press the flange tight against the ceiling and push the clamps into place with a screwdriver
- For a plaster ceiling, first adjust the clamps for the extra thickness

New-work Canister Lights

You can install a new-work fixture after a ceiling is in place if you have access from an attic. Cut a hole for the fixture, either from above or from below. Run the cables above or through the joists, as required by local code. Make the electrical connections in the box. Position the fixture so it slips down into the hole (there is no flange, as with a cut-in fixture). Slide the mounting brackets over to the joists; drive screws to attach the brackets and hold the fixture firmly in place. Then install the trim from below.

10 Install the trim

- Add the trim of your choice
- Trim like this uses coil springs that hook to holes in the fixture; work carefully to avoid overstretching them
- Once the trim is attached, you can usually adjust it on the ceiling by an inch or so

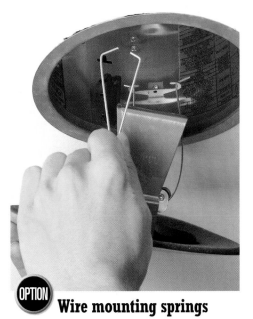

OPTION Wire mounting springs

- If your trim has wire mounting springs, squeeze them together and hook their ends to the holes in the fixture
- Attach both springs, then push the trim against the ceiling and slide it to adjust

Canister lights can be placed in a ceiling for general lighting or task lighting, as shown in this use of a canister light over a sink.

A New Light & Switch

If a room lacks an overhead light fixture, adding one may eliminate the need for floor lamps. Once the fixture box is wired and attached, you can install almost any type of light you want, including flush, track, pendant, or chandelier.

STOP!
Always turn off power to the circuits you are working on. Double-check before and after opening the receptacle box to make sure the power is off.

Wiring Methods

In the steps and photos on the opposite page, we show how to tap into a nearby receptacle for power using through-switch wiring. Before you do this in your home, make sure that the new lights will not over-load the receptacle circuit. In some cases, you may be able to tap into a nearby junction box instead.

PULL-CHAIN OPTION

If a fixture is controlled with a pull-chain switch (see illustration on opposite page), the power runs directly to the fixture box, so switch-loop wiring is called for. Shut off power to the circuit and test to verify that power is off. Remove the fixture. Unless you have access from above, you will probably need to remove the fixture box to run cable for the switch.

Through-switch Wiring

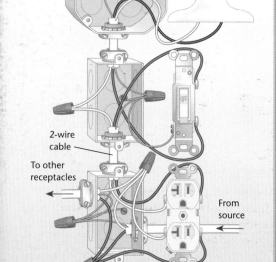

2-wire cable

To other receptacles

From source

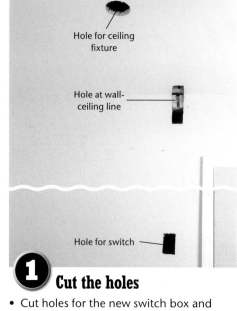

Hole for ceiling fixture

Hole at wall-ceiling line

Hole for switch

1 Cut the holes

- Cut holes for the new switch box and the fixture
- If the switch is right above the receptacle you're tapping into, the cable may run freely through the wall
- You'll probably have to cut a hole where the wall meets the ceiling

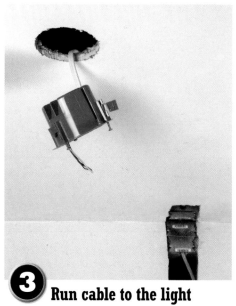

3 Run cable to the light

- Run two-wire cable into the ceiling box
- Strip 6 inches of sheathing and clamp the cable to the box

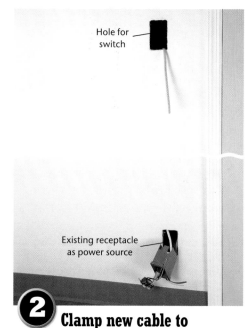

Hole for switch

Existing receptacle as power source

2 Clamp new cable to receptacle box

- Shut off power to the receptacle and test to confirm it's off
- Either pull out the receptacle box or remove a knockout
- Strip sheathing on a new piece of cable and clamp it to the box
- Leave about 6 inches of new wire in the box to attach later
- If you are tapping into a 20-amp receptacle for a 15-amp fixture and switch, check with your inspector regarding whether to use 12- or 14-gauge wire

Cut a hole for the switch box. Run two-wire cable from the switch box to the fixture box. Strip the sheathing, clamp the cable to the boxes, and then install the boxes. Mark the new white wire black in both the switch and the fixture box, and make connections for switch-loop wiring.

If you also want to add a receptacle, run three-wire cable from the fixture box to the switch box, and two-wire cable from the switch box to the new receptacle box.

Time Commitment

A weekend (including time for drywall repairs and paint)

Tools You'll Need

Screwdriver
Wire stripper
Lineman's pliers
Drywall knife
Jigsaw (for plaster ceiling)

Related Topics

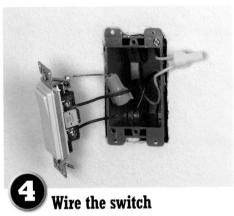

❹ Wire the switch

- Strip sheathing and run cables into the switch box
- Install the box
- Connect the grounds
- Splice the two white wires and connect the two black wires to the switch terminals

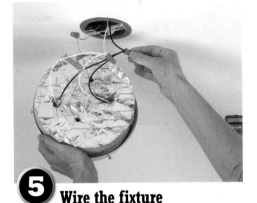

❺ Wire the fixture

- Attach the ceiling box and wire the light fixture
- Connect the grounds
- Splice the white fixture lead to the white wire and the black fixture lead to the black wire
- Mount the light

❻ Tap power from the receptacle

- Connect the grounds from the cable you ran into the receptacle box in Step 2
- If the receptacle has available terminals, connect the black wire to the brass terminal and white to the silver terminal
- Use pigtails if the receptacle does not have available terminals, or install a new receptacle that has extra terminals
- Fold the wires into the box, mount the receptacle, restore power, and test

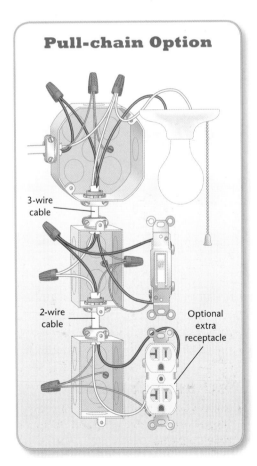

Pull-chain Option

3-wire cable

2-wire cable

Optional extra receptacle

The power source for the spotlights on this ceiling could be the receptacle near the floor. A switch interrupts the flow of power to the lights.

Hardwired Under-cabinet Lights

There are a wide variety of lights made to mount under cabinets, including low-voltage lights that simply plug in (see page 169). The following pages show how to install 120-volt hardwired fixtures controlled by a wall switch.

STOP!
Always turn off power to the circuits you are working on. Double-check before and after opening the receptacle box to make sure the power is off.

Lights under a cabinet illuminate task areas while calling attention to the design and color of a counter's backsplash.

Choosing Fixtures

A fixture with a plug-in cord can be modified for hardwiring, but it's easier and usually less expensive to use fixtures designed for hardwiring. Some xenon and halogen fixtures have cords for "daisy chaining"—you can hardwire the first fixture, then hook up the rest with the cords. But the cords cannot be cut to length, so you may need to bundle them up and hide them out of sight.

Fluorescent lights are usually the least expensive option, and offer other benefits as well. Long fluorescent tubes provide even illumination on a countertop, use little electricity, and stay cool. On the minus side, they flicker when they come on, and it's not practical to place more than one fluorescent fixture on a dimmer.

Xenon and halogen lights are efficient, their light is generally a little warmer in color, and they can be controlled with a dimmer switch. But they may produce circular pools or rectangular areas of light (depending on the type of fixture) rather than even illumination, and they cost more than fluorescents. They also get hot—halo-gens are hotter than xenons. Some units can be swiveled so you can point the light forward or back toward the wall.

If your cabinets have lips on the bottom, then each light must fit between the lips, or you will have to cut away the lips to fit the lights in.

Tapping into Power

Route power to a wall switch, then to the under-cabinet lights. Whichever of the following methods you choose, check to be sure the new lights will not overload the circuit you tap into.

Time Commitment
A few hours, depending on location of existing wires

Tools You'll Need
Screwdriver
Wire stripper
Lineman's pliers

Related Topics
Calculating usage & capacity, 282–283
Common wiring methods, 28–31
Low-voltage interior lights, 82–83
Stripping & joining wire, 54–59
Tapping into power, 136–137
Testing methods, 52–53

- If there is an existing switch (such as for the overhead light) in a convenient location, and if power enters the switch box with through-switch wiring, you can remove the switch box, enlarge the hole, and install a two-gang box with two switches.
- If codes allow, replace an existing single wall switch with a double switch, or replace a conveniently located receptacle with a switch receptacle (in which case you will not need to enlarge the box).
- If codes allow, you may tap into a nearby receptacle, as shown on pages 136–137. Cut a hole for the new switch box and run cable from the receptacle to the new switch.
- If there is an existing receptacle in a convenient place for the new switch, remove the box, enlarge the hole, and install a two-gang box with both a receptacle and a switch, as shown above right.

Routing the Cables

Local codes may determine how you will run the cables. In some areas, it is OK to simply staple NM cable to the undersides of a cabinet. Some inspectors prefer that you use armored cable or raceway wherever the wiring is exposed. (As long as exposed cables are behind the lights, they will not be very noticeable.) In some cases, armored cable is run inside the cabinet, back against the wall. Be aware that armored cable requires a large bending radius.

Some codes do not allow you to use fixtures as junction boxes; you may need to run cable from a junction box to each of the fixtures.

Running cable through walls is easiest with the cabinets removed. That way, you can cut holes in the wall that will be covered by the cabinets. Even if you are not changing cabinets, you may wish to remove them for the wire installation so you won't have to patch the walls afterward. But it is often possible to cut small, strategic holes and run cable without removing the cabinets.

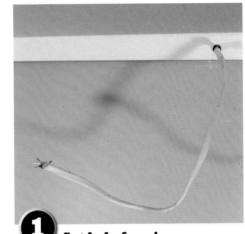

❶ Cut hole for wire

- Shut off power to the circuit and verify power is off
- Drill hole through lip at bottom of cabinet
- If power is nearby, bend cable and push it through hole and down wall toward source
- Leave plenty of cable for wiring

❸ Secure fixture to cabinet

- Double check that fixture is still aligned with hole in wall
- Before drilling in the underside of a cabinet, make sure screws are the correct length so that they don't poke through

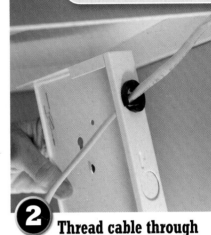

❷ Thread cable through fixture

- In this case, codes permit the fixture itself to be used as the junction box, so the hole in the fixture aligns with the hole in the wall
- Follow manufacturer's instructions to clamp the cable to the fixture

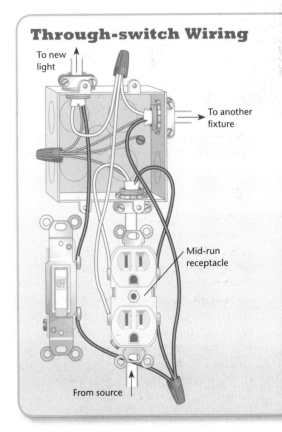

Through-switch Wiring

To new light

To another fixture

Mid-run receptacle

From source

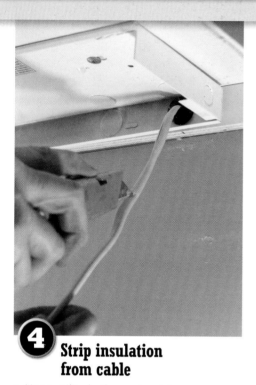

4 Strip insulation from cable

- Use a utility knife or wire strippers
- Be careful not to cut through insulation on wires inside cable

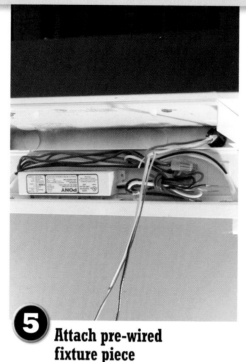

5 Attach pre-wired fixture piece

- The wired part of this fixture hangs from the main part on a simple hinge
- Strip enough insulation from cable wires to attach wires with nuts

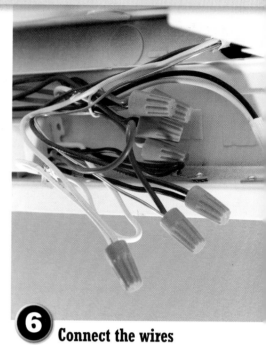

6 Connect the wires

- Follow manufacturer's instructions to connect house wires to fixture
- In this case, the black, white, and green fixture wires attach to the black, white, and copper wires in the cable

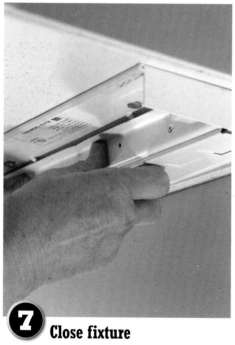

7 Close fixture

- Close the fixture's wiring housing
- This one snaps shut and also has screws to make sure it is secure

8 Install fluorescent bulb

- Slide the bulb into place and twist until it's secure in its holders
- If the light does not come on when you restore power, check to make sure you have installed the bulb properly before troubleshooting your wiring

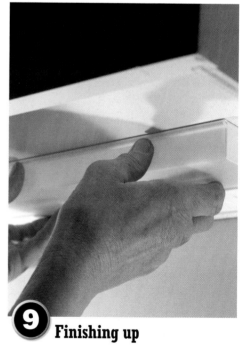

9 Finishing up

- Snap cover into place
- Connect fixture's hot wire to switch
- Connect the white wire and ground with pigtails
- Mount the switch, restore power, and test

A Plug-in Option

You probably don't want to have every fixture plugged into a receptacle, but it may look fine to do this occasionally. Other fixtures can be connected to the first with daisy-chain cables (for xenon lights) or cables run under or inside the cabinets, if code allows.

To control the first light with a wall switch, you can split a conveniently located receptacle. Following the safety precautions and the techniques shown on page 106, cut a hole for a new switch. Make sure the power is off and then run two-wire cable from the switch box to the existing receptacle. Break off the connecting tab between the hot (brass) terminals, and wire the receptacle as shown on pages 118–119. Mark the new white wire black to indicate that it is hot. The switched outlet (on top in the illustration) is controlled by the switch using switch-loop wiring.

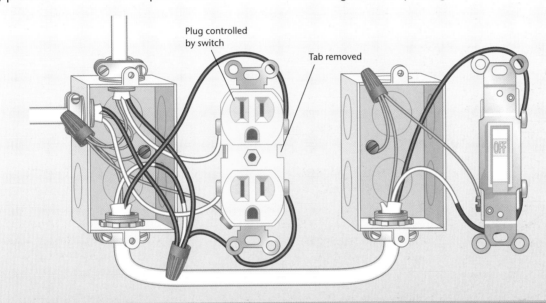

Plug controlled by switch

Tab removed

OFF

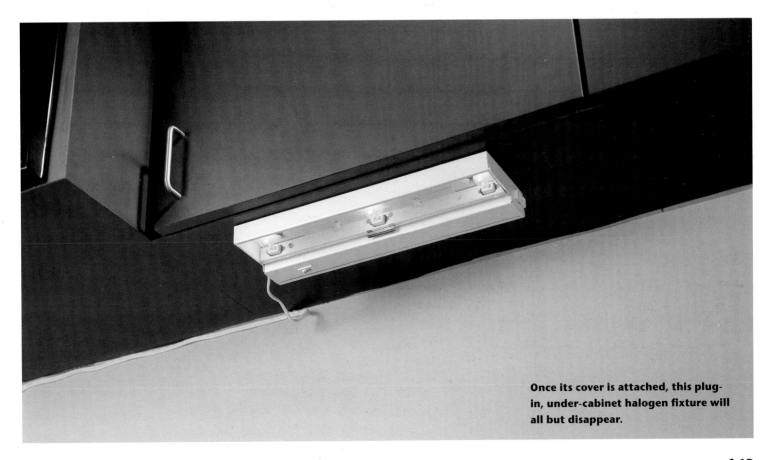

Once its cover is attached, this plug-in, under-cabinet halogen fixture will all but disappear.

Outdoor Wiring

Although low-voltage lighting is a good choice for modest illumination or marker lights, you'll need to run standard 120-volt service outdoors to install bright lights or to hook up a new receptacle outdoors. These pages show you how.

Outdoor Materials

The basic techniques for wiring are the same inside and outside. It's the materials that are different. Outdoor wiring materials are stronger and more resistant to corrosion. Also, the components must fit together tightly to prevent water from entering them, so heavy-duty gaskets or special fittings are often used to seal boxes. The outdoor light fixture and receptacle shown on page 172 is typical of outdoor components.

BOXES

Exterior electrical boxes come in two types, driptight and watertight.
- Driptight boxes are usually made of painted metal and may have a shroud or shield that sheds rain. These units are not waterproof, so they must be mounted where floods or even water from sprinklers can't touch them, such as under an eave.
- Watertight boxes are the best choice for a location that is likely to get wet. They are made of cast aluminum or another corrosion-resistant metal, and they have threaded entries to keep water out. All covers for watertight boxes are sealed with gaskets.

CABLE & CONDUIT

Most outdoor cable gets buried underground. Underground feeder cable (type UF) is waterproof and can be buried directly in the ground, although some local codes require that it be housed in conduit for additional protection from water and physical damage. UF cable must be buried at least a foot deep, and some codes require it to be buried deeper. Any cable that is above ground must be encased in conduit.

For most residential projects, conduit with an inside diameter of ¾ or ½ inch is large enough. An installation with multiple cables (which should probably be done by a professional) may call for conduit ranging up to 3 inches in diameter.

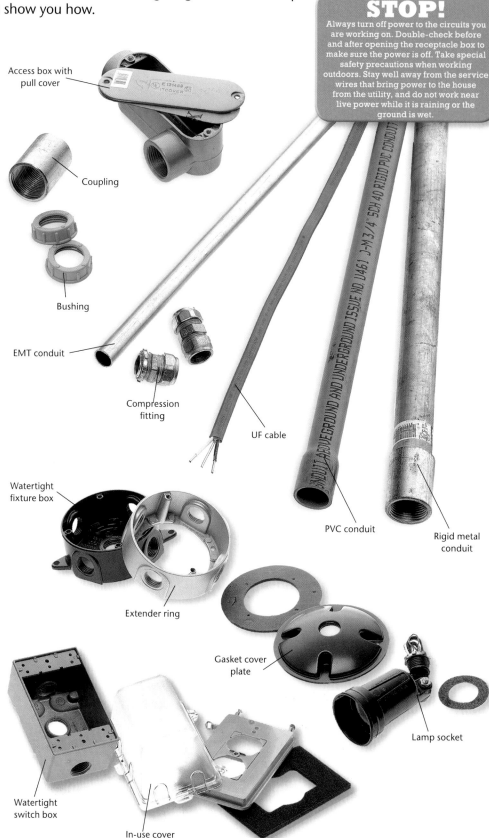

Access box with pull cover

Coupling

Bushing

EMT conduit

Compression fitting

UF cable

PVC conduit

Rigid metal conduit

Watertight fixture box

Extender ring

Gasket cover plate

Lamp socket

Watertight switch box

In-use cover

Time Commitment
An afternoon or a weekend, depending on the project

Tools You'll Need
Screwdriver
Wire stripper
Lineman's pliers

Related Topics
Calculating usage & capacity, 282–283
Common wiring methods, 28–31
Shutting off & restoring power, 50–51
Stripping & joining wire, 54–59
Tapping into power, 136–137
Testing methods, 52–53
Tools for running cable & installing boxes, 46–49
Wiring with conduit, 66–69

Plastic conduit (schedule 40 PVC) is a popular type of outdoor conduit. It is a good choice for direct burial because it's lightweight and doesn't corrode. Schedule 80 PVC is even sturdier.

Some local codes require rigid metal conduit, which is pricy and requires threaded fittings. It is tricky to install; consider hiring a pro. EMT metal conduit is not recommended for burial, but is sometimes acceptable for exposed locations above ground level, such as on the side of a house. Outdoors, EMT must be used with watertight compression fittings.

Extending Wiring Outdoors

Routing a circuit to the outside of your house requires the same procedures as extending an indoor circuit. You can tap into an existing switch, fixture, receptacle, or junction box, as long as doing so will not overload the circuit.

The illustrations on this page show how to extend a circuit outside to a new device. If you already have an outdoor receptacle or a porch light, you can use an extender ring. It adds space to the box for splicing the new wires, which run through conduit to the new device.

To bring cable from inside the house, the easiest way is to install a new receptacle box back to back with an existing box in an interior room, feeding the cable from the existing box to the new box. NM cable is often allowed because the cable isn't exposed to the weather. Another option is to tap into a junction box in the attic and run cable outside through an LB fitting to the new device.

You can, of course, install a new circuit for outdoor use. Run the cable directly from the service panel to a junction box on an inside wall near where the cable will exit, then run UF cable and outdoor conduit from the junction box to the outside.

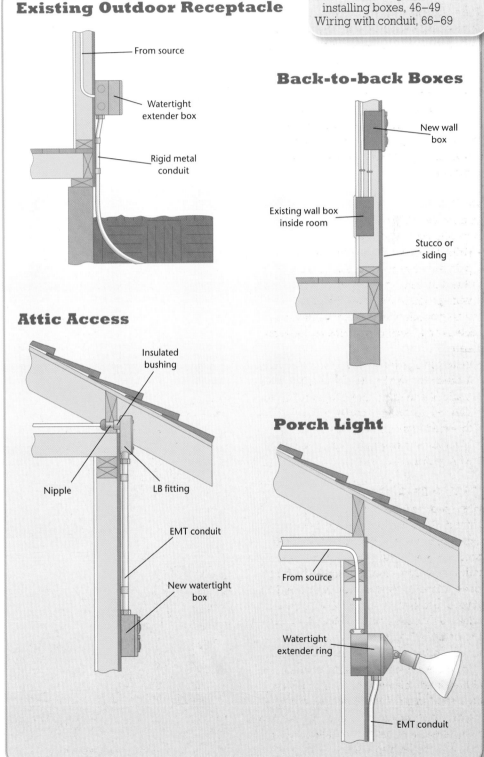

Exterior Fixtures

You can use an outdoor receptacle to power everything from low-voltage outdoor lights to an electric lawn mower. Pumps or filters for pools, spas, ponds, or fountains usually plug into outdoor GFCI receptacles.

STOP!
Always turn off power to the circuits you are working on. Double-check before and after opening the receptacle box to make sure the power is off.

Outdoor Receptacle Parts

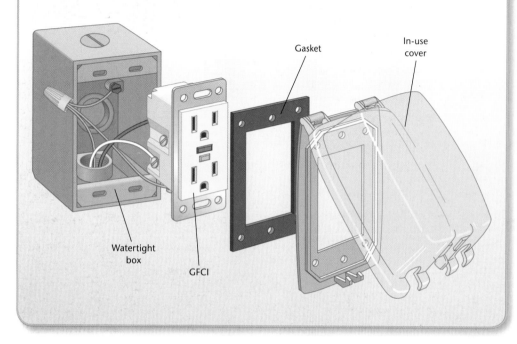

Gasket

In-use cover

Watertight box

GFCI

Wiring an Outdoor Receptacle

While you're installing a receptacle, it's easy to run conduit and cable from the box to other outdoor electrical devices and fixtures. A new receptacle should be GFCI protected. Make sure to locate it where it won't get bumped by a lawn mower, and out of the reach of small children.

In most cases you can use PVC conduit, but use rigid metal conduit if it's required by local codes. Cut and dry-fit the pipe lengths and fittings, then disassemble them carefully, keeping the parts in order. For each joint, apply PVC wiring cement to the inside of the fitting and the outside of the pipe, push the pipe into the fitting, add a partial turn, and hold for 10 seconds or so. Work carefully, because the connection is quick and permanent.

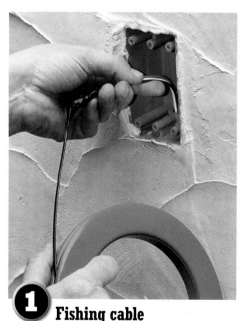

1 Fishing cable

- Fish individual wires of UF cable through the conduit
- If the cable runs are short, simply push the cable through the pipes
- If the run is long, or if you have several turns to make, use a fish tape

2 Wire receptacle

- Wire the GFCI receptacle just as you would inside the house
- Here we show the wiring for single-location protection

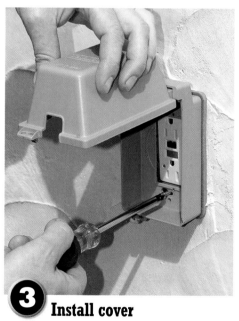

3 Install cover

- Mount the receptacle and then add the in-use cover
- Position the gasket so it seals completely around the perimeter of the box
- Take care to keep it in place as you screw on the cover

Time Commitment
A few hours

Tools You'll Need
Screwdriver
Wire stripper
Lineman's pliers

Related Topics
Calculating usage & capacity, 282–283
Common wiring methods, 28–31
Shutting off & restoring power, 50–51
Stripping & joining wire, 54–59
Tapping into power, 136–137
Testing methods, 52–53
Tools for running cable & installing boxes, 46–49
Wiring with conduit, 66–69

Switch to Bypass Timer

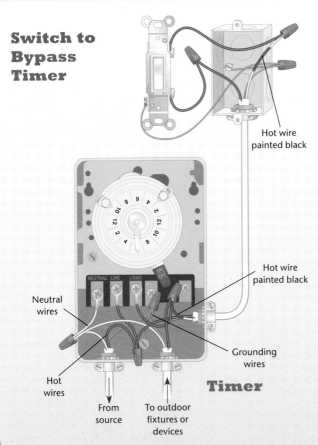

Hot wire painted black

Hot wire painted black

Neutral wires

Grounding wires

Hot wires

From source

To outdoor fixtures or devices

Timer

Wiring a Timer

By wiring an indoor switch and timer to an outdoor lighting circuit, you can turn on outdoor lights and other devices from inside the house or let the timer turn them on automatically. If you wire the switch to the automatic timer in a switch loop, you can bypass the timer and turn the lights on or off directly as well.

Connect the incoming black hot wires to the "line" terminal of the timer and the outgoing hot wire and switch wire to the "load" terminal. Some timers may have wire leads instead of screw terminals. Set the timer according to the manufacturer's instructions.

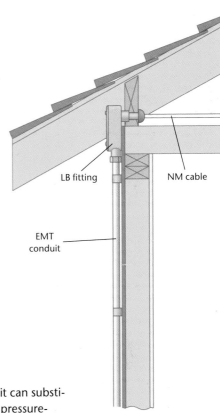

LB fitting

NM cable

EMT conduit

Driptight subpanel

Running Underground Cable

This drawing shows some typical uses of three types of conduit and UF cable. Follow local codes regarding the depth at which conduit and cable must be buried. In the installation shown here, rigid metal conduit with a sweep elbow is run into a trench, and UF cable runs through it. Once the approved depth is reached, PVC conduit can substitute for the metal conduit. A pressure-treated board can help protect the PVC.

In some areas, it is common to run rigid metal or PVC conduit into the trench, then run bare UF cable once the required depth is reached. Again, a rot-resistant board may be required. EMT conduit cannot be used underground, but it may be used to protect aboveground wiring runs, as shown.

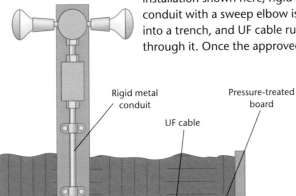

Rigid metal conduit

Pressure-treated board

UF cable

PVC conduit

Watertight bushing

Rigid metal conduit

Wiring an Outdoor Kitchen

Yesterday's simple grills have, for many people, grown into full-scale outdoor kitchens, with counters, storage, grills, and sinks with faucets. More ambitious kitchens include many features that call for electrical service.

Running Outdoor Lines

Outdoor kitchens may include receptacles for countertop appliances, lighting and overhead fans, garbage disposers, water heaters, refrigerators, and even home-entertainment systems. Some outdoor cooking equipment, such as infrared grills, needs standard-voltage wiring as well.

Many of the wiring techniques for an outdoor kitchen are described in the preceding section. Often, however, outdoor kitchen wiring runs not only underground but also through poured concrete or concrete block. PVC conduit is usually employed for wiring in these situations.

To build such a kitchen, you'll need a permit that covers the framing and masonry work, as well as the plumbing and electrical components. Often, the conduit will run alongside other lines, such as the water supply, water drain, and gas lines. In many cases, the utility lines emerge from the concrete inside the counter structure, below the sink.

No matter how well an outdoor counter is built, rainwater can seep in. Slope the concrete away from the utility lines, and keep all connections and devices at least a foot above the ground.

Connecting to Receptacles & Fixtures

From inside a counter structure, you can chisel or drill holes through the concrete block to run conduit to the outside wall of the counter, or to the backsplash behind the countertop. These lines can attach to outdoor boxes that are set in the block or the backsplash so that the front edges come flush with the finished stucco, stone, or other facing material.

Bringing electricity directly to a backyard barbecue allows you to see what you are cooking without the harsh glare of floodlights.

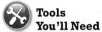 **Time Commitment**
Several weekends

 **Tools You'll Need**
Screwdriver
Wire stripper
Lineman's pliers
Chisel
Drill

Related Topics
Calculating usage & capacity, 282–283
Common wiring methods, 28–31
Stripping & joining wire, 54–59
Tapping into power, 136–137
Testing methods, 52–53
Tools for running cable & installing boxes, 46–49
Wiring with conduit, 66–69

Before a pour

Utility lines—from water to gas to power—are laid out amid the rebar before concrete is poured.

After a pour

Lines for gas, water, and power emerge through the concrete under a future counter.

Working with PVC

PVC wiring cement should be applied to the inside of fittings and the outside pipe.

Under counters

Here the conduit is exposed and runs through a receptacle box that supplies a garbage disposer and water heater.

On structures

Lines for standard-voltage lights have been run to each side of this pizza oven.

On counters

A low-voltage transformer can plug into a receptacle inside the counter structure; the thin wires are encased in conduit where they run through the masonry structure.

7

Installing Fans, Heaters, Appliances

In this chapter, we show you how to cool your home with a roof or house fan, vent a bathroom, and replace a range hood. We also provide step-by-step instructions so you can install a wall heater, baseboard heater, or even a heated floor. Finally, we show you how to install a new garbage disposer with a shock-proof air-activated switch, as well as a money-saving tankless water heater.

Chapter Contents

Smoke & Carbon Monoxide Alarms
page 193

Wiring Appliances
page 194

Garbage Disposers
page 197

Tankless Water Heaters
page 198

page 190

Roof & House Fans

Combined with good insulation, a roof fan is a great way to keep a house comfortable and energy efficient. Whole-house fans pull warm air from your home into the attic, where it can escape. Roof fans pull warm air from the attic to the outside.

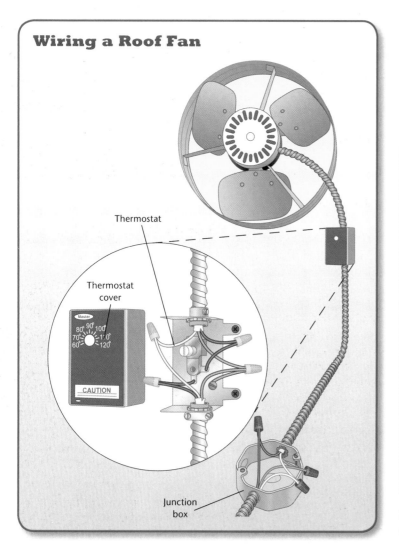

Wiring a Roof Fan

Thermostat

Thermostat cover

Master
80° 90° 100°
70° 110°
60° 120°

CAUTION

Junction box

Pulling hot air out of an attic with a roof fan helps cool your entire house, which can reduce expensive air-conditioning use.

Keys to Attic Ventilation

To allow air to flow freely through the attic, there should be vents near the base of the attic walls—usually at the eaves—and near or at the roof peak. Local codes can tell you how much attic insulation you need.

If an attic is appropriately insulated and vented but still gets stiflingly hot in summer, a gable or roof fan may help. A fan is rated by the amount of air it pulls, measured in cubic feet per minute (CFM). Which unit you choose depends on the size of the attic.

The fan should be wired to a thermostat (included with most models), which kicks on when the air gets hot. You may also want to wire the fan to a switch in the attic or in the room below so you can turn it on and off yourself. Use in-line rather than switch-loop wiring so you can disconnect the fan from the circuit.

To bring power to the fan, you may be able to connect to a junction box in the attic. If not, run cable from a receptacle or switch box in the floor below. Consult the fan's literature to find out how many watts (or amps) it pulls.

Installing a Gable Fan

Position a gable fan fairly near the roof's peak. If there is an existing gable vent with louvers, you may be able to install the fan against the vent. Make sure the existing vent is protected from rain, however, or the fan could be ruined within months. Ideally, there should be an overhang that keeps vertical rain from hitting the vent, plus closing louvers that shut out wind-blown horizontal rain.

For a new louvered vent, drill locator holes from the attic to the outside of the house and cut out a section of siding for the vent. Attach the vent to the siding with screws (above).

Consult the manufacturer's literature for the dimensions of the frame required to hold the fan. If a stud is in the way, you must cut it and add replacement framing. Measure 1½ inches below and above the opening to cut the stud. Then securely attach horizontal 2-by headers and vertical 2-by support pieces between the top and bottom headers. Attach the fan. Some models mount to the framing; others also require a mounting board.

Drive screws to mount the thermostat to a nearby framing member. Run two-wire cable from the power source to the thermostat, but do not connect to power yet. At the thermostat, strip sheathing and clamp the cable. Strip wires; connect the grounds, the hot wire, and the neutral wire. At the junction box, receptacle box, or switch box, shut off power and verify that power is off. Strip sheathing, clamp the cable, and splice the ground, neutral, and hot wires. Restore power and test the fan.

Roof Fan

A roof fan moves air more efficiently than a gable fan, because it sucks air directly out of the roof. It is wired like a gable fan, but is more difficult to install. From inside the attic, drill a locator hole near the peak of the roof, centered between rafters. On the roof, use a reciprocating saw to cut a hole according to the fan instructions.

Work carefully to achieve an installation that won't leak later on. Cut back shingles as needed, then slip the fan into place, with the upper part of the flange covered by shingles and the lower part resting on top of the shingles (right). Nail the flange to the roof, then cover the nail heads and the perimeter of the exposed flange with roofing cement.

In the attic, attach the thermostat to a nearby framing member. Run cable and make connections as for a gable fan.

Whole-house Fan

A whole-house fan can pull hot, sometimes moist air from the house and into the attic, where the air can vent outdoors. In medium-hot weather, it's an economical alternative to air conditioning, reducing the indoor temperature by about 5 degrees and creating a gentle breeze in parts of the house. You'll need to open a screened window or two on the first floor for the fan to work successfully.

To install a whole-house fan, you must cut a hole in a hallway ceiling under the attic. With most models, you need not cut through joists, just through the drywall or plaster. Inside the attic, build a 2-by-4 frame on top of the joists and mount the fan on top of the frame. To keep attic insulation away from the fan, you may be able to use baffles from the manufacturer, or you might add framing pieces between the joists.

Once the fan is attached, wire it to power as you would a gable fan. Some models have pull-chain switches. Alternatively, run cable into the room below and install a fan switch, which could be a timer switch.

Finally, attach the shutter unit to cover the hole in the hallway ceiling. Make sure the shutters easily open and close when the fan turns on and off.

Bathroom Vent Fans

Bathroom fans remove odors and the moist, warm air that can promote mildew. If a bathroom lacks a fan, or the current fan does not reduce the humidity, installing a new fan is a smart and economical improvement.

The ceiling fan in this bathroom ensures that a person in the bathtub will be able to watch TV, even if someone else is taking a steamy shower.

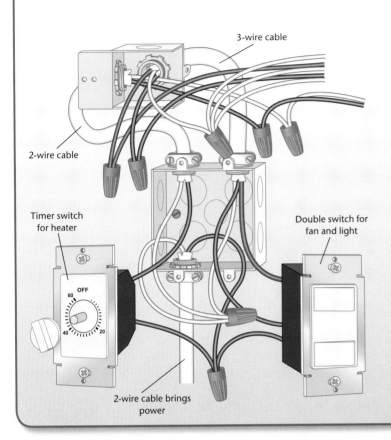

3-wire cable

2-wire cable

Timer switch for heater

OFF
60
40   20

Double switch for fan and light

2-wire cable brings power

Planning the Wiring

Before buying a unit with multiple features, make sure to plan the wiring.

- To replace a light fixture with a fan unit, check the wattage and make sure that the fan will not overload the circuit. If there is no existing light, you'll need to run cable and tap into power.
- If the unit only has a fan, or if it has a light and a fan that always come on together, you only need two-wire cable between the switch and the fan and you can use a standard single-pole switch.
- If you want to control a light and a fan separately, you'll need three-wire cable from the switch to the fan, and you will install either a two-function fan/light switch or separate switches for the fan and the light, requiring a two-gang box for the two switches.
- If the unit has a fan, a light, and a heater, you will need to run either a three-wire cable plus a two-wire cable, or three two-wire cables, between the switch box and the fixture. One common arrangement is to control the light and the fan with a two-function switch and to put the heater on a timer switch, as shown at left. A heater pulls plenty of wattage, so you may need to run a new, dedicated circuit from the service panel.

Choosing a Fan

Replacing an existing fan with a new one is about as easy as replacing a light fixture, if you can reuse the existing ductwork. Make sure that the new unit fits the existing opening and that its vent opening is in the same position as the old one. Here are some other things to consider when you are choosing a bath fan.

FAN POWER

Before buying the fan, determine the room size. If the ceiling is 8 feet high, multiply the room's width times its length, and then multiply that number by 1.1. The result is the minimum rating, measured in cubic feet per minute (CFM), of the fan you should buy.

Be aware, however, that a fan's ability to remove air depends on the ductwork. If there is a short, straight horizontal run with smooth, solid ducting, then the fan can pull air easily. If the duct has to travel more than 6 feet, uses ribbed flexible ducts, or travels upward, circulating the air will be tougher. When in doubt, buy a more powerful fan.

THE NOISE FACTOR

A bath fan may come with a sone rating, which tells you how noisy it will be. Two sones is about equal to the amount of noise a refrigerator makes. "Ultra silent" bath fans are often rated at less than one-half sone.

AUTOMATIC FEATURE

Because of increased concern over mold and volatile organic compounds (VOCs) in modern, airtight homes, some bathroom fans turn on automatically when a sensor detects a certain level of humidity. If the passive vents in your bathroom are not removing enough humidity, consider installing one of these automatic units.

LIGHTS & HEATERS

Many bathroom fans also have lights, and some even have heating units. It's a good idea to put a heating unit on a timer switch so it doesn't accidentally get left on, gobbling electricity, for a long time.

Fan-light with Duct Fitting

Fan-light with Pewter Finish

Installing a Vent Fan

Before you install a vent fan in a bathroom, spend some time in your attic to determine the best route for the fan's ductwork.

Good ventilation is especially important in small bathrooms with limited air circulation.

Planning the Vents

To install a new fan in place of a light fixture, you'll need to cut a hole in the ceiling where the fixture is, then route ducts to an exterior wall, cut through the wall, and connect a vent cap. If the vent work is beyond your skill level, call in a heating contractor.

Make vent runs as straight and short as possible—ideally, a solid horizontal vent that goes straight out the wall. However, you may need to use flexible ducts for part or all of the run, or go through the roof. This is more work than going through the siding, but sometimes there is no easy way to exit the siding.

Venting Through a Wall

Venting Through a Roof

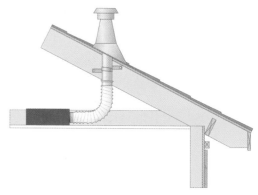

Stuff to Buy

BATHROOM FAN
DUCTWORK Also buy duct tape and self-tapping sheet metal screws
BASIC SUPPLIES Exterior caulk, wire nuts, electrical tape

Time Commitment

Most of a day

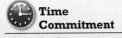
Tools You'll Need

Stud finder
Drywall saw
Drill
Reciprocating saw
Tin snips
Screwdriver
Wire stripper
Lineman's pliers

Related Topics

Cable connections, 144–145
Calculating usage & capacity, 282–283
Common wiring methods, 28–31
Replacing a range hood, 184–185
Stripping & joining wire, 54–59
Wiring in finished rooms, 130–135

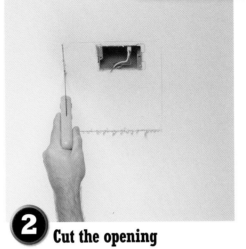

① Mark the opening

- With the power off, remove the old fixture
- Position the template or housing on the ceiling, aligned with the ceiling joist
- Trace around the template or housing to mark the opening
- If you have access from the attic, position the housing or template next to the joist and trace around it

② Cut the opening

- Use a stud finder, or probe with a bent wire, to be sure no framing will obstruct the fan
- Cut the opening according to the manufacturer's directions, using a drywall saw

③ Run ductwork

- Plan the location of the ductwork
- At the wall, drill locator holes from inside
- From the outside, cut a hole in the siding for the duct
- Attach the ductwork to the end cap; make sure you can reach the other end later to attach the duct to the fan unit
- Caulk around the hole, press the end cap into the caulk, and drive screws to attach the cap

④ Install fan

- Attach the ductwork to the fan unit
- If there is insulation in the attic above, tuck it around the ductwork

⑤ Connect the wires

- Depending on the fan, you may be able to re-use ceiling-light wires
- Strip sheathing and clamp the cable or cables to the box
- Make the wiring connections at the fan
- Screw the housing to the joist

⑥ Finish installation

- Attach the fixture to the housing and attach the grille to the fixture
- Screw in a light bulb and attach the diffuser
- Make the connections at the switch box
- Restore power and test

Replacing a Range Hood

A range hood, installed directly above a range or cooktop, is designed to clear away smoke and odors. Since a hood also has a light, it should be positioned about 58 to 60 inches above the floor to prevent glare in the eyes of a person standing at the range.

Common Duct Paths

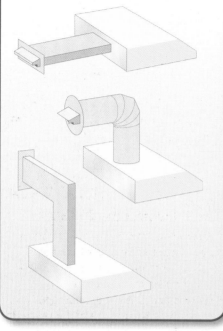

In some kitchens, a canopy range hood is the architectural centerpiece of the room.

Choosing a Range Hood

Most range hoods are 30 inches wide and fit under short cabinets. Like other vent fans, range hoods are rated according to the speed with which they are able to move air, measured in cubic feet per minute (CFM). An average 30-inch-wide hood is rated at 100 CFM; a 200-CFM unit is more effective. As with a bathroom fan, the type and length of ductwork will affect efficiency. If the duct is short, made of solid venting, and horizontal, it will work better than if the run is long, uses flexible lines, or rises upward.

If you use the fan often, you will want one that is quiet. Most vent hoods produce between 3 and 8 sones (the lower the number, the quieter the fan).

Where running ductwork is difficult—for instance, in an old building with double-brick walls—you may be replacing a ductless range hood. Instead of expelling air to the outside, it simply runs the air through a filter and back into the kitchen. If you rarely burn food or create unpleasant odors, it may be all you need.

Some higher-end range hoods have exposed ductwork for a sleek, modern style. A canopy range hood is in some ways simpler to install than an under-cabinet model, but it is heavy and requires a large roof cap, making it a job best left to professionals.

Doing the Job

Remove the old hood and take it to the store to find a new one that will fit. Make sure that the existing ductwork will attach to the new hood and that there is a knockout for the cable in a convenient place. Depending on the configuration of your existing range hood, you may have to purchase either 3¼-by-10-inch rectangular duct or 6-inch-diameter round duct. The illustration at above, left, shows some arrangements. In addition to the ducts, buy any fittings, as well as an end cap or roof cap, that might need to be replaced. You'll also need self-tapping sheet-metal screws and professional-quality duct tape.

A modest-size range hood may use less than 2 amps (240 watts), but commercial-type models can use much more. If the new hood uses more wattage (amperage) than the old one, check to be sure it will not overload the circuit.

Stuff to Buy

UNDER-CABINET RANGE HOOD

DUCTWORK Also buy duct tape and self-tapping sheet metal screws

BASIC SUPPLIES Wire nuts, electrical tape

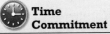 **Time Commitment**

Half a day

Tools You'll Need

Tin snips
Screwdriver
Drill
Wire stripper
Lineman's pliers

Related Topics

Cable connections, 144–145
Calculating usage & capacity, 282–283
Common wiring methods, 28–31
Stripping & joining wire, 54–59
Wiring in finished rooms, 130–135

A new range hood makes a nice complement to a new stove, resulting in a relatively low-cost kitchen remodel.

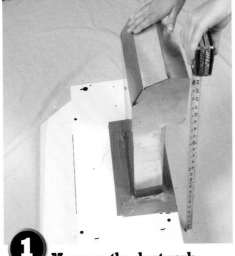

1 Measure the ductwork

- If necessary, cut openings in the cabinet or wall for the ductwork
- Plan how you will assemble the pieces—you may need to make the final connection inside a cabinet
- Dry-fit the pieces

2 Connect the ductwork

- Assemble as much of the ductwork as possible before you install the hood
- Drive four or more self-tapping sheet-metal screws into each joint
- Wrap joints tightly with duct tape
- If you can't use screws and duct tape (for example, inside a wall), have one piece slide at least 4 inches into the other

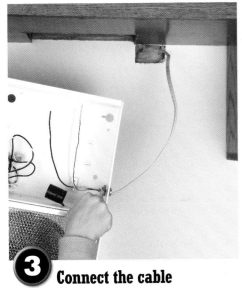

3 Connect the cable

- Without connecting the power, run two-wire cable from the existing power source
- Remove the cover from the hood's electrical box
- Strip 8 inches or so of sheathing and then clamp the cable to the hood

4 Attach the hood

- Slip the range hood into place, threading the cable into the wall as you go
- Attach the hood by driving short screws into the cabinet above

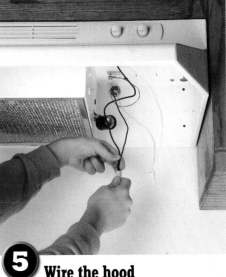

5 Wire the hood

- Make the electrical connections, splicing the grounds, the black wires, and the white wires
- Replace the hood's electrical cover
- Shut off power to the box you will tap for power, then make the connections
- Restore power and test

Wall Heaters

Degree of Difficulty

● Moderate

This wall heater has a built-in blower, so even though it's small, it can heat a medium-sized bathroom. Once you've decided how to bring power to the unit, installing the heater is relatively easy. Most models have a built-in thermostat.

Installing a Wall Heater

In choosing a wall heater, the first step is to decide how many watts of heat you need—and that depends mainly on the room size. In general, a 1,500-watt heater effectively heats 100 to 150 square feet. For a smaller room, buy a 1,000-watt unit. A 2,500-watt heater can handle a room up to 250 square feet. If the room is drafty or has high ceilings, you may need extra heat; if it is on a top floor and gets some heat from the rest of the house, you may need less. The wall heater shown here can be modified to pull from 375 to 1,500 watts (see Steps 2 and 3).

Make sure the heater you choose will not overload the circuit you tap into. If there is no conveniently located receptacle, junction box, or switch on a circuit with enough available wattage, you will need a new circuit. A unit rated at 2,500 or more watts requires a 240-volt circuit.

If you are working in unfinished framing, position the housing with its front edge protruding from the stud by the thickness of the finished wall material (in most cases, ½ inch for ½-inch drywall).

This slate-surface, energy-saving radiant wall heater with towel racks is designed for the bathroom.

1 Cut the hole

- Choose a location that's out of reach of small children, several feet from where people will sit or stand, and not too high
- Use a stud finder to locate a stud
- Trace the housing of the heater flush to the side of the stud
- Cut the shape you traced

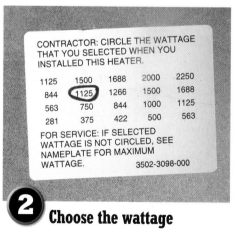

2 Choose the wattage

- Disassemble the motor and heater from the housing
- Select the correct wattage as described in the text at above, left
- Circle the correct number on the inside information tag

3 Set the wattage

- To lower the wattage, snip one or two of the jumper wires
- Consult the installation literature for the numbers
- Cut wires with diagonal cutters as close to the terminal as possible

 **Stuff to Buy**

WALL HEATER
BASIC SUPPLIES Cable, wire nuts, and electrical tape

 **Time Commitment**

Three to four hours

Tools You'll Need

Stud finder
Drywall saw
Diagonal cutters
Screwdriver
Wire stripper
Lineman's pliers

 Related Topics

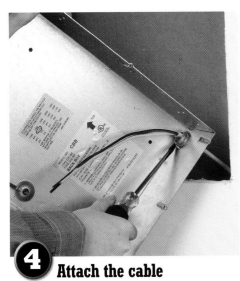

4 Attach the cable

- Run cable from your chosen source through the hole in the wall, but do not make the final connection to power yet
- Strip the sheathing so there is plenty of wire to reach the heater's leads
- Clamp the cable to the housing

5 Secure the housing

- Slip the housing into the hole, its front edge flush with the wall surface
- Drive screws securely through the housing and into the stud

6 Wire the heater

- For a 120-volt heater, use wire nuts to splice the ground wire to the green lead connected to the housing
- Splice the white wire to the neutral lead (which in this case is red)
- Splice the black wire to the black lead

7 Install the heater and grille

- Slip the motor and heater into the housing
- Drive screws to secure the unit in place
- Attach the grille and push on the control knob
- With the power still off, connect to the power source
- Restore power and test the heater

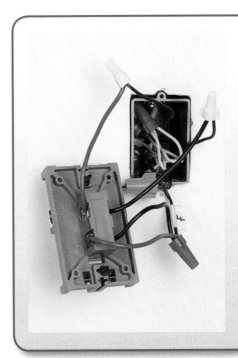

Thermostat Option

Most wall heaters have a built-in thermostat. If yours does not, cut a hole and install a box for a thermostat as described on page 257. Run power through the thermostat box, then on to the heater, and wire the heater.

Baseboard Heaters

Baseboard heaters come in 120- and 240-volt versions. Most 120-volt heaters require a separate circuit. A 240-volt hardwired heater shown here is the most energy-efficient option and will probably require a dedicated 240-volt circuit rated at 20 or 30 amps.

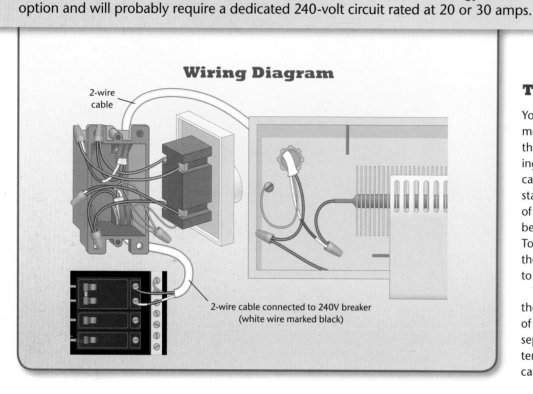

Wiring Diagram

2-wire cable

2-wire cable connected to 240V breaker (white wire marked black)

Thermostat Options

You can buy a unit with a built-in thermostat or plan to install a separate wall thermostat as shown here. The cable bringing 240-volt power has two hot wires, each carrying 120 volts. A double-line thermostat, as shown at left, is connected to both of the hot wires and has an "off" position because it can completely shut off power. To wire it, run power into the line side of the thermostat, out the load side, and then to the heater.

The steps show how to wire a single-line thermostat, which can interrupt only one of the two hot wires. It does not have a separate off position, but simply sets the temperature at which the unit automatically comes on.

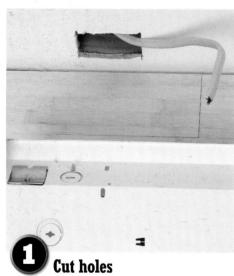

1 Cut holes

- Cut a hole for the thermostat's switch box
- Do not connect 12-2 cable to the service panel yet, but run it from the vicinity of the panel to the hole
- Remove the baseboard at the heater location
- Cut a hole for the cable where the cable can enter a cable clamp or knockout on the heater

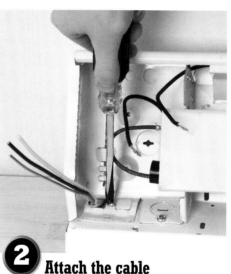

2 Attach the cable

- Remove the electrical cover plate from the heater
- Strip 8 inches of sheathing from the cable, remove a knockout in the rear of the heater, and run the cable through the hole
- Inside the heater, connect the ground wires
- Mark the white wire black, then splice the white and black wires to the heater leads
- Replace the cover

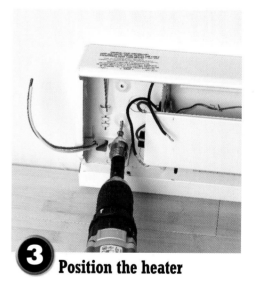

3 Position the heater

- Locate and mark wall studs
- Run cable through the hole in the wall
- Position the heater against the wall and on the finished floor; if more flooring or carpeting will be added, raise the heater that amount
- Drive screws through the heater and into studs
- To avoid creaking sounds as the heater works, back off each screw by half a turn from full tightness

Stuff to Buy	 **Time Commitment**	**Tools You'll Need**	**Related Topics**
BASEBOARD HEATER **SINGLE-LINE THERMOSTAT** **BASIC SUPPLIES** Cable, wire nuts, and electrical tape	Three to four hours	Drywall saw Stud finder Screwdriver Wire stripper Lineman's pliers	Cable connections, 144–145 Calculating usage & capacity, 282–283 Common wiring methods, 28–31 Stripping & joining wire, 54–59 Wall heaters, 186–187 Wiring in finished rooms, 130–135

In the future, if you need to do work on the unit, make sure to shut off power to the circuit. A single-line thermostat shuts off power to only one of the wires, leaving the other one hot.

Installing a 240-volt Baseboard Heater

It is possible to connect a 240-volt heater to an existing 240-volt circuit, if that does not overload the circuit. But it is more common to install a new 240-volt circuit. If a heater or any other appliance will be on for more than three hours at a time, the circuit rating must be reduced to 80 percent of its normal value. A normal 20-amp circuit, for instance, is then rated for 0.8 × 20 amps = 16 amps. If your eyes just glazed over, that's a pretty good sign that you should hire an electrician to help you complete this project.

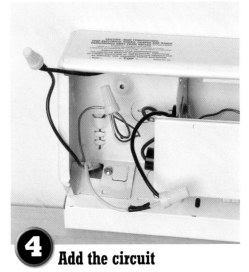

4 Add the circuit

- Shut off the main breaker to the service panel and test to confirm it is off
- Strip plenty of sheathing, clamp the cable, and run the wires neatly around the perimeter of the panel
- Connect the ground wire to the ground/ neutral bus bar
- Connect the white wire and the black wire to each of the terminals on a double-pole breaker, then install the breaker

5 Wire the thermostat

- Strip sheathing from the two cables, clamp them to the box, and anchor the box
- Connect the grounds
- Mark both white wires black (to indicate they are hot) and splice them together
- Splice each black lead to a black house wire
- Mount the thermostat
- Restore power to the circuit and test the thermostat and heater
- Cut the baseboard as needed and re-install pieces beside the heater

Because baseboard heaters are usually rather plain in their design, they blend easily into their surroundings.

Heated Floors

Warming mats, installed under flooring, provide steady, evenly distributed heat in a room. They may not generate enough heat to warm an entire home on a extremely cold days, but they are a good supplement.

Anatomy of an Electric Mat

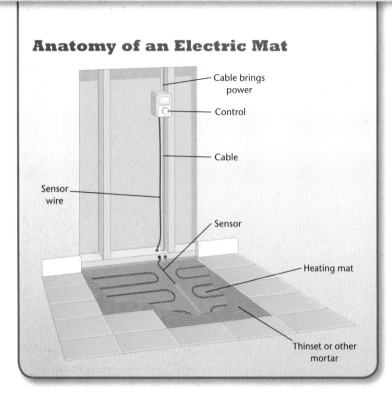

- Cable brings power
- Control
- Cable
- Sensor wire
- Sensor
- Heating mat
- Thinset or other mortar

About Electric Mats

Electric mats can be installed in any room where the floor will be finished with ceramic or stone tile. They cannot be installed, however, in rooms that will have carpeting, wood, vinyl, or other resilient flooring.

The most common method is to attach the mat to a concrete backerboard substrate. Thinset mortar (not an organic tile mastic) can then be troweled over the mats and tiles set in the mortar. You can also set the mats on a concrete slab substrate, troweling a bed of thickset or self-leveling mortar over the mats.

Mats come in 1-, 2-, and 3-foot widths and in lengths ranging from 5 to 40 feet. Make a scale drawing of the room and choose the mat sizes carefully, since you cannot cut a mat's blue power line to shorten its overall length. (You can, however, cut and arrange the orange matting to fit rooms of various shapes.)

You also cannot splice two mats together. If your floor is too large to be covered by one mat, you will need to use additional mats with separate power cables, each running separately to a controller.

Running Power

The circuit for any mat must be GFCI protected. The larger the mat, the more amperage it pulls. Small mats may pull as little as 1 amp, while larger mats can pull 8 amps. Once you have found out how many amps your mat will use, find a circuit that will not overload and plan how you will tap into it. If there is no circuit that can supply the extra amperage without overloading, add a new circuit.

Locate the new box for the controller in a place where it is convenient to run the power lead. Without connecting to power as yet, run two-wire cable from the power source into the box.

In addition to a thermostatic sensor, you may also install a timer to turn the heat on and off at certain hours. The timer will require another box.

A heated floor is a luxurious touch in a bathroom.

Stuff to Buy

RADIANT HEAT MATTING
STAPLES If you are not using a staple gun, get double-sided tape
THINSET MORTAR MIX
BASIC SUPPLIES Cable, wire nuts, and electrical tape

 Time Commitment

A weekend

 Tools You'll Need

Digital multitester
Drill
Snips or cutters
Staple gun
Hot glue gun
Screwdriver
Wire stripper
Lineman's pliers
Trowel for mortar

Related Topics

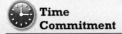

1 Test the mat

- Before installing a mat, use a digital multi-tester to test for breaks or shorts in the power line
- Touch the multitester's probes to two wire ends and make sure your readings are within the mat manufacturer's recommended range
- The manufacturer may supply a device that sounds an alarm if the wiring gets damaged during installation

2 Run the lines

- Cut two holes in the bottom plate of the wall for the power lead and sensor wire
- Make sure the holes are low enough so that the mortar will cover the lines
- Avoiding a sharp bend in either line, run both lines up and into the controller box

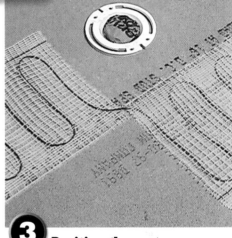

3 Position the mat

- Sweep and vacuum the substrate, then roll out the matting
- To fill spaces, cut the matting—but not the heating line—when you come to a wall or another stopping place
- The power lead must not cross over itself or come within 3 inches of itself
- Flip over one portion of the mat to offset the pieces

4 Alternate positioning

- Mat pieces can also be placed at right angles
- Remember: you can always cut the matting but never the heating line

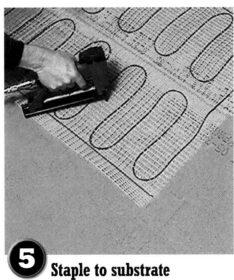

5 Staple to substrate

- Staple through the mesh matting to hold it in place
- Never use a stapler to secure the heating line to the substrate

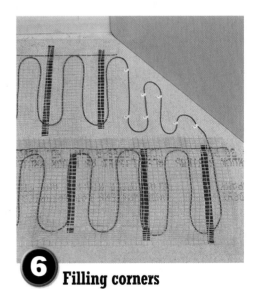

6 Filling corners

- At angled walls, carefully cut away matting and fill in voids with the heating line
- Secure heating line to substrate with clips provided by the manufacturer

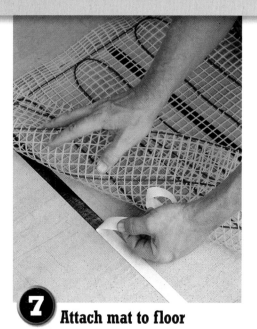

⑦ Attach mat to floor

- With the mat in position, lift up an end, apply double-sided tape, and press the mat onto the tape
- Alternatively, use a staple gun, stapling the matting only and not the heating line

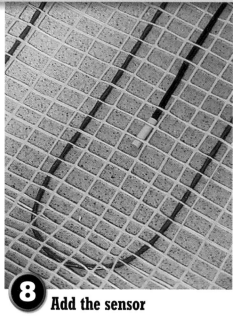

⑧ Add the sensor

- Weave the sensor line into the mat so it extends several feet into the room
- Place the sensor line halfway between two heating lines

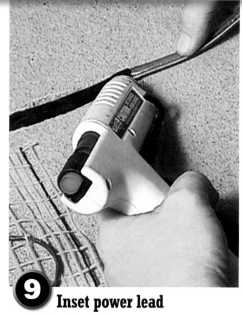

⑨ Inset power lead

- Chisel a channel in the substrate for the power lead
- Use a glue gun to adhere the power lead to the substrate

⑩ Wire the controller

- In the sensor box, use a multitester to check the mat again for resistance and shorts
- Use wire nuts to connect sensor controller to power source, then connect power leads and sensor
- Shut off power to the circuit and make the connections to power
- Restore power and turn the controller on briefly to make sure it heats, then turn it off

⑪ Add mortar and tile

- Trowel thinset or thickset mortar over the mat
- Lay the tile
- Take care not to damage the heating line as you work

Electric Heating Cable

Instead of installing mats with integral cables, as shown in Steps 1 through 7, you could install just the cable, available in long rolls. This allows you to create your own layout, which may be suitable for a space with lots of angles. You'll need to work carefully to keep the cable fairly consistently spaced, but galvanized straps are available that help maintain even spacing.

Smoke & Carbon Monoxide Alarms

In new construction, smoke detectors are required in each bedroom and the adjoining hall. You'll also need at least one on every floor, including the basement. Retrofitted detectors may be battery operated, but new installations must be hardwired models with battery backups. These will work even if you forget to change the batteries, and even if a fire damages the electrical circuit.

Carbon monoxide (CO) is an odorless gas emitted by fireplaces, furnaces, gas appliances, water heaters, and other combustion appliances. Under normal circumstances, it is carried safely out of the house by vents and chimneys. But it can build up to dangerous levels when a chimney becomes clogged or a vent pipe is disconnected. Even well-sealed ductwork may leak CO, if the parts are assembled wrong. Since residents won't smell or detect a CO build-up, detectors are especially important.

Codes call for CO detectors at various parts of the house. Carbon monoxide rises up through floors, so, for instance, a room directly above a boiler or water heater with malfunctioning ductwork may get nearly as much gas as the boiler room itself.

If a detector goes off, indicating high levels of CO, leave your house and call your gas company immediately. It should send a technician out for a free evaluation. If the detector

Wiring a Smoke Detector

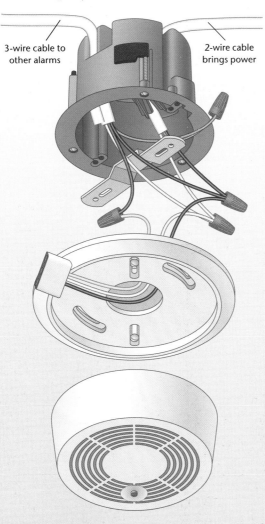

3-wire cable to other alarms

2-wire cable brings power

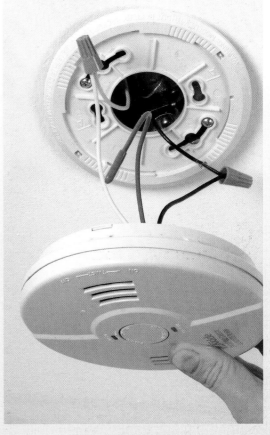

The wiring for a combination smoke and CO detector is essentially the same as the wiring for a detector that only senses one hazard or the other. Many newer detectors have a button so you can test them periodically.

sounds only while a fire is burning in the fireplace, call in a chimney sweep or a mason with chimney experience for an inspection.

The wiring for detectors should always be hot, not controlled by a switch or GFCI protected. In new construction, units must be wired together so that any alarm signal will be transmitted downstream and set off all the other alarms. To do this, run three-wire cable between the detectors, as shown in the illustration at left.

Install a detector powered by household current the same way you would a flush ceiling light, except that the box should provide always-hot rather than switched power. Turn off the power as usual before you begin the installa-

tion. The detector's body attaches to the electrical box via a mounting strap. Connect the ground to the box only, and then splice the black and white wires. Restore the power and use the button to test the detector.

Wiring Appliances

Many stationary appliances—electric water heaters, cooktops, or wall-mounted ovens, for instance—are hardwired directly to the circuit's wires without a receptacle. Connections are typically made inside a splice box on the appliance.

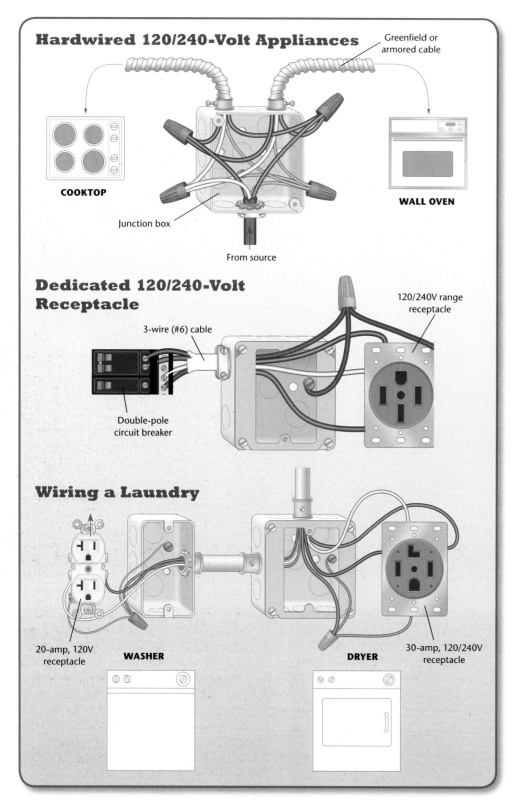

Hardwired 120/240-Volt Appliances

Greenfield or armored cable

COOKTOP

Junction box

From source

WALL OVEN

Dedicated 120/240-Volt Receptacle

3-wire (#6) cable

Double-pole circuit breaker

120/240V range receptacle

Wiring a Laundry

20-amp, 120V receptacle

WASHER

DRYER

30-amp, 120/240V receptacle

Ways to Wire Appliances

Most new appliances are not hardwired during installation. These days, it is more typical for an electrician to wire an appliance with a plug. An electric range, a heavy-duty air conditioner, or an electric dryer is plugged into a 240-volt receptacle on a dedicated circuit. Dishwashers, washing machines, smaller air conditioners, and garbage disposers usually plug into a 120-volt receptacle, which may or may not be on a dedicated circuit. Dishwashers and range hoods often plug into a 120-volt circuit that is not dedicated. A microwave oven plugs into a 20-amp, 120-volt receptacle; if the microwave's nameplate rating is more than half the capacity of the circuit, you may be required to put the microwave on its own circuit.

Wiring for a new high-voltage receptacle or hardwired appliance is run as for any new circuit. However, the job will be more difficult because you will either be running very thick cable, or thick wires inside large-diameter conduit or Greenfield. Plan the cable paths to avoid any sharp turns and consult your inspector to be sure you are running the right gauge of wire.

KITCHEN RANGES

Most electric kitchen ranges require a dedicated 120/240-volt circuit rated for either 40 or 50 amps (depending on the range's wattage) and a receptacle on a wall or on the floor. A gas range may need a 120-volt receptacle to power the lights and timer.

WALL OVENS & COOKTOPS

In most cases, separate electric wall ovens and cooktops share a 120/240-volt circuit that's rated for 40 or 50 amps. Cable is first routed from the service panel to a central junction box. From there, smaller wires branch off to the appliances. Most ovens and cooktops come with their own flexible cables, called whips. If yours do not, you can run individual wires inside Greenfield.

This laundry room shares space with a home office. Circuits for the washer and dryer are dedicated.

WASHERS & DRYERS

Most electric dryers plug into a receptacle on a dedicated 30-amp, 120/240-volt circuit. The receptacle may be mounted on the floor or on a wall.

Be sure the receptacle you buy satisfies codes and matches your dryer. Since the 1990s, dryer receptacles have been required to be wired with cable that has three wires plus a ground—a black, a red, a white, and a separate ground. Older installations may have just two-wire cable, with the white wire used as a hot and the ground wire used for neutral. The plug configuration has changed so that the old three-wire plugs will not work with newer, four-wire receptacles. If you are replacing an old dryer with a new one, you may be allowed to modify the plug, but it's a good idea to run new cable and install a new receptacle instead.

A washing machine needs a 20-amp, 120-volt receptacle. Codes often require the receptacle to be on a dedicated circuit; make sure that lights and other receptacles in the laundry area are not on the same circuit as the washer.

If the wiring will be exposed, conduit is a good choice. It's acceptable, and convenient, to use a single conduit for the wires for both appliances. The 120-volt circuit for the washer passes through the dryer's receptacle box, but the circuits are not connected to each other.

Garbage Disposers

Degree of Difficulty

● Easy

Replacing a garbage disposer is one of the simplest wiring (and plumbing) jobs you can tackle. The project on the opposite page includes an air-activated switch, which many codes now require for disposers and other appliances near sinks.

Switched-receptacle

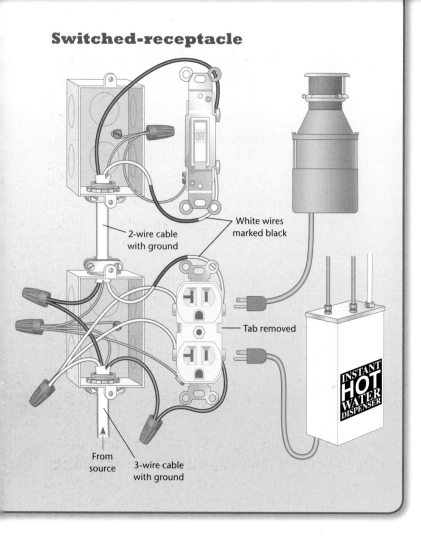

White wires marked black

2-wire cable with ground

Tab removed

From source

3-wire cable with ground

Wiring for Multiple Appliances

Most garbage disposers plug into a receptacle under the sink, either directly or via an air-activated switch controller, as shown in the photo at right and on the opposite page. A disposer may share a circuit with a dishwasher and perhaps a hot-water dispenser.

To wire for a disposer using a regular switch and a second appliance that does not require a switch at all (see illustration at above), split the receptacle. Wire it so that one of its plugs is controlled by a switch above the counter and the other plug is always hot. Plug the disposer into the switched plug and the other appliance into the always-hot plug. Place the wall switch near enough to the sink for convenience, but at least a foot away to keep it from getting splashed.

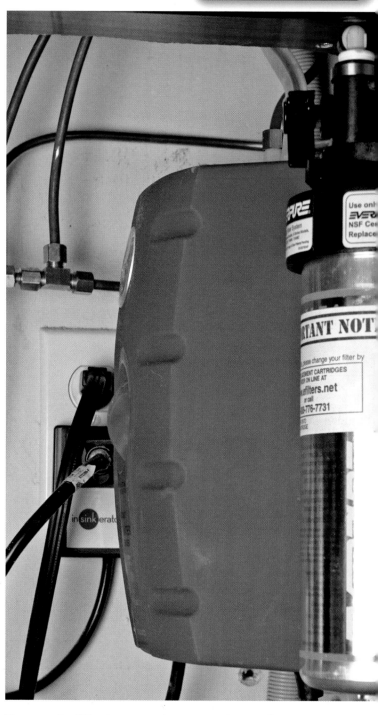

Here a water filter is mounted next to an instant-hot-water dispenser. Note that the garbage disposer is actually plugged into an air-activated switch, which is plugged into the same receptacle as the dispenser.

Stuff to Buy

GARBAGE DISPOSER
AIR-ACTIVATED SWITCH
BASIC SUPPLIES Wire nuts,
electrical tape, silicone

**Time
Commitment**

Two to three hours

**Tools
You'll Need**

Screwdriver
Drill, with bit for counter
material
Wire stripper
Lineman's pliers

**Related
Topics**

Cable connections, 144–145
Calculating usage & capacity,
282–283
Common wiring methods,
28–31
Replacing a split-circuit recep-
tacle, 118–119
Stripping & joining wire, 54–59

1 Assess connections

- Remove access plate from bottom of disposer
- Pull out hot and neutral leads; green screw is for plug's ground wire

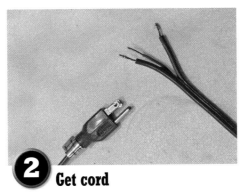

2 Get cord

- Most manufacturers supply a plug with cord attached
- Make sure your cord is three-pronged and includes a ground wire

3 Insert cord

- Push cord through cable clamp
- Attach ground to green screw

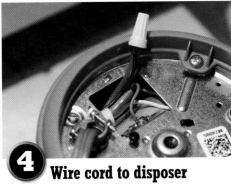

4 Wire cord to disposer

- Connect hot and neutral wires with wire nuts
- When pushing wires into disposer, be careful not to scratch insulation on metal edges

5 Attach access plate

- Secure plate with screws provided by manufacturer
- Tighten cable clamp on cord

6 Install air-activated switch

- Secure switch controller to wall under sink
- Make sure the air switch will reach the counter, and that the controller's plug will reach the receptacle

7 Install switch in counter

- Use a drill bit designed for your counter material
- The switch should have gaskets to prevent counter water from leaking under sink

8 Plug devices together

- After completing plumbing for disposer, plug the controller into the receptacle
- The disposer plugs into the controller

9 Test switch

- Run water and test the switch
- If you notice leaks, remember to unplug the disposer before making plumbing repairs

Tankless Water Heaters

In recent years, as energy costs have continued to skyrocket, an increasing number of homeowners have replaced their traditional storage-tank water heaters with tankless ones. For most homeowners, the savings average 30 percent per year.

STOP!
Always turn off power to the circuits you are working on. Double-check at the project site to make sure the power is off.

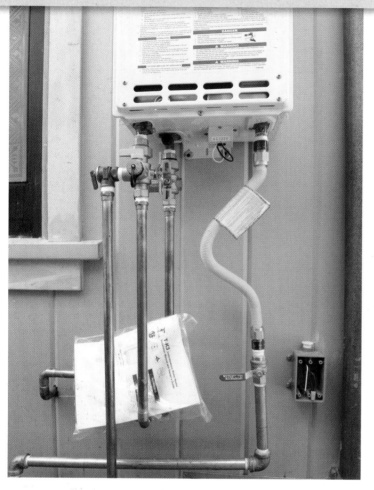

Installing a Tankless Water Heater

The device shown on the following pages heats up water using natural gas. A 120-volt switch is required for electronic ignition. Even though the switch does not require a great deal of power, codes may require you to give it a dedicated circuit. If codes permit you to put the switch on a shared circuit, it may be a good idea to dedicate a switch anyway so that you can turn off a breaker to, say, the ceiling lights in your kitchen without also shutting down your home's hot water.

Because this home is located in a mild climate, its hot-water heater has been installed on an exterior wall, which frees up about a closet's worth of space inside the home that would have been consumed by a traditional, bulky hot-water heater. Exterior installation also makes venting simple—a vent cap supplied by the manufacturer replaces potentially complicated duct-work and cutting a vent hole through a wall or roof.

Not all of the Steps that follow will necessarily apply to the system you install. For example, if your water heater is installed indoors, you will obviously not need to use exterior wiring techniques and hardware. In any event, always follow the manufacturer's instructions.

Before any electrical work is performed, the tankless hot-water heater should be mounted on the wall and connected to water and gas. The open electrical box to the right of the gas-line lever will be fitted with an outdoor-rated receptacle before being connected to a second box housing the heater's new switch.

① Cement PVC

- The heater switch will be connected to the receptacle box by a short length of flexible PVC pipe
- Apply PVC cement to ends of PVC pipes

② Attach switch box

- Level switch box before securing it to the wall with screws
- Measure a second piece of flexible PVC and attach its bottom end to the top of the switch box using PVC cement

 **Stuff to Buy**	**Time Commitment**	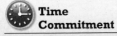 **Tools You'll Need**	**Related Topics**
TANKLESS WATER HEATER BASIC SUPPLIES Wire nuts, electrical tape, PVC conduit, PVC cement, watertight switch and receptacle boxes	Two to three hours	Screwdriver Drill with screwdriver bit Level Wire strippers	Cable connections, 144–145 Calculating usage & capacity, 282–283 Grounding, 22–23 Outdoor wiring, 170–171 Stripping & joining wire, 54–59

③ Push wire to switch box

- Since the distance is short, manually push a white neutral wire from the receptacle box, though the switch box, and to the heater
- Push a slightly longer length of green wire just as far as the switch box

④ Push wire to heater

- Tape the green wire to a length of colored wire and push both to the heater
- The switch that will be installed here does not have a ground screw, so the ground wire runs directly to the heater, but a future switch may have a ground, so leave a small loop of extra green wire in the switch box

⑤ Label load wires

- Push a short length of black wire from receptacle box to switch box
- Label the hot and neutral wires that go to the heater so there's no confusion when wiring the receptacle

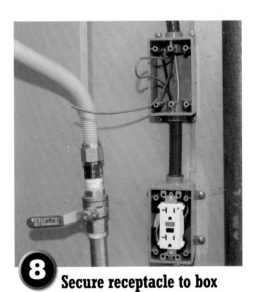

⑧ Secure receptacle to box

- In the switch box, there should now be an unattached black wire from the receptacle, an unattached red wire leading to the heater, an extra-long piece of green wire, and the white wire continuing uninterrupted from the receptacle to the heater (neutral wires are not attached to switches)
- The extra amount of green wire in the switch box is so it can be cut later for use on a switch that requires a ground

⑥ Wire receptacle from source

- Splice a green pigtail for the GFCI receptacle
- Attach source green from pigtail, white, and black wires to bottom of receptacle

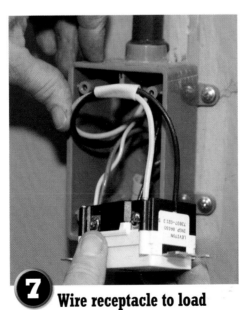

⑦ Wire receptacle to load

- Attach white and black wires marked in Step 5 to top of GFCI receptacle
- Gently push wires into receptacle box, being careful not to scratch insulation on box edges

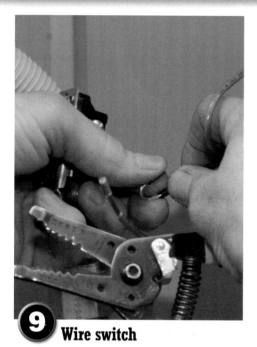

STOP!
Always turn off power to the circuits you are working on. Double-check at the project site to make sure the power is off.

9 Wire switch

- When working with twisted wire, trim about 1" of insulation from the wire's end, then cut the insulation again about ¼" in and slide it to the end of the wires so they are easy to handle
- Loop wires over terminals and tighten

10 Check connections

- This switch does not need to be grounded, but the extra green wire in the box gives you the option of replacing this switch with a different one in the future
- Don't push wires into the box just yet, but bend them into position so it will be easy to close the box in the next step

11 Attach outdoor-rated cover

- Because this switch is outside, it needs a special cover
- Screw cover to switch
- Make sure position of inside switch toggle is the same as outside switch cover

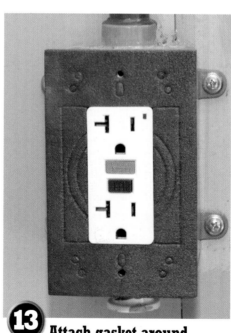

12 Attach cover to box

- Push wires into switch box
- Make sure waterproof gasket is visible around all edges before attaching the switch cover to the box

13 Attach gasket around receptacle

- The receptacle gasket fits completely around the receptacle and covers the edges of the box
- Poke out perforated holes for screws to secure the receptacle cover

14 Attach receptacle cover

- Screw the receptacle cover to the receptacle box
- As with the switch cover, make sure the gasket is visible all the way around so that it seals the box

15 Almost done

- You have now installed a weatherproof receptacle and switch
- The next step is to connect the wires to the water heater

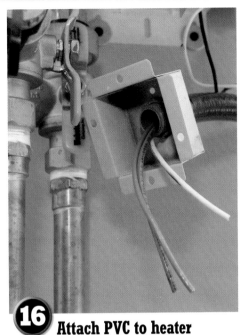

16 Attach PVC to heater

- This water heater has a small junction box so you can clamp the conduit to the box, and tabs so you can to screw the box to the unit itself
- Use PVC cement to join the threaded nipple to the end of the conduit

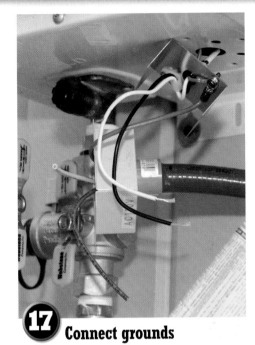

17 Connect grounds

- In this case, local code requires the ground wire that's attached to the heater to be secured by a special grounding ring; check codes in your area
- Be careful not to nick the soft wire insulation on the sharp metal edges of the heater's junction box

18 Wire and attach box

- Connect white neutrals and colored hot wires to each other
- Secure junction box to heater

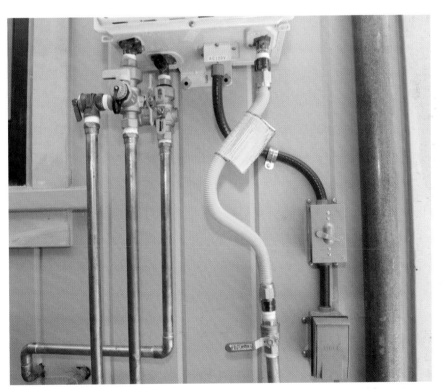

After securing the flexible PVC conduit to the wall with a strap, and pending approval of gas and electrical inspectors, the tankless water heater is now ready to be turned on.

8

Home Entertainment & Communications

I n this chapter, we show you how to wire and splice CAT and coaxial cable, as well as how to run speaker wire without losing audio quality along the way. We also give you tips on home-theater installations, teach you how to hang a flat-panel TV on a wall, show you the latest surge-protection products, and conclude with a section about when it makes more sense to go wireless.

Chapter Contents

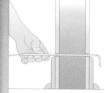

Coaxial Cable
page 218

**Running
Speaker Wire**
page 220

**Surge
Protection**
page 222

**When to Go
Wireless**
page 224

page 204

Wires for Communications & Entertainment

Even though wireless systems are on the rise, most of us will continue to rely on wires to transmit at least some of the data, voice, audio, and video signals throughout our homes.

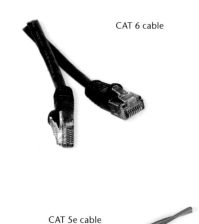

CAT 6 cable

CAT 5e cable

Manufactured CAT 5e cord

Site-made CAT 5e cable

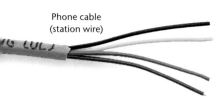

Phone cable (station wire)

RJ 45 data connectors

RJ 11 phone connectors

Overview

Telephones, computers, televisions, and speakers use different kinds of cable. However, they are all similar to electrical wires in that they are metal (usually copper) and encased in plastic insulation. Like electrical cable, communications cable contains two or more insulated wires wrapped in protective sheathing. Coaxial television cable is shielded with an additional thin layer of metal so that, for example, the signal from a nearby radio does not bleed into the TV signal. A connector attached to the end of a cable is used to link the wires in the cable to a jack in a wall or device.

DATA & TELEPHONE WIRING

New data and telephone lines use cables that have four twisted pairs of wires inside a plastic sheathing. Until a few years ago, CAT (category) 5 and 5e (enhanced) cable was considered state of the art. CAT 5 can move voice and data at up to 150 Mbps (millions of bits per second), with CAT 5e performing better than standard CAT 5. Either can carry up to four telephone lines or two data signals.

Today, CAT 6 (which is twice as fast as CAT 5 or 5e) and CAT 6a (twice as fast as CAT 6) are the standards, although it's a safe bet that something speedier is bound to come along. The good news is that the connectors for CAT 5, 5e, 6, and 6a have not changed, so CAT 5-era jacks will work if you decide to upgrade.

Older phone systems with single phone lines use standard phone cable, also called station wire, which has only four wires. (It is also often called two-pair, though the pairs are not twisted together.) To repair or extend service in a home with standard phone cable, you can use the same wire, CAT 3, or CAT 5e. If you purchase standard phone cable, choose #24 solid-core wires because cheaper stranded-wire cables can be difficult to connect.

DATA & PHONE CONNECTORS

The standard connector for computer data in a home network is a type RJ 45, which has eight conductors. Some RJ 45 jacks come in colors, making it easier to find the right one when you are plugging in a device.

Telephone systems use type RJ 11 connectors to link telephone sets, answering machines, fax machines, modems, and other devices to wall outlets. RJ 11 connectors and jacks are only a bit narrower than RJ 45 data jacks, so it's easy to get them mixed up. If possible, use a different colored jack for each type of service.

VIDEO CABLES

A video signal contains a lot of information, so a video cable must handle a much higher bandwidth than telephone or data cables. Video and cable-modem services use RG6 and RG6/U coaxial cable, which carry signals in a central copper wire surrounded by insulation and metal shielding. Coaxial cables use a threaded connector called Type F. Some F connectors use twist-on compression rings to hold the connector to the cable, while others have a housing that must be crimped permanently onto the cable. The crimp connection is more reliable, so it is worth the extra cost to purchase a crimping tool, which is often sold in a kit that includes a number of F connectors.

Analog component video cables are on their way out as all home electronics migrate to digital, but many of us still have an old DVD or VHS player hooked up using these cables. Some cables, such as the ones on the opposite page, are bundled with audio cables.

DVI (digital video interface) cables, move digital video signals from a cable box or dish to a digital television. Most DVI cables are like the one on the opposite page, which means it can move either analog or digital video. The only downside of DVI cables is that they do not deliver audio signals.

HDMI (high-definition multimedia interface) cables are the complete package, delivering digital audio and video signals from a cable box or dish to an HDTV. Like all new technologies, HDMI is a work in progress—the first versions had less bandwidth than current versions, which caused sometimes confusing delays in commands sent from, say, a cable box to an HDTV.

RG6/U cable

Crimp-type
F connector

Twist-on
F connector

Component video &
audio cables

DVI cable

HDMI cable

AUDIO WIRE

Household audio wiring comes in two forms: the familiar unshielded wire pairs (speaker wire) that carry sound from central amplifiers to remote speakers, and line-level cables, a type of shielded cable that contains two or more wires that typically run from a CD player, digital audio server, or tuner to amplifiers located in the same room as the speakers they control.

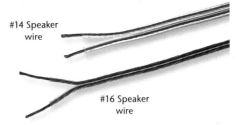

#14 Speaker
wire

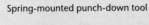

#16 Speaker
wire

Tools

STRIPPERS

In addition to general-purpose strippers, diagonal cutters, and lineman's pliers, you may find a small stripper handy for installing speaker wire or a few data cables. However, the best choices for data and video work are specially designed strippers—like the yellow pair shown below, left, which can quickly strip both CAT 5-6a sheathing and individual wire insulation, and the coaxial stripper below, right, which simultaneously makes the three delicate cuts necessary for stripping RG6 or RG6/U video cable.

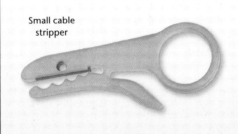

Small cable
stripper

Coaxial
stripper

PUNCH-DOWN TOOLS

Many telephone and data connectors use special terminal strips into which wires are pressed. This is a convenient system because it eliminates the need to strip insulation. Some data and telephone connectors come with cheap plastic punch-down tools, like the one below, left. These are fine for connecting a few wires, but they do require the additional step of trimming the excess wire after you attach them. A better choice is a spring-mounted punch-down tool, like the one below, right, which automatically cuts off the excess as it punches a wire into place.

Plastic punch-down tool

Spring-mounted punch-down tool

Sound & Vision

With the arrival of high-definition television sets into our homes comes the attendant problem of mounting those flat-panels on our walls and corralling the seeming miles of wire that connect to everything from speakers to amplifiers.

The Truth About Speaker Wire

Audio wire has a lot in common with wine—and not just that they are one letter apart. There are aficionados who claim that you have to spend big bucks for the best, and others who say that Two Buck Chuck does the job just fine.

When it comes to either, the only way to really tell if you are getting what you want is a blind test. That's common for wine, but listening tests are less easily arranged. In one widely reported (but not independently verified) experiment arranged by a mischievous audio engineer, a group of listeners couldn't tell the difference between speaker wire made from four coat hangers and the top-of-the-line wire made by a highly-marketed brand.

Which isn't to say that you should wire your home stereo in coat hangers. In fact, home-theater expert David DeFord believes that skimping on wire simply makes no sense.

"Dropping $200 on digital cable from the source to the receiver is one of the easiest ways to get better sound," he says. "What you lose up front, you never get back."

As for that brand-name speaker wire that couldn't be distinguished from coat hangers, he adds: "They would have been able to tell with wire from Tara Labs, Audio-Quest, Cardas and Tributaries," companies he champions, and happily pays $12.95 a foot for.

The things DeFord looks for in good speaker wire include how tightly the individual copper strands are crushed together, which minimizes "roll-off" at high frequencies. DeFord uses 16-gauge wire when connecting speakers up to 125 feet away from their source, and 14-gauge for speakers that are farther away.

Bottom line? If you are buying your components from a high-quality store, have them demonstrate different priced wire and see if you can hear the difference.

This sliding base rotates so you can get to the wires and cables connected to the rear panels of your cable box, DVD player, receiver, and other home-theater components. Designed for small cabinets and available in 14- and 18-inch depths, the base is designed not to rotate any more than 60° to prevent strain on cables. Cable-management accessories are included.

Not everyone can hide all their component wires like the installation on the opposite page. That's where a cover like this one can come in handy. Available in textured or smooth surface, the cover is primed and ready to paint, can hold up to 10 cables, and is easy to install.

Split-loom corrugated plastic tubing keeps cables neat and tidy, but how to get all those wires in the tube? This tool is designed to slide through the split in the tubing, leaving the cables inside.

Mounting a Flat-panel TV to a Wall

One of the hidden costs of a flat-panel TV, be it LCD or plasma, is the installation. But the hardware is not that expensive (a stationary mount should not cost more than $100; articulating models are around $200) and attaching it to your TV is not too difficult if you plan carefully and work with a helper. The only tricky part is making sure that you secure the mount firmly to the wall, but since the wall-bracket part of most mounts have wide openings at 16-inch intervals, you should be able to find studs to screw into.

① Assess parts

- Before you put anything together, check to make sure you have all parts
- This mount came with an extra pair of adjustable TV brackets (at right)

② Mount brackets to TV

- If you must lay the TV on its face to mount hardware, make sure the surface is soft and flat
- Measure the distance from the bottom of the bracket to the bottom of the TV

③ Measure at wall

- Mark for the bottom of the TV
- Measure up using the distance calculated in Step 2
- Make several marks along the wall

④ Level before you drill

- Use a stud finder or make pilot holes to locate studs
- If no studs can be found, use molly bolts, toggle bolts, or expansion anchors
- Use the bracket as a guide for your level

⑥ Hook up and hang

- A large flat-panel TV is heavy, so find a helper to assist you
- It's usually easiest to make connections before you hang the TV
- Make sure there is slack in all wires

⑤ Secure bracket to wall

- This bracket is secured to the wall in eight places
- Note the bracket's proximity to wires, which will be hidden behind the TV once it's mounted to the wall

Home Theaters

There are so many types of home theaters these days, at so many price points, it's a wonder anyone goes to a movie theater anymore.

Your Choices

As digital home-theater systems have become more common, their prices have dropped dramatically. Today you can get a great one installed for as little as $2,500. The same system might have cost you $10,000 just a few years ago.

It's not just the cost of the TV that has become more reasonable. You can spend $200 for a one-speaker audio set-up that imitates the feel of a large surround system. Or you can cough up Steven Spielberg bucks—tens of thousands are not unheard of—for a sound system that will have you flinching at the special effects that seem to swirl around the room.

The best news is the rising quality of the so-called HTIBs (home theater in a box). First piece of advice: don't fall for marketing. Salesmen are often stunned

TOP: An old-school record collection coexists with a new home theater. ABOVE: In this entertainment room, a flat-panel TV floats above an antique sideboard, which has been gutted to house electronic components, including a speaker where the top drawer used to be. Wiring for the speakers and TV behind the sideboard are hidden inside the wall.

RIGHT: This stand-alone mahogany cabinet has doors that can be closed to hide its flat-panel TV, which is mounted on a pivoting, retractable arm.

This flat panel is surrounded by speakers and components that are housed within a wall that's designed to accommodate them.

One clever way to hide the machined look of contemporary home electronics is to put them in a deliberately retro shell.

LCD vs. Plasma

The biggest question mark for most would-be home-theater owners is the type of TV: LCD (liquid crystal display) or Plasma. Here are a few arguments for each:

LCD

- Uses about half the power of plasma screens
- Performs better in rooms with lots of light
- Lasts longer than plasma

PLASMA

- Provides a wider viewing angle than LCD, which means more people in a room can see the screen clearly
- Color detail is better than on LCDs, so viewing experience is more like that in a movie theater

when people ask for heavily advertised brand-name systems, when cheaper, less expensively marketed systems often sound much better.

For example, when David DeFord, of the California company Audio Ink, was asked to recommend components for an $8,500 home-theater system for a client, he chose four small 6.5 × 11.5 × 3.5-inch speakers that cost only $450 a pair. The relatively inexpensive quartet in wooden cabinets delivered a more pure, lifelike sound than some smaller plastic ones that cost many times more. "The most important thing," says DeFord, "is to listen for yourself and figure out what you like. Don't make this an impulse buy. Do the research."

When it comes to actually delivering the sound to the speakers, wireless is not a great option because wireless signals are too prone to interference. That means owners will have to be more cagey about hiding wires, particularly on back speakers. DeFord has installed systems whose wires went outside a house to link the back speakers. Running wires through attics and in crawl spaces is also common.

A sliding panel with a full-width drawer pull makes it easy to hide this TV when it's not in use. Columns flanking the screen hold a track and counterbalance mechanism.

Running Data Cable

If you've installed outdoor lights, you already know how easy it is to work with low-voltage wiring. Running the data cables needed to connect computers to a home network is just as simple.

STOP!
Some manufacturers make faceplates that do not match up with standard network plastic boxes. Before you install a box, check to be sure your equipment will mount to it.

Today's typical home office is often wired with some form of CAT cable for data, a phone line, and electrical wires to power lights and computer hardware.

About Low-voltage Wires

Low-voltage wires do not need the insulated mounting boxes used for higher voltage electrical receptacles and switches, but the wall faceplates that hold the jacks do need a box or bracket to which they can be fastened.

In new construction, low-voltage cable is typically run after plumbing pipes, heating ducts, and electrical wiring has been installed. If you are adding low-voltage cable to a finished room,

keep the network outlets that you install a foot away from household wiring to avoid interference. As with electrical wires, make sure your low-voltage cable runs where it won't be nailed through (use nailing plates wherever the cable is less than 1½ inches from the finished wall surface).

Finally, unlike electrical wires, which can be run as far as they need to, CAT 5 to 6a cables can only be run 100 meters at a time (as a practical matter, even a bit less since part of the overall length is used up at junction boxes and making connections to devices).

Brackets

In finished walls, you can use a light-weight plastic bracket like the one at left as a mount for the plates that will hold connecting jacks for CAT, phone, and coaxial cables. As on a cut-in electrical box, plastic wings can be rotated and then tightened to secure the bracket to the back of the drywall. Metal brackets like the one shown at right with bend-able metal tabs are also available.

Permanent Labeling

Labels will help you keep cables sorted as you make your connections, and they'll be even more valuable in the future should you need to tie new devices into the network. Use ready-made self-adhesive labels. To ensure they won't drop off, add transparent tape or, even better, transparent heat-shrink tubing.

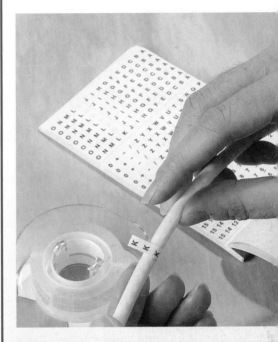

Boxes

In existing walls, use backless, plastic cut-in boxes, which are secured to the back of the drywall by small plastic wings. In new construction, use lightweight plastic brackets or "rings," which generally have no backs. Installation is similar to that used for plastic electrical boxes, with integrated nails that attach to framing.

Telephone Lines

Many people are switching from traditional phone lines to cell phones, cable phones, or voice-over-Internet (VOIP) connections because they are cheaper. But for those in areas prone to natural calamities or electrical outages, standard phone lines can be lifesavers.

"Our power was out for two weeks and the only thing that worked in the house was the phone," said Reid Bourdet, an engineer with Cisco Systems, who lives in northern California's Santa Cruz Mountains. "No matter what happens with new technologies, I'll never give up that phone." Even phone lines provided by cable companies, which get their signals from the Internet, quit in a blackout.

Standard, wired phones have other benefits: they can be instantly traced by 911 emergency operators, alerting rescue crews to an address, even when the dialer can't speak. Cell phones don't reach all coverage areas and wired connections carry better sound for professional uses, such as radio broadcasts or conference calls.

Wiring Methods

You can wire a phone system in one of two basic ways. Each has its advantages, so consider which option better meets your needs.

- **Daisy-chain wiring** is easily installed. It connects all rooms of a house on one circuit to the phone company's network interface jack.

- **Home-run wiring** connects each room and jack to a common point, such as a junction or splice box adjacent to the network interface jack. It is recommended for larger homes or homes with an office. Home-run wiring is easier to upgrade than daisy chain, and it is easier to find the location of a broken or shorted-out wire since the runs are individual rather than part of a chain.

WIRING TIPS

To ensure a clear connection, jacks should be no farther than 200 feet from the point where wiring enters your home. Because telephone cable is so thin, it's relatively easy to route along baseboards or inside walls (avoid steam, air ducts, and water pipes to protect from corrosion).

To reduce interference, separate phone wiring and jacks from electrical receptacles by at least 3 inches, and don't run phone wires with electrical wires through the same conduit.

Wires & Color Coding

A telephone circuit requires that at least two wires be used at all

A message center just off the kitchen is the sort of place where phone and electrical wires converge.

Connecting Phone Wire to a 6-pin RJ 11 Jack

Pin	Standard 2-pair Wire	Alternative Wire Types
1	Not Used	
2	Black	White with orange bands
3	Red	Blue with white bands
4	Green	White with blue bands
5	Yellow	Orange with white bands
6	Not Used	
Pin	Standard 3-pair Wire	Alternative Wire Types
1	White	White with green bands
2	Black	White with orange bands
3	Red	Blue with white bands
4	Green	White with blue bands
5	Yellow	Orange with white bands
6	Blue	Green with white bands

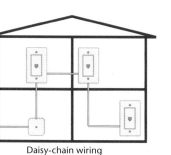

Daisy-chain wiring

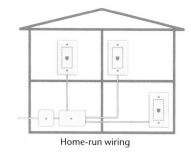

Home-run wiring

times: a "tip" wire (usually green) and a "ring" wire (usually red). You must maintain this color coding throughout your home.

Jacks & Adapters

Phone jacks are connection points between the telephone's line wire and the phone cable. New construction calls for flush-mounted jacks, which install onto boxes fastened to studs. In finished rooms, you can install flush-mounted jacks cut into electrical boxes, but it's more common to use surface-mounted jacks. They attach via short screws. A dual or triplex adapter allows you to add a phone, modem, or answering machine to a single phone jack.

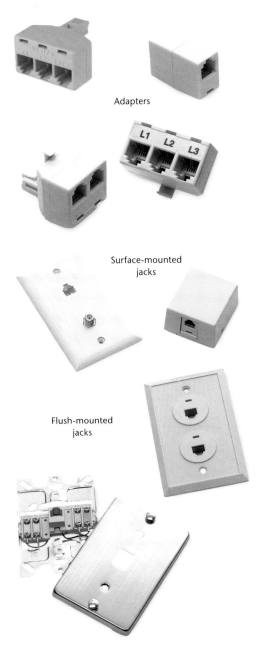

Adapters

Surface-mounted jacks

Flush-mounted jacks

Converting Old Jacks

In an old home, you may find jacks that do not accept a modern RJ 11 plug. Making the transition to modular is largely a matter of finding the right adapter.

- **Hardwired jacks** The most common type of telephone connection installed before 1974 is referred to as "hardwired" because the telephone cannot be unplugged. There are two kinds of hardwired connections: the block, which is attached directly to the wall or baseboard, and flush-mounted connections, which are actually in-wall boxes and can have either round or rectangular faceplates.

  You can convert a hardwired block connection to modular by simply removing its cover and replacing it with a modular-jack converter. Back off the terminal

screws, slip the converter's wire ends under the screw heads, and tighten the screws. Take care to keep the old wires in place as you work. In most situations, you need to attach only the red and green wires. Leave any other wires unstripped and fold them out of the way. Do not cut them short, as you may want to use them in the future.

A flush-mounted conversion is made in much the same way, using a different converter.

- **Four-prong jacks** These were once used for portable extension telephones. You may find one mounted on a wall or baseboard, or flush-mounted in a box covered by a faceplate. You can change a four-prong jack using a flush-mounted or wall-phone jack (see facing page). Or use a plug-in adapter.

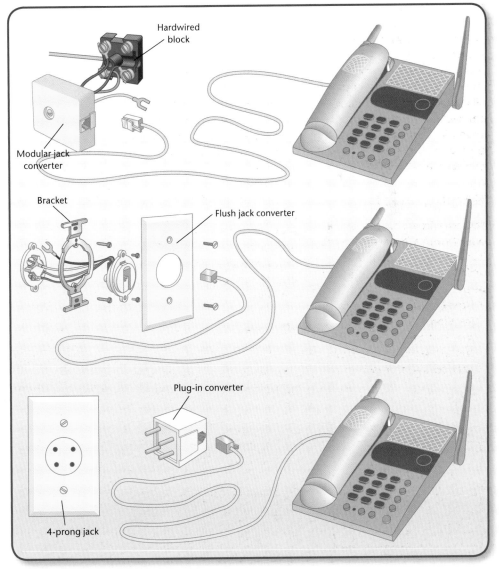

Hardwired block

Modular jack converter

Bracket

Flush jack converter

Plug-in converter

4-prong jack

Extending Your System

The easiest way to extend your system is by daisy-chaining, (described on page 212). If there is a jack where you want to put in new wiring, simply plug a dual-outlet adapter into the jack. Plug your phone into one of the outlets and a new line into the second. Run the new line at least 2 inches away from the existing jack and install your new jack wherever you need it (see illustration at right).

Sometimes a nearby phone line with no jack on it has enough slack in it to accommodate a jack (check baseboards, closets, cabinets, or joists in an attic or basement). If you can get just 3 inches of slack, you can cut the line, attach a modular jack, and add a new run of cable to it. To get slack, remove some of the staples holding the wire in place and gently pull on it. Don't pull so hard that a staple rips into the cable.

Lines look best tucked away under floors, above a ceiling, or in a wall. Exposed wire can be routed under paneling, behind baseboards, or inside hollow corner trim. Pull it taut and anchor with telephone cable clips for less visibility. Phone lines also fit under carpets in areas that don't get a lot of traffic. Use lineman's pliers to pull up carpet attached to a tack strip. If carpet tacks were used, pull them out and re-drive them after installing the cable.

Routing Cable Through Walls

When extending a phone line, you can save a great deal of time and trouble by leaving the new wiring exposed. However, routing wiring beneath a floor, above a ceiling, or in a wall

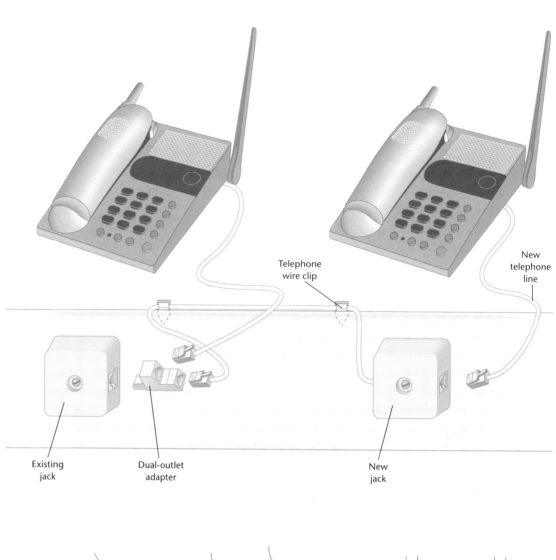

Telephone wire clip

New telephone line

Existing jack

Dual-outlet adapter

New jack

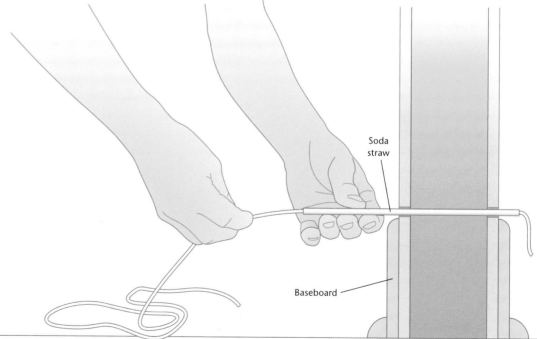

Soda straw

Baseboard

requires less wire, is more attractive, and provides better protection. It's definitely the way to go when walls are unfinished.

Drilling through a wall is often the easiest way to route wire from room to room, especially if the walls are covered with drywall. Use a wall sensor to find a hollow spot between studs, then use an extra-long ¼-inch drill bit to drill through the drywall just above the baseboard.

Phone cable is limp and difficult to fish through a hollow wall, so push a soda straw through first, then thread the cable through the straw. Once the cable is through, remove the straw. After the cable has been attached, seal the holes with caulk.

Floor-to-Floor Wiring

Running wire horizontally within walls is nearly impossible without cutting holes in the wall. However, running a line vertically is somewhat simpler, and a route from floor to floor is often the most practical way to take a phone line from one room to another—even when both rooms are on the same

floor. Usually, you'll be running the wire through one wall into the attic or basement, and from there into the wall of another room.

To run cable up a wall for a wall jack, cut the hole for the jack box and drill a hole directly below it and near the floor, where the cable will enter. Tie a few washers or some other small weight to the end of a string; lower the weight until it hits the floor. Insert a bent wire into the lower hole and fish out the string. Tape the cable to the string and pull it up through the jack hole.

Wiring for Two Separate Jacks

It does look more professional to have a face plate with two jacks, or to have separate jacks for each line than to use an adapter, as shown on the opposite page, so you may prefer this method. To wire two jacks, connect all four wires and attach the red and green leads to the line 1 jack. Attach the yellow and black wires and the yellow and black leads to the line 2 jack. You can also buy modular jacks and line cord that handle six conductors, for three phone lines.

Snag the string

Bent wire

Washers for weight

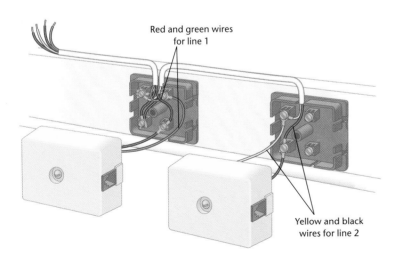

Red and green wires for line 1

Yellow and black wires for line 2

Data Lines

By routing CAT 5e or 6 cable to various points in the house, you can connect multiple computers to one Internet source. A home network allows files to be sent to a single printer from multiple computers, or it can be configured to control household systems.

Making the Connection

Where possible, use pre-connected jacks for data lines. If you run long lines through the house, however, you will need to make jack connections yourself. Carefully follow installation instructions supplied with your connectors, as a single wire in the wrong slot can make an entire system fail and can be very difficult to trace. The instructions below are for wiring RJ 45 data outlets with CAT 5e cable—the most common connection.

1 Expose the pairs

- Use a cable stripper to remove about 2 inches of the sheathing
- If the cable has plastic inside, snip it away as well

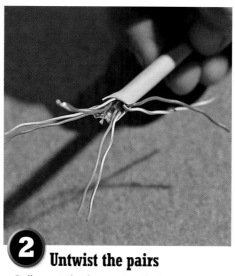

2 Untwist the pairs

- Pull apart the four pairs of wires
- Notice that each pair consists of wire with a solid color and another with that color plus white

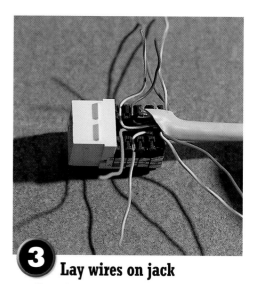

3 Lay wires on jack

- Follow the instructions provided with the connector
- Be sure that the sheathing extends into the jack

4 Punch down the wires

- If you are using a spring-loaded punch-down tool, it will cut off any excess wire ends

5 Check your work

- Make sure the wire order matches the instructions and the color codes on its side

6 Close up the jack

- A separate cover provided with the jack snaps onto its back

Stuff to Buy

RJ 45 JACKS
BASIC SUPPLIES CAT 5e or
6 cable

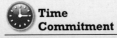 **Time Commitment**

Less than an hour

 **Tools You'll Need**

Diagonal cutters
Punch-down tool
Screwdriver
Small cable stripper

 Related Topics

Wires for communications &
entertainment, 204–205

Connecting a Data & Phone Jack

In general, it's a good idea to run separate lines for data and phone, if only so you will have more options in the future. However, CAT 5e and 6 cable contain four twisted pairs, and only two of those pairs are needed for a data circuit, so you can certainly hook up a phone and a data line using only one cable.

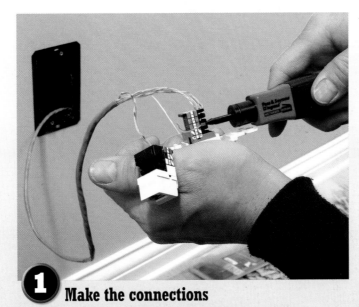

1 Make the connections

- Strip sheathing and separate the wire pairs
- On the RJ 11 (telephone) jack, use a punch-down tool to connect the solid blue wire to pin 3 and the blue-and-white wire to pin 4
- Connect the remaining wires to the RJ 45 (data) jack, following the manufacturer's instructions for color coding

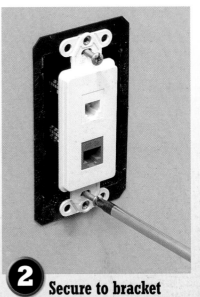

2 Secure to bracket

- Wrap the exposed wires with electrician's tape
- Snap the plugs onto an outlet plate designed for phone and data lines
- Fold the cables back into the box or bracket and mount the plate

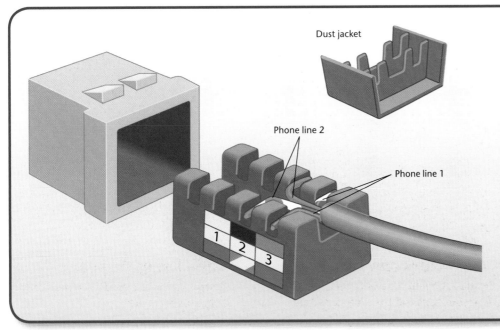

Dust jacket

Phone line 2

Phone line 1

1   2   3

Wiring a Phone Jack with CAT Cable

If you run CAT 5e or CAT 6 cable instead of telephone station wire, connect it to a RJ 11 plug as shown here. If you have two telephone lines, line 1 connects to pins 3 and 4 of the RJ 11 connector, while line 2 connects to pins 2 and 5.

Coaxial Cable

Video cables are extremely sensitive to interference from nearby radio transmitters, electric motors, and other devices. To minimize such interference, video cables and connectors have a continuous shield around the central copper wire.

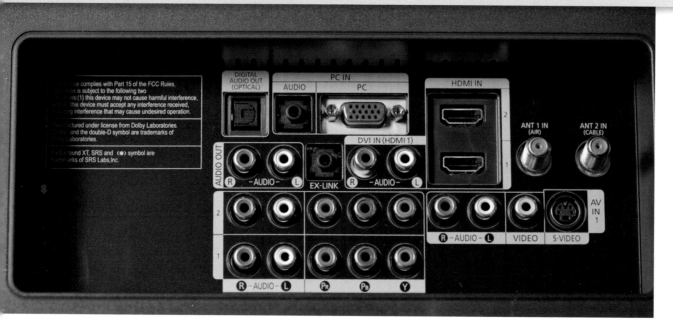

Many older TVs have two inputs for coaxial cable. If you get your signal via an antenna on your roof, use the input labeled "AIR." If you use a satellite dish, are a cable subscriber, or run your video signal through some sort of digital video recorder, use the input labeled "CABLE."

Making the Connection

To install a video outlet on a wall plate, you will need to attach an F connector to the RG6/U cable and plug that connector into the mating jack inside the wall plate. F connectors come in several forms, each with a different method for attaching the connector to the cable. Most use some variation on the process of stripping the cable, inserting the connector over the center wire, and crimping the sleeve of the connector around the shield. In addition to the crimping tools shown here, look for the type of F-connector tool that holds the plug on a threaded extension.

A No-strip Connector

One alternative to the strip-and-crimp method is the RCA center-pin connector. These are more expensive than standard connectors but don't require a special stripper or crimper. Trim the cable straight across, then push on the connector cap until ½ inch of cable shows. Use pliers to push on the other half of the connector, pressing the six prongs evenly into the insulation. Finally, pull the cap forward and thread it over the prongs.

Maximum Cable Bends

Stiff coaxial cable should not bend to less than a 2½-inch radius. A tighter bend could inhibit the cable signal. Run cables so they do not need to make tight turns. This may mean, for example, looping a cable above or below a room rather than making a tight turn at a corner.

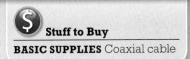

Stuff to Buy	Time Commitment	Tools You'll Need	Related Topics
BASIC SUPPLIES Coaxial cable	Less than an hour	Coaxial stripper F-connector tool Long-nose pliers Small crimper	Wires for communications & entertainment, 204–205

1 Strip coaxial cable

- Use a stripping tool (shown), the stripping teeth on a coaxial crimper, or, trickiest of all, a utility knife
- Even with a coaxial stripper it takes a knack to get this Step right, so practice on a piece of scrap first

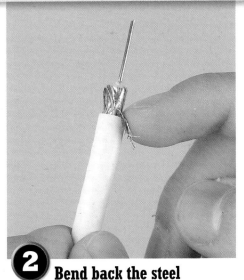

2 Bend back the steel

- Strip the cable so there is about ¼ inch of the braided shield and at least ¾ inch of cleanly stripped copper wire
- Carefully bend back all the steel braiding against the end of the cable sheathing

3 Place the connector

- Push a crimpable F connector onto the cable
- Make sure the turned-back steel braiding slips into the connector
- The white insulation that surrounds the copper wire should be pushed all the way into the connector

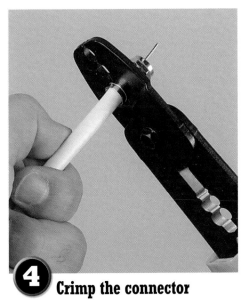

4 Crimp the connector

- Squeeze the F connector firmly with a crimping tool
- Give the connector a firm tug to confirm that it is fastened
- Trim the center copper wire so it protrudes about ⅛ inch beyond the connector

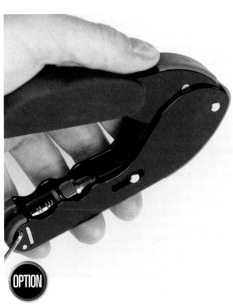

OPTION

- This crimping tool works by squeezing the back of the connector toward the front, resulting in a very strong connection
- Note: It works only with F connectors specially designed to be used along with the tool

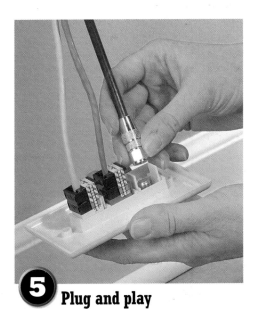

5 Plug and play

- F connectors allow you to connect a coaxial cable to a device like a digital video recorder or a TV
- They also connect to the back of a jack, as shown above

Running Speaker Wire

Speaker wire can distribute sound from any audio source to speakers throughout the house. Home audio networks can be configured to play different programs in different rooms, but in most cases the sound you hear will be the same from room to room.

Many newer receivers offer connections for far more speakers than a mere pair.

Impedance & Polarity

When you're talking about stereo wiring, two terms matter: impedance and polarity. Impedance, measured in ohms, is the resistance a speaker offers to the signal passing through it. The greater the impedance, the more sound quality will be compromised. Speakers are rated at anywhere from 4 to 16 ohms, with 4 being the best (least impedance).

If your receiver supports multiple channels—such as A, B, and A+B—you can wire two sets of speakers directly from the receiver in home-run fashion. Simply wire the speakers to the correct terminals. However, if you wish to run multiple speakers in series (or daisy-chain) fashion, the impedance rating will now be the sum of the individual speakers' ratings. Two 8-ohm speakers will become a 16-ohm load. So even though home-run wiring uses more cable, serial wiring can put more of a strain on your music source. In fact, an amplifier or receiver of moderate wattage that would be

This small, remodeled basement features speakers hidden in the ceiling to leave room for toys and the inevitable clutter created by the homeowners' growing family.

plenty powerful for home-run wiring may not be able to power your daisy-chained speakers adequately.

Polarity refers to the direction that current flows through a device. The ports or terminals on a receiver, speakers, and other components are polarized. Each set should have one input marked "1" or "L" and one marked "2" or "R." Your wiring hookups must match up at both ends. That is, if a wire is connected to a negative termi-

This speaker is rated at between 4 and 8 ohms, which means its impedance is relatively low.

nal on a speaker, it should also be connected to the negative terminal on the receiver. If polarity is switched, the sound quality will suffer. Most speaker cables are color-coded or have one ribbed and one smooth wire, which can help you be sure that they are connected to

a terminal of the same polarity on both ends.

Remember, use 16-gauge wire when connecting speakers up to 125 feet away from their source, and 14-gauge for speakers that are farther away than that. For more about speaker wire, see page 206.

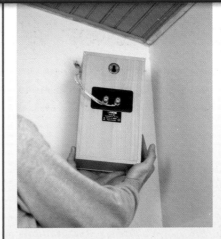

Plan Ahead

If you are running electrical cable through unfinished walls, it's a good idea to run audio cable as well, so you can easily hook up speakers in the future. Route speaker wires at least two feet away from electrical wire to minimize interference.

An Alternative to Flush

Mounting a speaker flush into a wall is a great way to go, but sometimes it's not practical, too much work, or a budget buster. The next best thing is to mount the speaker so that its profile is as flat against the wall as possible. This speaker has a bracket on it with a recessed space behind it for a nail or screw head so you can do just that. The speaker wire runs through the drywall—as you position the speaker in place, simply push the excess wire into the wall.

Remote Volume Controls

While it's not absolutely necessary, a volume control that regulates the sound levels of both speakers is a convenient addition. The volume control can be built into the wall or placed in a box on a tabletop or bookshelf between the speakers.

To install a wall-mounted volume control, run the speaker cables inside the walls to the volume control location, then run separate cables from the volume control to each pair of speaker terminals. If you're working in a finished room, you may be able to avoid extensive fishing by placing the speaker outlet's wall plate directly above the volume control so that you don't have to run the wires across studs.

Label Your Wires

Here's a simple time saver: Before you pull speaker wires through an attic or basement to get them to the other side of a room, label them first. That way you won't have to spend hours of trial and error to make sure that the right rear speakers are connected to the correct set of wires. Getting this right is especially important when installing a surround-sound system.

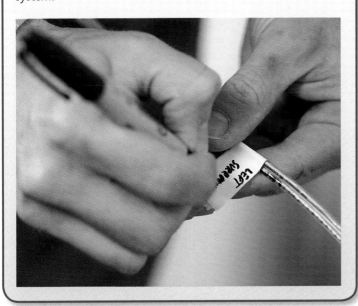

Eliminate Needless Connections

Home audio experts used to recommend that their customers install audio jacks in their walls to ensure that the connection from the stereo receiver to the speaker wire was as strong as possible. But with the proliferation of multispeaker audio systems requiring numerous strands of speaker wire, many pros simply run their wire directly from the receiver into the wall. The custom face plate above was made by drilling through a solid junction-box cover with a hole saw. The edges of the hole were filed to prevent the wire from being nicked, and though the appearance of the plate is certainly not objectionable, it will be covered up by a component cabinet, so its appearance was not especially important.

Surge Protection

To get a picture of what happens during a power surge, think about holding your finger over the garden hose when you were a kid. The water flow stopped for a second before it forced your finger off the nozzle and spurted out hard.

Ways to Prepare

When the power shuts down and then turns back on again, the resulting surge can produce a spike in voltage that can fry sensitive electronic devices, which are only designed to handle 120 volts, the current that flows through most household wires. It doesn't take long for a spike to do its damage—three nanoseconds (a nanosecond is just one billionth of a second) is enough to qualify as a surge.

With brownouts due to overloaded power grids and blackouts caused by increasingly unpredictable weather on the rise, it's less a question of whether a surge will happen but when, which is why it's well worth the cost of a few simple precautionary devices.

IN-ROOM SURGE PROTECTION

Surge protectors are rated in joules—the higher the joule rating, the more protection. Some come with insurance policies of up to $300,000 for your equipment.

At the bottom end is a power strip like the one below, right, for under $15 that will give basic protection, but will usually burn out after one surge. Make sure any protector you buy has an indicator light to let you know when it has failed.

Better power strips cost around $25 and have better ratings and features. Some use a metal oxide varistor and two semiconductors to channel excess power into a ground wire. A second type uses inert gas to conduct the surge to a ground.

Surge stations that sell from between $30 to more than $100 offer superior voltage protection, line conditioning, and may even feature built-in circuit breakers.

Uninterruptible power supplies (UPS) use batteries to keep power consistent when there is a shut down, giving you time, for example, to save your work on a computer. Depending of course on the model, prices for many of these devices are under $100.

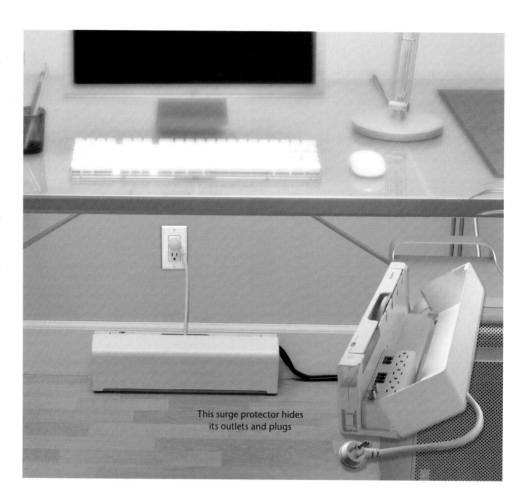

This surge protector hides its outlets and plugs

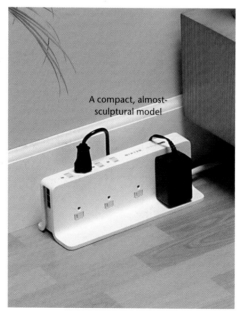

A compact, almost-sculptural model

The standard

Isolated-ground Receptacles

For even more protection, install an isolated-ground receptacle, which is often used in hospitals for extremely touchy diagnostic equipment. It provides a clean grounding path to the service panel and reduces electromagnetic noise that can interfere with your equipment's operation. To install one, you will need to run #12 three-wire cable directly to the service panel. At the panel, you will need to connect to and install a new circuit breaker, which may be GFCI equipped for even greater protection.

Whole House Protection

Whole-house protectors, which start at $300, connect to your circuit box and can protect all the lines in your house (although plug-in protectors are still recommended). You will need to install two 15-amp breakers with the protector. With some models you can install one double-pole, 240-volt breaker instead.

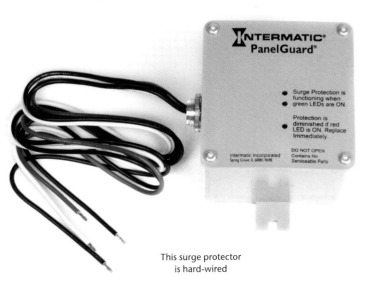

This surge protector
is hard-wired

DSL Filters

DSL service utilizes one set of wires for both broadband Internet access and standard telephone service. The two operate independently, but an always-on DSL connection can add noise to the phone line and interfere with modems, fax machines, and caller ID. To eliminate the interference, connect a simple filter to every telephone set or other device that shares the line with the DSL modem.

A phone-monitored security system requires a special DSL alarm filter like the one at bottom. Because the filter requires specialized testing equipment to make sure it has not compromised the effectiveness of the security system, it should be installed only by a licensed alarm service provider.

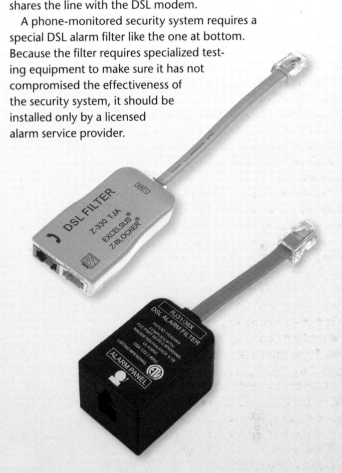

What They Don't Do

No home surge protector will protect against lightning, but lightning is the least common cause of surges. The best protection in an area with a lot of electrical storms is to shut off and unplug your equipment during a storm.

When to Go Wireless

Up until now, this book has focused on connecting wires to switches, receptacles, fixtures, and other wires. But every day, new wireless products come to market, eliminating the need for wires at all. Indeed, wireless is often the smarter way to go.

A 5.8 GHz cordless phone is a space-saving companion to a wireless laptop, which operates at 2.4 GHz.

Cordless Phones

Few household appliances have changed as much as the telephone. Long gone are the days when almost every home had a bulky, rotary-dial box mounted on a kitchen wall, or the era when only the luckiest and wealthiest teenage daughters got their own pink princess phones in their bedrooms. Today, many households do without traditional telephones entirely, relying instead on cell phones.

As discussed on page 212, there are still plenty of reasons to have a regular telephone in your home that's connected to actual telephone wires, but that doesn't mean its receiver needs to be tethered by a cord. Similarly, extra lines are more easily added by purchasing a phone system that includes a base phone plus satellites that rest in chargers, rather than by running wires all over your house.

Still, many people have had bad experiences with cordless phones, which have notoriously spotty reception. As with any other purchase, the key to getting a cordless phone that works well for you is to know what you are buying.

FREQUENCY & TYPE

Cordless phones are sold in four frequencies and two types. The frequencies are 900 MHz, 1.9 GHz (the frequency for the latest DECT 6 phones), 2.4 GHz, and 5.8 GHz. Just to makes sure your choices are as befuddling as possible, 2.4 GHz and 5.8 GHz phones come in either analog or digital models, and of the digital models, you may be asked to choose from phones identified as DSS (digital spread spectrum) and FHSS (frequency-hopping spread spectrum).

A popular misconception is that any digital phone will work better than an analog one. In fact, the frequency of the phone, as well as the frequency of other devices and appliances in your home, is more important. For example, if you have a wireless modem, a baby monitor, or a microwave, there are already a lot of 2.4 GHz radio waves bouncing around your house. In this case, a 5.8 GHz cordless phone is a better option since there will be no interference from these other devices.

Of course there's a catch: Some cordless models that are labeled, say, 5.8 GHz may actually send or receive sound at 2.4 GHz, which defeats the purpose of a 5.8 GHz phone 50 percent of the time. Before you buy, make sure your phone sends and receives at the same frequency.

Analog phones are still around because they are inexpensive, but if you are concerned about someone listening in on your phone calls, don't get an analog phone. Better are digital phones that use DSS or FHSS, which are designed to thwart eaves-

dropping by seamlessly switching channels in patterns known only to a phone's transmitter and receiver. That means the spies in the dry-cleaning truck outside your house will notice a bit more background noise as they try to eavesdrop, but they will not be able to hear you and your spouse make dinner plans or argue about whose turn it is to pick up the kids from soccer practice.

DECT 6 phones (DECT is the acronym for digital enhanced cordless telecommunications) send and receive signals at 1.9 GHz, a frequency designated for cordless phones in the US and Europe. These powerful phones are state of the art, providing clear reception and excellent security.

A Wireless Charger

You can cut the cords to your cell phone's battery charger with a device made by Wildcharge. The flat panel sits on a counter. All you have to do is put your battery-powered device on the panel, and it automatically begins to recharge, saving you the hassle of managing numerous charging plugs and remembering to plug in your various devices.

DECT 6 phones send and receive information at 1.9 GHz, a frequency reserved for cordless telephones.

If you do not have a wireless computer connection in your home, then a less expensive 2.4 GHz phone may be right for you.

This Uniden digital phone operates at 5.8 GHz, which is a different frequency than the one used by wireless modems and other devices that can cause interference. Its frequency-hopping protocol prevents eavesdropping.

Products like this one from Plantronics operate at 1.9 GHz and allow you to switch between incoming calls on your analog home phone and your cell phone.

As people have gotten more comfortable wearing headsets to talk on their cell phones, headsets for home cordless phones are becoming more common.

Home Entertainment

Though still in its infancy, the wireless-home-entertainment industry promises to change the way you listen to music, watch TV, and play video games in your home. In fact, in the not too distant future, your home's heating and cooling systems, as well as its entertainment centers, will probably all be controlled by a device that fits in the palm of your hand.

Today, some home-entertainment entrepreneurs have chosen to focus on delivering sound throughout the home while others have staked their futures on video. Prices for most of these products will probably remain relatively high for some time, but once competition and technology catch up to the business opportunity, the cost of such products should drop dramatically.

APPLE TV

To be clear, this is not a device that lets you do whatever you would normally do in front of a computer screen (check email, retouch photos, update your blog, etc.) from the comfort of your couch. Rather, Apple TV is designed to wirelessly stream anything you have stored in iTunes, as well as to wirelessly download movies and TV shows for purchase or rental. It also gives you wireless access to free content at YouTube and Flickr, all of which you can watch on your TV or listen to through your home-entertainment system's speakers. Apple TV is not a pure wireless device, though—it must be connected to your TV via an HDMI or other type of cable.

FLYWIRE

Like the Apple TV, the Belkin FlyWire is not a purely wireless device. The back of the FlyWire is designed to accept cables from your DVR, DVD player, and all of the most popular video-game players. But the breakthrough is that the FlyWire sends high-definition video signals wirelessly to a thin receiver that can be attached to the back of your flat-panel TV. This means you leave your existing cable or satellite receiver and stereo system right where it is and relocate your TV to the other side of a room, or another room entirely, if that's really the best place for you and your family to watch TV or play games.

SONOS

Wireless audio signals are prone to interference from other wires and wireless devices in your home, as signals travel from your home stereo to speakers. Sonos gets around this problem by creating a unique wireless network that communicates with ZonePlayers throughout your home, any of which can be controlled by a wireless remote. The speakers are then connected by wire to each ZonePlayer. Listen to music on CDs, your computer, or digital music player, or choose from hundreds of free Internet radio stations.

FUZE

Here's another device that requires wiring but then, once wired, can be controlled by a wireless remote. The expandable FuzeOne Media Server is big enough to store all your home movies, DVDs, digital photos, and music files, and allows you to access your entertainment by remote control from as many as seven locations for video and nine for audio throughout your home.

Wireless Safety Devices

There are two chief benefits of installing a wireless smoke alarm or carbon-monoxide detector. First, there are no wires to route through the attic or between ceiling joists, which makes installation a snap. Second, if your region is struck by a natural disaster that causes a loss of power for an extended period of time, your alarm or detector will still be able to warn you of a potentially life-threatening situation.

SMOKE ALARM

Most smoke alarms are powered by an inexpensive 9-volt alkaline battery, which lasts about a year. If you are the kind of person that does not want to have to think about changing batteries every year, put lithium batteries in your smoke alarms—they cost more but last about 10 years.

CARBON-MONOXIDE DETECTOR

This wall-mounted carbon-monoxide alarm from First Alert has a digital display that gives you both the hazard level and amount of charge left in its battery. An optional remote lets you silence so-called nuisance alarms.

Wireless Energy Savers

Even simple things like light switches and surge protectors can help you save energy and money.

DIMMER SWITCHES

Dimming a light switch by 50 percent results in an energy savings of 40 percent, which is not a one-to-one ratio but significant nonetheless. When savings like that are made convenient we are more likely to take advantage of them, which is why a set of wirelessly controlled dimmer switches like these from Lutron could pay for itself quickly. A central controller lets you turn off a light that you forgot to switch off upstairs, while the remote is designed to be clipped to the visor of your car so you can turn lights on when you arrive home before you get out of your car.

SMART SURGE PROTECTION

One of the biggest wastes of energy is the power consumed by appliances like televisions and home-entertainment components when they are in standby mode. The Conserve surge protector from Belkin lets you plug, say, your DVR into an unswitched outlet so that you can record your favorite shows while you are out or asleep. Everything else can be plugged into switched outlets, all of which are controlled by a wireless remote. Cleverly, the remote is designed to be installed next to a wall light switch, making the habit of turning off the TV as natural and as obvious a thing to do as turning out the lights.

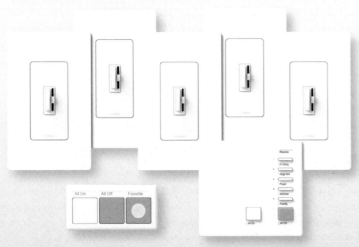

9

Off the Grid

In this chapter, we help you get off the grid. Because power outages are increasingly common, we provide a buying guide to help you select the best generator for your home. Considering solar panels on your roof? We explain how to get it done, as well as surfaces other than the roof that may work just as well. Finally, if you live in a cloudy climate, we introduce you to ways in which you can harness the wind.

Chapter Contents

Backup Generators

Aging power-grid infrastructure and increasingly unpredictable weather have made backup generators fixtures in many homes. Prices have come down, the generators have gotten quieter, and fuels have become more eco-friendly.

Can you spot the boathouse with the power generator?

Your Choices

These days, blackouts and brownouts are fairly common occurrences. In many homes, a day or even two without power is not much of a problem. Food actually stays fairly cold as long as you only occasionally open the refrigerator or freezer, and we can all use a break from TV.

But many homeowners have good reasons for a backup power generator.

- Many home heating systems—not just electric ones but also hot-water systems—need elec-tricity in order to function. If you live in an area with cold winters, a power outage could cause major problems.
- You may need to use a computer or other electronic equipment for work.
- In some rural areas, power outages can last a long time.
- If you have vital electric health-care equipment in the home, a generator could save a life.

The simplest solution is to buy a portable backup genera-tor that has several receptacles. When power goes off, position the generator outside near the house. Run heavy-duty water-proof extension cords from the generator to your most impor-tant appliances and lamps, then start the generator. This is a only stopgap solution, but it may be adequate for a short-lived outage.

For more serious backup pro-tection, and to ensure power will come on if you are away during an outage, have a pro-fessional electrician install a permanently mounted genera-tor near your house. The generator is wired to a transfer switch, which connects to your home's service panel. The switch will turn the generator on automatically when it senses a drop in voltage. Such a gener-ator, which is more expensive than a portable one, can be set up to restore power to selected circuits. It will also need to be hooked up to a line that sup-plies natural gas or propane.

Buying Guide

Prices for generators range from $700 to $7,000, but price is not the only factor to consider. Keep in mind that communities concerned about air quality have targeted portable gasoline and diesel engines as major polluters and have sought to limit their use. Beyond the fuel there's the noise. When comparing generators, be sure to check their decibel levels.

Here are a few other general guidelines:

- **Small portable generators** 3,000–6,000 watts. Designed for household appliances, including your refrigerator and furnace fan, but not necessarily at the same time. Price range: $1,000 and under.
- **Medium portable generators** 7,000–9,000 watts. Will power multiple rooms, but not a central air conditioner. Price range: $1,400 and under.
- **Large portable generators** 10,000 watts. Restores full power to small homes and some central air conditioners. Price range: $2,500 and under.

A generator's ability to power an air conditioner is often listed as its "A/C ton rating." To power a central-air-conditioning unit, you generally need a generator that produces the following amounts of power:

- If the A/C unit is rated at 3 tons (30-amp/36,000 BTUs), you need a generator that produces a minimum of 10 kilowatts.
- If the A/C unit is rated at 4 tons (40-amp/48,000 BTUs), you need a generator that produces a minimum of 15 kilowatts.
- If the A/C unit is rated at 5 tons (50-amp/60,000 BTUs), you need a generator that produces a minimum of 17.5 kilowatts.

Briggs & Stratton 30334. 8,000 watts; gasoline powered (US Forestry Department approved spark arrest); four 20-amp 120V outlets, one 30-amp 120/240V outlet; runs for eight hours on seven gallons of gas. $2,000 retail.

Winco HPS12000HE. 10,800 watts; runs on LP gas, natural gas, or gasoline; four 20-amp GFCI 120V outlets, one 30-amp 120/240V outlet, one 60-amp 120/240V outlet; 78 decibels. $3,500 retail.

Guardian 5525. 20 kW; runs on LP or natural gas; hard-wired to selected circuits; 66 decibels. A/C rating = 5 tons. $5,200 retail.

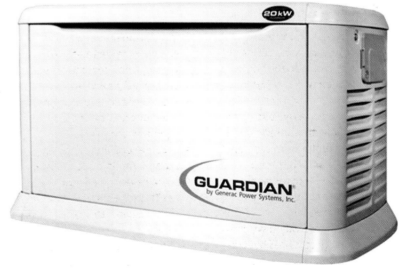

Solar & Wind Solutions

Alternative-energy technologies are hardly new. Solar power has been with us for decades, while wind power has been a staple on farms for centuries. Now, new incentives and pricing models are making these technologies more affordable.

Achieving Energy Independence

Two key economic events of 2008—high oil prices and declining home values—probably did more to promote energy awareness than 100 Academy Award-winning documentaries and Nobel Prize-winning politicians. As the price of gasoline crested $4 a gallon and people wondered if they could afford the oil to heat their homes, Americans started driving less (5 percent less in June of 2008 compared to June of 2007) and waking up to the many money-saving steps they could take in their homes (according to the EPA, sales of compact fluorescent light bulbs doubled between 2006 and 2007, and the numbers continue to climb).

Homeowners have been helped on the road to energy independence by a number of innovative companies who have decided to make it their business to cut our collective reliance on the power grid. In particular, some solar companies will now pay for the solar panels that they install on your roof (you choose the design you like). The company then sells you the power that their panels generate at a fixed rate that's less than what utilities are charging now, and certain to be way less than what they will be charging 5, 10, or 20 years from now.

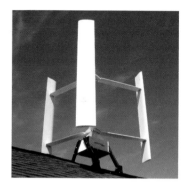

The phrase "small wind" refers to home-scale wind turbines that are either mounted on a roof or attached to the top of a tower. The ECO 1200 from Windterra (above) is a vertical-axis wind turbine that is designed to generate power even at low wind speeds. The Skystream 3.7 (above left) harnesses more wind because it sits atop a tower above wind-breaking trees. Both of these models will set you back $10,000 or more installed, but a new roof turbine (below) dubbed Democratic Ecology by acclaimed designer Philippe Starck will sell for under $1,000, plus installation.

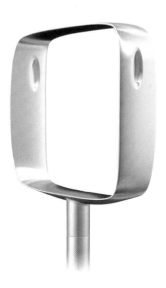

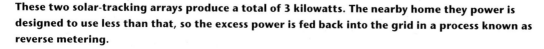
These two solar-tracking arrays produce a total of 3 kilowatts. The nearby home they power is designed to use less than that, so the excess power is fed back into the grid in a process known as reverse metering.

For More Info

For details about incentives in your area for alternative energy power sources, go to www.dsireusa.org, the Database of State Incentives for Renewable Energy.

To find a solar contractor, visit www.findsolar.com, which is sponsored by the U.S. Department of Energy and other solar energy associations. In addition to contractors, the site lists incentives in your area and calculates your savings and return on investment based on your current utility rates and your solar rating (i.e., the amount of sunshine you get).

To learn more about wind power, visit www.awea.org/smallwind/.

The traditional place for solar panels tends to be on the roof, as seen in this residential installation below, but shade structures like the one at right can support solar panels, too. After all, if you need to install a shade structure somewhere, that's probably because it's in a location that gets a lot of sun.

Going Solar

Photovoltaic (PV) cells convert light ("photo") into electricity ("voltaic"). Typically PV cells are made of a semiconductor material such as silicon, which absorbs the light while metal contacts on the top and bottom of the cells draw off the resulting electrical current. PV cells are bundled in groups of about 40 to make up modules, and the modules are organized into groups of about 10 to form panels, or arrays, measuring several yards in length and width. The result is a large, rectangular plate that can be mounted on a roof or in a yard at an angle that will maximize solar-energy collection. Generally 10 to 20 arrays are needed to power a home, and adding arrays over time is not difficult.

Solar systems are designed to last 20 to 25 years. Prices vary considerably, depending on the installation requirements, the number of panels needed, and incentives that may be available in your area. Many solar systems cost between $15,000 and $20,000, but rebates and new economic models can substantially lower upfront costs.

HARNESSING SOLAR POWER

Solar energy is collected as direct current (DC), so it needs to be transferred to alternating current (AC) for home use via an inverter. Newer solar panels have built-in inverters; otherwise a large central inverter is needed.

The wiring for solar panels is not especially complicated, but it is a job for a certified electrician. Basically, a bundle of wires runs from the panels on the roof down to the inverter. Other pieces of hardware needed to handle the incoming power are disconnect switches, grounding equipment, over-current protection, and a second meter. These can be attached to a basement wall or exterior wall near the service panel, and they typically take up 20 square feet or so of wall space.

METERS

Most utility companies are required to let a home connect its private solar system to the power grid. The question to ask is whether the utility will buy the home's surplus energy at a retail or a wholesale rate. If it pays the retail rate (the same rate that you pay the company), then a "net metering" setup can be installed. This requires only one meter, which spins in either direction (buying or selling). But it's more common for the utility company to pay a wholesale price for surplus energy (a few pennies per kilowatt hour as opposed to the higher rate you probably pay for the same amount), and for this a second meter must be installed to record surplus energy.

New Economic Models for Solar

In its earliest days, homeowners who wanted to use solar electricity had to pay high upfront costs. Installing panels, an inverter, and batteries could run to $30,000.

New companies have sprung up to take advantage of economies of scale and government incentives. PPAs (Power Purchase Agreements) have cut upfront costs and helped spread solar power more widely—home installations increased by 45 percent in both 2007 and 2008.

The model used by a company called Sun Run in San Francisco is fairly typical. For an upfront fee of less than a quarter of the cost of installing the panels themselves, a homeowner can hire Sun Run to install panels at their home and then purchase the energy the panels generate back from Sun Run. This way, the homeowner can pay off the initial costs of the installation in 10 years of electricity-bill savings. In addition, the homeowner signs a 20-year contract that locks in low electricity rates, which means the savings increase as energy costs rise, as is expected. Best of all, Sun Run maintains the system and replaces parts as needed. Other companies, SolarCity among them, contract with cities to do "group buys" and become an all-in-one solar utility, offering permitting, design, financing, tax-rebate processing, installation, and maintenance. Homeowners can lease the solar system from the company at a significant savings.

The solar installation at top is notched for a south-facing skylight. A second set of panels is mounted to a west-facing roof to catch the late-afternoon sun. The installation above faces only one direction, but the sheer number of panels facing southwest guarantees that it will generate a lot of power.

The installation of solar panels on a roof is best left to experienced professionals.

Here's a good idea: This deck needed a shade-giving pergola, so the homeowner had a structure built that was oriented to capture as much sunlight as possible. Instead of a roof, solar panels were installed.

A Skystream 3.7, just prior to installation in Pennsylvania.

Wind Energy

Another alternative source of energy is the wind. Currently the small-wind movement is still in its infancy, but new products (see page 232) could quickly change that. The main barrier to efficient wind production on a residential scale is getting the turbine high enough to work efficiently. For example, a 1,000-square-foot

An inverter and disconnect switch is getting to be a common sight next to the standard service panel (which, in this location, is behind a latched door).

home needs a small wind turbine mounted as high up as 40 to 100 feet to effectively generate power (the taller the tower, the greater the wind speed and the resulting electricity). Zoning laws tend to limit such towers to lots of an acre or greater. Then there's the effect on the neighbors, who sometimes complain about the appearance of the towers and the noise of the turbines—they make a repetitive *whop-whop-whop* sound—as well as concerns about the effects of turbines on birds. Rooftop models, while appealing and less expensive, will probably never work as well, especially if you live in a wooded area.

That said, per watt, wind power is cheaper than solar, and the manufacturing process is less of a drain on the earth's resources than making solar panels. That's why large-scale wind fields hold such promise. The Department of Energy reports that 20 percent of U.S. energy could be produced by wind power alone, which would be an enormous step away from dependence on fuels such as coal and oil.

As Bob Dylan once sang "You don't need a weatherman to

know which way the wind blows" but you may want to buy or rent an anemometer, a device that measures wind speed, and watch it for six months to determine whether or not wind power will work for you. That's the other truth about wind power: Not all areas have enough wind to make installation worthwhile. If you don't want to wait six months to make a decision, go to www.eere.energy.gov/windandhydro/windpoweringamerica to download a free wind map of your state.

Heat Pumps

While geothermal heat from natural hot springs has been a part of the green power arsenal for some time, the use of heat pumps to tap the benefits of below-ground heating and cooling is quickly spreading. Indeed, contractors who install heat pumps for a living say that installations have tripled in recent years.

Heat pumps take advantage of the constant temperatures that are found as little as 6 feet underground to heat homes in the winter and cool them in the summer. The systems use a network of water-filled pipes laid either horizontally (6 feet under) or vertically (often 200 to 300 feet down) that attach to a heat exchanger. Depending on where you live, a heat pump can save you anywhere from 25 to 65 percent on your energy costs.

Solar Roof Shingles

PV shingles offer an aesthetically appealing alternative to cumbersome panels. Lightweight and flexible, shingles are made of a thin film material. They can be used along with asphalt shingles to provide weather protection. The downside is that the shingles are more expensive and less energy efficient than solar panels.

Each shingle has two 12-inch-long 18-gauge lead wires that exit from the underside. These pass through the roof deck and are connected in the space below. To install solar shingles a roofing contractor first installs conventional shingles, leaving spaces for the solar ones.

Holes are drilled for the solar shingle wires, and then the solar shingles are installed so they overlap the asphalt shingles. An electrician wires the solar shingles together in the space below to form a unified array.

Steps to Solar

The first step in this solar installation was to install the mounts that would hold up the framing for the solar panels. The homeowner used this as an opportunity to replace the roof. Next came the framing, which is custom-made to connect to the mounts and the fittings on the solar panels. Finally, the panels were secured, which took just a day once the mounts were in place.

1 Installing the mounts

2 Attaching the framing

3 Securing the panels

Basic Repairs

I n this chapter, we help you make such basic repairs as replacing a light switch, installing a switch on a cord, and replacing a plug at the end of a cord. Also in this chapter is a step-by-step project to rewire a lamp, as well as the instructions needed to repair fluorescent fixtures, door chimes, and both low- and line-voltage thermostats. The chapter ends with a section on repairing existing wiring.

Chapter Contents

Troubleshooting Thermostats
page 256

Repairing Wiring in Boxes
page 260

page 240

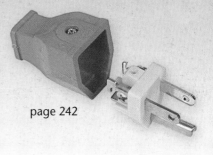

page 242

Fixture & Cord Switches

If a fixture or a lamp has a switch operated with a chain, a toggle, or a button, don't be surprised if the switch fails after years of heavy use. Such switches are not as hardy as wall switches. Fortunately, replacing one is neither difficult nor expensive.

Repair Choices

You can replace a fixture switch with a duplicate, or make a change—for example, replacing a toggle with a push button. The wiring is simple, and the hole required for mounting is a standard size. If a lamp's switch is hard to reach, you may choose to install a plug-in switch, or install a cord switch (opposite page).

Replacing a Fixture Switch

These steps show how to repair a light fixture switch. Repairing a lamp switch is similar: disconnect the power by unplugging the lamp, then remove the base to expose the wiring, detach the switch leads, and replace and rewire the switch.

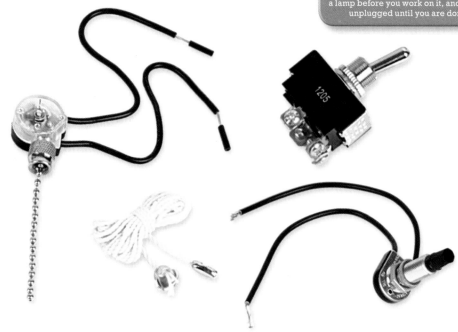

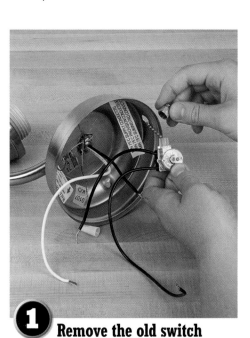

❶ Remove the old switch

- With the power off, pull out the fixture from the wall or ceiling
- Detach the two switch leads from the fixture's two hot wires
- Remove the mounting screw holding the switch to the fixture body; pull out the old switch

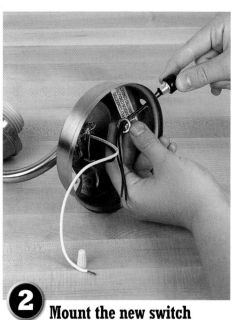

❷ Mount the new switch

- Insert a new switch into the hole
- Screw on the mounting nut

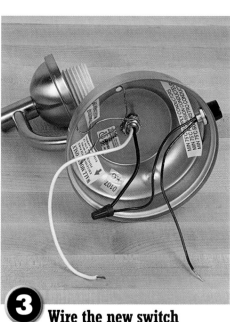

❸ Wire the new switch

- If necessary, strip insulation from the lead ends
- Twist the bare lead wires so they are fairly tight, then twist them onto the fixture wires
- Screw a wire nut on each connection
- Reinstall the fixture, restore power, and test

 **Stuff to Buy**
FIXTURE OR CORD SWITCH
BASIC SUPPLIES Wire nuts,
electrical tape

 **Time Commitment**
Two hours

 Tools You'll Need
Screwdriver
Wire stripper
Lineman's pliers
Utility knife

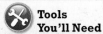 **Related Topics**
Grounding, 22–23
Replacing a single-pole switch, 106–107
Stripping & joining wire, 54–59
Testing methods, 52–53

Installing a Cord Switch

These steps show how to install a new cord switch. To replace a broken cord switch, substitute a new one of the same type, or upgrade from a small rotary switch (see Steps below) to a larger rocker switch, like the one shown here.

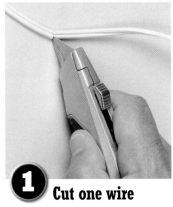

1 Cut one wire

- Place the unplugged lamp cord on a wood surface it's okay to cut into
- Slice through the smooth wire (not the ribbed one) with a sharp utility knife; the smooth wire is hot, and the ribbed wire is neutral

2 Pull apart

- Cut a short slit in the channel between the wires
- Pull away about 1 inch of the smooth wire on each side
- Strip ¾ inch of insulation from each smooth wire end
- Twist the bare wires tight to avoid fraying

3 Wire the switch

- Remove the screws to disassemble the switch
- Tightly wrap the wire ends clockwise around the switch's terminal screws
- Tighten the screws

4 Close cover

- Reassemble the switch and test

Installing a Rotary Cord Switch

A rotary cord switch is not very durable, but it is easy to install, with no wire stripping required. It's appropriate for a lamp that uses 100 watts or less and that you won't need to turn on and off too often.

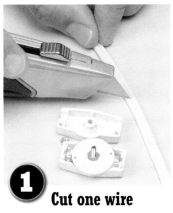

1 Cut one wire

- With the cord unplugged, cut only the smooth (hot) wire
- On each side, pull about ¾ inch of the smooth wire away from the ribbed wire

2 Insert wires into switch

- Push the wires into the switch
- No other internal steps are needed; metal barbs make connections after the switch is reassembled

3 Reassemble the switch

- Tighten the screws securely to make good electrical connections inside

Replacing Cords & Plugs

Cords and plugs carry 120 volts, just like household wiring. If a cord or plug looks worn or old (brittle and cracked), or it feels hot while in use, it should be replaced—preferably with heavier-duty parts. That precaution may avoid a dangerous short circuit.

Available Repair Parts

If a lamp or appliance is more than 6 feet from a receptacle, do not supplement the cord with a household-type extension cord on a long-term basis, especially if you notice the cord getting hot. If possible, install a new receptacle nearer the lamp or appliance. At a minimum, use a thick appliance-type extension cord to avoid overheating. A variety of cords and plugs are available at home improvement stores. Many more can be ordered online or special-ordered at a home improvement or hardware store.

CORDS

Buy a replacement cord with at least the same size wires and the same insulation as the original. If you cannot read the cord's specs, take the old cord with you and ask at the store. If the existing cord or plug got hot during operation, you need a cord with thicker wire or insulation rated for higher temperatures. Lamp cord is usually 18 gauge. You can use thicker 16-gauge wire (the size of a household extension cord) if it fits through the lamp's openings. Attaching it to terminals will be tricky but not impossible. Buy a foot or two more cord than you think you'll need.

REPLACEMENT PLUGS

The two common kinds of plugs are screw-terminal and self-connecting, both of which are appropriate for lamps and small appli-

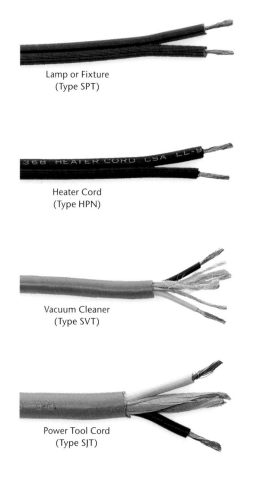

Lamp or Fixture
(Type SPT)

Heater Cord
(Type HPN)

Vacuum Cleaner
(Type SVT)

Power Tool Cord
(Type SJT)

ances. In plugs with screw terminals, the wires attach to screws inside the plug body. Self-connecting plugs clamp onto wires, making an automatic connection. Three-prong grounding plugs are most often used for appliances and power tools.

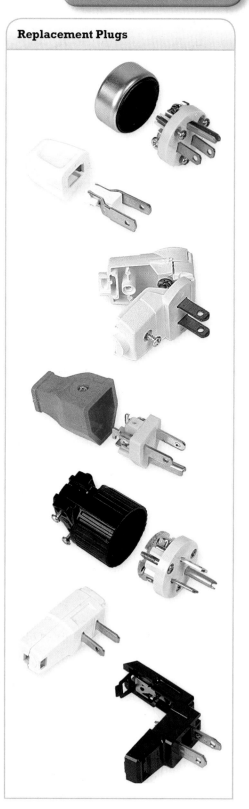

Replacement Plugs

Replacement Cords with Integral Plugs

The best solution is often to replace the cord and the plug at the same time. If possible, get a replacement cord that has the plug attached, rather than buying the parts separately.

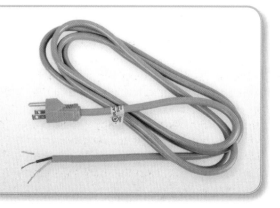

Stuff to Buy
CORDS OR PLUGS

Time Commitment
10 to 30 minutes

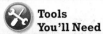
Tools You'll Need
Screwdriver
Wire stripper
Utility knife
Lineman's pliers

Related Topics
Fixture & cord switches, 240–241
Grounding, 22–23
Stripping & joining wire, 54–59

Zip Cord

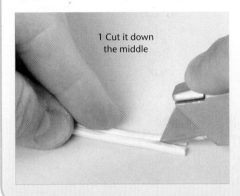

1 Cut it down the middle

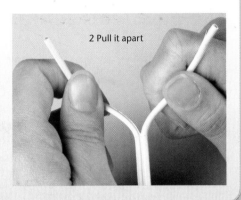

2 Pull it apart

Smooth (hot) wire   Ribbed (neutral) wire

Grounded Cord

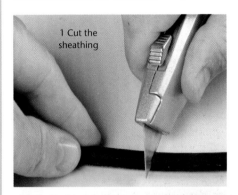

1 Cut the sheathing

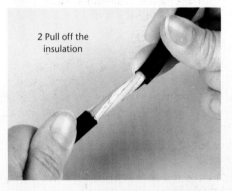

2 Pull off the insulation

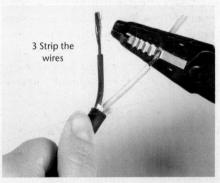

3 Strip the wires

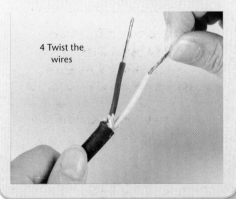

4 Twist the wires

Working with Cord

Electrical cord may be ungrounded zip cord or grounded cord.

Ungrounded zip cord has only two wires, with the insulation for both molded together. The hot wire insulation is smooth and the neutral wire insulation is ribbed. Grounded cord has three insulated wires—a black hot, a white neutral, and a green ground—encased in plastic sheathing.

To get to the wires, you separate the zip cord or remove the sheathing from grounded cord. Work carefully at a well-lit table with a wood surface you don't mind cutting into. When you strip the wires, don't nick the insulation, and avoid cutting away more than two or three wire strands.

ZIP CORD

To separate the two sides of zip cord, use a utility knife to make a cut in the channel between the wires. You may continue the cut with the knife, or pull the wires apart with your fingers.

In zip cord, the wire with ribbed insulation is the neutral wire; the one with smooth insulation is the hot wire. Be sure to connect the ribbed wire to the wider (neutral) prong and the smooth wire to the narrower (hot) prong. Otherwise, the lamp or appliance will not be correctly polarized and power will be present even when the switch is off.

GROUNDED CORD

You may be able to use the large hole in your wire strippers to remove sheathing. Alternatively, slice carefully around the sheathing with a utility knife, making certain not to cut the insulation of the underlying wires. Then make another slice, just as carefully, along the length of the sheathing and pull off the sheathing.

STRIPPING & TWISTING WIRES

To prepare either zip-cord or round-cord wires for attaching to terminals, strip about ¾ inch of wire insulation (depending on the type of terminal). Be sure you are looking at the "stranded" side of the strippers when choosing the stripping hole. If you lose more than three strands, cut and re-strip. Use your fingers to twist the strands so they are compact.

Replacing Plugs

If a plug sparks when it's pushed into or pulled out of a receptacle, examine the wires. You may need to tighten the connections.

Any plug with a cracked shell or with loose, damaged, or badly bent prongs should be replaced. Also replace plugs that transmit power erratically or that get warm when you use them. Be sure a replacement plug is at least as hefty and has the same number of prongs as the old one.

Many old-style plugs with screw terminals have a removable insulating disk covering the terminals and wires. The NEC now requires "dead-front" plugs, with a rigid insulating barrier rather than a removable one, to ensure that people cannot throw out the barrier. As long as you leave the barrier in place, an old-style plug is safe.

An Easy-connect Plug

There is no need to separate or strip wires for an easy-connect plug. This type of plug works only for zip cord, however.

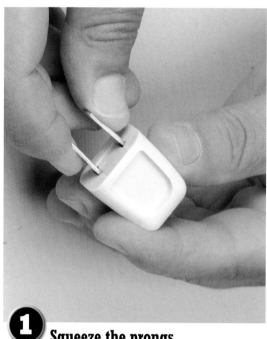

1 Squeeze the prongs

2 Pull out the prongs

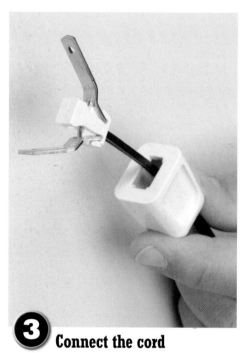

3 Connect the cord

- Spread the prongs
- Thread the cord through the body
- Poke the cord into the terminal hole behind the prongs; the ribbed wire goes to the wide prong and the smooth wire to the narrow prong

4 Squeeze the prongs

- Squeeze the prongs to clamp down on the wire and make the connections

5 Close up the plug

- Push the prongs back into the plug body

A Two-wire Plug

1 Prepare the cord

- For zip cord (shown here), pull the wires apart for 1 inch; for ground cord, strip that much sheathing
- Strip ⅝ inch of insulation from each wire

2 Attach the plug

- Remove the face screw from the plug
- Pull the inner part of the plug from the plug body
- Wrap each wire around a terminal screw; the hot wire goes to the smaller prong, the neutral to the larger prong
- Tighten the terminals, keeping the wire strands together

3 Reassemble the plug

- Push the plug pieces back together
- Reattach the face screw to the plug

A Three-wire Plug

1 Prepare the cord and plug

- Strip sheathing and wire insulation, removing the amount specified by the manufacturer
- Disassemble the plug; in this case, a single screw holds the two pieces of the plug together

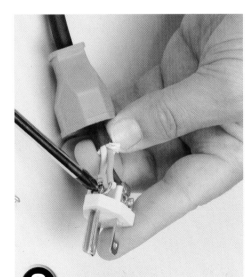

2 Wire the plug

- Attach the stripped wire ends
- White wire to silver terminal, green wire to green terminal, black wire to brass terminal

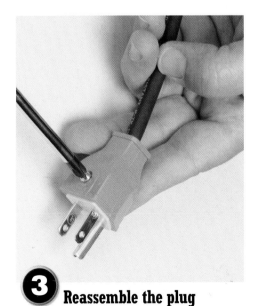

3 Reassemble the plug

- Push the plug pieces back together
- When the plug face lines up with the edge of the plug housing, tighten the screw

Rewiring a Lamp

Most plug-in lamps have a socket, switch, cord, and plug. Any one of those four parts may require repairs. The troubleshooting steps on these four pages can help to keep your favorite lamp burning bright.

STOP!
Always unplug a lamp before you work on it, and keep it unplugged until you are done.

Anatomy of a Lamp

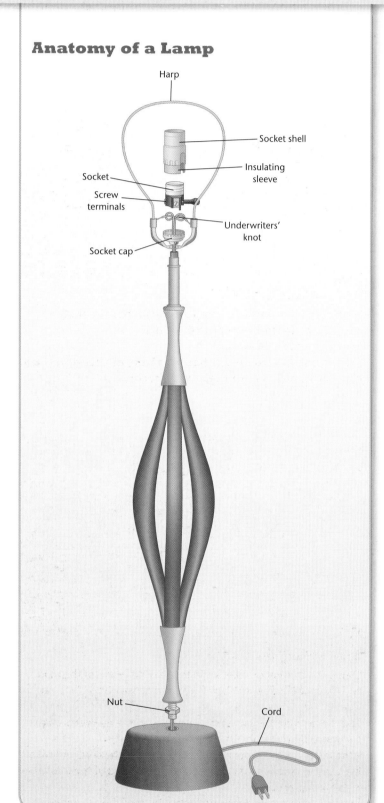

Harp

Socket shell

Insulating sleeve

Socket

Screw terminals

Underwriters' knot

Socket cap

Nut

Cord

Lamp Repair Basics

In the lamp shown here, the socket has an integral twist-type switch. A socket may also have a pull-chain switch. A lamp can also be controlled by a fixture switch in its body, or a cord switch, or several kinds of easy switches that plug or screw in.

If a lamp isn't working, first check the light bulb to make sure it isn't loose or burned out. Next, plug the lamp into another outlet to be sure the wall outlet isn't at fault. Check the plug and cord for wear.

If your old socket, cord, and plug are looking a bit dated or suspect, replace them all. The lamp will look better, and you'll have no doubts about its future performance.

Cleaning & Adjusting the Socket Tab

If the bulb, cord, and plug are in good shape, make sure the lamp is unplugged, then take out the bulb and inspect the socket tab (the raised metal piece inside the socket). If it's dirty or rusty, use a screwdriver to scrape it clean. The tab needs to be somewhat raised to make contact with the base of the bulb. If it's too flat, pry up gently with the screwdriver.

Adjusting the Tab

Stuff to Buy

SOCKET, CORD, PLUG as needed
BASIC SUPPLIES Electrical tape

Time Commitment

One to two hours

Tools You'll Need

Screwdriver
Continuity tester
Wire stripper
Utility knife

Related Topics

Fixture & cord switches, 240–241
Replacing cords & plugs, 242–245
Stripping & joining wire, 54–59

Basic Lamp Repairs

Repairing a lamp is a simple process you can do one step at a time.

❶ Remove the socket

- With the lamp unplugged, remove the small mounting screw (if any) near the socket tab
- Press or squeeze on the shell where it says "press," then slide out the shell and insulating sleeve
- Unfasten the wires from the socket's screw terminals
- If the socket shell's paper insulation is damaged or fragile, discard the socket instead of testing it, and skip ahead to Step 3

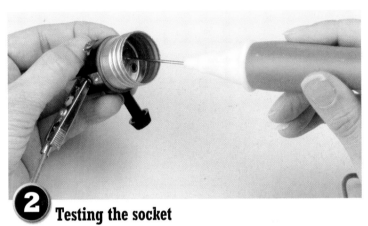

❷ Testing the socket

- For a socket with a switch, clamp the clip to the brass (hot) terminal and touch the probe to the contact tab
- Turn the switch on and off
- The tester should glow when the switch is on, and not glow when the switch is off; otherwise, replace the socket

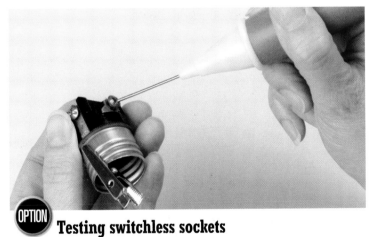

OPTION Testing switchless sockets

- If the socket has no switch, clamp the clip of a continuity tester to the brass (hot) screw and touch the probe to the brass tab
- Next, clamp the clip to the socket's metal threads and touch the probe to the silver (neutral) terminal
- If the tester doesn't glow in both tests, replace the socket

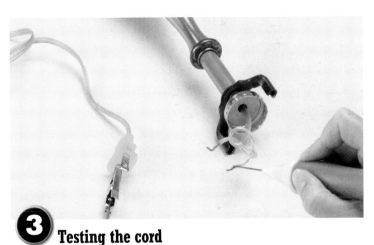

❸ Testing the cord

- Clamp the continuity tester's clip to the wide prong of the plug and touch the probe to the stripped end of the ribbed (neutral) wire
- Test the hot wire the same way, clamping to the narrow prong and touching the probe to the smooth wire
- If the tester doesn't glow in both tests, replace the cord and plug
- Replace any cord (or a damaged portion of a cord) if the insulation is visibly damaged
- Lamp repairs usually involve replacing the cord, but if your cord does not require replacement, skip ahead to Step 7

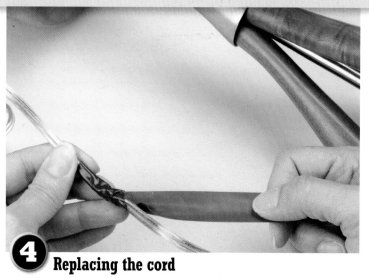

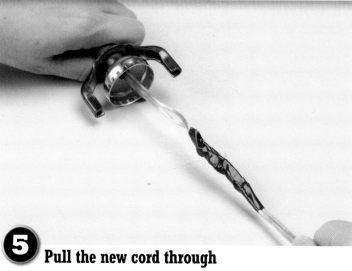

④ Replacing the cord

- Confirm the cord is still unplugged; at the socket, pull outward to see whether the cord is loose, but don't pull it through yet
- If it's not loose, loosen the setscrew (if any) in the socket cap; you may also need to remove the cap
- Cut the plug off the old cord
- Tape the replacement cord (preferably with a plug already on it) to the cut end of the old cord
- Make the connection secure but slender enough to feed through the lamp

⑤ Pull the new cord through

- At the socket end, pull on the old cord until the new cord appears
- Remove the tape and discard the old cord

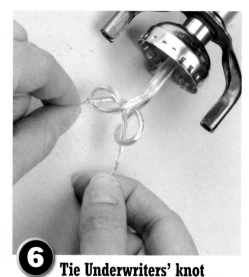

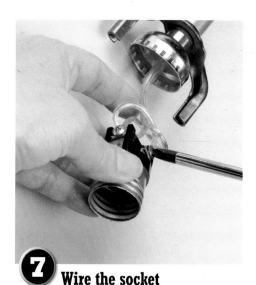

⑥ Tie Underwriters' knot

- Split 3 inches of the new cord
- Make an Underwriters' knot: form a loop in each piece of cord, then pass the loose ends through the loops, pulling fairly snug
- If the cord does not have a plug, install one

⑦ Wire the socket

- Install the socket and cord the same way whether they are new replacements or original pieces
- Strip just enough of the wires to wrap around the terminal screws
- Twist the strands together and wrap them around the terminals, with the hot wire on the brass terminal and the neutral wire on the silver terminal
- Tighten the terminal screws and pull on the other end of the cord to tighten the knot

⑧ Reseat the socket

- Press the socket into place
- Push the insulating sleeve over the socket, then push the shell in until you hear it click
- Screw in a light bulb, plug in the lamp, and turn on the switch to test

This graceful table lamp lends a stylish touch, general illumination, and localized reading light to a small area within a room.

Repairing Fluorescent Fixtures

✓ Degree of
Difficulty
● Easy

CFLs may be new to many homes, but energy-efficient fluorescent tubes have been lighting up workrooms, basements, and garages since the middle of the last century. Repairing a fluorescent fixture is as simple as fixing a lamp, but involves different steps.

STOP!
Always turn off power to the circuit you are working on, then double-check at the project site before and after removing the fixture to make sure the power is off.

Fluorescent Fixture

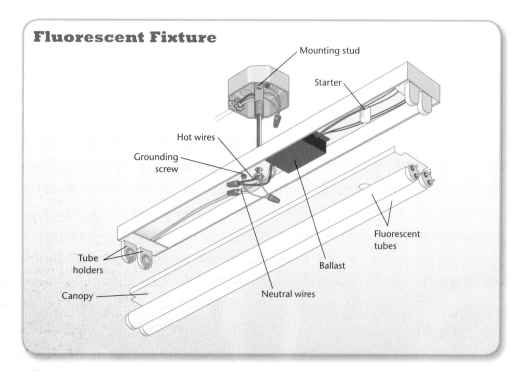

- Mounting stud
- Starter
- Hot wires
- Grounding screw
- Tube holders
- Canopy
- Neutral wires
- Ballast
- Fluorescent tubes

Fluorescent fixtures are popular above garage work tables because they produce a lot of light and are inexpensive to operate.

Anatomy of a Fluorescent Fixture

A fluorescent fixture consists of fluorescent tubes, a ballast that steps up the household voltage briefly to get the tubes started, tube holders (sockets), and, on some older fixtures, a starter that assists the ballast in the initial start-up process. Most fixtures have a diffuser, essentially a translucent plastic sheet, to reduce glare and spread light more evenly.

There are three types of fluorescent light fixtures. In a preheat fixture—an older style—you can see a starter, which looks like a miniature aluminum can. In a rapid-start fixture—the most common type—the starter is built into the ballast. In both a preheat and a rapid-start fixture, the tubes attach to tube holders via two pins. An instant-start fixture has no starter and uses tubes with a single pin on each end.

Older magnetic (or reactive) ballasts are heavy and may hum or ooze a somewhat caustic black goo when they fail. Avoid touching the goo if you can. Newer electronic ballasts are lighter and longer-lived. In some cases you may be able to replace a magnetic ballast with an electronic one.

Changing a tube or a starter is easily done, but you may want to take the fixture down and work on a table when replacing a tube holder or a ballast.

Mercury Alert

The insides of fluorescent tubes are coated with a tiny amount of mercury, so handle them carefully to avoid breakage. If a tube does shatter, wear gloves before handling it, open a window to vent the room, and wrap the shards in a double plastic bag. Many states and municipalities require you to recycle old fluorescents tubes, including CFLs. Even places that don't require recycling strongly encourage it.

 **Stuff to Buy**

FLUORESCENT TUBES For warm light, choose tubes with Kelvin ratings of 5,000 or more
STARTER, TUBEHOLDERS, BALLAST
BASIC SUPPLIES Wire nuts

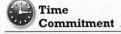 **Time Commitment**

One to two hours

 Tools You'll Need

Screwdriver
Wire stripper
Lineman's pliers

 Related Topics

Fluorescent fixtures, 78–79
Stripping & joining wire, 54–59

About the "Flicker Effect"

Fluorescent tubes flicker very quickly, perhaps at the rate of 120 times per second—too fast for people to really see. Still, some people are uncomfortable with fluorescent lighting. A good diffuser panel can minimize this discomfort. Newer fixtures with electronic ballasts also greatly increase the flicker speed, thus producing a light that very few people find objectionable.

Troubleshooting a Fluorescent Fixture

If your once-reliable fluorescent fixture flickers noticeably or doesn't light, try these steps to solve the problem.

- Check at the house service panel to see if a breaker has tripped or a fuse has blown.
- If a tube end is blackened, replace the tube.
- If a tube is discolored (but not black) on one end only, remove it, turn it end for end, and reinstall it.
- If tubes are not blackened, but will not light, try twisting the tubes to realign them in the tube holders.
- If the fixture is in a room colder than 50 degrees F (10 C), warm up the room or slip a clear plastic cold-weather sleeve (also called a tube protector) over the tubes.
- If the fixture has a starter, try replacing it.
- If a tube holder is cracked or damaged, replace it.

- If the fixture hums, or if you see black goo coming from the ballast, replace the ballast or replace the fixture.
- If the fixture will not light even with new tubes and (for a preheat fixture) a new starter, replace the ballast or replace the fixture.

REPLACING A STARTER

Unlike more modern fixtures, preheat fixtures contain a separate starter. To replace a starter, shut off power to the fixture and remove the tubes. Rotate the starter a quarter turn counterclockwise and pull it out of its socket. Buy a new starter with the same rating number and install it.

REPLACING OR REALIGNING A FLUORESCENT TUBE

If a tube is blackened at its ends, it should be replaced even if it still lights. For a tube that fails or flickers but is not blackened, first try rotating it to seat its pins in the tube holders. If that doesn't work, replace the tube.

Changing a tube is the equivalent of changing a light bulb. As with a lamp, you don't need to turn off power to the circuit if you are sure that the fixture is switched off. Rotate the tube about a quarter turn (it may be tight) until you can slip the pins out of the holders. You may need to wiggle it a bit.

REPLACING A TUBE HOLDER

It's relatively simple to replace tube holders (also called sockets) on most fluorescent fixtures. First, of course, make sure the power is off. The tube

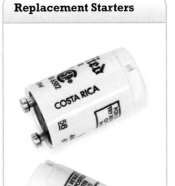

Replacement Starters

holder typically slips on and off the fixture body via slots in its sides.

If the holder has push-in terminals, poke the slot with a small screwdriver and pull the wires out. If the holder attaches directly to the fixture's wiring, cut the wires close to the holder and strip the ends. Install a new holder that has push-in terminals.

REPLACING A BALLAST

To replace the ballast, buy a new one that matches the numbers on the old one. You may need to special-order the ballast or go to an electrical-supply store.

Make sure the power is off to the fixture. Then hold the new ballast next to the old one and make sure you know which wires go where; you may need to tag one or more wires. If possible, disconnect the ballast's wires by removing wire nuts.

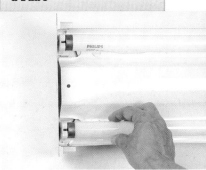

Rotating and Reseating a Tube

Replacing a Tube Holder

Replacing a Ballast

Otherwise, you'll need to cut the wires and strip wire ends.

Remove the mounting screws and the old ballast. Then install the new ballast in the same location. Screw on wire nuts to make the connections and restore power to the fixture.

Incandescent Light Fixtures

STOP!
Always turn off power to the circuit or circuits for the fixture you are working on. Double-check at the fixture to make sure the power is off.

When an incandescent fixture doesn't work, first check the light bulb to make sure it isn't loose or burned out. Then check the circuit and the light switch. If those are fine, the problem may be in the fixture wiring or in the socket.

First Steps

With the power off, detach the fixture, pull it out, and check for a loose connection. Tighten if necessary. Check the socket as you would for a table lamp (see pages 246–248); clean the socket, pry up its tab, and test it.

If the fixture still doesn't work, you'll have to either repair or replace it. If you prefer not to make the repairs described here—or if you don't like the fixture anyway—follow the instructions in Chapter 3 (see pages 74–81) to put in a new fixture.

Testing & Repair

Repairing the fixture involves removing and replacing the sockets, the wiring, or both. Sockets in all types of fixtures may have screw terminals like a lamp socket, or they may have permanently attached wires.

ABOVE: There are a lot of reasons why a chandelier like this one might be on the fritz, but if none of the bulbs are working, then they probably aren't the culprits. RIGHT: When troubleshooting a faulty track light, check to make sure that all fixtures are tight in their tracks and that all connectors are secure.

Pendant lights like these are fragile, so work methodically and carefully from the bottom up, removing glass pieces first, if possible, before removing the canopy to inspect the wires.

When you replace a socket, ensure the proper polarity by connecting wires of the same color. To replace a pre-wired socket, first disconnect the socket wires from the circuit wires, then unclip the faulty socket from the fixture. Attach the new socket by reversing these steps.

On a chandelier, the sockets and the socket wires in the arms connect in a central junction box to a main cord that runs to the house's ceiling box. You will probably need to remove a cover in the junction box to access these connections. Test each arm cord as well as the main cord with a continuity tester, as you would a lamp cord. If one cord is faulty, it's usually a good idea to replace them all.

Chandelier

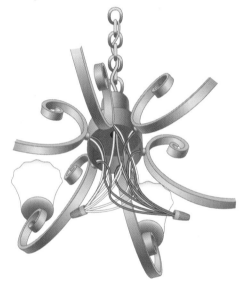

Ceiling Fixture

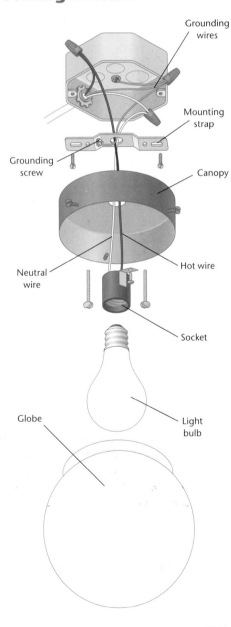

Grounding wires

Mounting strap

Grounding screw

Canopy

Neutral wire

Hot wire

Socket

Globe

Light bulb

Track Fixture

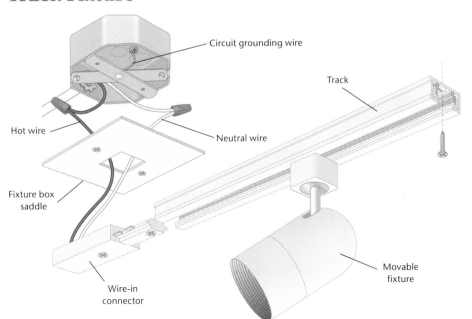

Circuit grounding wire

Hot wire

Neutral wire

Fixture box saddle

Track

Movable fixture

Wire-in connector

Repairing a Door Chime

A door chime system has four components: the push button(s), the noise element (a chime, bell, or buzzer), the transformer, and the thin wires that travel between them. The transformer steps down the voltage to between 6 and 24 volts.

Anatomy of a Door Chime

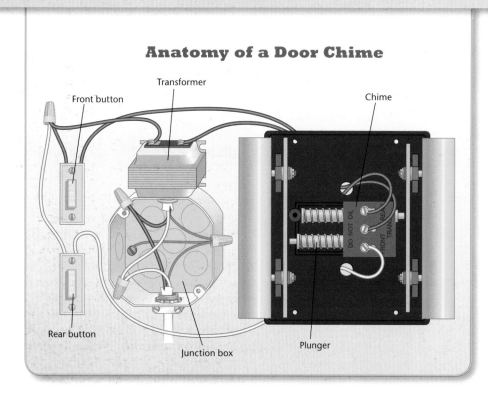

Transformer

Front button

Chime

Rear button

Junction box

Plunger

How Door Chimes Work

On many systems, pushing the front-door button produces two tones ("ding dong") and pushing the rear-door button produces only one ("ding" or perhaps "dong"). If you get only one tone when you push the front button, the front and rear wires may be switched in the chime.

The transformer sends low-voltage power to the front-door button via one wire. Another wire runs from the button to the "front" terminal on the chime, and a third wire completes the circuit by traveling from the chime's "trans" terminal back to the transformer. The button acts as a switch, turning power on when it is depressed. If there is a rear-door button, it is connected in the same way but uses the "rear" chime terminal.

Troubleshooting a Silent Chime

If a door chime does not sound, first check the button. Remove the button's screws and pull it out—taking care that the wires, which may come loose, don't slip into the wall. Tighten any loose terminal connections. If a wire is broken, strip it and reattach it to the terminal. Clean out rust or other debris with a brush.

If the problem persists, strip the ends of a short piece of wire and touch the bare ends to the bare ends of the bell wires. If the chime sounds, replace the button. If you see a small spark but the chime does not sound, the problem is with the chime; confirm this as shown in Steps 1 and 2. If there is no spark and no chime, the transformer is likely the problem (Steps 3 and 4). The transformer is also the likely problem if the chime got worse slowly.

Finding the transformer may be tricky. It could be in a basement, crawl space, or utility area, inside a cabinet, or mounted near or against the service panel. Trace wires to make sure the transformer you find is the correct one. There could also be one for a low-voltage thermostat or a sprinkler system, for example.

Wireless Chime

To install a wireless chime system, simply plug the chime into a receptacle. The button is battery powered.

Most wireless chimes have an electronic sound that is a matter of taste; many people prefer a standard chime or bell. However, some models allow you to choose among a number of tones or even melodies.

If there is an area of the house where you cannot hear the door chime, consider installing a wireless chime extender, which is triggered by the sound of the standard chime.

Stuff to Buy

BUTTON, CHIME, OR
TRANSFORMER as needed
BASIC SUPPLIES Wire nuts

 **Time Commitment**

One to two hours

 Tools You'll Need

Screwdriver
Brush
Multitester
Wire stripper
Lineman's pliers

 Related Topics

Grounding, 22–23
Stripping & joining wires, 54–59
Testing methods, 52–53
Inspecting your wiring, 36–39

Checking the Chime & Transformer

❶ Open the chime

- Remove the chime's cover (most covers pull off)
- Clean away dust and debris with a brush and vacuum, especially around the chimes and at the terminals

❷ Check the plunger

- If the chime has a plunger mechanism, pull back on it and release it; the plunger should slide easily, producing a tone
- If there is grime holding up the works, clean it out with a degreaser

❸ Check the power

- If the chime's voltage rating is not printed on it, check the transformer to find out the voltage
- While someone pushes the button, press the probes of a multitester to the "front" and "trans" chime terminals (for a two-button system, also touch the "rear" and "trans" terminals)
- A reading within 3 volts of the rating means the transformer is fine; replace the chime
- In case of a lower reading, replace the transformer

❹ Test the transformer

- With the transformer in its box, touch the probes of a multitester to the terminals
- If the reading is more than 3 volts below its rating, replace the transformer
- If you get no reading, check the circuit breaker or fuse
- If the circuit is live, shut off power to the circuit, confirm it's off, remove the cover plate at the junction box, and check the connections inside the box
- If the transformer checks out, a wire is broken; run new wires as needed
- Alternatively, install a wireless chime

Replacing a Chime

Make sure your new chime or bell has the same voltage rating as your transformer. If possible, get one that is as large as or larger than the old chime, to avoid touching up the wall after you install it. Before you remove wires from the old chime, tag them to show which terminal they go to. Then loosen the terminal screws and remove the wires. Take out the old chime's mounting screws and remove the old chime. Thread the wires through the hole in the new chime, drive mounting screws, and connect the wires to the terminals.

Replacing a Transformer

With the power off, remove the junction box's cover plate and confirm again the power is off. Unscrew the wire nuts and disassemble the transformer's leads from the house wires. Remove the bell wires from the transformer, remove the mounting nut inside the box, and take out the transformer. Mount the new transformer, splice its leads to the house wires, replace the box's cover plate, and attach the bell wires. Restore power and test the door chime.

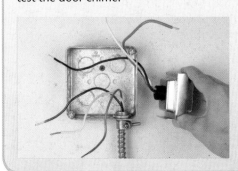

Troubleshooting Thermostats

Degree of Difficulty
● Easy

A thermostat may control a boiler, furnace, heat pump, air conditioner, electric heater, or other heating or cooling source. Most thermostats described here use low voltage, but some use standard 120-volt household current.

Discreetly placed thermostats, whether in a formal dining room (below, left) or a central hallway (below, right), can control the temperature for the whole house. Thermostats in locations like a bathroom (above) can be installed to control heat in a particular room.

Stuff to Buy

THERMOSTAT if needed
BASIC SUPPLIES Wire nuts

Time Commitment

15 minutes or so

Tools You'll Need

Screwdriver
Compressed air can
Level
Wire stripper
Lineman's pliers
Voltage detector
Continuity tester

Related Topics

Grounding, 22–23
Shutting off & restoring power, 50–51
Stripping & joining wire, 54–59
Testing methods, 52–53

Anatomy of a Thermostat

A thermostat is essentially a switch that senses temperature and turns the heating or air-conditioning on and off accordingly. Many older thermostats have a bimetal coil, which expands and contracts with changing temperatures. These changes rotate a small glass vial filled with mercury, causing the mercury to shift and thereby turning the power on or off. Newer thermostats use other sensing and switching mechanisms. A low-voltage thermostat also has a heat anticipator, which shuts off the boiler, furnace, or heat pump just before the desired temperature is reached to avoid overshooting the mark.

In a low-voltage thermostat, a transformer sends a small amount of current to the thermostat via a thin wire. If a thermostat only controls the heat, it is connected to only two wires—one from the transformer and one leading to the heating system. If it also controls an air-conditioning unit and a blower unit, there will be additional wires for those.

Because the voltage is so low, working on a low-voltage thermostat's wiring is safe. The following pages show some simple maintenance and testing procedures that should take only a few minutes to perform. If the thermostat still does not work, replace it; it's not worth trying to fix.

Repairing a Low-Voltage Thermostat

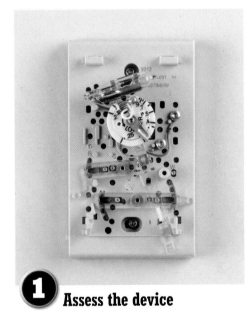

1 Assess the device

- Remove cover plate
- Look for loose or disconnected wires
- If the thin metal contacts are dirty or grimy, wipe them gently with a piece of paper

2 Clean the inside

- Use a soft brush or canned air to clean away dust or other debris, which can impede the connections
- Move control levers back and forth as you spray or brush

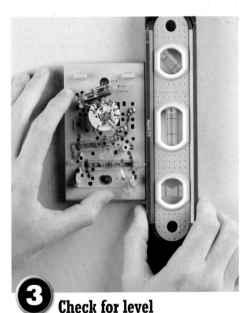

3 Check for level

- If house is overheated or underheated, use a level to make sure the thermostat is plumb; a round one will have marks for leveling
- If the thermostat is not level, remove the mounting screws, reposition it, and drive screws in new locations
- Mount the thermostat firmly, so it won't be bumped out of plumb

❹ Do an arc test

- If cleaning and leveling don't solve the problem, loosen the mounting screws and pull the thermostat away from the wall
- Strip insulation from the ends of a short length of wire and touch one end to the R terminal and the other end to the W terminal
- If system comes on and didn't before, replace the thermostat
- If the thermostat controls other functions, touch the short wire to R and each of the other terminals to which a wire is attached; if units come on and didn't before, replace the thermostat
- If nothing comes on, the transformer may be faulty

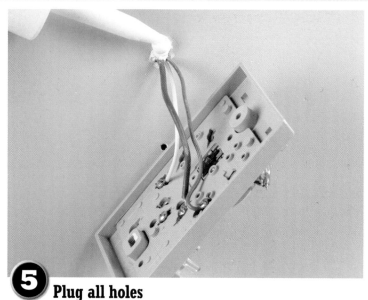

❺ Plug all holes

- To be sure air inside the wall doesn't affect the temperature reading, plug all holes
- Latex caulk is a good material for sealing wire holes

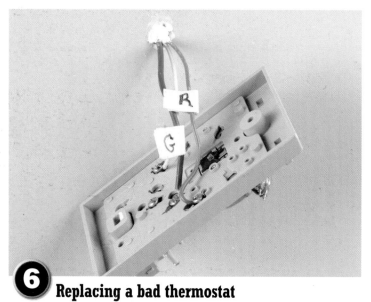

❻ Replacing a bad thermostat

- If the hole in the wall is large, first attach a clip to the wires so they don't slip into the wall
- One at a time, loosen the terminal screws, remove the wire, and tag the wires with tape indicating the terminal to which each belongs

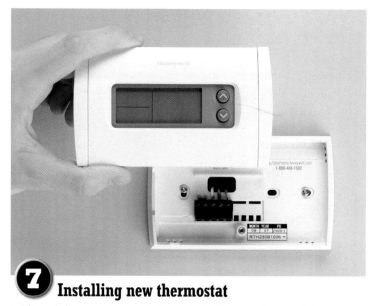

❼ Installing new thermostat

- Thread the wires through the hole in the new thermostat
- Cut and restrip the wire ends, bend them into loops, and attach them to the terminals, making sure no stray wire ends contact other terminals
- Press the base plate onto the wall, level it (Step 3), and drive screws to mount it
- Attach the thermostat body, then test

Testing a Line-voltage Thermostat

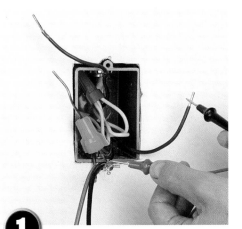

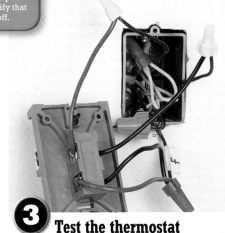

❶ Pull out the thermostat

- Shut off power to the heating unit at the service panel
- Remove the thermostat's cover and test with a voltage detector
- Pull the thermostat out, and test again for power

❷ Label the feed wire

- Tag the house feed wire so that you can splice it with the correct leads if you need to install a new thermostat
- This thermostat is wired like a wall switch, except that the power travels via a black house feed wire (F) to a pair of red and black "line" leads, and exits toward the heaters via two "load" leads; the house's neutral wires are spliced together

❸ Test the thermostat

- Clamp a continuity tester's clip to a "line" lead, then touch the probe to a "load" wire on the same side of the thermostat; the tester should glow when the thermostat is on and not glow when it is off
- Test the other side the same way
- If the thermostat fails the test, replace it; use wire nuts to splice the house wires to the correct leads, fold the wires into the box, press the thermostat into place, and attach it with mounting screws
- If it passes the test, have an electrician or heating contractor evaluate your heating units

Programmable Thermostats

A programmable thermostat can turn the temperature up or down several times a day, making it comfortably cool for sleeping but nice and warm when you arise—and save energy costs in the process. Install one in the same way you would a standard thermostat. Consult the owner's manual to be sure you are attaching wires to the correct terminals. Install batteries, then program the thermostat.

Savings from such a thermostat are greater if you are away from the house on a predictable schedule and if your heating source warms the house quickly—for instance, with forced-air or steam heat. Savings will be less if someone is home most of the time and if you have hot-water or radiant heat, which heat slowly.

Testing a Transformer

The transformer is probably attached to or near the heating or cooling unit. To make sure you are dealing with the right transformer (and not one for a door chime or sprinkler system, for example), trace the wires. One wire comes from the thermostat, and one goes to the heat or air-conditioning unit.

In older units, the transformer may be attached to an electrical box much as a transformer for a door chime would be. If this is the case with yours, touch the probes of a multitester to each of the low-voltage terminals. If there is no current, or if the current is more than 3 volts lower than the level printed on the transformer, the transformer needs to be replaced.

Often, however, the transformer is located behind a panel in the boiler or furnace, and the wiring can be complicated. You may be able to test the transformer, but it is probably a good idea to call in a heating professional to install a replacement.

Repairing Wiring in Boxes

Most wiring problems inside electrical boxes are due to age. Wire insulation gets brittle with age, which can leave the wire inside the insulation unprotected. If the wires were packed too tightly in a box, this can cause shorts.

STOP!

Some of the wiring in electrical boxes can only be checked with the power on, as described here; in such cases, work with great care. For tasks that don't require power, shut off the power to the circuit, and double-check at the project site that the power is off.

Examining an Existing Box

Look where wires enter a box to make sure they are not rubbing against a sharp metal surface. With NM cable and a metal box, there should be some sheathing visible; that is, the cable clamp should be on the sheathing and not directly touching wire insulation. With armored cable, there should be a plastic bushing (usually red) protecting the wires.

Old wiring insulation may become brittle and cracked inside a box, but wiring inside walls is usually in better shape. In most cases, the wires in a box are more exposed to heat and air, while wires encased in cable are protected.

A pipe in a ceiling or wall-sconce box may have originally been used for gaslights. If you have these pipes, there is a chance that they are still connected to live gas lines, and they might even have some gas in them. Have your gas company come out and test to be sure.

Here are several other wiring repairs you may have to make.

Checking for a Switched Ground	Installing a Sleeve	Shrinking a Sleeve	Enlarging a Box

CHECKING FOR A SWITCHED GROUND

Old insulation sometimes becomes so blackened that you cannot tell a black (hot) wire from a white (neutral) wire. As a result, it is not uncommon to find wiring mistakes, especially when a do-it-yourselfer has replaced a switch. If a switch is connected to neutral rather than hot wires, power will be present in the fixture box even when the fixture is switched off.

To make sure you know which wire is hot, shut off power to the circuit. Remove and separate the wires so they cannot touch each other, and have others leave the room.

Restore power. Touch one probe of a voltage tester to the metal box and one to a wire. When the tester glows, you've found the hot wire.

REPAIRING DAMAGED INSULATION

Missing or cracked insulation can cause shorts and perhaps a fire, so insulate any bare wire. Shut off power to the circuit before working. Usually, it is best to remove the device or fixture before making the repair.

You could wrap the wire with pro-quality electrical tape, but it's hard to get the tape tight and to cover all areas. A better solution is to use insulating sleeves made for the purpose. Make sure the sleeves you buy are large enough to slip easily over the wires. Slide a sleeve over a wire and push it down as far as possible to protect the wire where it enters the box. Direct a hair dryer or heat gun at the sleeve. Once it shrinks, stop heating it right away.

ENLARGING A BOX

Some boxes are only large enough for a standard switch or receptacle and its wiring. If you find a thicker than average device (like a special-duty switch or a GFCI receptacle) crammed into a box, you may be looking at a dangerous situation.

You could remove the box, pull out the wires, and replace it with a larger box, but that is difficult and messy. An easier solution is to use surface-mounted components, also called raceway. The box will protrude a bit into the room, but it can be painted.

ADDING A GOOF PLUG

All knockout holes in boxes and service panels pose serious dangers, so codes require them to be filled. Purchase goof plugs, which come in different sizes to fill holes of various diameters. Simply tap them in.

Aluminum Wiring

Especially during the 1970s and 1980s, a number of homes were built with aluminum wiring. You can recognize aluminum wiring by its thick, aluminum-colored wires. "AL" may be printed on the wire or sheathing insulation and is engraved on aluminum devices.

Aluminum expands and contracts, so connections tend to come loose after some decades. Also, aluminum oxide can form on the wire surface, making for poor conduction. This can cause flickering lights, poorly performing receptacles, and even house fires due to overheated wires.

If you have aluminum wiring, consult an electrician. It's a good idea to go through the house every so often and tighten all the splices and terminal screws. This is a time-consuming task that must be performed systematically, so you should probably hire a pro to do it or supervise you as you do it.

Special wire nuts are now recommended to make more permanent aluminum-wire connections. All switches and receptacles should be labeled CO/ALR, meaning that they make better connections with aluminum wires. An antioxidant paste should be squirted onto any connection between aluminum and copper.

Adapting an Old Ceiling Box

An older pancake box may have a pipe protruding down its center, making it impossible to install a standard strap for a ceiling box. Removing and replacing the box or disconnecting the pipe requires cutting a large hole in the ceiling and perhaps adding framing. There are two simpler solutions, however.

If you have a fixture that mounts via a center threaded rod (called a stud or a nipple), buy a piece of hardware, sometimes called a hickey, that can be screwed onto the old pipe at one end. At its other end are female threads that can receive the fixture's threaded rod.

To install a fixture whose canopy attaches with two screws, mount a standard strap that is off center. To securely attach the strap to the box, you will need a tap wrench, a #8-32NC tap and a $9/64$-inch drill bit (also called a #29 bit and possibly sold with the tap). Hold the strap in position, insert the drill bit through the strap's mounting slots, and drill holes through the box. Insert the tap into each hole and twist clockwise until you poke all the way through. You now have holes that will accept $8/32$ machine screws—a standard size for mounting hardware.

Drill bit

Tap wrench

Machine screw

CHECKING FOR GROUNDING

If your home has receptacles with only two slots, it's probably on an ungrounded system. Such systems can be basically safe. Any new wiring needs to be grounded, but the old ungrounded service will likely be allowed to remain. It's also possible your boxes are grounded after all, in which case you can install grounded receptacles. If not, you can install GFCI protection. You can also separately ground a single receptacle.

First, check if the box is grounded. If you're lucky, metal conduit or sheathing provides a ground path. With the power still on, remove the cover plate. Working carefully, insert a multitester's prongs into the receptacle's two slots and note the voltage reading. Then insert a prong into the short (hot) slot and touch the other prong to the metal box. If this reading is within 5 volts of the first reading, then you have a ground path and can install a three-slot, grounded receptacle.

Don't assume that because one receptacle is grounded the others are, too; test each one individually. After installing a grounded receptacle, use a receptacle analyzer to make sure it is properly grounded and polarized.

If the box is not grounded, you could run a green-insulated ground wire from the receptacle box to a grounding clamp attached to a cold-water pipe. Since each receptacle must be grounded separately, this is practical only if you need to ground just one or two.

A better solution is to provide GFCI protection, which is in most respects more effective than grounding. You can install a GFCI receptacle at the beginning of a series of receptacles to protect all the receptacles downstream. For durability, purchase a commercial-grade GFCI. Test the GFCI receptacle once a month or so using its built-in button.

Adding a Goof Plug

Checking for Grounding

11

Help Section

In this chapter, we help you prepare for a power blackout, give you easy formulas for calculating electrical capacity, and list some of the most common electrical codes. In addition, we've created illustrations of more than two dozen of the most frequently used wiring configurations, as well as plans to get you started on whole-room electrical remodels. Finally, the chapter concludes with a useful glossary.

Chapter Contents

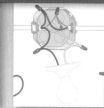
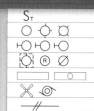
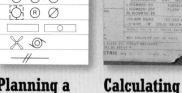

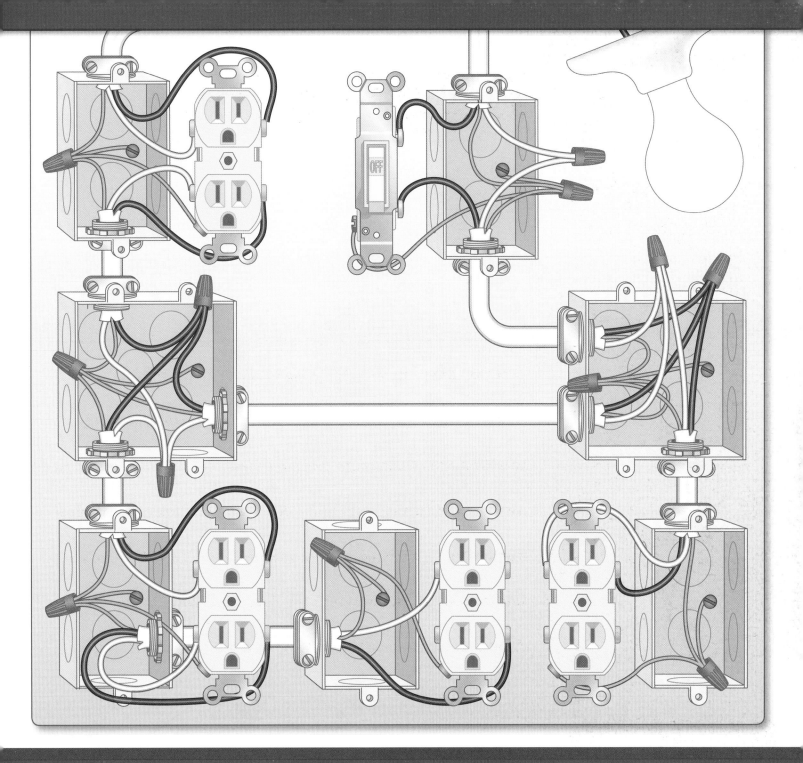

When the Lights Go Out

It's annoying and even a little scary when you lose power to all or part of your home. But these guidelines will help you isolate the cause of the problem.

To weather a power outage, keep plenty of matches and candles on hand, as well as flashlights, extra batteries, and a hand-crank radio (some models accept plugs for cell phones so you can keep them charged during prolonged outages).

What Can Cause an Overload

A short circuit, perhaps caused by a bad lamp or cord, can cause a breaker to trip or a fuse to blow. So can a damaged receptacle or switch, or loose wiring in a box. In such cases, the culprit is usually fairly easy to identify, because the overload occurs when a particular device or appliance is used. If the circuit often overloads even when usage is light, the breaker may be faulty. If overloads occur when two heavy-use items are on at the same time—or while all the lights are on and you plug in an appliance or tool—it's time to evaluate the circuit.

Tracing a Short Circuit or Overload

A tripped breaker or blown fuse is a signal that you may have either a short circuit or an overload. A short circuit may be easy to spot. Look for black smudge marks on switch or receptacle cover plates, frayed or damaged cords, or damaged plugs on lamps and appliances. There may even be a telltale burning smell. If the circuit goes dead after an appliance has been on for a short time, you probably have an overloaded circuit.

If you find none of these trouble signs, you'll have to trace the circuit. First turn off every switch and unplug every lamp or appliance on the dead circuit. Then reset the tripped breaker or install a new fuse.

If the breaker trips or the fuse blows right away, the problem may be a short circuit in a switch, receptacle, or junction box. With the circuit dead, inspect each device and its wiring. Look and smell for charred insulation, see if a loose wire is touching a metal box, and inspect the device.

Assessing the Problem

If your entire home is without electricity, you either have a local power outage, a blown main fuse, or tripped main circuit breaker. A local power outage could be caused by damage to the wires leading to the house, whether from squirrels or a rubbing branch. Such damage can kill as much as half of a home's power—or even all of it.

If you're in partial darkness or one or more receptacles in the same area do not deliver power, the first possibility to consider is an overloaded circuit. When a lamp or appliance doesn't work, the source of the problem may be the device itself, faulty wiring connections, or an overloaded or short circuit.

If the circuit does not blow right away, turn on the wall switches one by one. If a breaker trips or a fuse blows, there's a short circuit in a fixture or receptacle controlled by that switch, or there's a short circuit in the switch wiring. With the circuit dead, check for charred wire insulation or a faulty connection. Or call an electrician.

If the switches don't trip a breaker or blow a fuse, plug in and turn on each lamp or appliance, one at a time. If the circuit doesn't go dead while only one lamp or appliance is plugged in and turned on, it was overloaded. If the circuit goes dead just after you've plugged in a particular lamp or appliance, then you've found the offender—either the cord or the lamp or appliance itself.

Next Steps

If you have an overloaded circuit, the solution may be as simple as plugging an appliance or tool into a receptacle on a different circuit. If you have a split duplex receptacle with outlets on different circuits, you may only need to switch the plug from one outlet to the other. Also consider using lower-wattage bulbs, or perhaps switch to fluorescent bulbs, which require a fraction of the wattage. If an appliance is the problem, you may be able to buy a new unit that uses less power, particularly in the case of window air conditioners and microwave ovens.

If you've found a damaged cord or plug, replace it, then replace the fuse or reset the breaker. If you found faulty wiring or a defective device, replace it. If these simple solutions are not feasible, you may need to install a new electrical circuit.

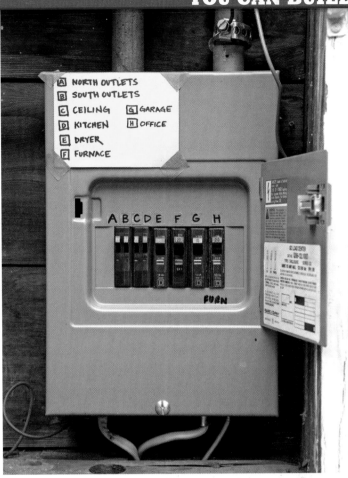

Troubleshooting an Outage

Problem	Possible Cause	Possible Remedies
No power in the house or nearby houses; fuses or breakers are fine	Local power failure	Report outage
Power out, but nearby houses have power	Main fuse has blown or main circuit breaker has tripped, or service lines to house damaged	Check your service panel; if the main is intact, call the power company
Half of electrical service out	One of two main fuses out, or damaged or down service line	Check your service panel; if the mains are intact, call the power company
Some lights or receptacles on a circuit won't work	Loose wiring or damaged switch or receptacle	Tighten connections at switch or fixture; replace switch or receptacle
All lights on a circuit won't work	Overloaded circuit, short circuit, loose wiring, or defective breaker	Test for overload and for short circuit; tighten connections at switch or receptacle; replace switch, receptacle, or breaker
Light fixture won't work, but bulb or tube is fine	Faulty fixture wiring or switch, or (for fluorescent) bad starter, tube holder, or ballast	Repair fixture wiring or parts as needed, or replace switch
Appliance or lamp (with good bulb) won't work	Overloaded circuit, damaged socket, plug, or cord, or defect in appliance	Test for overload; move item to another circuit; make lamp repairs

Avoiding Overloads

Before you add a receptacle, light fixture, or appliance to an existing circuit, make calculations to ensure that the additional loads will not overload the circuit. Your electrical inspector will likely want to see your calculations.

Home-theater equipment can consume a lot more power than you'd think, and if your flat-screen TV is plugged into the same circuit, you are asking for trouble.

Planning Ahead

First, determine which electrical box is easiest to tap into for power. Then follow the steps on these pages to make sure the circuit will not be overloaded when you install the new service. If it would be overloaded, look for a box on a different circuit, or plan to install a new circuit. When in doubt, err on the side of safety.

If you see three-wire cable or two sets of hot wires in a box, two circuits may be present in a single box (a split receptacle; see pages 118–119). If you don't understand the wiring, call an electrician.

Getting the Numbers You Need

To find which circuit runs through a box, start with the service panel's index, but don't trust that it's accurate. To verify that the index is correct, shut off power to the circuit and test to be sure that the power is off. Also verify the other items on the circuit without relying on the index.

Make a list of which devices and fixtures are on that circuit, then add up the wattages or amps to determine how much available "space" there is on the circuit. You can find the wattages of bulbs and check the information plates on appliances and tools that you plug into the circuit's receptacles. The plates may indicate wattage, amperage, or both.

Be sure to take into consideration any special uses you may sometimes make of a circuit. A large Christmas light display, for example, can easily cause overloads.

Add up the following:
- Wattages of all light bulbs for ceiling and wall fixtures on the circuit
- Wattages of bulbs in any lamps plugged into the circuit's receptacles
- Wattages or amperages of any appliances plugged into the circuit's receptacles, including those used only occasionally (such as a hair dryer)

Even something as innocuous as a waffle maker can cause a circuit to overload if the circuit is maxed out to begin with.

Working Up to Code

Even if you are adding only one receptacle or light fixture, be sure to comply with local electrical codes. Go to your building department with a drawing of your proposed installation, find out about codes, and schedule any required inspections.

In addition to loading the circuit correctly, you need to install cable, boxes and devices that meet code. In some cases, components of the new service will be different from the old. For instance, newer codes may require you to install metal boxes, even if the rest of the boxes in your home are plastic.

- Wattages or amperages of appliances that are hardwired into the circuit, such as a garbage disposer or wall heater; appliances that create heat—like office printers—often pull big loads
- Wattages or amperages of the new service you want to install, such as light bulbs in lamps or fixtures, as well as appliances you are likely to plug into receptacles

Appliances with motors—such as refrigerators, air conditioners, heating units, and whole-house fans—often surge when they turn on; for a second or so, they use more power than their ratings indicate. These appliances are often placed on their own circuits, with no other devices to cause an overload when the appliance surges.

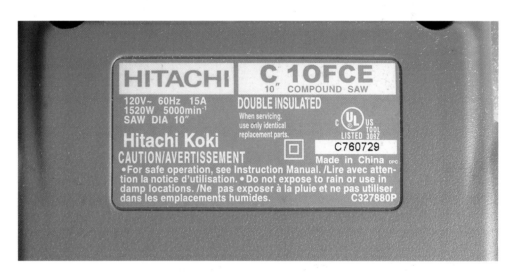

The wattage of this compound saw is over the suggested safe capacity for a typical 15-amp receptacle.

Calculating for Safe Capacity

Watts ÷ volts = amps. This means that a 15-amp, 120-volt circuit, for example, can theoretically handle lights, plug-in appliances, tools that total 1,800 watts (1,800 ÷ 120 = 15). However, for safety, electricians and inspectors usually try to balance circuits so they never exceed "safe capacity," which is 20 percent less than the total capacity. It works out like this (all figures are for 120-volt circuits):

- 15-amp circuit: total capacity = 1,800 watts; safe capacity = 1,440 watts, or 12 amps.
- 20-amp circuit: total capacity = 2,400 watts; safe capacity = 1,920 watts, or 16 amps.
- 30-amp circuit: total capacity = 3,600 watts; safe capacity = 2,880 watts, or 24 amps.

Three- & Four-way Switches

The following four pages present wiring configurations for three-way and four-way switches. Three-way switches let you turn lights on or off in two places. Four-way switches are good for rooms with multiple doorways.

STOP!
Always turn off power to the circuit you are working on. Don't start any actual installations until you have finished planning and have gotten your plans approved by the building department.

Drawing Cable Routes

If you want to be able to turn a light fixture on and off at two locations, such as at the top and bottom of a staircase or at either end of a hallway or long room, consider installing a pair of three-way switches. They're called three-ways because there are three possible combinations of positions: Both toggles are up, both toggles are down, or one is up and one is down.

Three-way switches have two terminals of the same color (brass or silver). These are called traveler terminals. A third terminal, of a darker color, is called a common terminal. They also have a grounding terminal. A three-way switch can be installed with either end up. It's important to observe, though, which terminal is the common

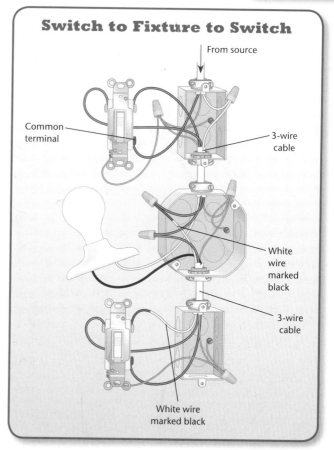

Switch to Fixture to Switch

From source

Common terminal

3-wire cable

White wire marked black

3-wire cable

White wire marked black

Three-way switches make it possible to control lights from the bottom or the top of a stairway.

one. The exact placement may be different from what is shown in the drawings on these pages.

To power a pair of three-way switches, there are a few options. Wiring is different for each arrangement, as the illustrations above and on the opposite page show. As a general procedure, first connect the hot wire that brings power (the feed wire) to the common terminal of one switch. Then connect the hot wire from the fixture or receptacle to the common terminal of the other switch. Finally, run hot wires from the two remaining (traveler) terminals on one switch to the two remaining terminals on the other. This procedure is often obscured by various wiring arrangements, so specific instructions follow for each configuration.

SWITCH TO FIXTURE TO SWITCH

Wiring from switch to fixture to switch is the most common method because it is usually the most convenient way to run the cables. The power comes into the first switch box. Three-wire cables from each of the two switch boxes run into the fixture box. At both the fixture box and the second switch box, the second cable's white wire is marked black. Grounds are connected in all the boxes.

Switch to Multiple Fixtures to Switch

Fixture to Switch to Switch

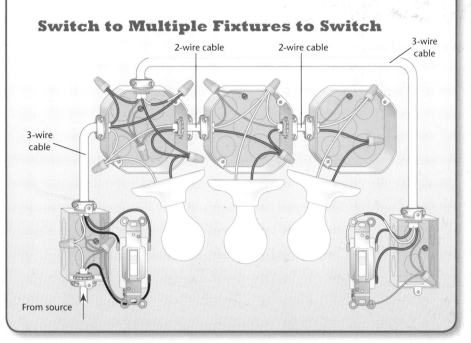

At the first switch box, the two white wires are spliced. The feed wire attaches to the common terminal on the three-way switch, and the red and black wires from the first three-wire cable connect to the two traveler terminals. At the second switch box, the black wire connects to the common terminal, and the white-marked-black and red wires to the traveler terminals.

Inside the fixture box, the red wires are spliced and the black wire from the first cable is spliced with the white-marked-black wire from the second cable. The remaining black and white wires are spliced to the fixture's leads.

FIXTURE TO SWITCH TO SWITCH

If you have an older home with an existing fixture box and switch-loop wiring, then two of the three cable runs for this arrangement are already in place. When a three-way switch is added, a new section of three-wire cable simply runs from the first switch to the second.

In this arrangement, the power enters at the fixture box, from which a two-wire cable goes to the first switch box (the wire's white wire is marked black in both the fixture box and the switch box). A three-wire cable goes from the first switch box to the second. Both ends of the three-wire cable's white wire are marked black. Grounds are connected in all the boxes.

The first thing to notice is that black feed wire connects to both three-way switches

before it reaches the fixture. Upon entering the fixture box, the black feed wire is spliced to a white-marked-black wire, which is connected to the common terminal on the first three-way switch. From there, it goes from one of the traveler terminals on the first switch to a traveler terminal on the second switch. Then, a black wire connected to the common terminal on the second switch runs through the box for the first switch (note how the black wires are spliced together) before emerging in the fixture box to deliver power to the fixture itself. A red wire connects the two switches to each other via the remaining traveler terminal on each. Finally, the white feed wire is attached directly to the fixture.

SWITCH TO MULTIPLE FIXTURES TO SWITCH

If you want to control two or more fixtures with a pair of three-way switches, the general idea is that the switches and the first fixture are wired in the normal way. Two-wire cable then runs from the first fixture to the others.

For this configuration, power runs into the first switch box, and three-wire cable runs between the first fixture box and each of the switch boxes. Two-wire cable runs from the first fixture box to the second fixture box, and from there to any other fixture boxes.

The white wires of the second three-wire cable (the one running to the second switch) are marked black at both ends. Grounds are connected in all boxes.

At the first switch box, the two white wires are spliced. The feed wire attaches to the common terminal and the red and black wires from the first three-wire cable connect to the two traveler terminals. At the second switch box, the black wire connects to the common terminal and the white-marked-black and red wires connect to the traveler terminals.

At the first fixture box, the two red wires are spliced. The two unmarked white wires are spliced to the fixture's white lead, and the black wire from the first three-wire cable is spliced to the white-marked-black wire from the second three-wire cable. The remaining black wires are spliced to the fixture's black lead. At each fixture box in the middle of the run, the black wires are spliced to the fixture's black lead and the white wires to the fixture's white lead. At the fixture box at the end of the run, the wiring is a bit simpler. The white wire is spliced to the fixture's white lead and the black wire to the black lead.

Switch to Switch to Fixture

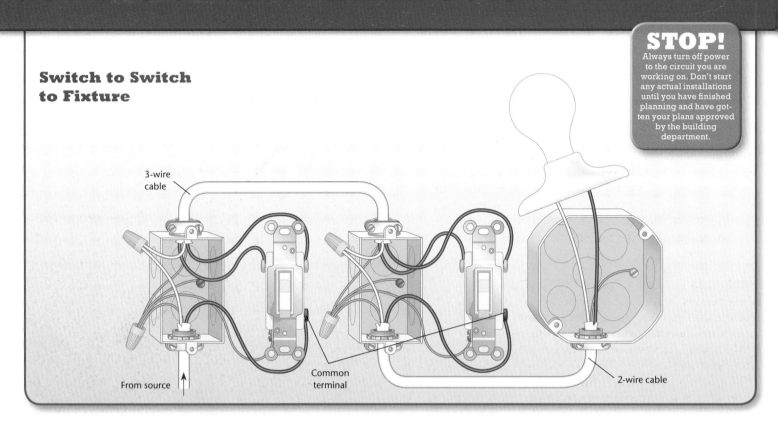

3-wire cable

From source

Common terminal

2-wire cable

SWITCH TO SWITCH TO FIXTURE

The switch to switch to fixture method can be the logical choice if it is easier to run cable through walls than through a ceiling. The wiring is the simplest of all the arrangements.

The power enters at the first switch box. A three-wire cable connects from the first switch box to the second, and a two-wire cable goes from the second switch box to the fixture box. Grounds are connected in all the boxes. For once, there is no need to mark any of the white wires black.

In the first switch box, the white wires are spliced. The feed wire connects to the common terminal, and the three-wire cable's black and red wires to the traveler terminals. In the second switch box, the white wires are spliced. The black wire from the fixture connects to the common terminal, and the remaining black and red wires (from the three-wire cable) connect to the traveler terminals. At the fixture box, the black and white wires connect directly

Switch to Switch to Multiple Fixtures

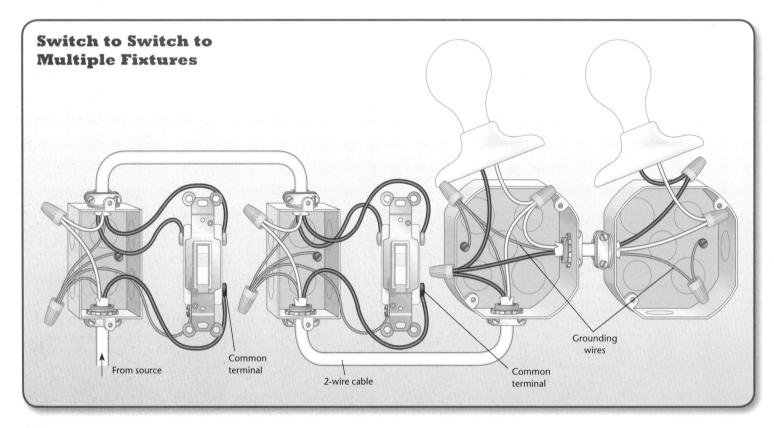

From source

Common terminal

2-wire cable

Common terminal

Grounding wires

to the fixture, as shown on the opposite page, or to the fixture's black and white leads (if supplied).

SWITCH TO SWITCH TO MULTIPLE FIXTURES

In this scenario, cables and wiring are exactly the same as for the "switch to switch to fixture" option on the opposite page, except for the addition of the other fixture boxes and wiring. At the first fixture box, the two black wires are spliced to the fixture's black lead and the two white wires are spliced to the fixture's white lead. At the second fixture box, the black wire is spliced to the black lead and the white wire to the white lead.

RADIATING FROM FIXTURE TO SWITCHES

If it is easy to run power to the fixture, and if running new cable to the two switch boxes is not a problem, the best option may be radiating from the fixture to the switches.

The power enters through the fixture box, from which three-wire cables extend to each switch box. The white wires are marked black in each box, and the grounds are connected in each box as well. The wires in each box are connected in the same way: black wire to the common terminal, and the remaining two wires (red and white-marked-black) to the two traveler terminals.

At the fixture box, the feed wire is spliced to either of the black wires. The two white-marked-black wires (from the switches) are spliced, as are the two red wires. The remaining black and white wires are spliced to the fixture's black and white leads.

Radiating from Fixture to Switches

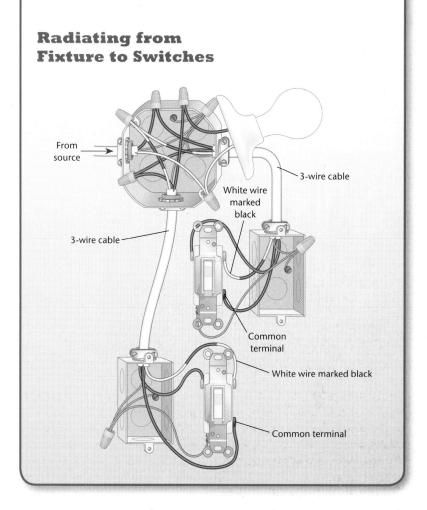

From source

3-wire cable

White wire marked black

3-wire cable

Common terminal

White wire marked black

Common terminal

Four-way Switches

A four-way switch works in tandem with a pair of three-way switches to control a light from three locations, such as from three doorways in a room. The four-way switch is always placed in the middle of the wiring run, with the three-way switches on the ends. You can even add more four-way switches, as long as the three-way switches remain on the ends.

Four-way switches have two pairs of screw terminals—usually one brass pair and one copper pair. The pairs are commonly found on opposite sides at top and bottom, as shown, though some brands differ.

In a four-way arrangement, the three-way switches are wired as for standard three-way wiring, and the four-way switches interrupt the wiring as it travels from three-way to the fixture. One pair of wires connects to the four-way switch from the traveler terminals on the three-way switch closest to the source. A second pair connects to the traveler terminals on the three-way switch at the end of the run.

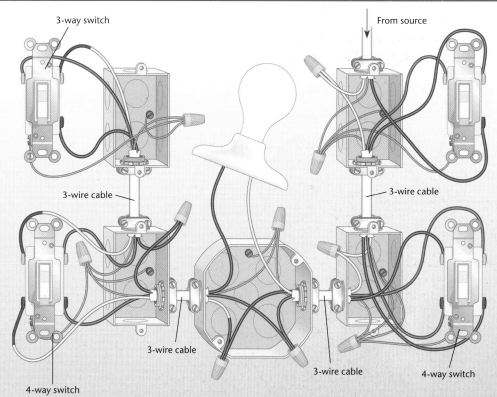

3-way switch

From source

3-wire cable

3-wire cable

3-wire cable

3-wire cable

4-way switch

4-way switch

Common Wiring Configurations

When designing a wiring project, you will need some ingenuity to come up with the best arrangements for your particular needs. In most cases, however, your wiring plan will include some of the configurations shown on the next eight pages.

STOP!
Always turn off power to the circuit you are working on. Don't start any actual installations until you have finished planning and have gotten your plans approved by the building department.

Before You Begin

As always, be sure to check local codes. For example, some configurations shown here use switch-loop wiring, which may not be allowed in your area. These diagrams show metal boxes and NM cable, but you can also use plastic boxes, armored cable, or conduit, depending on local codes. Some diagrams show light fixtures being wired directly, but some areas require wires to be connected to leads.

All these configurations start with a cable that brings in power. Make sure your plan will not overload an existing circuit; if it will, choose a different circuit. For some projects, you may need a new circuit.

DIAGRAM NOTES

The diagrams show light fixtures, but other fixtures, such as ceiling fans or vent fans, could be installed in the same locations. Similarly, the diagrams show ceiling fixtures, but sconces can be wired in the same way. The diagrams do not indicate the wire size. Use 14-gauge wire for 15-amp circuits and 12-gauge wire for 20-amp circuits.

The overall diagram at right shows how power can be distributed to a circuit that combines receptacles and switched light fixtures. The total amperage of the devices and fixtures must not exceed safe capacity for the circuit.

Circuit with Receptacles & Switched Light Fixture

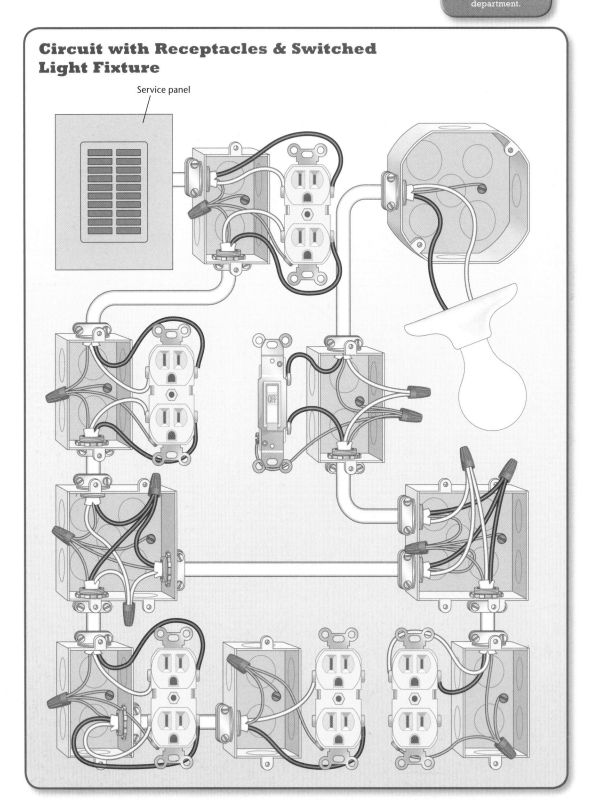

Service panel

Switch with Multiple Fixtures

This configuration uses through-switch wiring to deliver switch-controlled power to two fixtures. The switch is connected to the hot wires only. The arrangement can be used for as many fixtures as you wish. For the first and any other mid-run fixtures, wires are spliced to the outgoing cable as well as to the fixture leads. For the final fixture, they can be wired directly, depending on local codes.

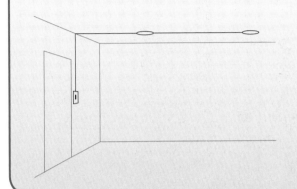

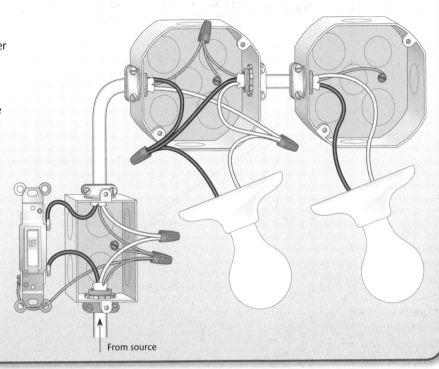

From source

Multiple Switches & Fixtures

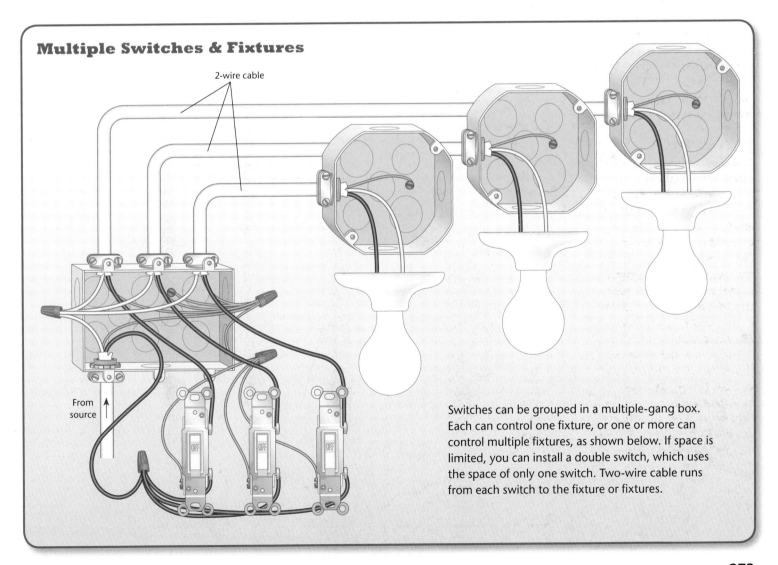

2-wire cable

From source

Switches can be grouped in a multiple-gang box. Each can control one fixture, or one or more can control multiple fixtures, as shown below. If space is limited, you can install a double switch, which uses the space of only one switch. Two-wire cable runs from each switch to the fixture or fixtures.

Multiple Receptacles

This basic arrangement, used in almost every room of the house, is particularly easy to run when the framing is unfinished. The most common method is to wire mid-run receptacles with wires attached to four terminals, as shown.

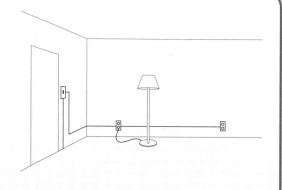

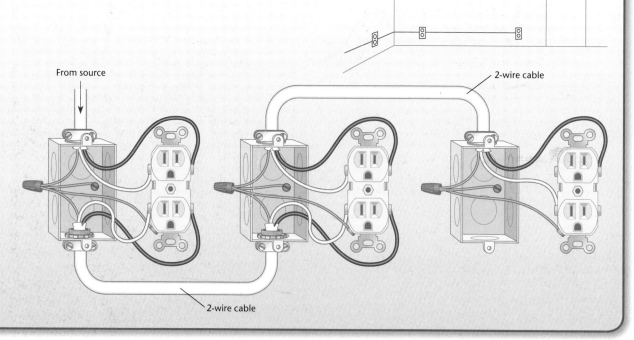

From source

2-wire cable

2-wire cable

Switched Receptacle, Through-switch Wiring

If power runs first to the switch box, you can arrange the wiring so that you control one of the receptacle's plugs with the switch. In this configuration, a three-wire cable runs from the switch to the receptacle. As described elsewhere in this book, the receptacle's tab is removed to separate its two hot terminals. A pigtail arrangement in the switch box sends unswitched power, via the black wire, on to the receptacle. The red wire, meanwhile, runs switched power to one of the plugs. Unswitched receptacles can be added downstream.

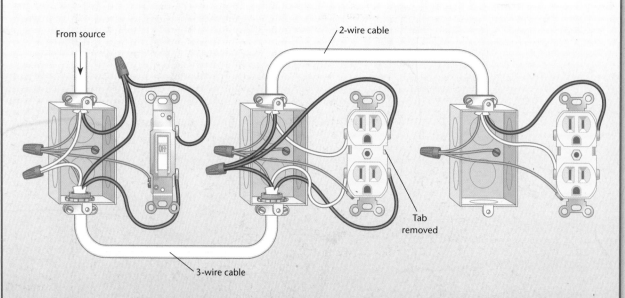

From source

2-wire cable

Tab removed

3-wire cable

Switched Receptacle, Switch-Loop Wiring

If power runs first to the receptacle box, you can make use of switch-loop wiring to control one of the receptacle's plugs with a switch. In this arrangement, the receptacle's tab is removed to separate its two hot terminals. Two-wire cable runs from the receptacle box to the switch box, and the wires are attached so that the switch controls only one of the plugs.

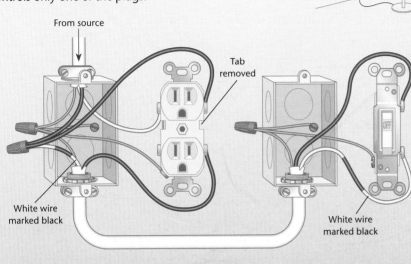

From source

Tab removed

White wire marked black

White wire marked black

Switch & Receptacle Sharing a Box

This arrangement places a receptacle right next to a switch, which may be handy in a bathroom or kitchen. Use a GFCI receptacle if the location is damp or if codes require one. Note that the fixture controlled by the switch will not be GFCI-protected, however—just the receptacle itself. One way to provide GFCI protection for the fixture as well would be to tap into another GFCI receptacle when you bring power into the switch box.

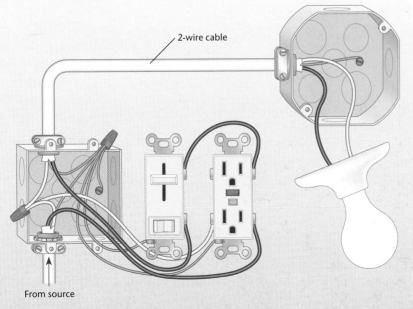

2-wire cable

From source

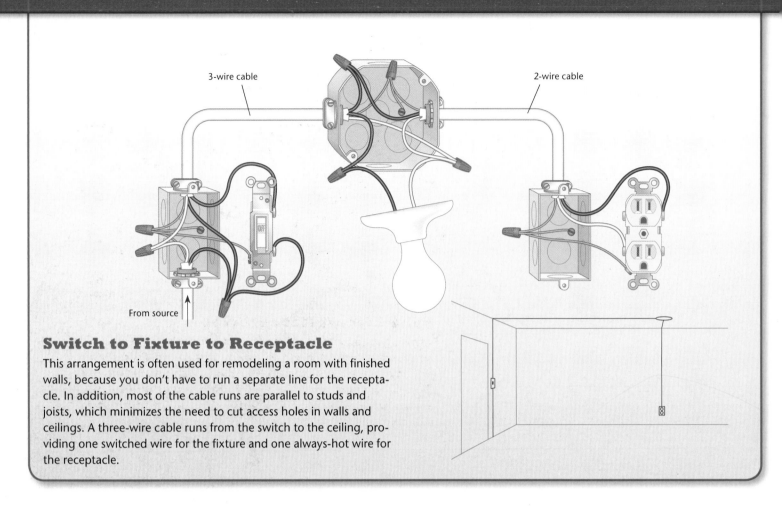

3-wire cable

2-wire cable

From source

Switch to Fixture to Receptacle

This arrangement is often used for remodeling a room with finished walls, because you don't have to run a separate line for the receptacle. In addition, most of the cable runs are parallel to studs and joists, which minimizes the need to cut access holes in walls and ceilings. A three-wire cable runs from the switch to the ceiling, providing one switched wire for the fixture and one always-hot wire for the receptacle.

Switch with Multiple Fixtures & Receptacles

This is essentially the same arrangement as the one shown above, but it allows for more than one fixture and one receptacle. Three-wire cable runs from the switch box to the first fixture box, and also from fixture box to fixture box. The receptacles are wired just as you would normally wire mid-run and end-run receptacles.

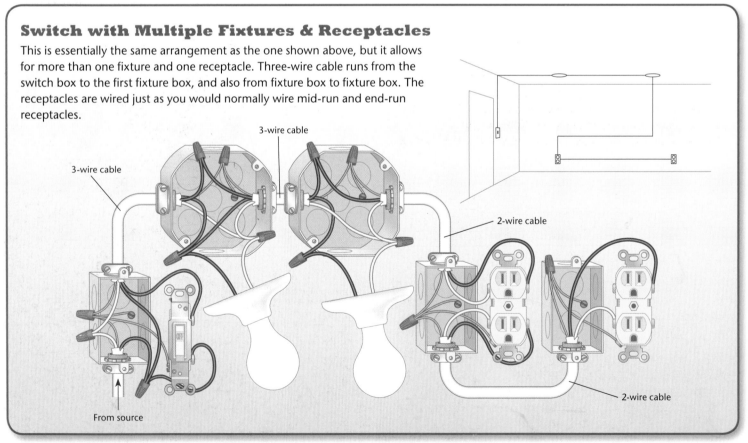

3-wire cable

3-wire cable

3-wire cable

2-wire cable

2-wire cable

From source

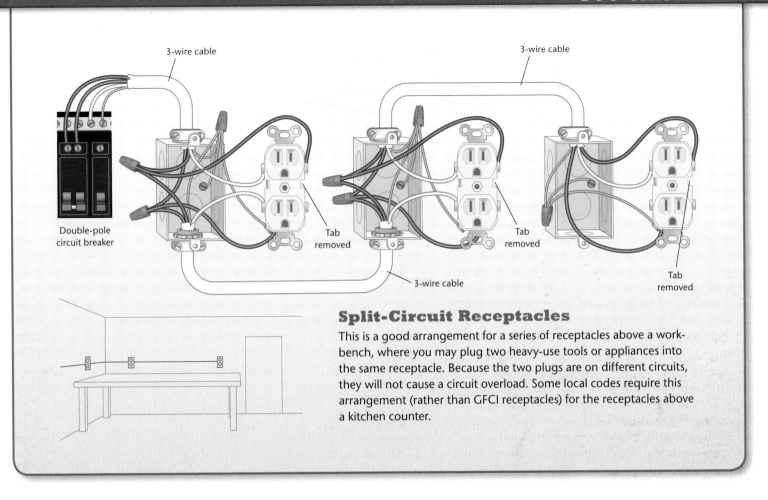

3-wire cable

3-wire cable

Double-pole
circuit breaker

Tab
removed

Tab
removed

Tab
removed

3-wire cable

Split-Circuit Receptacles

This is a good arrangement for a series of receptacles above a work-bench, where you may plug two heavy-use tools or appliances into the same receptacle. Because the two plugs are on different circuits, they will not cause a circuit overload. Some local codes require this arrangement (rather than GFCI receptacles) for the receptacles above a kitchen counter.

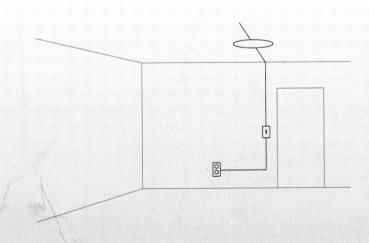

Fixture to Switch to Receptacle

If power first enters the fixture box, you can plan to wire a downstream switch and an always-hot receptacle. In this arrangement, three-wire cable runs from the fixture box to the switch box. A pigtail arrangement in the switch box supplies power to the switch and keeps power running to the receptacle. The red wire completes the switch loop back to the fixture. Two-wire cable connects the switch box and the receptacle box.

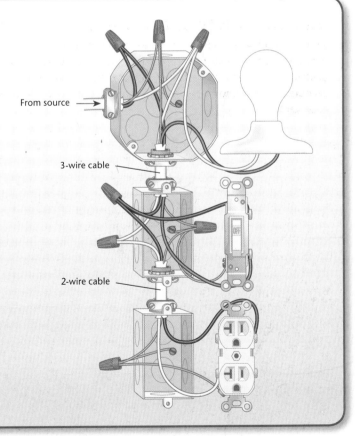

From source

3-wire cable

2-wire cable

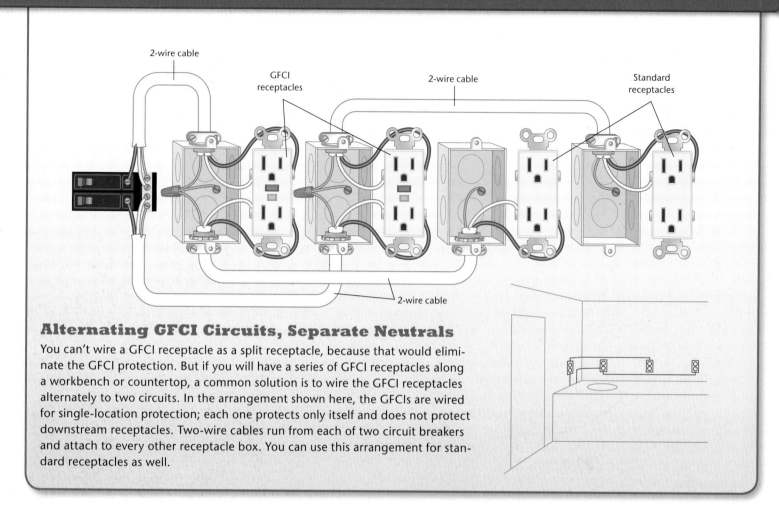

Alternating GFCI Circuits, Separate Neutrals

You can't wire a GFCI receptacle as a split receptacle, because that would eliminate the GFCI protection. But if you will have a series of GFCI receptacles along a workbench or countertop, a common solution is to wire the GFCI receptacles alternately to two circuits. In the arrangement shown here, the GFCIs are wired for single-location protection; each one protects only itself and does not protect downstream receptacles. Two-wire cables run from each of two circuit breakers and attach to every other receptacle box. You can use this arrangement for standard receptacles as well.

GFCIs on Alternating Circuits, Shared Neutral

This arrangement is much the same as the one shown above, and it serves the same purposes. The difference is that this configuration uses a single three-wire cable rather than a pair of two-wire cables, and the hot wires connect to one double-pole breaker rather than to two separate breakers. As a result, when one of the GFCI receptacles switches off, all the downstream GFCIs will also be de-energized. You can use this arrangement for standard receptacles as well.

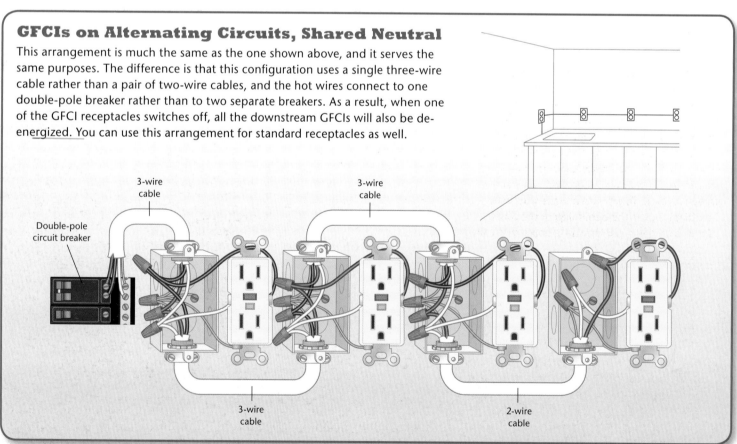

Switch Box with Power to Other Switches

A lighting circuit often travels from one end of a room to another, or to different rooms, so you often need to continue power from one switch box to another. You could send power through the fixture box, but it is more common to run power from one switch box to another. At the first box, a pigtail connects power from the feed wire to the switch, and also the feed wire is spliced to the black wire leading to the next switch box. All the neutrals in the switch boxes are spliced together.

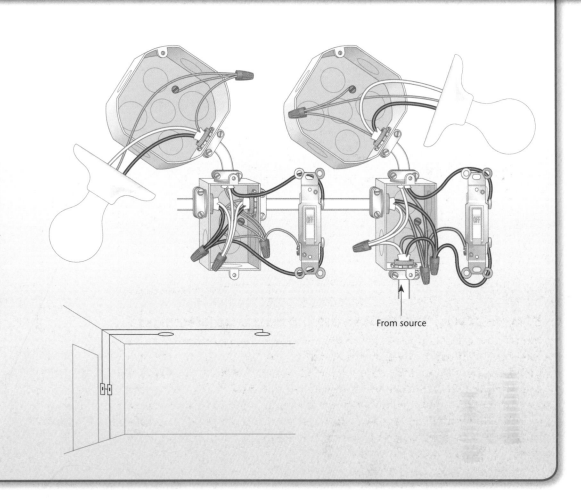

From source

Tapping into a Three-Way Switch

It is possible to tap into a three-way switch box in order to run power for a new receptacle or a new switch with fixture. The feed wire does not run directly to the three-way switch's common terminal; instead, it's spliced with a pigtail so that power can go to the new receptacle. The new receptacle's neutral and ground wires are spliced to the neutral and ground wires in the three-way box. To tap into a three-way switch box that is not at the beginning of the run, a pigtail is used in a similar way to splice into the wire that runs to the common terminal.

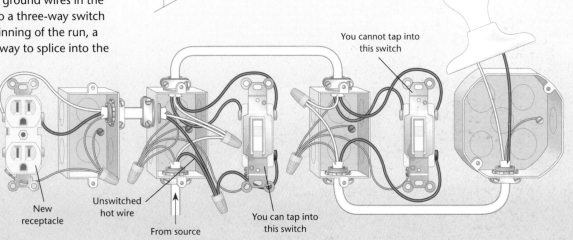

New receptacle

Unswitched hot wire

From source

You can tap into this switch

You cannot tap into this switch

Planning a Large Project

A major remodeling project like a kitchen or bathroom renovation calls for extensive planning. Your plans will likely start with nonelectrical items, such the locations of cabinets or walls and new plumbing and heating; the electrical system comes next.

Drawings & Plans

First make rough drawings, then draw up final plans. Start by planning the final locations and types of fixtures and devices you will need. Consider practical matters, such as placing lights where they shine on work surfaces without glare, putting switches in convenient locations, and placing receptacles where you can easily plug in lamps and appliances without extension cords. When in doubt, add an extra receptacle. If a room has more than one entry point, you will probably want to put some light fixtures on three-way switches so you can control them from two points.

In some cases, codes will determine device and fixture placement. Be sure, for instance, to comply with your building department's requirements for the spacing of receptacles.

LOADING THE NEW CIRCUITS

Once you know where you want all the devices and fixtures, plan the circuits to supply power to them. Some items, such as a refrigerator or a 240-volt appliance, will need to be placed on separate, dedicated circuits. Most items will need to be distributed onto 15- or 20-amp circuits. Many building departments prefer or require that light fixtures be on one 15-amp circuit and receptacles on another 15- or 20-amp circuit. This book will help you with many specific situations, but be sure to consult your inspector as well.

THE SERVICE PANEL

After you determine how many circuits of which amperage you need, you'll need to calculate whether your house's total amperage will be sufficient to handle the new circuits. If it won't be, you may need a new, higher-amperage service panel, and you may even need new service wires from the utility company. Solving these problems is a job for an electrician.

In this large kitchen, light is supplied by pendants, canisters, under-cabinet fixtures, and the clerestory windows near the high ceiling.

In most cases, a laundry combo like this one will have a dedicated 120-volt circuit for the washer and a 240-volt circuit for the dryer.

Permits & Inspections

For many projects, you will need to pull a permit and place it on a door or in a window where it will be clearly visible from the sidewalk or street.

You will also need to schedule inspections. There will likely be a rough inspection to make sure the boxes are correctly installed and the cable is correctly run. It is important not to cover any wiring with drywall until you have passed this inspection. A finish inspection takes place after the walls and ceilings are finished and the receptacles, switches, appliances, and fixtures are installed. If you are doing work to the service panel or adding a subpanel, there may be a separate inspection for that as well.

Pulling a permit, following an inspector's instructions, and going through the required inspections may seem onerous, but the inspection process is there for a reason: to ensure that the electrical installations are safe and durable. It's not only required; it's also in your best interests to do as the inspector says. Always find out ahead of time just what your building department mandates. Specific codes on materials and procedures can vary from town to town.

At the beginning of the planning process, also find out whether you are allowed to do the work you propose. You may need to hire an electrician for work that involves new circuits. Or you may be able to do most of the work yourself as long as an electrician supervises and signs off on the work. You may also need to pass a test before you are allowed to do certain types of work.

WORKING WITH AN INSPECTOR

Ask at the building department for literature related to your project; information sheets and brochures often answer basic questions about materials and plans, so you won't end up asking the inspector unnecessary questions. Some inspectors provide free advice, but most are too busy to do so, and some simply have little patience for homeowner questions. Inspectors are hired to inspect, after all, not to create your plans. Whenever possible, have a drawing and a list of materials that the inspector can examine. Make your drawings clear and easy to follow, and use professional-style symbols (right). If there is something you don't understand, at any point, don't hesitate to ask the inspector.

	Duplex receptacle
GFCI	GFCI receptacle
WP	Weatherproof receptacle
	Split duplex receptacle
C	Clock receptacle
D	240v dryer receptacle
R	240v range receptacle
J	Junction box at wall
SD	Smoke detector
T L	Line-voltage thermostat
T LV	Low-voltage thermostat
	Door bell
CH	Door chime
	Push button
	Telephone/data outlet
S	Single-pole switch
S₃	3-way switch
S₄	4-way switch
S DS	Dimmer switch
S P	Pilot-light switch
S T	Timer switch
	Ceiling light
	Sconce
R	Recessed light
	Surface-mounted fluorescent light
	Ceiling fan with light
	2-wire cable
	3-wire cable
	Home-run cable
	Switch-leg cable

Calculating Usage & Capacity

When planning a remodeling project, you need to determine whether the overall capacity of your electrical service can handle the extra amperage. An addition may increase your requirements enough that you'll need a new service panel or even new service wires.

Assessing Your Current Load

The amperage rating on the service panel actually tells you how many amps each of the two hot bus bars supplies. A 100-amp service panel, for example, supplies 100 amps via each bus bar, for a total of 200 amps.

If you were to total the amperages of all the breakers in a panel, you might find that they add up to more than twice the panel's total amperage rating. That's OK because it's highly unlikely that all the users of electricity in your home will ever be on at the same time.

Instead, you can determine your current usage or current load using values established by the NEC (National Electrical Code) that represent typical electrical usage. For general-purpose circuits (general lighting and receptacles), the load is figured at 3 watts per square foot of living space. A nominal value of 1,500 watts is applied to each 20-amp small-appliance circuit (circuits that power receptacles in the kitchen, dining room, family room, and pantry) and to the laundry circuit.

By applying these values to your home, plus checking the values on plates affixed to major appliances, you can estimate your electrical load. The worksheet on the opposite page shows you how.

A Sample Home, 100 Amps or More

To understand how the formula in the worksheet is used, consider a house with 1,800 square feet of space—based on the house's outside dimensions—that is either finished or adaptable for future use. The first step is to multiply 1,800 square feet by 3 watts per square foot. The total is 5,400 watts for lighting and general-purpose circuits.

This sample house has two small-appliance circuits, a laundry circuit, an electric water heater (5,500 watts), a garbage disposer

Whether your space is large (above) or small (opposite), the way you calculate usage and capacity is exactly the same.

(600 watts), an electric range (15,000 watts), and a central air conditioner (5,000 watts).

Add a total of 3,000 watts for the two small-appliance circuits and 1,500 watts for the laundry circuit to your base figure of 5,400 watts, for a total of 9,900 watts. Next, add the values of all the major appliances, except the air conditioner, for a total of 36,000 watts.

The next step is to figure 40 percent of the amount over 10,000 watts: $0.40 \times 21,000 = 8,400$ watts. That amount plus the 10,000 watts gives a subtotal of 18,400 watts. Finally, add the 5,000 watts of the air conditioner for a grand total of 23,400 watts. This is your estimated load in watts.

To figure the capacity needed to carry that load, divide 23,400 watts by 240 volts. The total comes to 97.5 amps. The common service panel amperages are 60, 100, 125, 150, and 200, so the rating on the service panel of the sample house should be 100 amps or higher.

Estimating Loads Less Than 100 Amps

If your service panel's rating is less than 100 amps, use a different formula to calculate your load. To begin, compute the general-purpose circuits, small-appliance circuits, and laundry circuits exactly as in the worksheet.

Once you've figured the general-purpose circuit load (3 watts × number of square feet of living area), add 1,500 watts for each 20-amp small-appliance circuit and for the laundry circuit.

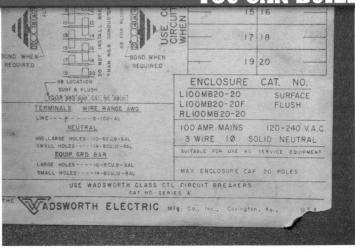

Many breaker panels have a label on them that lists the amperage. For example, this is a 100-amp panel.

120-volt service, you can find the current by dividing the total wattage by 120. For a house with 240-volt service, which is more typical, divide by 240 to find the current.

What to Do If You Need More Amperage

If it turns out that you need more power, either to handle your present usage or for the project you're planning, consult an electrician, your utility company, or your local building department. There are three basic scenarios:

- You may be able to increase total amperage with an added subpanel
- You may need a new service panel
- You may need, in addition to a new service panel, new, thicker service wires from the utility company

In any case, be sure to resolve this basic problem before you make any further plans.

Subtract the first 3,000 watts of this total and calculate 35 percent of the result. Then add that figure to 3,000. The result is that you are counting 100 percent of the first 3,000 watts and 35 percent of the rest.

Add to this value the ratings on the plates of all major appliances, such as each space heater, the garbage disposer, the dishwasher, and so on. This gives you your estimated load in watts. If you have

A Quick Way to Estimate Your Load

The following worksheet is for a 120/240-volt service of 100 amps or more. The first step is to add up your watts.

_____ sq. ft. of living area (outside dimensions)	
× 3 watts per sq.ft.	_____ watts
20-amp small appliance circuits	
× 1,500 watts each	_____ watts
Laundry circuit (1,500 watts)	_____ watts
Appliance nameplate values	
(if given in amps, multiply by volts to get watts)	
Water heater	_____ watts
Dryer	_____ watts
Dishwasher	_____ watts
Garbage disposer	_____ watts
Range	_____ watts
Other	_____ watts
Total watts of all entries listed above	_____ **watts**

Now calculate the amps you need.

1. Your total watts (see total at left)
   minus 10,000 watts _____ watts
2. Multiply Line 1 by .40 _____ watts
3. Add 10,000 watts to Line 2 _____ watts
4. Watts of air conditioner or heater(s),
   whichever has the larger value _____ watts
5. **Estimated load (the total of Lines 3 and 4)** _____ **watts**

Finally, convert the total estimated load to current by dividing by 240 volts.

6. **Line 5 ÷ 240 volts** _____ **amps**

Wiring a Bedroom

A bedroom typically has GFCI-protected receptacles and an overhead light controlled by a wall switch. Codes may allow you to control one plug of a receptacle, instead of the overhead light, with the switch.

This bedroom includes bedside lights, overhead recessed canisters, and switches within reach of the bed.

The wires in this bedroom bring power to bedside lamps, ceiling spots to illuminate an antique headboard, and a ceiling fan.

A convenient wall-mounted bedside light is for reading, a table lamp provides ambient light, and little puck lights illuminate top shelves.

Bedroom Plan

In the plan shown here, the overhead fixture is a fan with a light. It's on a circuit that supplies fixtures in other rooms; otherwise there would be an arrow indicating a home run to the service panel.

A pair of lights in the closet are controlled by a nearby wall switch (S). This is preferable to lights on pull-chain switches, which wear out and need to be replaced every few years. On the adjacent wall, a pair of wall-hung bedside lamps are controlled by wall switches, each within easy reach of a person lying in bed.

Three-wire cable runs from a switch box to the ceiling fixture make it easy to install separate switches for the fan and the light. For a standard overhead light, you would need only two-wire cable. If the bedroom has two entry doors, you may want to install three-way switching.

Under one of the windows there is a receptacle for a window air con-

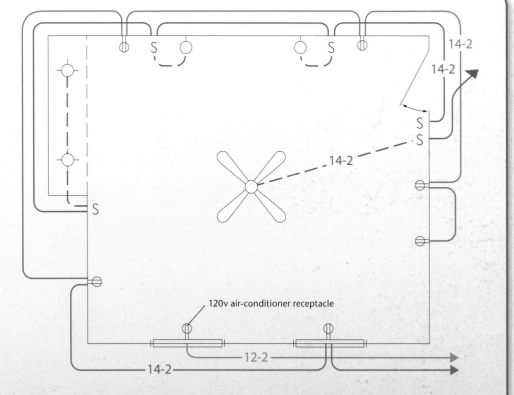

120v air-conditioner receptacle

14-2

14-2

14-2

12-2

14-2

ditioner on a dedicated 20-amp, 120-volt circuit. There is usually no need for a 240-volt air conditioner for a room this size. If the air conditioner does not use much amperage, it can share a circuit with other receptacles.

Wiring a Kitchen

A medium-sized kitchen typically uses five or more circuits (the one in our plan has six), so the drawing can get a bit complicated. Often, three-way light switches are part of the wiring plan, too.

This compact kitchen has a refrigerator, oven, range, range hood, dishwasher, under-cabinet lighting, and ceiling lights, among other wired features.

Kitchen Plan

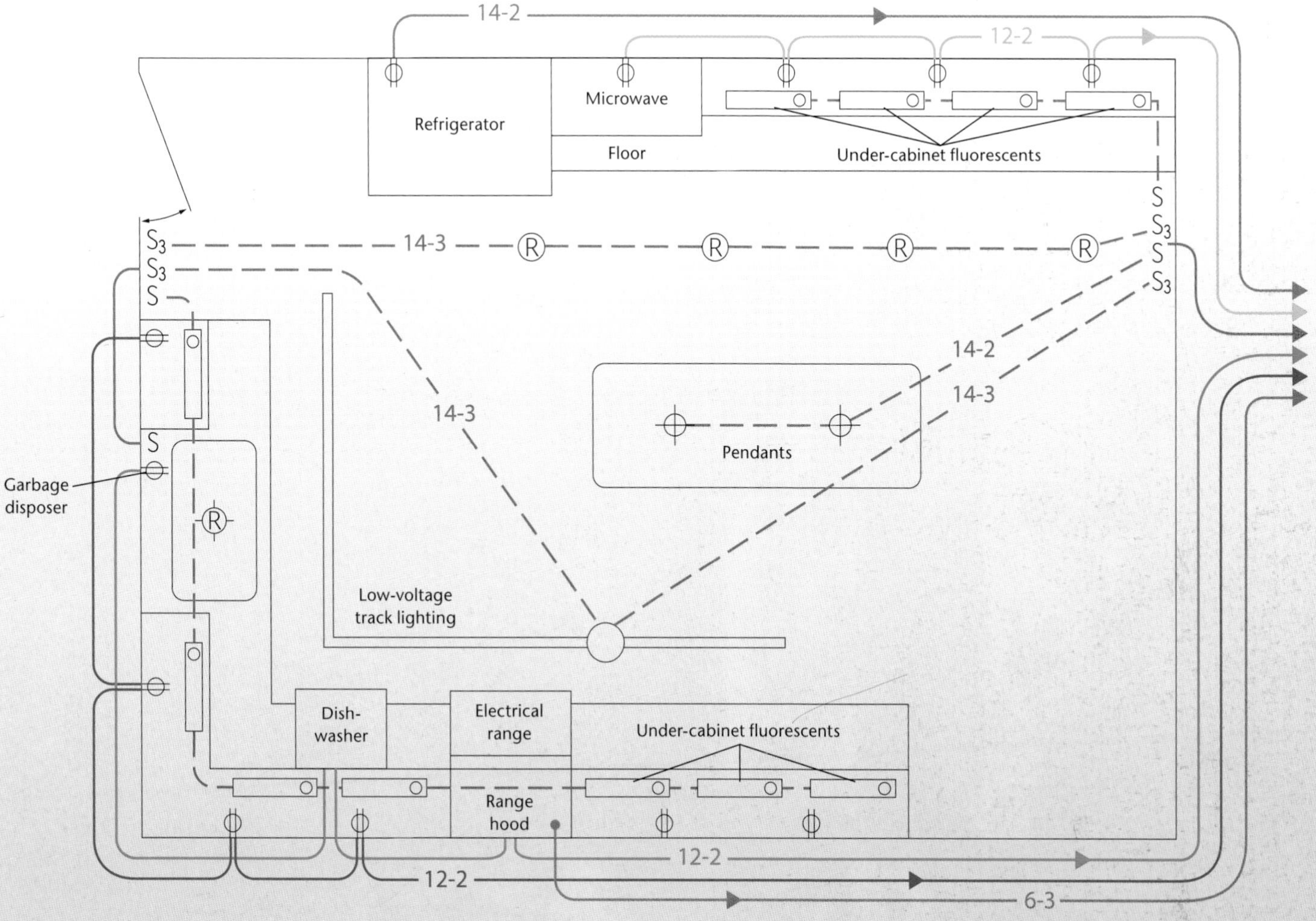

The kitchen illustrated in this plan includes a lot of lighting, but it fits nicely onto one 15-amp circuit because the lights are nearly all low voltage: fluorescent under-cabinet lights, halogen recessed canisters, and halogen track lighting. Only the two pendant lights are standard incandescents. Be sure to add up your wattages, as you may need two light circuits. Also remember that your inspector may call for more circuits than are shown here and may want receptacles and light fixtures distributed differently as well.

Think carefully about which lights you want to control with three-way switches. Here, you can use three-ways for the track lights and the recessed cans, with one switch at each end of the kitchen. The under-cabinet lights on either side have single-pole switches, as does the recessed light over the sink. You might choose to use more three-ways to control the under-cabinet or pendant lights from two locations. Don't make things too complicated, though.

A single 20-amp circuit supplies the garbage disposer, the dishwasher, and the range hood. Some codes may require additional circuits. The electric range needs its own 50-amp, 120/240-volt circuit and thick 6-3 cable.

There are two 20-amp circuits to supply GFCI receptacles above counters, one for each side of the kitchen. If you plan to plug in several heavy-use small appliances in one area, run another circuit. Note that some codes require that the receptacles alternate between two circuits. Or you may need to split each receptacle so that each of its plugs is on a separate circuit (something that is only permitted for regular receptacles, not GFCIs).

Wiring a Bathroom

Most bathrooms are small and tend to have moisture and misting, so the placement of receptacles and switches has safety implications. Codes often call for at least one GFCI-protected receptacle, which should be about 12 inches from a sink.

When fixtures are anchored through a mirror, as in this bathroom, the light is dispersed throughout the room.

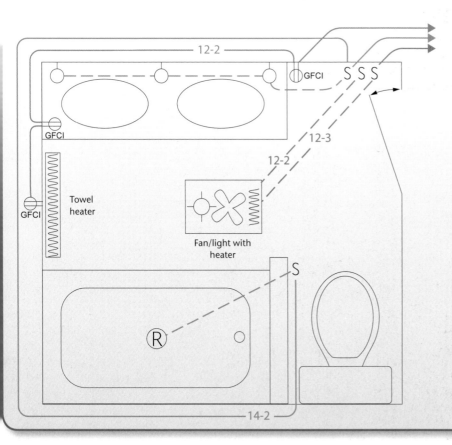

Bathroom Plan

In the medium-sized bathroom pictured in the plan drawing, two GFCI receptacles are placed just to the side of the double-sink vanity countertop, but it's OK to put them above the countertop as well. There is another receptacle for a towel heater. These units typically use only about 100 watts, so they do not require a separate circuit.

The combination ceiling fan and light with heater is on its own 20-amp circuit. It has three switches and requires two cables—one three-wire and one two-wire. If your fixture does not have a heater, it can probably be placed on a 15-amp circuit, with the other lights in the bathroom on the same circuit.

The recessed canister light above the tub should have a waterproof lens. It shares a lighting circuit with three sconces, positioned so that a person standing in front of one of the two sink bowls can see his or her face clearly. (Another option is to install a vanity strip light.) These lights do not use much wattage, so the circuit supplying them may also supply lights in other rooms; that's why there are no home-run arrows on the green line).

Three circuits are enough for a fairly large or medium-size bathroom. A small bathroom may need only two.

The white receptacle and motion-sensor light switch all but disappears against a background of white subway tiles.

This bathroom's wiring plan includes power and a cable connection to a small flat-screen TV.

Common Electrical Codes

Local electrical codes are based on the National Electrical Code (NEC), which describes in excruciating detail every possible situation for both residential and commercial wiring. However, local codes often contain modifications of the NEC.

In a kitchen, local electrical codes may dictate the wiring to receptacles for refrigerators, garbage disposers, dishwashers, and other appliances, as well as for countertop receptacles and even light fixtures.

SERVICE PANEL

- The panel must be connected to an approved system ground wire, which is attached to a grounding rod, a cold-water pipe, or both.
- A new service panel or subpanel must be of a type approved by code. To be safe, use whatever models are most often used by pros in your area.
- Circuits should be clearly labeled on an index (map) located on the panel door, or with individual labels next to each breaker or fuse.
- The panel must supply amperage sufficient for the home.

CABLE

- Inside walls, NM cable is up to code in many areas, but in some localities you may be required to install armored cable or even conduit.
- Where the cable is exposed, cable requirements may change. You may need to install armored cable (or Greenfield) or

Old vs. New

These are some of the most common code issues. If your existing wiring is not up to current code, check to see if you will need to upgrade it. In many cases, it's fine to leave it and just install the new wiring up to code. Of course, if the inspector considers the old wiring unsafe (or, if you do), you should change it even if you are not required to do so.

conduit in a garage or basement, even if the cable inside the walls is NM.

- Cable must be protected from nails or screws that will be driven into studs and joists. This usually means either running it through holes in the framing that are at least 1½ inches from the finished wall surface, or protecting the cable with a metal nailing plate.
- A number of rules govern how cable should be run through unfinished framing.
- NM cable should be stapled within 8 inches of an electrical box that it enters (or 12 inches if the box has a clamp), and it should be stapled every 3 to 4 feet whenever it runs along a framing member. Similar requirements apply to armored cable and conduit.
- Cable run underground should be underground feed (UF) type. It may be required to run through rigid metal conduit where exposed, and inside PVC conduit elsewhere.

WIRES, SPLICES, & TERMINAL CONNECTIONS

- Wire should be correctly sized. In most localities, 15-amp circuit should have 14-gauge wire, a 20-amp circuit should have 12-gauge wire, and a 30-amp circuit should have 10-gauge wire.
- Inside a box there should be a minimum of 8 inches of wire (with the sheathing, but not the insulation, stripped).
- All splices must be made with wire nuts. In some jurisdictions, the bottoms of the nuts must also be wrapped with electrical tape.
- Only one wire may be connected to a terminal. If you need to connect two or more wires, use a pigtail.

- Once wires are connected to screw-down terminals, some codes require that you wrap electrical tape around the device to cover all electrified metal.

BOXES

- Plastic boxes may be allowed, or metal boxes may be required. Boxes should be large enough for the wires and devices they house.
- Use cable clamps as required by your building department.
- Typically, receptacle boxes are 12 inches above the floor, and switch boxes are 48 inches above the floor. You may change positions—for a disabled person, for instance.
- Consult with your building department for the correct locations of receptacle and switch boxes above or near a kitchen or bathroom counter or sink.
- Boxes must come within 1/8 inch of being flush with the surrounding drywall, plaster, or tile. The drywall or plaster should fit fairly tightly around the box.

RECEPTACLES & SWITCHES

- Every receptacle and switch should be grounded.
- GFCI-protected receptacles are required for areas that get damp.
- Switches should be positioned within easy reach. In a hallway or stairway, a pair of three-way switches may be required.
- A receptacle used for an air conditioner, refrigerator, or other heavy-duty appliance may be required to be on a separate, dedicated circuit.

KITCHEN CODES

- The receptacle for the refrigerator may be required to be on a dedicated circuit. High-use items like large microwaves may also need their own circuits.
- The garbage disposer and dishwasher may be allowed to share the same 20-amp circuit, or they may need separate circuits.
- Many building departments call for two 20-amp circuits to supply countertop receptacles, which should be GFCI protected. Others specify 15-amp countertop receptacles that are split-circuit, so each plug is on a separate circuit. Countertop receptacles should be no more than 4 feet apart, and at least 6 inches above the

countertop. (Note that you cannot split a GFCI receptacle, however.)
- Light fixtures should be on a separate circuit. You may be able to put a range hood on the same circuit as the lights.
- An electric range, oven, or cooktop needs its own 240-volt circuit.

BATHROOM CODES

- Bathroom receptacle(s) should be GFCI protected and on a separate circuit.
- An exhaust fan is usually required. A fan/light might share the same circuit as other light fixtures, but if the fan unit includes a heater, it probably needs its own circuit.

LIVING ROOMS, DINING ROOMS, & BEDROOMS

- Along a living area wall, there should be at least one receptacle every 12 feet. If a wall is wider than 2 feet, it should have at least one receptacle.
- Bedroom receptacles, and perhaps living and dining room receptacles as well, should be on circuits that are AFCI protected.
- Light fixtures and receptacles may need to be on separate circuits, or you may need one circuit to supply all lights and receptacles in every 600-square-foot area.
- A bedroom must have either an overhead light controlled by a wall switch, or a switch-controlled receptacle so that you can turn on a lamp with a wall switch.
- Firmly attach fan-rated boxes wherever a ceiling fan will be installed.
- Smoke alarms and carbon-monoxide detectors are required. They may need to be hardwired.

STAIRS, HALLS, & CLOSETS

- You must be able to control a stairway light from both the bottom and the top. In most cases, this means installing two three-way switches.
- Any stretch of hallway that is 10 feet or longer should have at least one receptacle.
- A closet light should have a globe rather than a bare bulb, and be positioned away from combustibles. You may be required to place a closet light on a wall switch rather than on a pull chain (a switch will also last longer).

Glossary

alternating current An electrical flow that cycles (reverses direction) 60 times per second. Abbreviated as AC. Residential power is AC. Compare *direct current*.

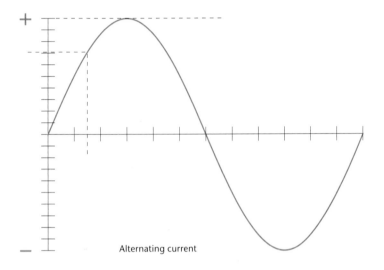

Alternating current

ampacity A word combining *ampere* and *capacity*. Expresses in amperes the current-carrying capacity of electrical conductors (wires).

ampere Often simply called an amp. A unit used to measure electrical current, based on the number of electrons flowing past a given point per second. Many elements of a wiring system are rated in amperes, indicating the greatest amount of current that they can safely carry.

antioxidant A paste that can be applied to aluminum wires and connections to limit corrosion and maintain a good electrical connection.

appliance An electrical appliance is any user of electrical current other than a light fixture. An appliance may be plugged into a receptacle or hardwired.

arc-fault circuit interruptor (AFCI) A circuit breaker that shuts off when it senses electrical arcing, which can be a fire hazard.

arcing An unsafe condition that occurs when electricity jumps from one conductor to another nearby conductor, such as from a bare wire to a metal housing or from one bare wire to another.

armored cable Cable with a flexible, metallic sheathing, sometimes called flex. Newer versions include AC and MC. Older armored cable is called BX.

ballast In a fluorescent light, a small transformer that supplies low voltage to the tube. Older, heavier ballasts are magnetic, while newer, lighter ballasts are electronic.

bell wire Thin wire (typically 18 gauge) generally used for door chimes, thermostats, and other low-voltage applications.

box Short for electrical box. A plastic or metal enclosure that houses electrical connections.

branch circuit Any one of many separate circuits distributing electricity throughout a house, originating at a fuse or circuit breaker in the service panel.

bus bar In a service panel, any of several metal strips to which circuit components are attached. See *hot bus bar* and *neutral bus bar*.

BX cable An older type of armored cable with a thin bonding strip rather than an insulated ground wire.

cable Two or more insulated wires (conductors) bundled together and covered with an integral insulating sheath. Most commonly NM cable.

circuit Two or more wires providing a path for electrical current to flow from the source, through a device (such as a light), and back to the source.

circuit breaker An overcurrent device installed in a breaker-style service panel. When current passing through the breaker exceeds a predetermined amount, it trips, thereby stopping the flow of electricity. Compare *fuse*.

CO/ALR A designation for devices approved for use with aluminum or copper wiring.

codes Electrical codes are rules emanating from both the National Electrical Code (NEC) and local building departments. They are designed to ensure safe electrical installations.

BX cable

common terminal On a three-way switch, the terminal to which is attached a wire that brings power or leads to a fixture. The common terminal is darker than the other terminals, which are called travelers.

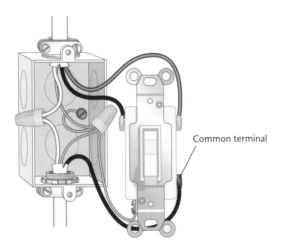

Common terminal

conductor The technical term for electrical wire.

conduit A metal or plastic pipe designed to shield conductors from moisture and physical harm.

contact The point or points inside a device where electrical conductors meet.

continuity A condition in which current passes continuously through a circuit, device, or fuse.

continuity tester A tool that determines whether there is a continuity break in a wire or a device.

cord Two or more flexible, stranded wires encased in sheathing, producing a wiring path that can be flexed many times, therefore suitable for a plug-in connection.

current The movement or flow of electrons through a conductor. Measured in amperes.

cut-in box A metal or plastic electrical box that can be mounted onto a finished drywall or plaster wall or ceiling. Also called a remodel box or an old-work box. Compare *new-work box*.

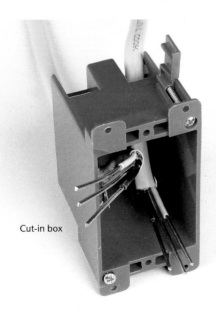

Cut-in box

device A switch or receptacle.

dimmer A switch that allows the brightness of a light fixture to be varied. *Rheostat* is an older term for a dimmer switch.

direct current Continuous flow of electrons from one electrical pole to another, as in a battery. Compare *alternating current*.

duplex receptacle The most common type of receptacle, with two plugs.

Duplex receptacle

EMT Electrical metal tubing. Easily bent thin-wall metal conduit suitable for indoor installations.

end-line wiring A wiring configuration in which power first enters the switch box, then travels to the fixture. Compare *switch-loop wiring*.

end-run Describes a switch or receptacle at the end of a branch circuit. Compare *mid-run*.

feed wire The hot (black or colored) wire that brings power into an electrical box.

fishing Pulling wires through conduit, or pulling cable through a finished wall.

fixture A light, fan, or other device that is permanently attached to a ceiling or wall and is permanently wired.

flex A term often used for Greenfield or armored cable.

fluorescent Describes light produced by electricity passing through a glass tube with a phosphor coating that changes ultraviolet to visible light. Compare *incandescent*.

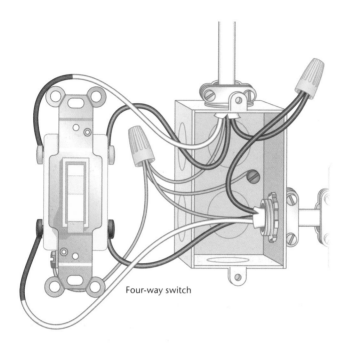

Four-way switch

four-way switch Used in a wiring configuration where a light or group of lights is controlled by three or more switches.

fuse A safety device installed in a fuse-type service panel. When current exceeds a predetermined amount, the fuse blows, stopping the flow of electricity. Compare *circuit breaker*.

gang Describes the size of an electrical box. A one-gang box is large enough for one device. "Gangable" boxes can be combined to accommodate multiple devices.

gauge A measure of wire thickness. The lower the gauge number, the thicker the wire. The symbol # is used as an abbreviation for gauge, as in 12#.

Greenfield Flexible metal conduit through which wires can be pulled. Also called *flex*.

ground A connection between any part of an electrical system and the earth. Typically, a ground wire or metal sheathing runs to the service panel, and from there to a grounding rod or cold-water pipe. In case of a short circuit, grounding provides protection against shock.

ground fault A flaw in an electrical system that occurs when a bare hot wire accidentally touches a grounded object, so that current escapes from its intended path. This leakage of current is also known as fault current.

ground-fault circuit interrupter (GFCI)
A receptacle or circuit breaker that senses minute differences in incoming and outgoing power (ground faults) and quickly shuts off, thereby providing an important safety measure.

grounding electrode conductor A conductor that connects the neutral bus bar of the service panel to ground. Sometimes referred to as a service ground.

grounding rod A metal rod typically driven 8 feet or so into the earth, to which the house grounding wire is connected.

ground wire A conductor that provides a ground but does not carry current during normal operation. Ground wires are part of the standard connections in modern devices and fixtures. If a metal component accidentally becomes energized, the ground wire will direct the current back to the service panel, where the circuit breaker or fuse will activate and stop the electrical flow.

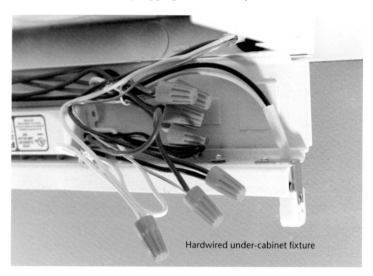

hardwire To connect a fixture or appliance directly to the household wires, rather than plugging it into a receptacle.

Hardwired under-cabinet fixture

hickey A special threaded fitting used to connect light-fixture hardware to an older electrical box that has a center stud (short length of threaded pipe).

hot bus bar A solid metal bar connected to the main power source in a service panel or subpanel. Branch circuit hot wires are connected to hot bus bars via circuit breakers or fuses. They convey power from the main conductors to the branch circuits.

hot wire A wire carrying electrical current from the power source. Usually identified by black or red insulation but may be any color other than white, gray, or green.

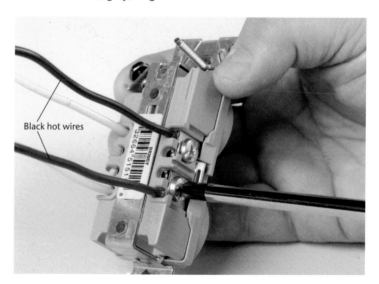

Black hot wires

incandescent Describes light produced by electricity passing through a filament. Compare *fluorescent*.

insulation A protective material that does not carry current, such as the color-coded thermoplastic insulation on wires.

isolated-ground receptacle A receptacle—typically 120-volt, 20-amp—connected to its own dedicated grounding wire. It is most commonly used in commercial applications to protect sensitive equipment from power surges.

Isolated-ground receptacle

joist A horizontal wooden house-framing member placed on edge, as in a floor or ceiling.

jumper See *pigtail*.

junction box An electrical box that houses spliced wires, sometimes from more than one circuit, and that may or may not house a device or a fixture.

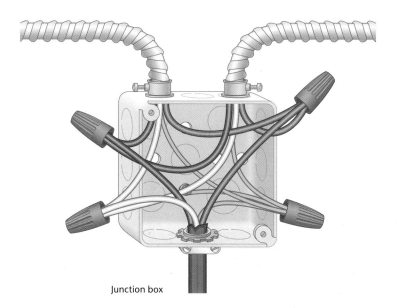

Junction box

kilowatt A unit of electrical power equal to 1,000 watts. Abbreviated kw.

kilowatt-hour A unit that is used for metering and selling electricity. One kilowatt-hour equals 1,000 watts used for one hour (or any equivalent, such as 500 watts used for two hours). Abbreviated kwh.

knockout A pre-stamped circular impression in a metal electrical box that can be easily removed to accept standard cable clamps.

lamp A light fixture that is plugged into an electrical receptacle, rather than being hardwired.

LB connector Short for L-body, an elbow fitting for making a right turn with metal or plastic conduit.

lead Pronounced "leed." A short, usually but not always stranded wire attached to a fixture. A lead is spliced to house wires.

lightning rod A metal rod, typically positioned at the top of a roof, connected to a grounding wire that in turn runs to a ground rod; transmits the electricity from a lightning strike harmlessly to the ground.

load A technical term for any device, fixture, or appliance to which electrical power is delivered.

low voltage Voltage between 4 and 30 volts.

low-voltage transformer A device that steps power down from standard 120 volts to 30 volts or less.

main breaker The circuit breaker that controls all power in a service panel; shutting it off stops power throughout the house.

MC cable See *armored cable*.

mid-run Describes a switch, receptacle, or junction box through which power flows to other devices.

network A general term for a system of connections between computers, telephones, and other communications devices.

neutral bus bar A solid metal bar in a service panel or subpanel to which all neutral wires are connected. It provides a route for power to return to the neutral service wire supplied by the utility, thereby completing the circuit. In the service panel, it is bonded to the metal cabinet and is directly connected to the earth through the grounding electrode conductor. In a subpanel, it is not bonded to the cabinet, so only neutral wires are connected to it.

neutral wire A grounded conductor that completes a circuit by providing a path for current to return to the source. Neutral wires must never be interrupted by a fuse, circuit breaker, or switch. Always identified by white or gray insulation.

new-work box An electrical box made to be attached to unfinished framing, before drywall or plaster is applied. Compare *cut-in box*.

NM cable Short for nonmetallic cable, which has two or more insulated wires plus a bare ground wire encased in thermoplastic sheathing.

NM cable

ohm The unit of measurement for electrical resistance or impedance. See *resistance*.

old-work box See *cut-in box*.

outlet Any place that enables a connection to electricity. Often a receptacle is called an outlet.

overcurrent protection device The generic term for fuses and circuit breakers.

overload More current than a circuit is designed for.

pancake box A thin, round electrical box often seen in older homes. A pancake box may be used if the box must rest against a ceiling joist.

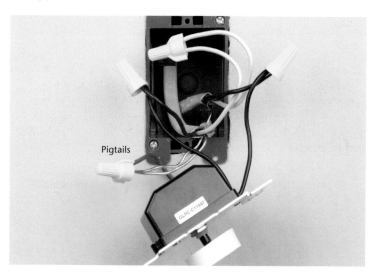

Pigtails

pigtail A short length of wire that is stripped at both ends, used to connect two or more wires to a single terminal. Also called a jumper. The connection thus made is called a pigtail splice. As a verb, to connect via a pigtail.

polarization A system that keeps current flowing in a single direction, to the fixture via the hot wire and from the fixture via the neutral. Polarized plugs have different size prongs for hot and neutral wires, matching different size slots in polarized receptacles, so the system cannot be foiled by an incorrectly inserted plug.

pulling elbow A conduit fitting that has removable plates so you can reach inside to pull wires through. Wire splices cannot be made inside a pulling elbow.

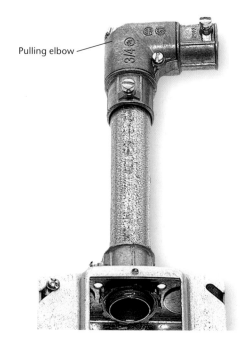

Pulling elbow

PVC Short for polyvinyl chloride, a thermoplastic material often used for nonmetallic ("plastic") electrical conduit, boxes, and fittings.

programmable switch Any of a variety of switches that can turn lights or appliances on and off according to a preset schedule.

R

raceway Technically, raceway refers to any conduit through which wires can pass. But the term is most often used to refer to nice-looking conduit that attaches to finished wall and ceiling surfaces.

receptacle Often called an outlet (and sometimes a plug); a device with at least one set of slots into which a lamp or appliance can be plugged.

remodel box See *cut-in box.*

resistance The property of an electric circuit that restricts the flow of current. Measured in ohms.

rheostat See *dimmer.*

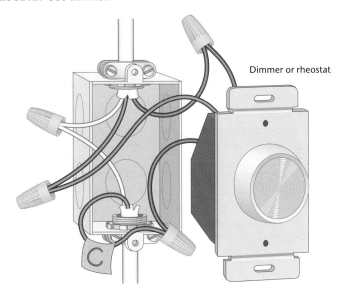

Dimmer or rheostat

S

screw terminal A screw found on sockets, switches, and receptacles that is used to make wire connections.

service drop A common term for the service entrance conductors and their connections to the house.

service entrance conductors The main wires bringing power to a house, via either the service drop (overhead) or the service lateral (underground).

service panel or service entrance panel The main cabinet through which electricity enters a home wiring system. It houses the service entrance conductors, a main disconnect breaker or fuse, and the grounding connection for the entire system. Sometimes called a fuse box, panel box, or main panel.

short circuit A fault in the electrical system that occurs when a hot wire touches bare metal or another wire of any sort. The malfunction creates a shorter path for the current than the intended circuit.

socket In a lamp, a threaded metal shell into which a light bulb is screwed.

spike A sudden and temporary surge of electrical power.

splice To join wires together, usually by twisting them together and then twisting on a wire nut.

splice box A housing for electrical splices that is integrated into an appliance or light fixture.

standby generator A generator that can supply temporary power to part of a house's electrical system.

station wire A common term for telephone cable, which has four wires.

strip To remove insulation from a wire, or sheathing from a cable.

stud A vertical wooden house-framing member. Also referred to as a wall stud.

subpanel A panel with circuit breakers, separate from the main service entrance and from which some or all branch circuits are routed. The wires that connect the main panel to the subpanel are called subfeeds.

surge arrestor or suppressor A device that diverts a small temporary surge in electrical power to the grounding system, so it cannot damage electronic equipment. A house surge arrestor protects the house's electrical system in case of a lightning strike.

switch-loop wiring A wiring configuration used when power enters the fixture's box, rather than the switch box, first. Compare *end-line wiring.*

T

terminal On a device or appliance, a point of connection where wires are attached.

transformer A converter that raises or lowers voltage to the amount required by a device.

type UF (underground feeder) cable A multiconductor cable consisting of three or more wires that are contained within a single nonmetallic outer sheathing. Used for exterior wiring only.

UF cable

UL Stands for Underwriters Laboratories, an independent agency that tests electrical products for safety. A UL-listed item is approved for its intended use.

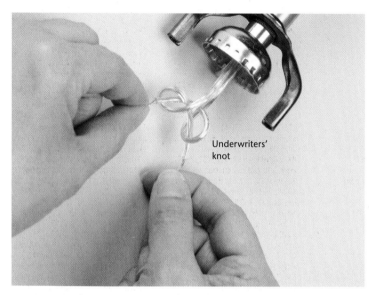

Underwriters' knot

Underwriters' knot A type of knot that relieves strain on the screw terminal connections in lamp sockets and some plugs.

volt A unit of measure denoting electrical pressure. Abbreviated V.

voltage The pressure at which a circuit operates, expressed in volts.

voltage tester A tool used to detect the presence of electrical power. When one probe touches a hot wire and the other probe touches a neutral wire, a ground wire, or a metal component that leads to ground, the tester's light glows.

watt A unit of measurement for electrical power. One watt of power equals one volt of pressure times one ampere of current. Many electrical devices are rated in watts according to the power they consume. Abbreviated W.

wire A single electrical conductor, usually made of solid-core or stranded copper and wrapped in a nonconducting color-coded insulation.

wire nut A plastic or plastic-and-metal connector used to splice two or more wires without solder.

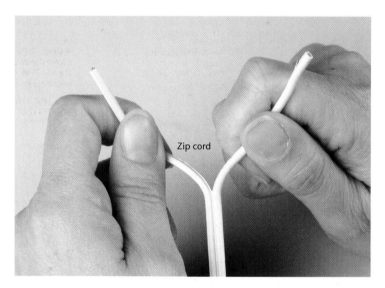

Zip cord

zip cord Two-wire cord, commonly used for lamps or household extension cords, that is flat; the two wires can be easily zipped apart for stripping and attaching to terminals.

Resources & Credits

Acknowledgments

We'd like to thank Gaye Carlson and the crew of Carlson Electric, Al Larsen of Larsen-Hoffman, David DeFord of Audio Ink, and Kinya Pollard of Wil-Cal Lighting for their help and expertise. Thanks also to Steve Cory and Scott Atkinson for their contributions to previous Sunset books on wiring.

Resources

Page 40
When & How to Hire a Pro
Carlson Electric
650-529-1774

Audio Ink
831-372-0100

Larsen-Hoffman, Inc.
650-424-0456

Page 72
Light Bulbs
Ledtronics, Inc.
800-579-4875
ledtronics.com

Pages 75, 82, 87–88, 148–151, 166, 169
General Lighting
Sea Gull Lighting
800-347-5483
seagulllighting.com

Page 96
Low-voltage Outdoor Lighting
Lighting New York
866-344-3875
lightingnewyork.com

Page 149
Choosing Light Fixtures
Royce Lighting
www.roycelighting.com

Page 151
Choosing Ceiling Fans
Hunter Fan
800-313-3326
hunterfan.com

Page 152
Smart & Wireless Switches
Lagotek
425-455-2165
lagotek.com

Page 179
Roof & House Fans
Airvent Inc.
800-AIR-VENT
airvent.com

Page 181
Bathroom Vent Fans
Broan
800-558-1711
broan.com

Page 185
Replacing a Range Hood
Broan
800-558-1711
broan.com

Page 186
Wall Heaters
Smarthome

Plantronics
800-544-4660
plantronics.com

Sonos
800-680-2345
sonos.com

Uniden
uniden.com

WildCharge Inc.
888-494-5324
wildcharge.com

Page 231
Backup Generators
Electric Generators Direct
866-437-7998
electricgeneratorsdirect.com

Pages 234–237
Solar & Wind Solutions
Occidental Power
888-49-SOLAR
oxypower.com

SolarCity
888-SOL-CITY
solarcity.com

Southwest Windpower
928-779-9463
windenergy.com

Starck Network
starck.com

Windterra Systems, Inc.
windterra.com

800-762-7846
smarthome.com

Page 189
Baseboard Heaters
Cadet
360-693-2505, ext. 500
cadetco.com

Pages 190–192
Heated Floors
SunTouch
888-432-8932
suntouch.com

Pages 205
Home Entertainment Cables
Optimized Cable Company
866-966-1733
optimization-world.com

Page 206
Cable Management Products
866-222-0030
CableOrganizer.com

Page 209
Home Theaters
Wilkerson Furniture
wilkersonfurniture.com

Pages 220–221
Speakers
Canton Electronics Group
612-706-9250
canton.de/en-home.htm

Page 222
Surge Protection
Belkin
800-223-5546
belkin.com

Page 223
DSL Filters
Excelsus
858-674-8100
pulseeng.com

Page 224–227
When to Go Wireless
Apple Inc.
800-MY-APPLE
apple.com

Belkin
800-223-5546
belkin.com

First Alert
800-323-9005
firstalert.com

Fuze Media Systems
877-FUZE-MEDIA
fuzeav.com

Lutron
888-LUTRON1
lutron.com

Photo Credits

T = *top*, B = *bottom*, L = *left*, R = *right*, M = *middle*

All photographs by Jim Bathie unless otherwise noted.

Courtesy *Airvent Inc.:* 11BR, 176BL, 179Tr, 179 MR, 179BR; Courtesy *Apple:* 226TL, 226ML; Courtesy *Belkin:* 203BM, 222T, 222BL, 222 inset, 226BM, 226BL, 227BM, 227BR; Courtesy *Broan:* 176 2nd from BL, 181MR, 181BR, 185TL; Bill Brooks/ *Alamy:* 236MR; Courtesy *CableOraganizer.com:* 202 2nd from BL, 206TR, 206BR, 206BL; Courtesy *Cadetco:* 189 inset; *Jared Chandler:* 159TR; *Beatriz Coll:* 150L; Andrew Bordwin/Beateworks/Corbis: 154L; *Tim Street-Porter/Beateworks/Corbis:* 156TL, 252R; *Craig Lovel/Corbis:* 122BR; *David Frazier/Corbis:* 10T; *Elizabeth Whiting & Associates/ Corbis:* 160BR; *George Gutenberg/ Beateworks/Corbis:* 174L, 180; *Joe Schmelzer/Beateworks/Corbis:* 154R; *Wayne Cable/Beateworks/Corbis:* 163BR; *Jim McDonald/Corbis:* 178R; *LWA-Stephen Welstead/Corbis:* 176BR, 190B; *William Geddes/Beateworks/ Corbis:* 182L; *Corbis:* 262BR, 208TL, 250B, 284; *Olson Photographic/ Corner House Photo Stock, Inc.:* 156BL, 189TL, 253T, 268BL; *Alan Shortall/ Corner House Photo Stock, Inc.:* 134L, 256BL, 256BR; *Carolyn Bates/Corner House Photo Stock, Inc.:* 256T; *Jessie Walker/Corner House Photo Stock, Inc.:* 120TL; *Russ Widstrand/Corner House Photo Stock, Inc.:* 11TR, 102BR; *Steve Cory:* 6 2nd & 4th from BL, 9MR, 9BR, 14TR, 14TM, 18BL, 19TL, 19BL, 23ML, 28TR, 29BR, 36BR, 37 all, 38R, 39 2nd from BL, 39BR, 39 2nd from BR, 42 2nd from BL, 42 4th from BL, 43B (4), 45BL, 45 2nd from BL, 45MR, 45BR, 46 all, 47T, 47BR, 47MR, 47ML, 47BL, 48ML, 49ML, 49TL, 49TR, 50BM, 50BL, 50TL, 51TR, 52TR, 53ML, 53TR, 53BR, 54TR, 55BL, 56TL, 58MR, 59TR, 59BM, 61 2nd from TR, 62TR, 63–65 all, 66BL, 66BR, 67 all, 69 all except BR, 71 3rd from BR, 72R, 73T, 73B, 73 inset, 100 2nd and 4th from BL, 101 3rd from BL, 101 2nd from BR, 102TL, 102BL, 103 all, 104BR, 105 2nd from ML, 105MR, 105 BL, 108Bl, 108BM, 108BR, 109BR, 109BR, 109TML, 112BL, 115 2nd from BL, 115TR, 123BL, 123BR, 126–127 all, 128BL, 128 3rd from BL, 128 2nd from BL, 129B, 131TR, 132BR, 138TR, 138MR, 139TL-TR, 142TL, 143–145 all, 146 2nd-3rd from BR, 153 all, 160TR, 161–162 all, 163TL, 163BL, 164TM, 164TR, 164BM, 165TL, 165TM, 165BL, 176 3rd-4th from BL, 176 2nd-3rd from BR, 177BL, 179TL, 183TR, 185 all except TL, 186 all except TR, 187 all, 188BL-BR, 189BL, 189BM, 193R, 219BM, 222BR, 223BR, 223TL, 238 3rd from BR, 238BR, 239 2nd from BL, 239 2nd from BR, 239BR, 240 all, 242R, 242B, 243ML, 251 all, 254B, 255 all, 259–261 all, 267 all, 283TR, 295TL, 296ML; *Sergio di Paula:* 175TL, 175TM; Courtesy *Electric Generators Direct:* 228BL, 231 all; *Cheryl Fenton:* 98 all, 99BM, 99TR; Courtesy *First Alert:* 203 2nd from BR, 227T; *Scott Fitzgerrell:* 48TR, 48MR; Courtesy *Fogazzo:* 175BL, 175BM; Courtesy *Fuze:* 226BR, 226MR; *Paul Glendell/ Alamy:* 235T; *John Granen:* 30L; Art Gray: 2BR, 166TR; *Steven A. Gunther:* 95TR; *Jamie Hadley:* 285TR; Courtesy *Harbor Breeze:* 151TR; *Daniel Harris:* 5 2nd–3rd from T, 6BR, 7BR, 15T, 23BR, 23BL, 23MR, 40T, 41T, 41B, 70BR–3rd from BR, 71BL, 71 3rd from BL, 80R, 81 all except BL, 82BL, 82 inset, 85 all, 86BR, 90–91 all, 93BR, 130R, 167–168 all, 177 3rd from BL, 177 2nd from BR, 196R, 197–201 all, 202BR, 203 2nd from BL, 207 all, 208ML, 216 all, 218T, 220TL, 220BR, 221 all except TL, 228BM, 236BL, 294TR; *Philip Harvey:* 146BR, 146 3rd from BL, 155BR, 156TR, 158T, 158BR, 159B; *Alex Hayden:* 78, 124; Courtesy *Hunter Fan:* 151TL; *Douglas Johnson:* 263BL, 282T, 286; *Naturbild/Jupiter Images:* 230; *Jupiter Images:* 210; *Rob Karosis:* 43T, 57R; *Muffy Kibbey:* 177T, 195; Courtesy *Kichler:* 149ML, 149MM, 149MR; Courtesy *Lagotek:* 146 2nd from BL, 152 all; Courtesy *Ledtronics:* 70BL, 72L; Courtesy *Lighting New York:* 71BR, 96 all; *David Duncan Livingston:* 158BL; Courtesy *Lutron:* 227BL; *Stephen Marley:* 157TR; *Daniel Nadelbach:* 280, 281TL, 285TL; *Greg Niemi/BigStockPhoto:* 7 3rd from BR, 34T; Courtesy *Optimization World:* 202BL, 203BR, 204TL, 205 3rd from TL, 205 2nd from BL, 205BL; Courtesy *Oxypower:* 234T, 235ML, 235MR, 235B, 237 all, Courtesy *Plantronics:* 235BM, 235BR; Courtesy *Portfolio:* 151 2nd from BL & BR; *Howard Lee Puckett:* 92L; Courtesy *Pulse Engineering:* 223TR; *Eric Roth:* 224, 266; Courtesy *Royce Lighting:* 149TL; *Mark Rutherford:* 4B, 8B, 11M, 17ML, 17BL, 25BL, 32 all, 33BL, 42BL, 42BR, 44 all, 45TL, 45ML, 45BM, 48BR, 48BL, 49BR, 49BL, 50TR, 50BR, 51ML, 52TL, 53BL, 59BL, 61 all, 62B, 66TR, 68L, 68R, 69BR, 70 4th from BL, 75 all except BL, 79 all except BL, 99BR, 99TM, 100 2nd from BR, 101T, 101BR, 104BL, 104BM, 105ML, 105 2nd from MR, 105BR, 108T, 109TMR, 109TR, 109BL, 114TL, 114BL, 115BL, 115BR–2nd from BR, 125T, 128 3rd from BR, 131BL, 131BR, 132TL, 132ML, 138ML, 138BL, 138BR, 139BL, 139BM, 139BR, 140TR, 140BR, 142TM, 140TM, 142TM, 142TR, 142BL, 142BR, 147BL, 147BR, 160BL, 163TR, 170T, 170B, 204 2nd from BL, 213 2nd from TL, 213BL, 242TL, 246R, 296BR, 297R; Courtesy *Sea Gull Lighting:* 19R, 71T, 75BL, 82TL, 87BR, 88R, 146BL, 148T, 149TM, 149TR, 149BL, 149BR, 149BM, 150R, 151 2nd from TL, 151 2nd from TR, 166TL, 169B; Courtesy *SmartHome:* 186T; Courtesy *Solar City:* 229, 233T, 233B, 234B; Courtesy *Sonos:* 226TR, 226 2nd from TR; Courtesy *Southwest Wind Power:* 5 3rd from B, 232TM, 236TL; *Robin Stancliff:* 129T, 140L; Courtesy *Starck Network:* 228BR, 232BR; *Bill Stephens:* 33BR; *Thomas J. Story:* 7T, 12, 17R, 21T, 23T, 24, 30R, 76BL, 80L, 81BL, 84L, 99ML, 118B, 147T, 155TL, 184R, 209TL, 209BL, 209BR, 212TR, 220TR, 232BL, 252L, 283TL; *Dan Stultz:* 1, 2TR, 2BL, 4T-3rd from T, 7 4th from BL, 7 2nd from BR, 8TL, 18BM, 18BR, 27 all, 28TL, 29BL, 33T-3rd from T, 35L, 35R, 36TR, 36MR, 37BL, 39 all, 42 3rd from BL, 44MR, 45M, 51BL, 51MR, 53BM, 55 all except BL, 59ML, 70 3rd from BL, 71 2nd from BR, 76 all except BL, 77 all, 79BR, 82BR, 83 all, 87 all except BR, 94 all, 95TL, 95BL, 202 3rd from BR, 203BL, 204 3rd from TL, 204BL, 204BM, 205TL, 205 2nd from TL, 205TR, 205M, 205MR, 205BM, 205BR, 211 all, 213TL, 217TM, 217TR, 218BL, 218BM, 218BR, 219 all except BM, 221TL, 292BR, 295BR; Courtesy *Sun Touch:* 177BR, 191–192 all; *Dave Toht:* 147 2nd from BL, 147 3rd from BL, 172BL-BR, 175TR, 175BR; Courtesy *Uniden:* 225ML, 225BL, 225M; *Christopher Vendetta:* 183 all except TR; Courtesy *Wallplates.com:* 100BL, 102TM, 102MR, 102ML, 102TR; *Greg West/ Corner House Stock Photo:* 20B; Courtesy *WildCharge:* 225TR; Courtesy *Wilkerson Furniture:* 202 3rd from BL, 209TM; *Michele Lee Willson:* 5T, 54BR, 70 2nd from TR, 74 all, 130L, 157TL, 184M, 203T, 208BR, 262BL, 263 2nd from BL, 263 2nd from BR, 265BL, 288, 289BL, 289BR, 290; *David Stark Wilson:* 157BR; Courtesy *Windterra Systems:* 232TR.

Index

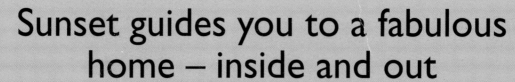